PEOPLE THROW ROCKS AT THINGS THAT SHINE

A CLERGY WHISTLEBLOWER'S JOURNEY

D1218293

VASHTI BOOKS

PEOPLE THROW ROCKS AT THINGS THAT SHINE

A CLERGY WHISTLEBLOWER'S JOURNEY

Rev. Beth Caulfield

VASHTI BOOKS

Mount Royal, New Jersey

 VASHTI
BOOKS
Mt. Royal, New Jersey

People Throw Rocks At Things That Shine

Book design by Pen2publishing

Cover Photo by Kara Raudenbush Photography

ISBN: 979-8-9861032-1-1

Acknowledgments

I want to thank God first, because without Him my journey would not have been possible. I also want to thank my forever loving husband, Tom, and our children, T.J., Amber, and Camille, who have been my continuous inspiration. I am also grateful to my mom, who has been with me all along, especially encouraging me to write this book. Throughout this writing process I have had glimpses of Dad cheering me on from Heaven, and I cannot wait to give him a big hug in appreciation. Thank you to Aunt Dot and other family who helped with family history. I so appreciate the women of my Wesleyan Covenant Band group who have walked with me through crucial final decisions in this journey and encouraged and gave feedback for the earliest draft of this retelling. I say thank you to the leaders of the Wesleyan Covenant Association, particularly here in Greater New Jersey, who have helped me get the story and facts right and supported me from the beginning of my UMC challenges and certainly through the writing of this book.

I want to thank my wonderful editor, Jamie Calloway-Hanauer, for her diligence, heart, and expertise; as well as Kara Raudenbush, whose awesome photography, patience, and vision for the cover I am forever indebted to. Janet Darnell is one of those angels God has sent along the journey at just the right time to give me clarity, prayer support, and to keep me grounded in God's love for me.

Her artwork in this book helped keep me on the path. To Lloyd Jassin for his legal counsel, I say "thank you, thank you, thank you!" I am grateful to Penn2Publishing for helping me get this story to the page, and to IngramSpark for working with me to polish and deliver the final product.

Finally, I would like to give a special shout of appreciation to my Seoulmate, Jisun Kwak, who has lived much of this clergy journey up close and personal with me. I have not always understood the paths God has led me down, but I am forever indebted that He has let our paths connect so that we could sharpen one another, bolster one another, and together cry many tears of joy and sorrow. I do believe we were brought together for such a time as this, and I am eternally grateful to God and to you.

Table of Contents

INTRODUCTION

This book is about my journey through the inner workings of the clergy world of the United Methodist Church, one of the largest Protestant denominations in the world, with over twelve million members. It is about my experience with abusive leadership and a toxic culture. It is a whistleblower's tale. It is not a story of fraud, theft, or any other criminal activity under U.S. laws, but it does call into question some civil wrongs. But mainly it is a call to attention of the demand to place loyalty to abusive bishops and other Church leaders over loyalty to Christ. It is about bad actors who, among other misdeeds, utilize and shape the theological wars surrounding LGBTQIA+ concerns within the Church to solidify their own power. It is about the naivety and failure of a Church governing system that lends itself to the abusive behavior and adverse employment action described. It is about careers and lives demolished and stolen as a result. Therefore, this is a whistleblower's tale about how bad actors are running the show.

According to the United Methodist Church's laws and regulations as described in its Book of Discipline (¶2702.1), Bishops, no different than all other clergy, including local pastors, are subject to disciplinary action for the following offenses:

1. Immorality, including but not limited to, not being celibate in singleness or not faithful in a heterosexual marriage;

2. Practices declared by The United Methodist Church to be incompatible with Christian teachings, including but not limited to: being a self-avowed practicing homosexual; or conducting ceremonies that celebrate homosexual unions; or performing same-sex wedding ceremonies;

3. Crime;

4. Disobedience to the order and discipline of The United Methodist Church;

5. Dissemination of doctrines contrary to the established standards of doctrine of The United Methodist Church;

6. Relationship and or behavior that undermines the ministry of another pastor;

7. Child abuse;

8. Sexual abuse;

9. Sexual misconduct or harassment, including, but not limited to racial and/or sexual harassment; and

10. Racial or gender discrimination.

In this book I share how, even if tried and found guilty, bishops whose offenses are outside of sexual misconduct and financial impropriety often suffer minimal if any repercussions for their behaviors. They instead remain in power with the ability to retaliate against their accusers and to continue further abuses. In this book I elaborate on this claim specifically in references to violations four, five and six detailed above. The result is that as such violations occur, clergy and others are reluctant to file complaints against bishops and other associated power leaders. It is upon this reality that I am blowing the whistle.

Who am I? Briefly, I am someone who discerned a call from God to enter the ordination process and serve the United Methodist Church in the Greater New Jersey Annual Conference. Greater New Jersey is one of fifty-seven regional decision-making bodies called "annual conferences" in the United States and of an additional seventy-six annual conferences internationally. It comprises over 500 congregations in New Jersey and parts of New York and Pennsylvania, and is proud to proclaim "a network of more than 50,000 disciples."[1] I was commissioned as a provisional elder in 2013 and spent eight years as such. A provisional elder is the terminology United Methodists use for a clergy who is seeking to be pronounced fully-ordained and has met basic requirements for such, but is in a probationary status until green-lighted by their conference's Board of Ordained Ministry. During my time as a provisional elder, I was blessed to lead ministry that bore much fruit for Christ, the local church, and the Annual Conference, including serving with distinction on the bishop's staff.

However, I was turned down for full orders (ordination) twice by the Board of Ordained Ministry, most recently in 2017. The second time was shortly after I was threatened by the bishop of the Greater New Jersey Annual Conference regarding my support for a clergy-woman who had been a candidate for bishop herself. I was soon thereafter removed from his staff and endured significant hardships in subsequent ministry appointments I was given by the bishop and his cabinet. As a result of my treatment, I refused to go before the Board of Ordained Ministry anymore.

Instead, I began work to break myself and countless others free from the system of abuse and dysfunction that the United Methodist Church has become in Greater New Jersey and elsewhere. While much of my tale transpires in New Jersey, the issues and treatment I describe are systemic to the entire denomination and represent global concerns. As a result, I concluded that the best solution to the escalated conflicts in theology, the bureaucracy, and the hostile work environment that limit the UMC's ministry and tarnishes its reputation was to start afresh with a new denomination. I want to be part of a denomination that covenants to uphold doctrines and disciplines that provide needed freedoms and safeguards for effective ministry as seen through the lens of traditional Wesleyan Christian theology. So, I settled on one specific strategy: I organized and became a founding member of the Wesleyan Covenant Association (WCA) Chapter of the Greater New Jersey Annual Conference.

The Wesleyan Covenant Association is a global connection of local churches, laity, clergy, and regional chapters that seeks to partner with like-minded orthodox Christians.[2] Members of the WCA hope for a renewed, orthodox global Methodist church. I was elected the first WCA Greater New Jersey Chapter President beginning in 2018, and in 2019 was elected a Global Council member. I also served as a member of the Next Steps Working Group that drafted the initial Book of Doctrines and Disciplines for a new expression of Methodism (2018-2019).

In early 2021, after more than eight years within an ordination system led by those intent on realizing the French proverb—*C'est seulement l'arbre chargé de fruits que les gens jettent des pierres à/* It is only the tree loaded with fruit that the people throw stones at—I surrendered all attempts at receiving full credentialing and incurred the professional, financial, and emotional impacts such surrendering implies. I have chosen to shake the dust off my feet and work to ensure that another system that breeds such toxicity does not get replicated.

To that end, I am writing this book as part of my ministry against injustice. My writing is not vengeance, bitterness, nor a neglect to explore my own mistakes or growing edges. Toxic cultures and narcissistic leaders need to be challenged, and the hope of this book is to do just that. This book is written to encourage others who suffer in silence and have been afraid to stand up. With the desire to help others being my primary objective, **I will donate more than a tithe of the profits from all versions of my book to disaster relief through the United Methodist Commission on Relief, (UMCOR).**[3] UMCOR is a worthy agency supported by Christians throughout the world, including progressive, centrist, and traditional UMC members.[4] It is my prayer that many will purchase and read this book so that many will benefit.

PEOPLE THROW ROCKS AT THINGS THAT SHINE

You are the light of the world. A town built on a hill cannot be hidden.

Neither do people light a lamp and put it under a bowl. Instead they put it on its stand, and it gives light to everyone in the house.

In the same way, let your light shine before others, that they may see your good deeds and glorify your Father in heaven.

Matthew 5:14-16 (NIV)

By adulthood, most of us have learned that, as Taylor Swift sings it, "people throw rocks at things that shine." We have been hit, we at times ourselves have thrown, we have seen others take aim, and we also have seen them struck. But in the Church of Jesus Christ? Among its holy leaders? At those who shine for Christ?

Across all denominations, abuse scandals have rocked Ecclesia and hastened secularism. Fraud and tax evasion by televangelists and even long-standing mainline denominational leaders are no longer news that garner much more than a fleeting headline. But what about the power struggles amongst those striving to be the leaders of religion?

We may watch the challenges actor Jude Law faces in HBO's *The New Pope* as he and other fictional church officials navigate the high stakes political waters of the Vatican. The over-the-top political jockeying, power abuse and contentious battles represented most surely are the fruits of creativity among stables of talented screenwriters. Or are they? Amid its numerous scandals, many have become jaded regarding the real-life actions, motivations, and scruples of Roman Catholic leadership.

But what about political machinations and tyranny within the infrastructures of the Protestant religious landscape? Does rock throwing occur there? Some may say "yes" and readily point only to the evangelical, mega-sized and mega-independent churches whose leaders' antics and falls have been chronicled of late.[1] But is this ancient form of combat really averted within the carefully constructed mainline denominations? Denominations that offer detailed policies and principles to ensure the importance of strong connection among its leaders and care for its clergy? Christianity is a sphere that claims the least shall be first and the first shall be last, yet those called to serve are too often exploited by bad actors at the top who manipulate and circumvent systems so their self-serving actions are protected, even at the expense of others. Perhaps this is best attested to by Wespath's Clergy Well-Being Survey published in September 2021 regarding United Methodists.[2] Wespath provides health, retirement and investment benefits management for the United Methodist Church. Their report shares disturbing information about clergy health. In its email sent to all clergy with the survey results, Wespath stated:

> Since the first survey in 2012, we have seen the results
> from the survey continue a downward trend in four of
> the five dimensions of well-being: physical, emotional,

social and spiritual. Key differences highlight disparities in age, race, gender and other areas.[3]

Just as telling, the last sentence of the survey states, "Cabinet-level
Church leaders (bishops and district superintendents) report better emotional, social, and spiritual well-being."[4] That comment, in
comparison to the reported decline in general clergy well-being,
speaks volumes and corroborates the concerns about the clergy
systems I address. I am not the only one concerned about these
systemic issues. In the email sent to United Methodist clergy
regarding the survey, Wespath stated, "Wespath sees these results
as alarming, and we are working to gain the understanding and
insight to some of the systemic issues impacting clergy well-being." My hope is that this book will be helpful to those endeavors
as well as to those of others who want to improve clergy well-being and performance.

The challenge is that the relevant clergy systems that need to be
addressed are oftentimes anchored in the First Amendment to the
U.S. Constitution and the sacred doctrines and policies legislated
by denominations themselves. These First Amendment and Church
polity wrinkles are exploited to the detriment of good ministry and
clergy well-being. I speak to the Church polity concerns throughout this book and share regarding the First Amendment challenges
in the latter chapters.

The story you are about to read gives insight to the reality of these
machinations. It is an account of the power abuse and toxic culture
that exists within the United Methodist Church. It is a personal
account that does not focus on billionaires, U.S. Presidents, or drug
cartels, but does involve the destruction of lives, careers, and even

souls. This story reveals those at the top of the organization who cling to power by attacking and undermining those perceived as threats to that power. It reveals persecution and hazing executed by those who hope to climb higher as they abuse their own power and mimic those at the top. It is also a story of those who turn a blind eye, keep their head down, and thereby assist the abuse and perpetuate the culture. It is a story about very real assaults on individuals' faith and ministry.

This tale is told not from the top, but from the bottom, beginning with the ugly entryway into the United Methodist clergy connectional system through the Board of Ordained Ministry. It tells of the mismanagement of the appointment system for clergy deployment, which is often used to manipulate, shape, and reward "yes men" and "yes women," and retaliate against those seen as threats. While my personal story is about those of us on bottom, I also tell of those whose mistreatment occurs much closer to the top.

My story tells of the unfettered power of rascally bishops, their abilities and propensities to abuse clergy and churches through the appointment system, and their undue influence over and manipulation of Boards of Ordained Ministry. With those powers they reshape the systems they are entrusted to protect and uphold.

Their carefully chosen insiders, i.e., those cabinet members, Board of Ordained Ministry members, and others placed in positions of power, are only too willing to aid and abet sordid agendas for political points. They frequently mimic the leadership that puts them in power. The result is clear misapplications of, as well as circumventing and deviating from, processes and procedures that result in violations of the letter and/or spirit of the UMC Book of Discipline. These actions constitute ungodly behavior, as do those that undermine the ministry of other pastors. I have seen and personally experienced so-called pastoral actions and responses from such leaders that were, in reality, thinly veiled attempts to bully, manipulate, and shut down perceived threats to power. I have been and seen others ground down until they capitulated to these leaders and their agendas. Occurrences I describe warrant grievances being filed through the UMC Judicial Complaint system, as they meet the offenses described in the UMC Book of Discipline ¶2702.[5] However, given that in many cases, including my own, the abusers are either legislated or de facto policers of the offenses they commit, it is no wonder that victims often see no recourse in filing complaints against them. I did not. In fact, many of us believe that filing a complaint will cause worse treatment.

It should be understood that these misdeeds are occurring amidst the theological wars raging within the UMC that are capturing much media attention. The story I reveal tells of those battles. While conflicts regarding LGBTQIA+ issues have been what has garnered the most attention, these wars more accurately revolve around the acceptance of the authority of Scripture and classical Christian creeds and doctrine. The challenges of differences on this include accepting the virgin birth and Resurrection of Jesus Christ, the existence of hell, many issues of human sexuality (not just LGBTQIA+ concerns), primacy of Scripture vs. primacy of social justice concerns, and many other core Wesleyan and Christian faith concerns. The best summation of classical Wesleyan faith within the UMC and the one that I have covenanted to can be found on the Wesleyan Covenant Association website.[6] The doctrinal matter of human sexuality, including whether bishops, their disciples and others are espousing and disseminating a doctrine contrary to the established doctrines of the UMC that states "the practice of homosexuality is incompatible with Christian practice,"[7] is a source of conflict that led to my, and others', isolation, and workplace harassment.

However, the sinister tactics I endured aren't just about the theological differences that continue to cause United Methodists to break away from the denomination. They are symptoms of a toxic culture rampant with narcissism from the top down. In a nutshell, hiding behind the zealousness for achieving a newly directed version of "inclusive" methodism is a cadre of bad actors who exploit systems within the church for personal gain and power. I submit that those bad actors are less interested in the theologically progressive or even centrist agendas they proclaim than in maintaining a privileged and legally entrenched system that they can continue to manipulate for their own personal interests. The job of a true leader is to use their spiritual gifts and special talents to build up others and the church, rather than push for the ministry and culture to be built around them.

Through sharing my personal story, I hope to spotlight problems in our current church systems that allow such shenanigans so that they can be rethought, rectified, and not replicated in the future denominations that are surfacing as the current United Methodist Church crumbles.

I also hope to inspire the development of clergy relations systems that protect and lead to the recruitment of better clergy. The current United Methodist system not only causes harm to those who do not conform to the whims of bad acting leaders, but also breeds mediocrity to the system and ultimately the fruit born by the Church, particularly the fruit that should emerge via the connectionalism and entrepreneurialism that John Wesley envisioned. I share more on this subject toward the end of this book.

In this telling, I reveal my concerns about the current overrun of progressive theology in United Methodist leadership. This theology pervades and indeed is a scapegoat to the difficulty that I encountered as a traditional Methodist. My experience demonstrates that there is a significant effort underway within the UMC to rewrite a gospel on hearts that turns the Church almost exclusively into a social action agency. A current primary goal of this effort is advancing a human sexuality theology agenda counter to traditional Christianity and the transforming power of Jesus Christ.

That progressive focus is not one I support: it is detrimental to the mission of the Church and its witness to the world. My ministry had a different and effective focus. But, as a result of its shine, there was backlash against it. The rocks that were thrown at me also served as a clear sign to other traditionalists to not stand up or stand out.

On a personal level, I tell my story to help heal myself and my family. The treatment my family has experienced over the past decade has been challenging to our faith and strained our relationships at times. Watching your mother, wife, or daughter be mistreated is heartbreaking. Seeing her choose to stay in a religious system that repeatedly hurts her despite your pleading for her to get out is even more difficult.

So, I write this book also to set the record straight for my family, so that they might better understand not only what has happened, but why I was called to endure it. For sure mine is a whistleblower's tale, but it is also a journal of the Lord's goodness and faithfulness in ministry despite the rocks that are hurled at His servants. My intent is to remind us all that we should never give up on God, that God never gives up on us, and that, as Paul declares, "all things work together for the good of those who love Him, who have been called for His purpose." Romans 8:28

What do I hope to get out of writing this? Peace. A sense that I did what I was called to do by telling the truth. I want to know that I did not aid and abet a system and people who are hurting others. I want to answer my call to stand up for justice for clergy. Therefore, I feel led to "Go where nobody else wants to go. Do what nobody else wants to do."[8]

I confess that my biggest struggle in publishing this memoir has been the fear of being judged. I have fought the concern of being labeled "sour grapes," or as one who just could not hack it in the UMC ordination process and clergy world. I have battled a sense that others will see me as unfit or unworthy of ordination because of the observations, experiences, and feelings I share. That some will say "she still has not learned her lesson" has haunted me as someone who fervently wants to move on to Christian perfection and recognizes it can only happen through discipline that desires God's grace.

My hope is also that my whistleblowing will not hinder but rather encourage the UMC General Conference's passage of the Protocol for Reconciliation and Grace Through Separation legislation. This Protocol is a "proposal to restructure the United Methodist Church by separation as the best means to resolve our differences. This agreement will allow each part of the Church to remain true to its theological understanding while recognizing the dignity, equality, integrity, and respect of every person."[9] That legislation provides the best vehicle for the amicable separation of the UMC and for the further development of the Global Methodist Church, a separate, traditional denomination.[10]

In her 2020 book, *A Church Called Tov: Forming a Goodness Culture That Resists Abuses of Power and Promotes Healing*, Laura Mcknight Barringer writes:

> How a church responds to criticism, or handles information that could damage the reputation of a leader of the church, reveals the culture of that church. Again, compassion, truth, and wisdom should be our guiding lights. But when a culture is toxic, priorities change and truth telling often takes a back seat…In a toxic culture, pastors and leaders tell stories that are false, while the congregation either goes along with the deception or lives in blissful ignorance.[11]

Finally, in light of the above statement, it is my prayer that this book be met with the grace, prayer and resolve for personal growth, glory for God, and institutional improvement that has gone into its writing. I confess additional concerns that this whistleblowing would instead be met with denial or attacks, including frivolous lawsuits. I have done my best to offer only what is helpful and true, even when the details cause pain as they are exposed and revisited. That pain includes my own.

In spite of these concerns, I have indeed persevered and distributed this book because if I do not, who will? Who will tell my story or the story of others' struggles against unjust powers in the United Methodist Church? I am only choosing to be this vulnerable by pulling back the curtain on Church leadership in hopes that my doing so helps in advancing God's Kingdom.

Here I am Lord, is it I Lord? I have heard you calling in the night. And I will go Lord, if you lead me. I will hold your people in my heart.[12]

MY CALL

I am no longer my own, but thine.

Put me to what thou wilt,

rank me with whom thou wilt.

Put me to doing, put me to suffering.

Let me be employed for thee or laid aside for thee,

exalted for thee or brought low for thee.

Let me be full, let me be empty.

Let me have all things, let me have nothing.

I freely and heartily yield all things to thy pleasure and disposal.

And now, O glorious and blessed God, Father, Son and Holy Spirit,

thou art mine, and I am thine. So be it.

And the covenant which I have made on earth, let it be ratified in heaven.

Amen.

— Wesleyan Covenant Prayer

The Wesleyan Covenant Prayer was adapted by John Wesley, the co-founder of Methodism (along with his brother, Charles), for the renewal of the believer's covenant with God. The prayer points to deep surrender of ourselves in complete trust to God.[1]

METHOCOSTAL ROOTS

I believe my faith journey began before I was born. One of the ways that my parents bestowed their abundant love on me was that I was taught that my salvation had been prayed for by my ancestors, in particular my great-grandfather whom I never met. My Christian faith was especially nurtured by my mother and grandmother, both of whom sought to make Jesus Christ the head of their lives and treasured their personal relationships with Him above all else.

Both my parents took Christian discipleship seriously. The dinner table was frequently a place where theology was worked out between my mother and father. My younger brother and sister and I sat there listening and learning while we gulped down my mom's southern cooking. My mother had been raised as what I now know to refer to as a "Methocostal." But in those days, she would just say that while her people were Methodists, her mom taught her to be Pentecostal and the Church of God was where she learned most about how to be close to God.

As we passed the cornbread, gobbled down fried salmon, pork chops, or chicken, scraped the last of creamed corn, green beans, fried potatoes, or turnip greens and drained the sweet tea, there was serious God talk. When was the rapture going to hit? Mom said it would be soon. Was it going to happen pre-, mid-, or post-tribulation? Dad says as believers we are not going to suffer. Mom says he's wrong. That we are going to be tested beyond our imagination. What was heaven going to be like? Mom says we're going to all have jobs. What kind of bodies would we have? Dad says he's going to finally be good-looking. What does grieving the Holy Spirit really mean? Mom says don't mess with this unpardonable sin. When

11

people speak in tongues, is it in heavenly languages or earthly ones? Mom says what's important is that you speak in tongues.

Me on left, mom, Jill and Max. Dad was always behind the camera. Danville, AL

A favorite point was my father's "once saved, always saved" notions. He would not bring them up, my mother just knew that they were still in his thinking. Sometimes she would suddenly declare,

> We can *all* backslide at *any* given moment! We always have a choice. That's free will. You've got to always be working at it. You have to learn your Bible and lean on the power of the Holy Spirit to stay true to God. If you're not Spirit-filled, you can make it to heaven, but it's going to be hard. And you're not going to get the best room. Everyone who cries 'Lord, Lord' isn't going to make it.

Her words were often delivered in a somber tone. I know now as I also understood back then that her intent was merely to impress upon our family the importance of the subject matter. She shared her thoughts often out of her love and concern for the well-being of our souls.

Dad would sometimes counter that if your choice is to go against God then you haven't really been saved anyway. Other times he would remark that if you've been saved and then walk away, you'll come back. Always. And God will always forgive you when your heart is right. Always. "That's what grace is," he'd say.

Mom talked about the needed power of the Holy Ghost. Dad spoke about the power of grace. She would say, "yes, God gives grace, but too many use it as an excuse to sin!" They usually both seemed to be right to me. It was pretty confusing at times.

Those supper conversations are where I was introduced to the concept that theology matters. What you think about God matters. All thoughts are not equally true; some are incorrect. But thinking about God is important. I also experienced that it can be satisfying to think about God with other people. At the same time, I learned that arguing about points of detail rarely convinced anyone. In fact, as I got older, such arguments really turned me off, and for a long time I shunned conversations that I feared might lead to such conflict. Later I learned how invaluable they were.

Nonetheless, such God talk was my normal. It started from well before I was ten years old. It wasn't until I got a little older that I understood this was perhaps not quite "normal."

13

My dad's people, the Waddells, were Methodists. My great-grandfather, Lee Polk Waddell, helped build and establish Salem Methodist Church in Hartselle, Alabama. But his son, my grandfather, Oscar, didn't go to church much as an adult. He married Maybel Prince, a Southern Baptist. She brought Dad and his sisters up in the Shoal Creek Baptist Church in Priceville, a crossroads town on the way to Huntsville. Dad "got saved" at a youth gathering at Shoal Creek and was baptized for the first time the following Sunday. He was fourteen. That was in 1961. But then as my mom tells it, he backslid real bad for a long time before returning to the Lord.

The Owens family, Mom's dad's people, were also Methodists. My grandfather, Alvis Chester Owens, grew up in the Lebanon Methodist Church in Speake, Alabama. But Mom's mom, Johnnie Azilee, was Solomon Walter Gray's daughter, though we knew him as "Papa Gray." Papa Gray raised their family in the Penn Church of God, a Pentecostal church on Rt. 36 in Danville. I have visited that church many times throughout my life.

As Mom tells it, that's where my real spiritual heritage comes from: Papa Gray and the Pentecostal church. I have heard many stories over the years about Papa Gray's faith and the way he taught his kids and grandkids to love the Lord. Mom tells of sitting on his lap and being told how in the last days they would have to fight hard to keep their faith.

Papa Gray is the one who prayed faithfully for my salvation and the salvation of all his great-grandkids. He died in 1959, seven years before I was born. Hearing about his devotion to the Lord and love for me has always been faith-bolstering. My faith is in part an answer to his prayer. I still believe that.

When I was in seminary, I spent a Thanksgiving break with our family in Alabama and as I rummaged through family keepsakes, I found Papa Gray's well-worn Bible. It was marked up heavily. From the stories Mom remembers, I expected to find the most notes made by him to be in Revelation, Daniel, and other passages of prophecy. That isn't what I found, though. I found the most underlining and comments in the Book of John, the book that uses the term "love" more than any other in the Bible. Every time I visit my mom, I thumb through that Bible. It gives me comfort and assurance as I contemplate my spiritual heritage.

So, my Christian faith was nurtured from before I can remember through my family's faith. I made my own personal commitment to Christ at the age of thirteen. It happened one summer that I stayed with my grandmother and had attended a weeklong church revival meeting with her. One night after returning from a meeting at the church, alone at my bed, I got down on my knees and asked Jesus into my heart.

The year I gave my life to Jesus, two personal gifts emerged. The first came out of adversity. My dad's management career with Monsanto Chemical Company had led to frequent moves all over the U.S. for our family. The summer I turned thirteen we moved from the Houston, Texas area to a St. Louis suburb. This was our seventh move. By the time I graduated high school five years later, I had attended 12 schools, including three different high schools: one in Concord, California; one in Fayetteville, North Carolina; and, finally, graduating in Westfield, Massachusetts.

While there were many blessings in the diverse experiences and education we received through that lifestyle, all the moving around also caused a lot of insecurity and time spent alone that resulted in loneliness. I was very pale skinned and had a lot of freckles. Having received my height early and being thin as a beanpole, I spent the ages of ten through thirteen adjusting to major changes in my body. I had a significant overbite that caused me to be teased and had to get braces to correct it. So by the summer I turned thirteen and asked Jesus into my heart, I was extremely self-conscious, shy, and withdrawn. Social interactions with kids my own age were especially hard for me. Adolescence is a difficult time for most people, and I was no exception.

My mother was determined to help me overcome this and the year I started eighth grade she insisted I choose public speaking as an elective in school. I was terrified and protested, but she did not relent. Through that class I discovered I had a gift for speaking, and at that age began honing it. I also believe I discovered and received that gift from the Lord at that time as part of my spiritual maturing as I was now choosing a relationship with God on my own.

Pine Forest Girl's Track Team 1986. I was in 10th grade (back row center). (Fayetteville, NC)

I have always enjoyed sports and was deemed a "tomboy," but had never really been in any organized sports. The following spring after accepting Jesus, while in the eighth grade, I joined a Catholic Youth Organization (CYO) track team in the San Francisco Bay Area town in which we lived. That changed my life drastically, as my sprinting and jumping talents took flight.

I could run extremely fast. Within months I was competing in the TAC Junior Olympic Nationals in Tempe, Arizona. I spent much of high school and college honing my gifts of sprinting and speaking, developing discipline, and gaining confidence. These gifts opened many doors for my ministry, and I thank God for them. I also had a keen appreciation that these gifts did not belong to me, but to God.

The running also led to practicing leadership skills as I served various teams as captain. I enjoyed many awards and was recruited by Division 1 schools, including several in the Ivy League. In my search for what my future career should be, I remember taking a student career interest survey in high school that analyzed and deduced my gifts and interests to be best suited to a career in sales. I balked at the results, believing there could never be a product I believed in enough to feel honest about persuading others to purchase it. I smile to myself now as I realize that I did go on to a career in sales as a minister intent on making disciples for Jesus Christ. That vocation has invoked passion in me as I believe in the person I introduce others to with all my heart and soul.

Nonetheless, at that time, all I knew was that I wanted to be a communicator and I did not want to be in sales. Between the running and that desire, my top three schools for college were Penn, Brown, and Syracuse University. I was offered admission by all three, but ultimately Penn and Philadelphia won my heart.

PENN PROUD

Penn vs. Princeton women's 4x200 relay, 1985. (Princeton, NJ)   *Penn Relays, Women's 4x800 relay, 1988. (Philadelphia, PA)*

At Penn I studied communications with the intent of pursuing a career in broadcast journalism. I worked hard to prepare for my future. I took a position at the university television station, interned in the summers at both a major national network television station and a magazine, and even went to finishing school and did some modeling to prepare for that career.

I was on the right track to obtain the future I thought I desired. Continuing in my track and field career, I excelled on a team that won the Ivy League Championships for four indoor seasons and three outdoor. The time in competitive sports refined my work ethic and disciplined my body to be healthy.

But in the middle of my junior year, an unexpected experience changed my course. I attended a small, intimate gathering on campus with celebrity television journalist Nancy Glass, today a six-time

Emmy award winner with many other accolades. This was not the first time I had seen or listened to such a television journalist, but this time I heard someone on a different level than I had before. Somehow, that night, I listened on a spiritual level.

The meeting was late, starting at 9pm. When Nancy arrived, it was obvious that she was very pregnant. I would later learn she was expecting twins. I remember being distracted, thinking that it was really a show of her commitment and focus that she would still be working at 9pm and beyond in her condition, and wondering if our little gathering would be worth her time at such a delicate moment in her life.

The more I listened to her speak, the more everything felt wrong to me. While she recounted her journey, triumphs, and challenges, I began realizing that the life she had passion for I somehow did not. I am not sure if I had been feeling that for a while, but the realization was poignant to me that evening. I could not escape it. It flooded me. It was unsettling as I recognized that I wanted to do something different than all I had planned so carefully to do, but what that was I had no idea. Furthermore, after the meeting, as I walked across campus back to my dorm, I had a strong sense that God was telling me that broadcast journalism was not for me. Looking back, I see that I had experienced a robust encounter with the Holy Spirit.

I ended up changing my coursework so that I could minor in both economics and marketing from the Wharton Business School while continuing and completing my communications major. I chose to pursue a corporate career in human resources management.

My first job put me on an executive training program with International Paper Company. I went on to work for other Fortune 50 companies including Honeywell and Lockheed Martin. For over ten years I honed my skills in employee and labor relations; career planning and counseling; employment law; sexual harassment management; organization design; management development; staffing; and other areas that gave me a successful human resources career at an early age.

My experience included developing a niche skill investigating discrimination claims and working to resolve issues. I look back at that training after the experiences that I have had with the United Methodist Church and its lack of practice providing such protection and advocacy and I am very saddened. As you read further into my story, you will understand why.

One of the important skills HR manager experience refines is consultation. I learned to be approachable, a good listener, methodical, and a safe place for people to share their professional and even personal burdens. I learned to do this with employees of all levels of the organization, from hourly, blue-collar workers to executives. At Lockheed Martin, Fred Moosally, then Vice President of Business Development but also a former U.S. Navy Captain of the USS Iowa, teammate to Roger Staubach at the Naval Academy, and future president of the company's MS2 division, called me his "priest." I look back now at how God used even that consulting component of my work as important training ground for the future.

Yet even though I enjoyed the work, I often felt restless and unfulfilled. I sensed that I was missing something or that I was not doing exactly what I was supposed to be. In 2000, when I was thirty-two and had given birth to our second child, my husband's career moved us to Paris, France. I decided to put my own career on hold to stay home with our children during our time there.

FRENCH CONNECTION

The first week in Paris, at our new church home, the American Church in Paris (led by Greater New Jersey United Methodist Rev. Dr. Larry Kalajainen), I was invited to attend Community Bible Study International (CBS), an interdenominational para-church ministry whose mission is to make disciples of Jesus Christ in communities throughout the world via caring, in-depth Bible study.[2] I was told I would get two hours a week of adult company and my children would be taken care of in a kids' program. I signed up right away.

On a busy weekday September morning I climbed into our Opel Zafira European minivan and drove across Paris, including the Etoile, which is the "no traffic laws seem to apply as traffic comes in and out of all directions" ring around the Arc de Triumph. My destination was 50 Ave. Hoche in the seventeenth arrondissement, the address of the Église catholique anglophone Saint Joseph. Later I would refer to it as Saint Joe's. But at that time I was frazzled by crying kids in the backseat, still acclimating to Parisian driving, refamiliarizing myself with piloting a standard transmission in city traffic, and nervous about what I would encounter.

What I found was a loving, reassuring, diverse gathering of people. We came from all over the world, spoke many different primary languages, and had almost as many skin colors. We came from a global variety of churches. We had economic statuses that ranged from homeless to the world's elite. We included nannies, government officials, political refugees, housewives, retired grandparents, businessmen and women, professional musicians, fashion models, a CIA agent, and an ex-prostitute, and those are just the few I can remember.

We were studying the Word of God in a very disciplined fashion with weekly lessons that required significant homework. We were held accountable for our attendance and our interactions with one another. What made this so special was not simply learning about other cultures, worldviews, and experiences, although that was pretty cool. Instead, the most transforming and faith-bolstering experience was when we gathered to share our responses to the Scriptures: in spite of our differences, we could see in each other that we were encountering the *same* Jesus Christ.

Our "God talk" left us all marveling not only at what we learned from each other's differently crafted lenses on the Bible, but also at how we recognized God's enlightenment in each other's understanding as we shared with one another. It was the Bible and our commitment to it that opened us up to one another and drew us closer to Christ in a most marvelous way.

That group caused me to grow so much, and I loved CBS and the good friends I met there. The kids and I brought our learnings home to my husband. Our faiths began to grow together. It was a particularly holy time for our family.

Having begun as a class member, I was soon asked to become a small group facilitator. I told them I did not think I could do it because I was not comfortable praying out loud. Because we had bonded so closely, they were able to bluntly say to me, "Beth, you're just going to have to get over that." And so I did, and learning to lead prayer empowered my life even further. I then was asked to be the Teaching Leader of the entire class. I felt especially ill-equipped to become the Teaching Leader. I had little Bible study experience, and had never even read most of the Bible, much less taught it.

In addition to these obstacles, the class met in a Roman Catholic Church and had only been led by Roman Catholic Teaching Leaders in the past. Yet as I prayed about it, I knew that God was calling me.

Sharing a devotion at a CBS luncheon at Église catholique anglophone Saint Joseph, Paris, 2003.

After I agreed to teach the class, I was informed that I was not to approach lecturing as presenting a research project or history lesson. I would be given minimal study materials and told that I should limit my study of commentaries. The point was for me to connect with God, understand what spiritual truths I was being shown to instruct others on, and just deliver that. The goal was to change lives.

I remember the first class I taught, just before my lecture, a French woman came up to introduce herself as a retired French literature professor from Wellesley College, one of the most prestigious institutions of higher learning in the U.S. She said she had studied many great works of literature but never the Bible and was now looking forward to doing so. I thought I was going to pass out. Yet I obeyed the call. I became quite fulfilled and more focused on my relationship with God than ever before and my entire family and the class were blessed.

During one class I felt led to give an altar call to encourage people to confess that they were sinners in need of a savior and invite Jesus into their hearts. I wrestled with the idea. One, I had never done such a thing and questioned my own competence for the skill. Two, altar calls were not listed in my job description, and I therefore questioned my own authority. Three, I was going to be standing in the pulpit of a Roman Catholic church where I was pretty sure altar calls were not practiced. Four, I was not sure how I felt about altar calls and wondered if they were manipulative and served the minister more than those who might be tempted to come forward. I also think I was grasping for excuses not to follow what the Holy Spirit was leading me to do. I look back at those concerns now and see a growing edge, as I was beginning to think a little deeper about the power entrusted to Christian leaders and the implications of our following of the Holy Spirit in public ministry.

As I prayed on the matter in the narthex of the church, Joan Minor, an American jazz, blues, and gospel singer who would become a lifelong mentor to me, asked if anything was wrong. I told her there was something that I thought God was asking me to do, but I was not sure, and it was frightening for me. She responded, "If God is telling you to do something, then you better do it." Many times since that day Joan has been a rock for me. Even living many miles away from one another, we have always had a spiritual connection that tells us just the right time to call. We can sense when the other needs prayer and a good talk. Joan is the longest running mentor in my life and I trust her spiritual judgement and wisdom.

Joan Minor, my spiritual mentor, singing for our CBS class. May 2003, Paris

I gave the altar call. Three women came forward and gave their lives to Jesus. Two were French, one was American. We celebrated. Any doubt I had about the power and importance of altar calls was erased that day.

The class grew from roughly twenty-five members to over fifty and I developed strong friendships with my leadership team and class members. Those experiences in Paris broadened my appreciation for the diversity within the body of Christ and taught me that all people, regardless of their background or culture, can and do experience the same kind of relationships with the same loving God. I began learning how to rely on God as I prepared each week to teach others passages that often I was reading for the first time. My passion for this type of in-depth Scripture study and ministry began in Paris.

Scenes from a Paris CBSI class luncheon. Members were from every tribe, tongue, nation, and age group.

JERSEY GIRL

When our family returned to the U.S, I joined a suburban New Jersey Community Bible Study class. After nine months as a class member, I was asked to become the Teaching Director. I struggled with the request because I believed it was time for me to move back into my career. But as my husband and I prayed about it, I once again knew that God was calling me.

CBS class leadership team, Flemington, NJ, 2005

By God's grace, over the years I led them the class doubled in size to 150 women plus 75 children. It also became more diverse in terms of the denominations represented, socioeconomics, race, and age. Our leadership team grew to 25 people. All Community Bible Study class leadership (including mine) was completely volunteer ministry.

My husband and I also became members of Clinton United Methodist Church in the Raritan Valley District of the Greater

New Jersey Annual Conference. I remember the first day that our family visited the church. It was the spring of 2006. Having outgrown its building, the church was offering a service at our children's elementary school gym. I had heard good things about the church and its senior pastor, Rev. Dr. Jeannie Pearson, a traditional Wesleyan theology pastor who had grown the church exponentially for seventeen years. That first day we visited, however, it was the also popular and deemed highly effective associate pastor who preached. Throughout the book I will refer to him as Rev. Andy Hoover, though this is not his real name. I would later learn that, in contrast to Rev. Pearson, Rev. Hoover was a progressive theology pastor with strong Wesleyan roots. My husband and I both enjoyed and were touched by his sermon that day, as he shared his love of the Philadelphia Eagles (my husband's favorite NFL team as well) and of personal tragedy that God had helped him through.

We were greeted by many friendly worshippers that day and there was a youthfulness about the service and its worship. We both felt drawn to the church as we participated in the service. At the end, however, both pastors stood before the congregation and announced both were being appointed elsewhere by Bishop Sudarshana Devadhar and would be leaving the church. I would later learn from various church members that there had been a power struggle between the two and it had caused division in the church.

This was my first real look at conflict between leaders in a church. The conflict, while not solely based on theological differences, had an air of such to it. The church had previously been highly successful with three services and at least several hundred members.

Yet even now, almost twenty years later, it has never recovered its pre-conflict size and ministry energy.

We decided to join the church anyway, and have had many friends, spiritual experiences, and ministry involvements with Clinton. My faith was fostered and mentored by their successor, Rev. Galen Goodwin, and then later by his successor, Rev. Dr. Lew Hiserote. All three of my children were baptized there on the same day in May of 2010 by Rev. Lew Hiserote. Our family stayed members of that church until I received my own appointment to pastor in 2013.

PRISON SCHOOLING

Early one morning in 2007, while tending my vegetable garden, I heard the Holy Spirit nudging me to prison ministry. Through some incredible circumstances, unlikely encounters, and God connections, I launched a Community Bible Study prison ministry sponsored by our church but led by an ecumenically and racially diverse leadership team from other churches who only God could have brought together. Rev. Goodwin and Clinton UMC were both highly supportive as we established and led a weekly Bible study class at Edna Mahon Women's Correctional Facility and shepherded the start of a class at Mountainview Youth Correctional Facility. The Bible study time there was rich as we developed solid relationships for in-depth sharing and learning from one another. Our Holy Ghost Dance Parties became a hit with the inmates, officers, and chaplain Rev. Estelle David. So did our pen-pal program with Clinton church members. I wish I had a photo of our Christian dance choreographer, Young Kim-Cedro, teaching us a dance to lead the prisoners into CC Winans' *Pray*. Her teaching me the dance was a feat unto itself.

Our CBS Prison leadership team, 2008.

The popularity of our classes grew as we expanded our offerings to the maximum security and mental illness units as well. We collected funds and purchased both English- and Spanish-language Bibles for the inmates and established a partnership with a local Christian bookstore that donated Christian greeting cards for the inmates to send their families and friends.

My faith grew exponentially through that experience in that God prompted me to follow Him into an environment that I had been afraid of and into ministry to people I had been most judgmental about in life—convicted felons. I learned a new sense of compassion and empathy, and a new view on social justice concerns. I found new friends and relationships. One special relationship that has endured over time was with the prison chaplain, Rev. Estelle David. Estelle and I not only keep in touch but continue to do ministry together. I would later write a short article about the experience for United Methodist Women's *Response* magazine.

Rev. David attending a fundraiser at Clinton United Methodist Church with her grandkids. The church held a cakewalk to raise money for Bibles for the prisoners.

DREAM DEAL

Dreams have been a significant factor in my faith journey. In February 2008, I experienced a vivid one. In it I was talking to a man at a business that was operating out of an old house. We were discussing some kind of employment for me. He asked me how much I thought I should be paid, so I told him how much money I had been making at my last corporate position. He laughed. I was embarrassed and told him that I did not have to start out making as much money as I used to make. He smiled and told me to pick up a toolbox that was on the floor next to me and look inside. There I found rolled up blueprints (plans) and bound documents that I perceived to be dissertations. He said to me, "Take the box and go to seminary." I woke up. I was very shaken. I cried. I woke my husband up and shared the dream with him immediately.

I prayed about the dream with my husband for a while. Seminary did not appeal to me and the thought of pursuing ministry as an actual career unnerved me, even though the truth is I had been doing close to (and frequently more than) full-time ministry work for over eight years. Somehow, I just always thought I was leading ministry efforts temporarily while raising our children.

While I struggled with this dream and how to respond to it, I experienced a "mystery" gastrointestinal illness that led to *many* medical tests and much concern. I also began seeking advice and counseling from my pastor, Rev. Galen Goodwin. He encouraged me to not be afraid of this calling. As my confidence grew that I was indeed being called into full-time ministry, my illness subsided as mysteriously as it began.

THE FOREST AT DREW

Rev. Goodwin encouraged me to look at the Drew Theological School, a Methodist institution founded in 1867. It was forty-five minutes from my home, and the closest seminary to me besides

Princeton, which was also forty-five minutes away. I understood that Drew was very progressive in its training, and I was skeptical of such an education. I was aware of Asbury Theological Seminary in Wilmore, Kentucky, that was soundly traditional in its Wesleyan approach, but with my family responsibilities I did not see it as a viable option for me.

I visited Drew Theological School the week of Memorial Day, 2008. I applied for admission in July and within one week was informed that I had been granted a 100% tuition scholarship. I enrolled in the MDiv program that fall full time.

My time in seminary, like many others have experienced, could be a book unto itself. But for the purposes of this one, it will suffice to say that I thoroughly enjoyed being a student. I had professors and colleagues I truly admired and respected, and I thank God for the education I received.

I was also challenged to my core by the progressive approach to the study of Christianity and the Bible in particular. It is said that seminaries and theological schools do this on purpose, to help rebuild students' theological foundation more solidly and give a surer footing for navigating theological matters. While I agree that the approach indeed shakes its recipient's core, I do not believe that the result brings about better faith leaders for ministry, which should be *a* goal, if not *the* goal, of a Master of Divinity degree program.

Among other deficits to the program, the minimal introduction to relevant scholarly materials from a traditional perspective was a real detriment. When introduced, I found it was done so usually in ways to not just critique it, but to delegitimize it with students. It was easier to be rewarded for criticizing such material than voice appreciation for it. It struck me as antithetical and hypocritical to a truly liberal educational methodology that such material was not afforded more respect. I remember approaching my New Testament professor, Dr. Melanie Johnson-DeBauffre, someone whom I respected and liked even though we disagreed on just about everything, and asking her if there were any scholars whose approaches I would have more affinity with and whose work I could read. She took pity on me and suggested I "go look up N.T. Wright." Even after over three years of seminary at that point, I had no clue who that preeminent, traditionalist New Testament scholar was. Discovering his work and the work of others was like receiving the balm of Gilead for my soul.

My initial plan had been full-time study and graduating with my MDIV in three years, the usual amount of time to receive such a degree. I had figured with my two children now being tweens, they were old enough and responsible enough to be without Mom, and not yet old enough to need constant chauffeuring from activity to activity. Yet God laughs at our plans when His are so much better.

SURPRISE BABY

As I finished my first year of full-time study, I was surprised to learn I was expecting our third child at age forty-three. I suddenly found myself navigating an unplanned pregnancy, the medical concerns of a later-in-life pregnancy, a radical lifestyle change, and a severing of relatability to many of my peers and friends. In terms of my call and ensuing education, this was a faith-challenging development. I wondered how I could continue and if I should. I was thoroughly challenged on my traditional beliefs about the sanctity of life and my God-given gifts and graces as a woman. I was in the right schooling environment to cause me to question everything.

Yet I had the right foundation, mentors, friends, and relationship with God to see me through. Camille Joy Caulfield, whose names combine to mean "perfect, unblemished joy," was born January 20, 2010. I ended up writing several published articles about the experience. The most extensive was for the Roman Catholic *Celebrate Life Magazine*,[3] another for *Prism Magazine*, which is a publication from Evangelicals for Social Action, and for United Methodist Women's (UMW) *Response* magazine.

The diversity and complexity of the waters I was learning to successfully navigate at the time was well represented in my journey to publication. First, I was published by a Catholic magazine that was adamant I did not mention in the article that I intended to go on to ordained ministry, given that women are not ordained as priests in their faith. I found a way to meet their request while still being true to my call.

United Methodist Women struggled to agree to publish my article for concern that they would appear to be endorsing an anti-abortion, pro-life political stance, which they do not. I found a way to make clear my own stance and how my mid-life pregnancy had cemented that for me, and yet comply with the restrictions UMW placed on my writing. After much personal grappling with the subject, it was clear to me that following God's lead regarding the preciousness of life above political concerns is crucial in all circumstances. God's lead sometimes takes different paths than expected, such as with me finding myself pregnant at the time and circumstances of my life that I did.

Of these publications, I found myself most aligned with the Evangelicals for Social Action, a group that follows a traditional faith with a strong emphasis on social witness. It was no surprise that they gave me the most freedom in crafting my convictions and true self in my article. It therefore also did not surprise me when years later, in 2020, they left behind their "Evangelical" title and became Christians for Social Action (CSA).[4] The term "evangelical" no longer offers an air of hospitality to a racially and culturally diverse world. CSA asserts, and I agree, that the term has been co-opted by a theo-political agenda that now weakens the witness of those who use it. As an important side note, I share at this juncture that I am a traditional, orthodox Christian steeped in the evangelical nature of faith, but I no longer utilize the label of evangelical.

After five years, on May 18, 2013, I graduated from Drew with my family by my side. My final GPA was 4.02. I received the *Order of St. Luke Hoyt Hickman Award* for excellence in liturgical studies and The Chalice Press Book Award for "Outstanding Achievement."

My graduation day from Drew Theological School, Madison, NJ, 2013. A big and busy day for our family. We also had a track meet for TJ and a dance recital for Amber that day. I was blessed that my parents could come up from Alabama.

"SHE" PREACHES GOSPEL

At this juncture, I suspect a clarification of Wesleyan theology, the United Methodist Church, and other Wesleyan heritage denominations' doctrine and polity regarding the ordination of women may be helpful. This chapter is a brief attempt at just that. I also address here concerns for those who question the rationale for a theology that supports the ordination of women and yet does not do so for openly practicing homosexuals. Clarity on these positions is important, especially at this juncture of my story because of the muddying of the waters I will detail in following chapters.

In 1761, John Wesley granted Sarah Crosby of Leeds, England a license to preach. Thus, it was the founder of Methodism who became the first within Methodism to authorize women preachers. Since his time there have been successful and even famed female preachers, church planters, and pastors throughout the Methodist/ Wesleyan movement. For example, in 1866, Helenor Davidson was an ordained circuit rider for the Methodist Protestant Church in Indiana. In the 1870s, Anna Howard Shaw was ordained in the Methodist Protestant Church in Michigan. There have been splits within the Methodist movement and politically-motivated and short-lived aberrations since Wesley's death that, among other shifts, resulted in some Wesleyan heritage denominations choosing polity that disallowed female ordination. However, today, of the approximately 80 Methodist, Wesleyan, and related denominations that belong to the World Methodist Council and represent over 80 million members in 138 countries, virtually all (if not all) have polity that supports female ordination. This includes the United Methodist Church. The new Global Methodist Church also affirms the ordination of women in its draft doctrines and disciplines. This practice is in line with Methodism's egalitarian position of women and their societal roles as part of God's good creation.

Most egalitarian churches have polity and teaching that support both women and men in church leadership positions, including as ordained clergy.[1]

I find within the report given by the *Task Force on Women in the Ministry appointed by the General Board of The Wesleyan Church* the best currently published summary of our Biblical understanding of women as ministry leaders. That report states:

> Scripture sets forth God's original plan and its redemptive renewal that provides equal standing to both men and women.
>
> 1. In the Beginning. The creation story reveals full equality of man and woman in God's original plan, as both were made in the image of God (Gen. 1:26-27), and the so-called "cultural mandate," giving them full authority over the earth and all earthly life-forms, was spoken to man and woman (Gen. 1:28-30). This plan of equality was interrupted by the Fall as human sin brought the wife's submission to her husband (Gen. 3:16). But even at that point God spoke of His redemptive plan as He foretold that Eve's descendant would crush Satan beneath His heel (Gen. 3:15). The redemptive purpose and mission of Jesus is to redeem all

humanity from the results of the fall, including the subjection of women. Jesus has provided equal forgiveness and redemption to both men and women.

2. In the Old Testament. God Himself initiated opportunities in the Old Testament period by His call to and use and blessing of women in ministry. God used Miriam as both a prophetess (Ex. 15:20) and a leader (Micah 6:4). He used Deborah as a prophetess and as a judge who led Israel; she directed Barak as to how military victory was to be won and even accompanied him into battle (Judg. 4:4ff.). God used the prophetess Huldah (even though Jeremiah and Zephaniah were prophets at the time) to spark a great religious revival during the reign of King Josiah (2 Kings 22:14ff.; 2 Chron. 34:22ff.). And God predicted through an Old Testament prophet the coming of the long-expected Day of the Lord when the Holy Spirit would be poured out on both men and women and they and their sons and daughters would prophesy (Joel 2:28-29).

3. In the Ministry of Jesus. The New Testament shows that Jesus differed from the prevailing culture in a very positive openness to women as co-laborers. He ministered to men and women alike without distinction. He violated several cultural taboos to share the good news with the Samaritan woman who then evangelized her village (John 4:7ff.). He was accompanied by women who ministered to Him and His disciples (Mark 15:40-41; Luke 8:1-3). And Jesus chose women to be the first to see Him after His resurrection and to be the first to carry the message of the resurrection to the male disciples.

4. At Pentecost. Both men and women were awaiting the ful-
   fillment of Jesus' promise that they would receive power for
   witnessing to the whole world when the Holy Spirit would
   come upon them (Acts 1:13-15). It was this group of men
   and women that was filled with the Holy Spirit on the day
   of Pentecost, and began to speak in many languages to the
   Jews assembled in Jerusalem for the festival (2:1-12). Peter
   took the occasion to declare that "this is that" which Joel
   had predicted: "Your sons and daughters will prophesy . . .
   and on my servants, both men and women, I will pour out
   my Spirit in those days, and they will prophesy" (2:17-18).
   So the birth of Christ's church was accompanied by the
   demonstration and announcement that men and women
   would both serve as God's voices to carry the message of
   Christ to the world.

5. In the Ministry of Paul. Paul reflected Jesus' openness to
   women as co-laborers. In what was probably the first epis-
   tle that he wrote, he declared that in Christ Jesus, "There
   is neither . . . male nor female, for you are all one in Christ
   Jesus" (Gal. 3:28). In writing to the Corinthians, he recognized that women prophesied and prayed in public
   worship under the new order (1 Cor. 11:5). When closing his letter to the Romans, Paul mentions ten women
   in chapter 16, seven of whom he speaks of with detailed,
   high commendation, referring to one as a "deacon" (not
   deaconess) who had been a great help to many including
   Paul himself, referring to one as "outstanding among the
   apostles," referring to one as a "fellow worker," and referring to those who had worked hard "in the Lord" or for

the Roman believers. In Philippians 4:2-3 he mentions two women who had "contended at my side in the cause of the gospel."[2]

Certain Scriptures are often cited against women leading men in ministry by non-egalitarians that include 1 Corinthians 11:5, 14:33b-35, 1 Timothy 2:11-15, and other passages in 1 Timothy and Titus. Egalitarians believe these scriptures are misused when interpreted in such a manner. For example, when Paul spoke to the Corinthians in the passages inappropriately reduced to "women should remain silent in the churches," he was addressing a specific and most likely localized problem that was disrupting the church meeting. That women are not forbidden to speak by Paul is evident also in 1 Corinthians 11:5 when he indeed acknowledges women having place to prophesy. His comments reveal him traversing the challenges of encouraging the Corinthians to navigate the culture around them (including their right to wear a head covering or not), as they were living out being both in that culture but not of it. The navigation of culture he was encouraging was intent on both attracting outsiders through the freedom displayed in Christ and yet also protecting the church from becoming a perceived threat to local authorities.

Paul also demonstrated the same concerns of sensitivity to worshipping amidst the surrounding culture in his correspondence regarding the Ephesians in the 1 Timothy letter. This includes the 1 Timothy 2:1-15 passage that is often reduced to and interpreted as "women are not to teach or have authority over men." But even more important to understand is that in 1 Timothy, Paul repeatedly refers to problems that are commonly interpreted by scholars to be signs of early Christian Gnostic teachings infiltrating the

Church at Ephesus. It appears they had especially been taught to and embraced by at least some outspoken women. I would note that Christian Gnosticism's emphasis on spiritual over bodily relevance and experience, i.e. asceticism, can be quite liberating to those living in corporeally oppressive conditions (like many of the women in Ephesus). Hence, I can understand the possible attraction to Gnosticism for women living in the Ephesian culture. Asceticism, that is, denying the body, also usually includes sexual abstinence. So when 1 Timothy 2:15 concludes with a reference to women being "saved through childbearing," I support the interpretation that Paul was telling the women to stop refusing sexual relations with their husbands in the cause of their faith.[3]

Finally, Paul communicates qualifications for "a bishop" (KJV) or "overseer" (NIV) in 1 Timothy 3:1, an elder/bishop/overseer in Titus 1:5-7, and "a deacon" in 1 Timothy 3:12. It is often cited by non-egalitarians that in all cases the passages include that those in such positions should be the "husband of but one wife." It is therefore concluded such positions are to be held by men alone. Such interpretation, however, ignores that Paul implies that he and Barnabas were not married (1 Cor. 9:5-6) and therefore not "husbands of but one wife." It also misses that Paul specifically calls Phoebe a deacon (Rom. 16:1). Those references help in clarifying that Paul's point was not to reinforce only men in leadership, but rather to exclude polygamous men from such positions of authority. He was setting a standard for Christian human sexuality and marital relationships of Church leadership. My thought is that such standards may have already been challenged.

This brings me to another question often posed: If traditional Wesleyans support the ordination of women, how do we not support the ordination of practicing homosexuals? Is our differentiation not antithetical?

In the most succinct language possible, firstly, we are not being contradictory as we differentiate being a woman from the behavior of same-sex intimacy. The trajectory for women in the Bible is redemptive, leading to full inclusion as leaders for Christ. For the practice of same-sex intimacy, the Bible offers no redemptive trajectory. It only condemns the practice as one of many sins to be overcome through the power/love/transformation offered in Christ.[4] Therefore it is not keeping with our understanding and beliefs to ordain those who knowingly and unrepentantly deny and teach others to deny through their public witness what is consistently and clearly asserted by Scripture regarding such practices.

We follow Scripture in our understanding that people are made in the image of God as male or female and that we are uniquely crafted out of all of creation with a biologically sexed body, and that body is consistently independent of our behavior, desires, or identity (our sense of who we are). Scripture teaches that all are loved by God[5] and all have sinned and fall short of the glory of God (Romans 3:23). While not everyone has a choice as to whether we experience same-sex attractions, there is a choice involved with acting on same-sex attractions, and we also have a choice as to whether or not we identify as LGBTQ+. Therefore, there is a categorical difference between being a woman and choosing to act on a temptation consistently deemed as sinful in the Bible (both Old and New Testaments).

Finally, I would add that identifying yourself by who you are attracted to sexually, or by what you're tempted by, is a relatively new social construct. It is an ideology that we do not believe holds up theologically, philosophically, or scientifically. Theologically, we follow Genesis 1:27 (CEB) for our identity: "God created humanity in God's own image, in the divine image God created them, male and female God created them." Also as Christians, we know our identity primarily in Christ. Philosophically, Michael Hannon points out:

> ...ultimately, the empirical problem with the sexual-orientation framework we have been handed is that it is too neat, that it works by oversimplifying an incredibly messy web of attractions and drives and temptations, and that it inhibits the taming of those desires by improperly amplifying their significance.[6]

Scientifically, studies have shown that same sex attraction is not an immutable (unchanging or unable to be changed) characteristic. Most people who experience same sex attraction do not do so exclusively across their lifetime. In other words, sexual orientation is fluid. It can be changed.[7]

Now for the muddy waters. The reality is that there are those in leadership of Wesleyan-identified churches who do not follow or teach egalitarian understanding of the Scriptures regarding women and women's ordination. Frequently they were first indoctrinated in churches that do not support women as ordained clergy or in other leadership roles that oversee men. Some are misinformed and believe traditional Methodism supports their views. Some just want to subjugate women. Some are even women who wrestle with deciding what God truly tells them about their roles. I, too, had to search prayerfully and theologically consider this point early in my walk and call by God into leadership.

Additionally, even though virtually every Wesleyan heritage denomination affirms the ordination of women, women, and especially
racial/ethnic women, are still unlikely to be called or appointed
by bishops and their cabinets to large churches or to have higher
salaries.[8] In fact, in keeping with other mainline denominations
who report similar statistics, in a 2017 release, the UMC's General
Commission on the Status and Role of Women shared that female
clergy salary was 16% less than male's, and our housing allowances
were 14% less.[9] As of this writing, a partially released updated survey shows some progress in 2020, but also continued obvious disparities.[10] There are also a few Wesleyan denominations, mostly
I believe in Africa, that, although they affirm female ordination,
do not affirm through their polity women reaching the Episcopal
office. So even though our theology and polity affirm women in
leadership, Wesleyans still send less than fully supportive messages
to female clergy and to their congregations and ultimately their
communities and world about female leadership.

Many United Methodist female clergy find progressive theologies
to be more supportive of these concerns. I understand that perception and its appeal. I do not, however, believe that the direction progressive theologies in general have taken are based on the historical
Christian faith and therefore limits its truth and power for the heart
transformation that is needed to correct the sinful challenges that
women face as clergy and otherwise. While many progressive theologies adhered to in the UMC tout understanding that is based on
Scripture, reason, tradition, and experience, by their own admis-
sions they focus foremost on experience, not the teachings and
hope of Scripture for all humankind that John Wesley and the vast
majority of Christians throughout history and still today rely upon

first. That experiential focus leads to a different Gospel, one that is less reliant on the transforming power of Christ.

In conclusion to this chapter, as a traditional Methodist, I uphold the following statement made in the report by the *Task Force on Women in the Ministry appointed by the General Board of The Wesleyan Church* cited previously:

We believe that our experience over the past 150 years affirms the fact that the Holy Spirit anoints and blesses the ministry of women. We can provide examples of pastors, evangelists, preachers, teachers, missionaries, church planters and church leaders who have rendered Spirit-anointed and Spirit-empowered service. They have won thousands of converts, recruited scores of ministers and leaders (both male and female), established scores of churches, developed mission fields, and taught entire generations of ministers in some overseas fields—often serving where no one else would go… To live within the teachings of Scripture, we must work counter-culturally to provide women with increasing opportunities to answer the call of God.

I look forward to a similar report being published by The Global Methodist Church .

ORDINATION PROCESS BEGINS

I am not certain about my call beyond what I have written. I am applying for ordination with the United Methodist Church because it seems logical. Whether I am to pursue a deacon or elder position, I am not sure. Whether I am being called to work in a church environment or some other agency, again, I do not know. However, I have complete confidence in my Lord and Savior Jesus Christ and the plans that God has for me. I look forward to experiencing what our loving God has in store for me next.

– Beth Caulfield, 3/29/09

That paragraph was included in the initial paperwork I forwarded to the Raritan Valley District Superintendent of the Greater New Jersey Annual Conference in 2009. I was requesting to enter the candidacy process and to receive a candidacy mentor. How I have pondered that paragraph written more than twelve years ago. Surely the Lord has been good to me even as the United Methodist ordination process has not.

I now genuinely believe revealing my journey in this book is indeed part of my call. My story through this system sheds light not only on me, my growing edges, and my own journey with the Lord, but also on the many failures of the United Methodist ordination process as it is currently administered, and of the failings of leadership who own that process.

I began exploring the candidacy process early in seminary, but it took several correspondences sent by me before the District Superintendent responded roughly nine months later. I was not alone in this experience. I had several discussions with colleagues in seminary about our not being responded to by the Greater New Jersey Annual Conference when we inquired about the ordination process. The conference was publicly touting their desire for good leaders, but we were being ignored. I have since heard accounts of similar experiences years later in the Greater New Jersey Conference as well as in others. The issue does not stem from one derelict District Superintendent.

While I do not believe my traditional Wesleyan theology was known or the cause of the problems I encountered at the time, I do believe adhering to traditional theology and coming from more conservative seminaries is a major cause of problems for others here in Greater New Jersey and elsewhere. I have colleagues with traditional Wesleyan theology who have waited months as their academic credentialing was looked into by the conference. Meanwhile they were or still are in limbo or, in some cases, have chosen to serve in another more accommodating denomination.

When I finally met the District Superintendent (DS) at his office for an interview in the Spring of 2009, I was surprised and saddened that much of our conversation turned to his own personal problems. This was a man who I had never met, yet with whom I immediately found myself in an already familiar pastoral role. We ended the conversation with me praying for him and his troubles, rather than about my calling. I felt a strong sense of compassion for him at the time, yet I also left that meeting feeling uneasy.

I shared the experience with my pastor, Rev. Galen Goodwin, a former DS himself. He was about to retire but made a point of interceding and finding a mentor for me. By June 2009, I was meeting with Rev. Dr. Vickie Brendler, then pastor of Bridgewater UMC, a former DS, and former GNJ Conference-endorsed candidate for bishop.

As far as mentors go within the UMC system, I do not believe I could have been given a better one. Vickie went above and beyond over the eight years that she mentored me. I considered her a friend and I believe the feeling was mutual. We had some theological differences, but I do not believe those hindered her mentoring me. Among other decisions, she helped me discern that my call was to become an elder rather than a deacon.

However, I do believe that as my influence grew within the United Methodist system, Vickie became less of an advocate for me. It was both politics and her loyalty to a progressive agenda within the UMC that ultimately led to our parting of ways. But while being loyal to a specific cause, person or church can be a good thing, I had to cut ties with her in response to injustices being done to me through the system and people with whom she held alliances.

Those alliances understandably included her own daughter, Rev. Jessica Brendler, who was working on her own career agenda as a bright and upcoming pastor, serving on the Greater New Jersey Board of Ordained Ministry and as a leading local member of the Reconciling Ministries Network, an organization that states it seeks "to advance justice and inclusion for all LGBTQ people in the United Methodist Church and beyond."[1] Vickie's adopted brother, Mark Miller, serves at Drew Theological School as Director of Craig

Chapel, Professor of Church Music and Composer in Residence. He is well known as an outstanding song writer/composer who, among many other contributions, wrote "Draw the Circle Wide, a popular song for United Methodists and in other religious and progressive settings. A gay father in a same-sex marriage, Mark has been very involved in bringing LGBTQIA issues to the forefront of UMC concerns. Again, I have much respect for the mentoring that Vickie gave me as I prepared for my calling within the United Methodist Church.

WHO SAID I WON'T MOVE?

Itineracy is a requirement in the United Methodist Church for its elders. As such, I had not intended to move forward in the elder candidacy process until after my oldest children were out of high school. Especially after my own relocating experiences as a youth in the later years of high school, I did not want to move them at such a critical time in their development. However, my candidacy mentor encouraged me to enter the process and begin serving in some capacity.

Also, and most importantly, in the Fall of 2011, Greater New Jersey Annual Conference Bishop Sudarshana Devadhar visited UMC students at Drew and assured us in a publicly held meeting that those with children in their last years of high school would not receive an appointment that required moving. He claimed that he and his cabinet would work with the candidate. Based on this proclamation, my husband and I decided I should move forward in the process.

I went before the Raritan Valley DCOM to be examined in the Spring of 2012. I was seamlessly recommended and my paperwork was forwarded to the Board of Ordained Ministry. I entered the provisional candidacy process and submitted the extensive paper-work and all other requirements to go before the Board of Ordained Ministry at their interview retreat in February 2013. During my home church's Fall 2012 Church Conference, I informed my then DS, Rev. Dr. Barbara Rambach (now deceased), that if I was approved by the Board I would only be seeking an initial appointment that was commutable from my current home as I had two high schoolers and a toddler and was not going to move at this time. My husband and I would be willing to itinerate once the older two had graduated. She thanked me for letting her know early and made a note of my comments.

What I did not understand, nor was ever explained to me, was the significance of there having been a change in bishops appointed to our conference (Fall 2012). Bishop John R. Schol was appointed to Greater New Jersey after serving eight years as Bishop of the Baltimore Washington Conference. In essence, what I now know is that Bishop Devadhar's policies for appointment making differed greatly from John Schol's.

I also am unclear whether the request I made not to move was ever communicated to the cabinet table. If it was, it was not honored. Nor was I ever told that it would not be honored. Thus, I went forward to the Board of Ordained Ministry Retreat to advance and serve to the best of my abilities.

I did well under examination at the retreat, and shortly thereafter received a call from my then pastor at Clinton and member of the Board, Rev. Dr. Andy Hoover, sharing the good news. All seemed well. Our family celebrated and looked forward to my next ministry opportunity being revealed.

Within a couple of weeks, however, I received a phone call from the District Superintendent of the Capitol District, telling me the bishop was offering me an appointment at Medford UMC as an Associate Pastor. This was a wonderful opportunity from a ministry standpoint, but Medford was an hour and a half from my home and would require relocating.

I was told to pray about this opportunity and that I had 24 hours to respond. This short time to decide on a major life decision is standard UMC practice. It hails, I am led to understand, from the days of the circuit riders, who were to be ready to preach across the land at a moment's notice. Life is a little different now, but this is not the kind of cultural context change that UMC leadership is interested in making. I believe not revising this approach is an abusive, and frankly lazy, mistake that leads to more problems than the nostalgic spiritual myth supposedly driving it is worth.

Nonetheless, I knew immediately in my heart that this was not a good choice for the church or for me. It was simply too far from my home. I therefore told her right then that I could not accept the appointment. She acted surprised when I explained why. I was not sure if she was reacting as one who had never heard that I had restrictions, or as someone who was shocked that I would say no to an appointment and do so immediately. The DS then told me I would receive further instruction.

The next day I was contacted by the Chair of the Board of Ordained Ministry. I was told that the conditions of me having been recommended as a provisional elder included that I would itinerate, and that it appeared I had not been honest with the Board about my willingness to do so. She told me that my case would need to be reviewed and that the recommendation might be rescinded.

So that is how I started out with the appointment process and the Board of Ordained Ministry. I was already a problem child for the intertwined system that supposedly valued compliance with the rules unless the bishop determined they did not apply. Which he had.

Meanwhile, a major life decision and a whole lot of work for being recommended by the Board of Ordained Ministry was now jeopardized. I was also hurting as my integrity was being challenged. Yet I naively believed this was all something that could be worked out, because even though the denomination might be a little antiquated and disorganized in its management practices and leadership, the end goal of bringing ministry leaders into the system to further the mission of Jesus Christ would prevail.

Within a few weeks I was contacted by the bishop's office for a meeting with Bishop Schol, the District Superintendent, and the Chair of the Board of Ordained Ministry. I had in the past heard the bishop speak but had never interacted with him personally. As one might imagine, preparing for such a meeting was quite stressful. I had a number of friends and mentors praying for me, however.

At the meeting I told the truth about all that had transpired between the District Superintendent and me, and what had been shared by Bishop Devadhar. No one disputed what I shared. I told them that I had honestly answered that I was willing to be a part of the itineracy system, but that my position on itineracy at this particular time in my family life had not changed and I had been truthful with everyone about that. I tearfully shared that I did not want to move my children at such a crucial time for my oldest two, and at a time when I would have to find new and significant support caring for my youngest.

Bishop Schol indicated he understood but told me there were probably no appointments available to me at this late juncture in the appointment season that would meet my needs. If the Committee on Investigation determined that I was to remain recommended for commissioning as a provisional elder, then he would see what he could do.

I was then examined by the Committee on Investigation. Hearing my story, they determined that I should remain a provisional candidate for ordination and be commissioned as originally indicated. From there I was sent to my Board of Ordained Ministry Debrief Team, who put together a Growth Plan for me. A Growth Plan is standard for all candidates and is created by using feedback from the Board. My Growth Plan had added to it that I must interview ten elders regarding the importance of itineracy and write a report to be submitted to the Board.

I then was instructed that I must appeal to the cabinet and the Board of Ordination for a full-time appointment. So as instructed, I wrote the following.

> *April 9, 2013*
>
> *Board of Ordained Ministry*
>
> *Greater New Jersey Annual Conference*
>
> *Rev. Shawn Callender Hogan, Chairperson*

Dear Rev. Callender Hogan and Board:

Given the current challenges for appointing me to a full-time elder position in the GNJAC this year, after prayerful contemplation, I would like to clarify and request consideration for the following:

It is still my primary hope to receive a full-time appointment that I could assume responsibilities for July 1, 2013. I have indicated my willingness to be creative about such an appointment to the cabinet and bishop and have ideas that could be beneficial for the Conference and local church for such an assignment. I would like to discuss these ideas with my District Superintendent.

If a full-time appointment is not possible, then I hope for and request a part-time appointment.

If no such appointments are directed, then I am requesting a one-year Leave of Absence effective July 1st. I will utilize this time serving God in other capacities and being available to appointment during the year.

In essence, it is my strongest desire to serve the conference as fully as possible. I look forward to doing so as the Board, bishop and cabinet see fit.

In God's Peace
Beth Caulfield

cc. Rev. Bobbi Rambach, Raritan Valley District Superintendent

The whole experience was incredibly challenging. I was a top student, had basically been drafted into the ordination process despite my original plan to wait, passed the strenuous ordination examination, and followed all instructions. And yet the process was already failing me and my ministry.

As I waited to hear if I would receive an appointment, I spent a good bit of time in prayer and fasting. I thought about going to another denomination at that point, that maybe God was calling me elsewhere. Why would God be calling me to a denomination with so much conflict around theology, and why did joining them have to hurt so much? I talked to pastor friends at the Church of the Nazarene and at the Assemblies of God. I wondered if I should just spend time writing rather than serving in a denomination. I really did not know what to do and nothing seemed clear from God. I have frequently wondered how different my story would be if I had just walked away at that time. However, are we not called to grace even when people treat us poorly? Michelle Obama put it like this, "When they go low, we go high." I have quoted her 2016 Democratic Convention statement in many sermons to illustrate Matthew 6:12, 7:12, 18:21-22. I chose obedience to God.

PART TIME?

In mid-May, on the day of the awards ceremony at Drew, my District Superintendent requested I meet her at her office. After receiving my awards, my husband and I drove over from the ceremony. She had news of an appointment. It was at North Hunterdon United Methodist Church, a half-time appointment church in our district. It was a ten-minute drive from my house. Because it was a less than full-time appointment, it meant that I would not be eligible to go before the Board of Ordained Ministry again for full orders for at least an extra year in the process, as you need two full-time years of service to be eligible for full orders. But a way had been found for me to serve near my home and I thanked God for it.

The previous pastor of the church had overseen a two-point charge (two churches), and thus the church had paid half her salary, half her benefits, and assisted with utilities at the parsonage she lived in that they also provided. She had also received travel and educational reimbursement expenses commensurate with a full-time appointment.

Because I had my own home and benefits through my husband, I negotiated with the church through the DS that the appointment be made ¾ time rather than ½ time, and that I would receive ¾ of the minimal salary for a newly-appointed provisional elder according to the conference established equitable pay guidelines. Therefore my salary was $29.7k annually. A full-time appointment would have paid at a minimum $39.6k. I was offered no housing allowance, which is an addition to your salary given in lieu of a parsonage . I was ignorant that housing allowances even existed at that time. The Book of discipline allots for housing allowances, but turns to annual conferences to set their own policies regarding them. In GNJ, part-time clergy are not required to receive housing allowances when a parsonage is available to them and they opt not to live there. However there is nebulousness around GNJ's policy for such situations and the DS's involvement is key.

Because it is a common misconception that clergy salary is tax-free, I share that this is not exactly true. It is an understandable assumption because it is well known that, in most cases, churches are tax-exempt entities. That means churches, who are the clergy's employers, are not required to withhold income tax from pastors' wages. A clergy, therefore, must pay taxes like a self-employed worker, yet they are not eligible for all the tax benefits many self-employed workers enjoy. However, ordained, commissioned, or licensed clergy, whether serving in a local church or elsewhere under appointment (called extension ministry in the UMC), can exclude a portion of their compensation when reporting gross income for federal income tax purposes that is used to provide housing for themselves. There are limits on what can be claimed as housing expenses. At North Hunterdon, I received no housing allowance, but was eligible to take a housing exclusion up to my full salary for tax purposes. As the compensation is so low, it is not uncommon for clergy who are part-time, have a very small congregation, or have another source of income to deduct 100% of their clergy compensation.

The church was happy because my salary as a part-time Provisional elder was less than their previous pastor had received, there was no housing allowance involved, they would not be required to contribute to any medical insurance for me, they would no longer have to pay utilities for a pastor not living in their parsonage, and they would be able to rent out the parsonage for additional income. There would be additional tax implications for renting the parsonage out, but North Hunterdon leadership determined the taxes were worth it. And all of us knew there is rarely such a thing as a ¾ time pastor: they would receive my full-time attention.

This is ministry as vocation, and those who follow its call are not doing it for the money. We believe that God will take care of us and, surely, He does. (Psalm 23:1-4, 6). I share this common belief at this juncture in my story for two reasons. One, the statement, "that I do not do this for the money but for greater reward," should be written on the heart of all who enter ministry. However, because that statement is in fact written on the hearts of many, I also point it out because clergy and others in ministry are often too timid to question the results of the DS's and church's salary negotiations and you have no real outside advocate to turn to when you have concerns. The implication is that if you question the process or results, there may be consequences in your future treatment. At a minimum, you may be characterized by your bosses to not be at the level of faith needed for the job, difficult to deal with, or inappropriately focused. Everyone should learn how to stand up for their own fair pay, however, for clergy in the UMC system, the challenge in doing so is a bit more complicated.

I was commissioned at Wildwood in May 2013 and humbly thanked the bishop for my appointment, even though the experience of receiving it had been painful.

Commissioning/Ordination Service with Bishop School, May 2013.

NORTH HUNTERDON

North Hunterdon was in a rural location and was mostly known in the community for its thrift shop. Yet the congregation was gracious and welcoming. My first Sunday in the pulpit there were only eighteen people in the pews, and four of them were my own family. Nonetheless, there was a desire expressed to be led and to grow the church.

North Hunterdon UMC's Harvest of Hope event

Within a couple of months, I recognized it to be a congregation that needed encouragement and ministry to unify and spark those within it to utilize their gifts. I began rallying the church around the idea of turning their poorly attended Fall Festival into a broader event focused on raising money for the conference's major mission effort at the time, A Future of Hope. This mission was dedicated to relief and help rebuilding for those suffering from the devastation of Superstorm Sandy that hit New Jersey in the fall of 2012.

From its inception, there has been much controversy around Bishop Schol's Future of Hope 501(c)(3), which was established during his first year as bishop of Greater New Jersey. The issues have never stemmed from concern regarding the humanitarian mission work the organization does. The issues have not been that it was designed to provide a legal buffer for the Annual Conferences repair mission and related matters. The concerns that have lent to distrust have been over how Bishop Schol initiated and established the effort. This is evidenced by the fact that shortly after its formation, GNJ Annual Conference members asked four questions of law of Bishop Schol that required rulings by the UMC Judicial Council, which is the denomination's equivalent to the Supreme Court. The Council's rulings are found in their Decision Numbers 1256-1259. The Digest for Decision 1257 accurately portrays the nature of all concerns registered and is a good example of denominational leadership's understanding of Schol's tactics and yet inherent lack of structural teeth for curtailing his out-of-bounds endeavors:

Judicial Council Decision 1257   Oct. 25, 2013

The ruling of law by the Bishop on Question 2 from the Greater New Jersey Annual Conference is not affirmed. The Primary Task Team, Conference Council on Finance and Administration and conference leadership including the Bishop and Cabinet had no authority to take actions to set forth a disaster response plan and budget including the establishment of the nonprofit corporation *A Future with Hope*, Inc., and to elect a Board of Directors on its own without prior Annual Conference approval. The campaign plan is legal as it was approved by the Annual Conference on a motion from the Conference Council on Finance and Administration. To rule that *A Future with Hope* corporation is null, void and without effect is impractical and probably impossible as it is a now a separately incorporated entity meeting a great humanitarian need. However, this ruling serves as a pronouncement to the Greater New Jersey Annual Conference to be cognizant of the importance of maintaining the role of the Annual

Conference in decision-making and in monitoring the future structure and strategic decisions of the Annual Conference and the actions of the conference entities between the sessions of the annual conference.[2]

Perhaps that Digest and those of the other questions raised serve as a hand slap to Bishop Schol, but there were no other formal consequences given. Additionally, the red flag of nepotism was raised at that time, when Bishop Schol's wife was immediately brought as an employee of A Future With Hope with significant management responsibilities. I speak further to concerns of nepotism in the chapter entitled "Cuba Gooding." So even as he began his tenure with Greater New Jersey, a seed of distrust was sown as Schol blatantly disregarded the church doctrine he had been entrusted to protect.

Poster we used all over the community and social media to advertise our event.

The Caribbean Steel Rhythms gave an amazing performance at our Fall Harvest of Hope

I was oblivious to those controversies as I planned our Harvest of Hope event to raise awareness of the good work being done and its need for human volunteers and financial support. In addition to our own inhouse family band, The Williams Boyz, we brought in a variety of church praise bands from the area, including from Clinton United Methodist Church, Bloomsbury UMC, and a Caribbean Steele Drum band from a church in Pennsylvania. We also featured local youth singers and a liturgical dance troop from Irvington's Christian Love Baptist Church who traveled across the state to be with us. We advertised throughout the community and invited local media and press as well as conference staff and local churches and their pastors.

We partnered with local businesses for product donations to be used at the event and to be auctioned off for the Superstorm Sandy effort. Our little church hosted roughly two hundred people that day. By the time it was over, we were on the map with the conference, the community, and local UMC churches, and the church's spirit, camaraderie, and confidence in ministry was high.

North Hunterdon Fall Harvest of Hope, 2013.

My traditional theology was clearly articulated through my ministry and the church began growing. We also began attracting visits
and new membership from Clinton UMC. By this time, the now
Rev. Dr. Andy Hoover had been brought back to Clinton as its
senior pastor by the previous bishop. It was a popular move for the
progressives within the church, but less so with more traditional
members. Those who came over from Clinton to North Hunterdon
had grown dissatisfied with the boldly articulated progressive messages and vocal disagreement with the Doctrines and Disciplines
of the Church around the subject of human sexuality espoused by
both him and the staff members he brought on board.

My work at the church in a short period of time caught Bishop Schol's
attention, as captured in a <u>video</u>[3] that was prepared for the North

Hunterdon congregation in January 2014 at the bishop's winter convocation. Clergy had been invited to sign up for a personal video message from the bishop to our respective churches. Having a church that needed encouragement, I signed up. What is also caught in the video are a couple of red flags that I sensed at the time but did not fully appreciate. In it, Schol praises the work of the church. However, his comments regarding me offered flattery and preceded those regarding the church. His words included "rarely have I encountered the kind of pastor who just comes out of seminary with the kind of experience, enthusiasm, depth, and commitment to serving the church," and "I'm grateful, Beth, for your leadership and all that you are doing..." At the time I thought perhaps this was a way of making up for the injustice that had been done to me with the appointment. I suppose it was also a way of encouraging the church to be satisfied with me as their pastor. Now, however, after years of experience with him, I recognize what Wade Mullen describes in his 2020 book *Something's Not Right: Decoding the Hidden Tactics of Abuse—And Freeing Yourself from its Power*. Mullen states, "The flatterer wants you to see something pleasant about yourself, not for the sake of encouragement or affirmation, but so that you think more highly of them," and "flattery redirects your attention: by focusing on your real, fabricated, or exaggerated positive characteristics, you are kept from seeing the true desires and agenda behind the compliments."

Schol and Caulfield, January 2014

The second indicator of something not right was that Bishop Schol did not invite me to speak. It felt awkward and disappointing, but as overall this was a wonderful compliment to the church and to my ministry, I buried the unsettled feeling. I remember one of my seminary professors commenting on the social media post of the video, saying "Great. Wish we could have heard from you, too." I later came to appreciate that the video was just one example of Bishop Schol's need to be the center, focus, and controller of everything. I also believe it depicts his true character for working with women.

My traditional ministry also caught the attention of Rev. Dr. Hoover, which I did not grasp the significance of at the time, but received warning of through a dream that I recorded but did not understand until later. Looking back, I believe the stark difference in my ministry and theology from Rev. Hoover's was on his radar for longer than I was aware. I remember he and his wife attending our Harvest of Hope event and feeling a less than supportive vibe from him. I did not register the significance of it at the time, however.

CONFERENCE CALLING

At the end of 2014, just seven months into my ministry at North Hunterdon, I attended the bishop's Convocation in Long Branch, NJ. This was an annual, three-day retreat for clergy to recharge and be ministered to by the conference, with invited guest speakers, preachers, and leisure time.

One of the leisurely activities offered during the conference was a tour of homes that were being rebuilt by the Future of Hope team. I signed up because of interest in the project and, frankly, to get outside and do something different. The tour ended up taking me and the few others on it to meet the Future of Hope staff, including the bishop's wife, Mrs. Beverly Schol.

Also during the conference, my email was hacked, and everyone in my contacts list received an email supposedly from me stating I was stranded in Italy, my purse had been stolen, and I was requesting money to return home. Several people at the conference received the email, including the bishop, who was the first to inform me my email had been hacked. This was a less frequent occurrence in 2014 than it is today, so it garnered me much attention throughout the conference. Suddenly many people were seeking me out, either teasing me in fun and/or expressing concern for me and anyone who might fall victim to the hoax. So, in less than a seventy-two hour period, I made a video about my work with the bishop, met and spent time with his wife, and was on many people's radar because of a fraudulent email. All I can say is if it was God wanting me to be seen, well, he does work in mysterious ways.

On the last day of the Convocation, I was approached separately by various conference staff and encouraged to apply for one of the five newly created Connectional Ministries team positions. These were staff positions that would report to the Director of Connectional Ministries and would work in partnership with the bishop's cabinet. I was aware of the positions but had not given any thought to applying for them as I was just starting as a provisional elder with less than six months experience. But by the time I left the Convocation, I understood that I had a very good chance of being placed in one of them. When I asked which one to apply for, I was told whichever one I thought was the best fit.

I went home, read the job descriptions, and talked to and prayed with my husband and kids. The next day I sent the following email:

Beth Caulfield <bcaulfield710@gmail.com>
Thu, Jan 30, 2014, 3:17 PM

to bhartman, John Schol

Hi Bruce -

As I've thought more about our conversation yesterday, I realize that I have not only skills but very relevant experience with small groups organization for faith formation - I was a Director for 6 years for the parachurch organization Community Bible Study International- setting up small groups internationally, in New Jersey and even in prisons.

I'd like to apply for the position if it is still available. Let me know and I will submit all the necessary paperwork.

Thank you,
Beth

These were prized positions, high profile, and well compensated within the UMC church world. My initial salary was $60k. I also received a housing allowance of roughly $20k, a housing exclusion allowance, and was allowed to opt out of the medical benefit plans (unlike other clergy in church full-time appointments in our conference, who are required to participate, paying for it out of their own salary as well as their churches paying the premiums). I received a $12k spending/travel allowance, a corporate credit card, a laptop, iPad, and an iPhone with all charges for service paid for by the conference.

Bishop Schol, now in his position for just over a year, was dismantling the staff put in place by his predecessor and bringing in his own. That appointment season he replaced seven of nine cabinet members, the Connectional Ministries Director, and the Connectional Ministries staff with four out of five of us becoming new members.

It is my understanding that there had been four different clergy who had already been signaled by conference leadership that they would be placed into the Connectional Ministries positions. Schol, however, with perhaps the advisement of his new Connectional Ministries Director Bruce Hartman and a couple of church leadership consultants, did an abrupt about face. In just a few weeks, hiring decisions were made to bring in an entirely different Connectional Ministries Team: Rev. Matthew Na as Director of Professions of Faith and Youth/Young Adults, Nicole Caldwell-Gross as Director of Mission and Multi-cultural Ministries, Rev. Hector Burgos as Director of Worship and Urban Ministries, and me, as Director of Small Groups and Spiritual Visioning. We joined Rev. Dr. Rich Hendrickson, who had been functioning as the Director of Stewardship and Visioning for a few years on the former Connectional Ministries team.

A few months into the job, a friendly District Superintendent who later retired whispered that me getting that job "was evil being repaid." She was referencing a problem that Carey Nieuwhof captures in his January 2018 blog, entitled "Jealousy, Envy, Insecurity and The Heart of a Pastor."[4] He asserts that jealousy and envy are the dark underbelly of ambition in church leaders and are a significant and troubling problem. She was confirming that what happened to me as I entered the ranks of UMC clergy with the Board of Ordination and appointment situation that led me to a less than fulltime position was the result of such feelings fueling bad actors. That was only the beginning.

THE SET UP

The new Connectional Ministries Team was introduced to the conference at a pre-Lenten clergy gathering of over 350 conference clergy in late February 2014. The event was carefully scripted to allot each of us a space to lead the service and share a little about our gifts, graces, and calls as they related to the positions we were about to begin. We were dressed well and an attractive bunch. The bishop and Bruce Hartman introduced us and praised us extensively. At one point, Bishop Schol shared from the pulpit a pet name for us that was repeated several times over the coming year. He called us "The Dream Team."

You could have heard a pin drop when that label was introduced. Everyone on the team would later recount how our stomachs tightened with that pronouncement. We all knew that we were going to have to work extra hard to overcome jealousy, resentment, and skepticism. There was already resistance to our positions having been created and the costs associated with them. There were already former staff members who had been displaced to make room for us. There were also at least four other people who had thought they were getting the jobs but were replaced on the roster at seemingly the last minute. Additionally, the new cabinet members were being told that they were to be in partnership with us and that we would very much be included in conference decision-making and leading initiatives that would be high profile. This added another layer of friction for us to navigate.

Hector and Matthew were already ordained elders and, in that sense, secure in the system. Nicole was also secure as a lay person who would later seek and achieve ordination in a Baptist denomination with a much less subjective and tedious process than the United Methodists'. Rich, also an elder in full connection (ordained), had been in his position for a while and the conference was used to him. His wife was also being named dean of the cabinet. That left me.

I was the only one on the stage (literally on a stage) who had an obvious vulnerability. I was seeking ordination and therefore laid open to subjective scrutiny by my peers. Yet by the grace of God, there I stood.

In the eyes of too many who at that point had never even met me, I was simply someone who was less than a year out of seminary, had been commissioned for less than a year, part-time in a tiny church, and now only seven months after entering my first appointment, was receiving one of the most sought-after positions in the conference. To others, I was also the one who had gotten away with being less than honest with the Board of Ordained Ministry. I was a person who had said no to not just any appointment, but a good one and the very first appointment I was given. Add in that I was physically fit and well-dressed, in a long-term marriage, and had three obviously well-adjusted children.

It is sad to say that, as has been noted by others and shared with me too many times, the truth was that the battle I would first and from then on face was not just proving my value to the conference. It was not just the theological one regarding progressive vs. traditional theology that would be later revealed. I would also need to overcome jealousy, envy, and the insecurities of those in power: specifically, the Board of Ordained Ministry and the cabinet. As I would later learn, the two were closely intertwined despite the provisions within the United Methodist Book of Discipline that attempt to dispel such power alignment.

As I would also learn, I would have no internal safe place or advocate built into the system to protect or advise me. There is no viable human resources department for clergy within the church. You are at the mercy and whim of the bishop, cabinet, and Board of Ordained Ministry. If clergy have a complaint, unless it is against the bishop directly (which is its own can of worms), they are to take it through one of those groups. Even advocacy groups, such as the GCOSROW (General Commission on Status and Role of Women), and its local affiliates, recognize their survival and power is closely meshed with pleasing bishops, cabinets, and Boards of Ordained Ministry, thus as my story will reveal, their assistance is limited at best.

Before I accepted the position, the new Director of Connectional Ministries, Bruce Hartman, and I discussed the possibility of me having trouble with the Board of Ordained Ministry. Bruce, a former CEO and CFO of major corporations such as Yankee Candle and Footlocker, had been shut down in the ordination process at the earliest stage, the District Committee on Ministry (DCOM). One of the most sincere and pastoral leaders I know, he was resented and treated as a rich man trying to buy a title (my words, not his).

Unlike me, Bruce chose to shake the dust off his feet at that early juncture. He later became Director of Connectional Ministries as a lay person.

Bruce was concerned for me. I was made aware that a previous member of the Connectional Ministries staff had been given a hard time with the ordination process while serving in the high-profile role of Youth Director for the conference. This is a familiar story for those going through the ordination process in other conferences as well.[5]

Bruce even put in a phone call to the Chair of the Board of Ordained Ministry to discuss if there would be issues due to my extension ministry position (a position serving beyond the local church). The chair assured Bruce that I would not, as the board had "learned a lesson" in how it had treated the former Youth Director. Bruce left the decision to me, and I trusted that a Godly process would be followed by the board and all involved.

I have tremendous respect and admiration for Dr. Bruce Hartman. He stayed on the bishop's staff for only six months, and while I am not privy to his full rationale for leaving, he did state that the demands of the position were more than he wanted to take on as a retired executive. He saw the position taking too much time away from his family, and he was not going to compromise that. He left, received a doctorate degree, and is now a prolific writer with blogs, podcasts, and books to his credit.

I remember a comment Bishop Schol made a couple months after Bruce left. I was in his office to discuss my work. When I mentioned something about Bruce, Bishop Schol's demeanor changed and his voice became course. He stated that what he learned from "that experience" was "never hire someone who does not need a job." I think he meant never hire someone you don't have undue power to control.

CONFERENCE STRATEGY

When he first joined the conference, Bishop Schol hired a consultant to work with conference leadership to develop a five-year strategic plan. That plan, as recorded in our GNJ Conference "Play Book," was as follows:

- Increase the number of highly vital congregations from 14% to 41%.

- Increase the percentage of churches growing in worship attendance from 33% to 51%.

- Start 90 new faith communities.

- Decrease the number of worshipers it takes to make a new profession of faith from 17 to 15.

- Increase the percentage of worshipers in small groups from 43% to 75%.

- Increase the number of young adults in small groups from 2820 to 3200.

- Increase our racial ethnic worshipers from 20% to 25%.

- Increase the percentage of worshipers engaged in mission from 8% to 40%.

- Increase local church dollars spent on mission from 8% to 40%.

- Raise $12 million through a mission campaign.

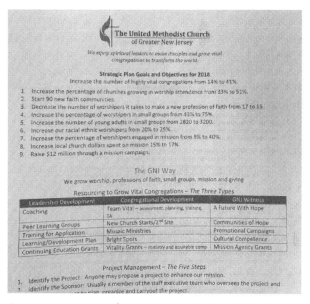

Greater New Jersey Conference Ministry Playbook 2014, showing the Five-Year Goal Plan set in 2013 to be accomplished by 2018.

DIRECTOR OF SMALL GROUPS

While staff worked together to lead the conference to achieve the above goals, as Director of Small Groups I was specifically responsible for increasing the percentage of worshipers in small groups from 43% to 75%, and the number of young adults in small groups from 2820 to 3200. I quickly excelled at my position.

For the purposes of this book, I do need to share the successes in the ministry I was given and how I carried it out. While I may talk about myself, the highest credit goes to God and God alone. God alone is worthy to be praised; I am just an unworthy vessel that is loved by the Lord and blessed to have a relationship with him. This love affair has many benefits, including the guidance of the Holy Spirit (Ephesians 5:5).

I was the first on the Connectional Ministries Team to develop a comprehensive strategy for my area of responsibility's Strategic Plan goals. I identified a team of diverse leaders, at least two in every district, who were laity and clergy, to be experts on a conference small groups ministry team whom others could reach out to for consultation and training. Team members included the now deceased Dr. Frank Fowler from Hacketstown UMC, Dr. Timothy Ahn from Arcola UMC, and Rev. Mike Bill from Sharptown UMC, as well as other leaders who were known for their successful small group ministries. No one else on the connectional ministries team formed such a team.

I kept a busy schedule preaching, speaking at churches and conferences, training, and encouraging leadership teams.

Photos taken at churches throughout New Jersey where I taught, consulted about small groups, and preached.

I developed my own training resource that I implemented for local church leadership teams and identified other tools for educating leaders and facilitators. I was the first to put together a helpful and easily followed webpage of resources for pastors and other leaders. I was a leader in utilizing social media to garner attention for churches who were developing their small groups. I championed a variety of ways that small groups could be contextualized and varied in format while also being consistently effective discipling tools.

I held a Small Groups Symposium at Drew Theological School with a panel of distinguished champions of small groups, including Dr. David Lowes Watson, the late Dr. Frank Fowler, Dr. Timothy Ahn, and others. The blogs I wrote on small groups consistently had the most hits of any written by our team and achieved award-winning status from the UMC Communicators.[1]

In 2015, Bishop Schol organized his staff to focus our efforts into three separate geographic regions. Those of us in connectional ministries continued to support the entire conference but concentrated our efforts on our regions. I was initially assigned to work as a part of the Northern Region Resource Team, with the plan being that I would move to support another region at the end of eighteen months. As part of my focus on the region, I led the development and organization of a regional training event at the largest UMC church in the state, the Korean Bethany Church. That resourcing and training event, to my knowledge, has yet to be surpassed in its depth, breadth, attendance (except by our same team the following year), or reviews by any other such event held by the conference. I was quoted in a conference article as stating,

> The organizing team was focused on creative, smart and bold action so that we could launch a new kind of event for Greater New Jersey. The goal is to provide content to our congregations that is relevant to the issues they are facing today in a format that is accessible and fresh. We look forward to offering more such events, building on what we have learned and what we anticipate as needs for the future.[2]

An example of the groundbreaking work we did was celebrating and highlighting the multiculturalism of the region. The Northern region of New Jersey is the most culturally diverse area of the most diverse state in the U.S. So, I opened the day by greeting the assembly in the eight different languages that are preached in the United Methodist Church there. We also offered interpretation services in Spanish, Korean, and Portuguese during the day. The Korean church provided amazing hospitality that included a delicious luncheon featuring Korean food. That event set a high bar for other regions to follow.

We brought in experts from around the country to lead our carefully crafted workshop topics. We entitled the event, "Growing the Church Younger – A Day of Learning." As detailed in the above referenced article,

> The day focused on equipping leaders to better understand, attract and build disciples of children, youth, young adults and young families. Workshops included focus on reaching millennials, covenant small groups for youth and young adults, spiritual growth for children in the digital world, holistic sexual education and values and mission partnership opportunities in Cuba. The event was tailored to and attracted UMC clergy, laity and Drew Theological students.[3]

We followed up the next year with an event entitled "Outbound: A Day on Evangelism." We achieved even higher attendance with a very exciting list of workshop leaders and, as evidenced by the number of views on the conference Facebook page promotion for the event,[4] garnered much attention.[5]

But most importantly, I exceeded the Strategic Plan goals used to evaluate my job performance. By year-end 2016, two years ahead of schedule, churches reported an overall increase of participants in small groups from 45% to 78%, exceeding the given goal of 43% to 75%. I was also making good strides toward accomplishing the young adult goal as we were putting more emphasis on affinity small groups to attract them.

TEAM VITAL CHAMPION

Additionally, by mid fall of our first year as the new cabinet plus Connectional Ministries Team (2014), in a single meeting the bishop introduced several resources that he wanted developed and implemented by us all in the coming years. We were given brief descriptions of those that had yet to be developed and asked to choose which of the resources listed in the photo at the beginning of this chapter that we wanted to lead.

I quickly surmised that Team Vital could become an impactful resource in developing congregations and that it would be the most challenging and comprehensive leadership responsibility of everything else listed. I watched as my colleagues scrambled to lead every other resource and no one chose Team Vital. I stepped up quietly and said I would take it on. No one challenged me for the role.

I discovered that a basic concept for Team Vital had been imagined after the Council of Bishops set a goal in 2010 of doubling the number of highly vital congregations after the results of a Vital Congregations Study in 2009. They had envisioned Team Vital broadly as a way to train congregations to improve their ministry performance around the indicators of vitality that had been identified in the 2008 study. In 2012, several conferences, including Greater New Jersey, had sent teams to quarterly meetings over a two-year period to discuss development of this resource.

As I dug into the work done, I was surprised to learn that although travel expenses had been incurred for several cabinet members and the Stewardship Director from GNJ and a number of other people to attend various conferences, there was no end product. So in

2014, I began leading a new effort from scratch. To my knowledge, no other conference had ever built a Team Vital resource or any other resource out of those Chicago meetings.

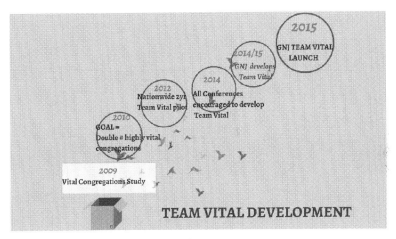

Personal PowerPoint

The bishop gave me an initial team of conference staff that included two district superintendents, two connectional ministries staff, the conference communications director, and three conference administrative personnel.

Personal PowerPoint

I began by building the team and our relationships. We always began our meetings with devotions and prayer, and we used humor and social opportunities to come together and build trust and dedication. We identified a core Scripture for the team to work from that I included in all correspondence with the team.

Team Vital Project Team

No one puts new wine into old wineskins. For the new wine would burst the wineskins, spilling the wine and ruining the skins. Luke 5:37

The first month we assembled, I gave everyone on the team and the bishop a Rubik's Cube. This was symbolic of the way we would solve the puzzle of building the Team Vital resource together. We identified some core principles of our work, and I also included a picture of the Rubik's cube and those principles on all correspondence.

TEAM VITAL PROJECT TEAM RUBIK'S CUBE CORE PRINCIPLES

- You have to give up what you have to get what you want
- You can never change just one thing
- Some things will stay constant
- It doesn't matter where you start to complete the pattern
- It IS solvable!

From the beginning my work was well received.

Bishop John Schol 　　　　　*Fri, Feb 13, 2015, 2:14 PM*
To: Beth Caulfield

Beth, I love the cube. It is inspirational, clarifying and championing. Good work.

John
John Schol, Bishop The United Methodist Church Greater New Jersey

We built Team Vital into a strategic action planning resource for up to seven church ministry leadership teams. These teams would come together in one location and learn from conference staff and each other about ways to build their church ministries in five markers of vitality:

Professions of faith

Worship

Small Groups

Mission

Giving

They would build action plans and goals for their respective churches, receive coaching and other resourcing including grants, and share their lessons learned through semi-annual group meetings over a two-year period. Not only would there be training and plans, but inter-church connectionalism would grow. Team Vitals could, and did, take place simultaneously and systematically across the conference twice a year. We translated Team Vital Resources into Spanish and Korean. We consistently assessed and improved it.

We pushed to build the resource quickly and launched in less than a year. We had our first meeting as a team in January 2015 and work-shopped a concept for Team Vital with a group of twenty conference leaders before the end of February. We launched a pilot Team Vital with five churches in early May of that year. By the Annual Conference, we were advertising Team Vital as a resource churches could engage in for fall 2015. In less than two years, we had over 100 churches participate in this rigorous resource. I credit the Lord first, but also a wonderful team spirit that rallied around our work.

My creative juices really flowed with Team Vital as I envisioned "Catching the Wave of the Spirit" when one joined. I worked with a vendor and designed a backdrop for a selfie station to put next to our Team Vital information table at the Annual Conference. It made a real "splash" at the event.

I enjoyed developing promotional materials and videos along with guiding the team, training the rest of the cabinet and staff as they became facilitators of the sessions and coaches to the teams, and putting together the entire resource. But I also enjoyed when we were implementing the resource and seeing leaders catch the wave of the Holy Spirit with their own contextualized plans for doing better ministry based on what they had learned and developed through their Team Vital experiences.

My work was noticed and rewarded. The initial promotional video I wrote, directed, and co-produced with our communications team received the UMC Communicator's Video of the Year Award. I received regular if not frequent public praise from the bishop. He mentions Team Vital as one of his achievements in his public bio.[6] I was rewarded with additional compensation beyond that given annually to the staff:

Team Vital memories made at various church, district, annual conference, and promotional events.

From Hector Burgos
Tue, Dec 1, 2015, 11:03 PM
To Beth
Dear Beth,

I give thanks to God for your leadership and ministry in GNJ. You are a valuable member of our team. I really appreciate your passion for the church of Jesus Christ and commitment to GNJ vision and strategic goals. Your leadership has been instrumental to the successful development and launch of Team Vital and significant progress in our strategic goals in the area of small groups. Please note that your 2016 salary reflects not only the 3% increase approved for all staff but also a well deserved adjustment of $5K. Let me know if you have any questions.

Thanks for all you do! Blessed to be in ministry with you.

Peace, Hector

Rev. Hector A. Burgos
Director of Connectional Ministries
The United Methodist Church of Greater New Jersey

As far as official performance appraisals go, however, I never received one. Never a sit down, never anything in writing except for the email above from Rev. Burgos, and sporadic "atta a girl" emails from Bishop Schol. I was not alone in this experience. As my colleagues on the Connectional Ministries team conversed, none of us received official performance appraisals in writing or meetings. The Discipline mandates that each clergy person be evaluated for performance (¶334.2).

Yet my pay was increased 21% in only two years from my start date. My salary when coming on conference staff had actually increased by 245% from my previous local church appointment, even more if you count the housing allowance and other perks that were added. For 2017, the last year I served on conference staff, my pay was as follows:

December 10, 2016

Dear Beth Caulfield,

It is with pleasure that I am able to announce that the Council on Finance and Administration has approved a salary increase for the Staff of the United Methodist Church of Greater New Jersey beginning January 1, 2017.

Your annualized 2017 salary will be $93,278 (salary: $72,060 + housing: $21,218)

With this letter you will find several payroll forms that need your attention:
o Premium Conversion Enrollment Form for those having their 2% health insurance contribution taken out of their pre-tax pay
o Housing Exclusion Form
o Voluntary Tax Withholding

All forms are due to Jay Kim by Wednesday, 12/21/2016. Thank you.

Sincerely, John Cardillo
Director of Administrative Services Conference Treasurer

Those outside the Greater New Jersey clergy world may need a better sense of the level of my compensation. Remember I only graduated from seminary in 2013. In an email to the entire conference dated January 16, 2015, Bishop Schol shared the following regarding conference clergy salaries:

Bishop John Schol bishopjohnschol.gnjumc@brtapp.com
Jan 16, 2015, 3:06 PM
…Also to keep expectations about appointments realistic, the following are the breakdown of salaries.

Salary Band 1 - $70,000 and above – 26 appointments
Salary Band 2 - $60,000 to $69,999 – 39 appointments
Salary Band 3 - $50,000 to $59,999 – 64 appointments
Salary Band 4 - Elder minimum salary to $49,999 – 154 appointments

I was not yet a full elder, yet my salary was at the Salary Band 1 listed above. I would note that nine of the twenty-six appointments listed at Salary Band 1 were the District Superintendents and one was the Connectional Ministries director. Assuming I was not being counted as I was not yet a full elder, together they represented 38% of the appointments at that salary level in 2015.

I point this out to make clear again three points and to add another. The first is that I was in a highly compensated role within the system as I was hired into it at $60,000 a year in 2014, which was at Salary Band 2. Second, I was clearly performing very well and above expectations. Three, my salary was public information (as is the salary of all clergy members), and therefore an "in your face" to those who resented me and would begin to cause me more problems. Fourth, the top heaviness of a bureaucratic institution that values administrators above its pastors is evident from these figures.

COSROW AND SEXUAL ETHICS

Another of my responsibilities was to be the staff liaison to two conference agencies: the Commission on the Status and Role of Women (COSROW) and the Commission on Native American Ministries (CONAM). While I enjoyed the charter and people on both these Commissions, I found their effectiveness limited in relation to their charges from their UMC General Agencies as directed in the UMC Book of Discipline.

According to the UMC's Book of Discipline, ¶2102:

> The primary purpose of the General Commission on the Status and Role of Women shall be to challenge The

United Methodist Church, including its general agencies, institutions, and connectional structures, to a continuing commitment to the full and equal responsibility
and participation of women in the total life and mission
of the Church, sharing fully in the power and in the
policy-making at all levels of the church life.

On their website The General Commission on the Status and
Role of Women (GCOSROW) states they "help the church recognize every person—clergy and lay, women and men, adults and
children—as full and equal parts of God's human family."[7] The Book
of Discipline also states in ¶644 that each annual conference shall
have a conference commission on the status and role of women or
other structure to provide the functions laid out for such commissions in the Discipline. One of those responsibilities is "to participate in connectional programs and plans initiated or recommended
by the general commission, and to utilize the resources available
from the general commission as needed." ¶644.1(f).

In Greater New Jersey, although we maintained a Commission on
the Status and Role of Women, we met sporadically, and meetings
were poorly attended. There was little focus, and few defined goals.
Choosing the winner of the Helen Alter Davidson Award was our
main activity for two of the three years I served with them. This
$500 award was to be given each year "to recognize a woman who
demonstrates vision, passion, resilience, sense of purpose, inclu-
siveness, perseverance, and a willingness to work with and stand
for the status and role of women in ministry." There were always
few, if any, people nominated for the award, and thus there was
more discussion around finding someone to nominate than vetting

and choosing a winner. I believe the lack of productivity of this commission is indicative of the lack of support and emphasis for COSROW's function by the bishop and conference leadership.

That is a big statement to make and not back up. So I will.

The UMC Book of Resolutions as is posted clearly on the UMC website, states the following:

> All clergy in The United Methodist Church are required to have "regular, up-to-date sexual ethics training to be in good standing for appointment" (BOR 2016, p. 140).

On their website, the UMC also gives very clear instruction and support to annual conferences for creating sexual ethics policies and even offers sample policies for assistance.[8] That webpage goes even further by including the following statements:

> *Each annual conference in The United Methodist Church must create its own policies regarding misconduct within ministerial relationships, within the guidelines and procedures found in The Book of Discipline. A* **policy** *outlines specific conduct or behavior that is inappropriate, while* **procedures** *describe the processes by which a concern or complaint should be handled. It is advisable to write separate documents for procedures (not to include them in a policy document).*

Also boldly printed in all caps on the page is:

"IT'S NOT ENOUGH TO HAVE POLICIES; THEY MUST BE CLEARLY AND CONSISTENTLY UNDERSTOOD."[9]

Finally, Resolution #2045, from the UMC Book of Resolutions includes:

> In 2006, a significant national symposium addressing sexual misconduct in The United Methodist Church, "Do No Harm," was held. At that critical event, participants asked episcopal leaders to focus on clergy training, lay leadership training, and early intervention with problem clergy. Advocacy and intervention teams have been working in many conferences but not all, and every episcopal area needs to maintain working, effective channels and procedures. We need and are grateful for strong episcopal leadership across the Church who maintain our achievements and forcefully address existing barriers to a harassment-free denomination.[10]

In the spring of 2016, the Chair of GNJ's COSROW, Rev. Michelle Ryoo, championed bringing Becky Posey Williams, Senior Director of Sexual Ethics and Advocacy from GCOSROW to Greater New Jersey to lead a sexual ethics training session. She had desired to offer that training for GNJ for several years but had not achieved the goal. When she brought it up in one of our meetings, I thought this was wonderful contribution from the COSROW team and was surprised that such training was not a regular offering and, in common memory, had not been done in the conference in many years, at least over ten, if ever at all.

As the Conference liaison to COSROW, I offered my service by raising awareness of this training desire with our conference staff, Board of Ordained Ministry, and Communications team. I suggested that the training be offered as co-sponsored by the Board of Ordained Ministry, the Episcopal Office, and COSROW. My comments were met with a tepid response. Neither the Board of Ordained Ministry nor the Episcopal Office sponsored or promoted the event. Space for the training was granted by the Conference office and advertising through Conference Communications' online publication "The Digest" was offered, but that was all, beyond my own and other COSROW members' personal social media posts.

As it had not been mandated for clergy or even strongly supported, attendance at the event was quite low. We were less than twenty-five people, including the few COSROW team members that attended and me.[11] I quickly learned this was not high on our conference staff or Board of Ordained Ministry's agenda, and therefore not on our clergy's radar. Given the serious proliferation of sexual misconduct cases associated with church leaders throughout the world, including the UMC in Greater New Jersey, and as a former Human Resources professional, I was shocked and disturbed that we would not offer such training and mandate that it be regularly repeated for all clergy.

After the event, I continued to lobby for more attention to this concern. When I approached the dean of the cabinet, she told me this was a responsibility for the Board of Ordained Ministry. The Board of Ordained Ministry chair told me it was something they would look at but did not make progress toward. I continued to lobby for such training, including with Bishop Schol in December 2016, eight months after our training event, as detailed in the chapter *Threatened*, but to no avail. The string of emails below show a concerted effort and my concerns raised. Yet, to date, six years later than the emails below, there is no discernable GNJ sexual ethics policy nor has there been any training offered or promoted by through the conference, including through the Board of Ordained Ministry.

To be clear on this, I offer the following: As I have searched the conference website (and retained screenshots thereof), nothing comes up as training or policies for "Sexual Ethics." Ironically the first thing that does come up is a blog that I wrote on the subject in 2017, entitled "Fifty Shades of Gray." I search "Healthy Boundaries 101", which is the online course recommended by UM/COSROW, and there is nothing. Even then one of my old blogs comes up, entitled, "Why Pastors should not be Small Group Leaders." I have searched on the website for other COSROW/sexual ethics offerings such as "The Way of Integrity," "A Sacred Trust," "Faith Trust Institute" and "Healthy Boundaries," and I see no evidence of GNJ following UMC guidelines by promoting or even retaining accessibility to such materials.

On January 23, 2018, GCSRW released a joint statement with the Council of Bishops in support of the #MeToo and #ChurchToo movement. After requests from the connection on how to address the #MeToo and #ChurchToo movements in local churches, GCSRW developed the #MeToo Toolkit. The toolkit was distributed to every annual conference in the United States and has been available at United Methodist events such as the UMW Assembly.[12]

A search of the GNJ website, again, returns nothing related to "#Me Too Toolkit" or "#ChurchToo." A brief perusal of other UMC conferences' websites shows that others, do indeed have clearly accessible policies and regular training available and/or required.[13] It has been hard to fathom that especially with the inordinate amount of energy that has been expended by the GNJ conference on LGBTQIA+ concerns, that justice and legal concerns for sexual ethics are so neglected.

Beth Caulfield   April 27, 2016, 5:43pm
To: Hector, Gina, Erica, Michelle

Hi All,

First - thank you Erica for your well considered reply. It seems to me that although we provide Safe Sanctuary Training that communicates the importance of following state laws in reporting incidents involving minors to legal authorities,

1) we are still unclear about <u>whether we have a specific GNJ policy in place or not</u> that mandates clergy to obey state requirements on reporting incidents involving minors

2) we are still unclear about <u>whether we have a specific GNJ policy in place or not</u> that mandates action regarding clergy sexual ethics concerns that are reported

3) We can not say that we have clear communication about such policies if they exist

My concern is that even if we make Safe Sanctuary and Clergy Sexual Ethics Training available that address our legal and moral responsibilities, without clearly communicated policies that state compliance with such laws is mandatory, we are at legal risk as well as are not being as effective as we should in addressing these serious issues.

It is my recommendation that we ensure that:

1) we have such policies and have all clergy sign off on having reviewed and received them

2) We mandate <u>AND enforce participation in</u> both Safe Sanctuary and Clergy Sexual Ethics Training over a reasonable time.

I do not know where ownership of this best lies, it seems to me to be a joint BOOM and Episcopal Office responsibility.

Below is the promised information on Conference Internet/social media policies from Becky Williams, which, to me, carry the same issues as mentioned above that we need to address.

I hope this helps and, as always, I welcome being of further assistance in these important issues.

Joy in Christ,
Beth

Rev. Beth Caulfield
Director of Small Groups Ministry /TEAM VITAL Champion

Hi Beth.

I am so sorry I am just now getting this information to you. I think this is some of what you asked me about. Please let me know if it was something different and also, any additional information you may need after looking over these two pieces. Hope all is going well in your world.

Peace today,
Becky

Becky Posey Williams
Sr. Director for Sexual Ethics and Advocacy
General Commission on the Status and Role of Women
3 Attachments

From: Beth Caulfield   Tuesday, April 26, 2016 11:28 AM
To: Becky Williams
Subject: Re: Policy resource

Thank you Becky- these are very helpful guidelines. Do you also have, or can you point us to sample policies from local churches an/or conferences?

Blessings,
Beth

From: *Becky Williams*   *April 26, 2016 1:30:38 PM*
To: *Beth Caulfield*
Subject: *RE: Policy resource*

Beth,

Here is North Carolina's. I am reviewing Tennessee's and it is much more detailed. I will ask for permission to send it to you as well.
Becky

Hector Burgos   *April 27, 2016 6:13pm*
To Beth Caulfield

Thanks for following up in this important (matter). I will consult with Gina before replying to all in the email.

Peace, Héctor
Rev. Hector A. Burgos
Director of Connectional Ministries

Michelle Ryoo   *April 27, 8:23pm*

To: Erica, Beth, Hector, Gina

I think we all need to work on this together. Since I am serving for BOOM this year on, I have an excess to address this issue directly to BOOM. COSROW also will also discuss about this at the right time. Meanwhile I will personally contact Becky and seek her wisdom one at a time. This won't happen overnight, yet we will definitely make it happen here GNJ through intentional efforts and fervent prayer! By the way, Hector, thank you for your leadership always. The training went really well and everybody there was blessed. She will get back to me probably after the general conference.

In Christ,
Michelle

Hector Burgos   *April 28, 2016 11:20 pm*
To: Beth, Michelle, Erica, Gina

Dear Michelle,

After consulting with Gina Hendrickson, dean of the cabinet, we agree with your assessment that the best place to address, at least begin this important conversation, is at the Board on Ordained Ministry. Please bring this concerns/ questions to the attention of the new board when it convenes in June. As a member of the new board and chair of COSROW, you will have a unique opportunity to provide leadership in this matter. In the meantime, we encourage you to reach out to Rev. Steve Bechtold, who is a past president of the board and has extensive experience on this matter to seek further clarity.

I want to share that yesterday I had a brief conversation with one of the pastors that attended the training and he was very appreciative for the time of learning.

Once again, thanks to all for lifting up this important matter for our conference, clergy and congregations. Please, let us know how we can support you as you work with BOOM on this matter.

Thankful for your transformation leadership.
Peace - Hector

Rev. Hector A. Burgos
Director of Connectional Ministries

NATIVE AMERICANS, SYNCRATISM, AND "TWO SPIRIT" PEOPLE

I also enjoyed getting to know the leaders and members of the Greater New Jersey Committee on Native American Ministries (CoNAM) and the Native American communities associated with the UMC within Greater New Jersey. I worked with conference communications to promote CoNAM events and to help them secure and build a webpage on the conference website. In 2015, I reminded the bishop and the Annual Conference Meeting planning committee leadership of the Bishop's 2014 public commitment that all future Annual Conference meetings would be opened by a Native American, helping the committee to plan accordingly. The bishop's spontaneous commitment had been made after a powerful Act of Repentance service had been led by the conference in conjunction with CoNAM. The reason I cite my effort is explained later in this section.

Beth Caulfield   *April 15, 2015, 9:14 PM*

To: dharding (an alias, explained later), Hector, Bishop

Hi All,

FYI- I was just in a CoNAM meeting this evening where it was brought up that last year a public promise was made that from then on an indigenous person would always be asked to open the worship for Annual Conference. I believe the group (chaired by Cyndi Kent) is waiting to be contacted by someone organizing the Worship so that they might supply a name.
Cyndi can be reached at: Cyndi Kent
May the Lord bless you and keep you,

Beth

Rev. Beth Caulfield
Director of Small Groups Ministry & Spiritual Visioning
TEAM VITAL Champion

Bishop John Schol   *April 15, 2015 10:54 PM*

To:Beth, dharding, Hector

Thanks Beth for passing this along.
John

From: *dharding*   *April 16, 2015 8:11 AM*

To: *Bishop, Beth, Hector*

This would be at the opening worship service, then? Where would you see this happening, Bishop Schol? Should I reach out to Cyndi or someone from the conference office?

Everyone's faith can be enriched when we utilize our Christian lens to appreciate, connect, learn from, support, and celebrate indigenous people and their experiences. We can also learn from and build better bridges for Christ by repenting of sins against them and work with Native Americans to address the many social justice issues they continue to face. I value Native American commitment to preserving their heritage and past, and educating others about them and their journeys. I appreciate and encourage Church support lent to such endeavors. I also believe the Church is called to action regarding the social justice concerns they face.

The Book of Discipline, in describing the UMC theological task, states that "To be persons of faith is to hunger to understand the truth given to us in Jesus Christ," "As United Methodists, we have an obligation to bear a faithful Christian witness to Jesus Christ, the living reality at the center of the Church's life and witness," "United Methodists as a diverse people continue to strive for consensus in understanding the gospel. In our diversity, we are held together by a shared inheritance and a common desire to participate in the creative and redemptive activity of God." (Book of Discipline, ¶105.4 – Our Theological Task)." That shared inheritance includes proclaiming the Gospel and to "spread scriptural holiness over these lands."[14]

My time with CoNAM, however, caused me to question if there were disconnects in the ambitions of some of its leaders and therefore CoNAM's focus in relation to our UMC inheritance as described above. I observed that the GNJ CoNAM spent much of their agenda, resources, and energy on raising awareness of, preserving, and providing vehicles for Native American culture and becoming involved with supporting Native American social justice concerns on a national level. That work is important, but as practiced through CoNAM, I sensed disengagement from furthering the Gospel being written on hearts. Furthermore, there became an increasing shift from traditional Christian teachings to embracing and promoting progressive Christianity concerns such as LGBTQIA+ issues. I was not alone in my observations.

To be sure, during the time I worked with them, Greater New Jersey's CoNAM had a significant and worth emulating commitment to supporting Native American youth, young adults, and children. They annually sponsored youth to attend the conference's weekend youth retreat, Ignite, and to Peg Leg Flamingo, a UMC weeklong, national Native American Youth Leadership Program. One of their youth members started and grew a Native American Youth Program at Bridgeton High School. With aid and sponsorship from CoNAM, Rev. Roy E. Bundy of the Nanticoke tribe and local pastor of St. Mark's UMC in Fordville, NJ, led the church in offering vacation bible study programs, after school learning programs (featuring young adults as teachers), community feeding programs and many other ministries for spreading the love message of the Gospel. That church was formed in 1841 by one of the UMC predecessor denominations, the Methodist Episcopal Church as a Native American church and has remained so since.

However, Rev. Bundy, and other Native American church leaders involved with CoNAM started expressing concern and dissatisfaction with the direction both CoNAM and the United Methodist Church had begun taking toward progressive theology and support of syncretism within Native American communities. Before he died in July 2021, Rev. Bundy had for several years expressed his growing desire to leave the United Methodist Church because of these concerns.

One of the people he expressed this wish to was Rev. Dr. John Norwood, a CONAM member at the time and a long-standing minister and leader from the Nanticoke-Lenope Tribal Nation.[15]

Norwood has shared with me that there became a growing concern among some CoNAM members and other Native American Christians that CoNAM's focus was becoming increasingly removed from promoting Christianity. Furthermore, according to Norwood, CoNAM leaders and members began to include both Native Americans and non-Native Americans "whose Christianity not only differed from traditional Christian teachings, but also included those who did not profess to be Christians and even some who were openly hostile to the faith."

Reflecting this concern, in 2015, First Light Mission was formed. "First Light Mission is a non-denominational outreach, originally established in partnership with the Tribal Christian Prayer Circle Ministry of the Nanticoke Lenni-Lenape Tribal Nation. The site provides resources for Christian worship, witness, and spiritual formation in addition to guidance for non-Natives on interacting with American Indian people, groups, and governments."[16] The "primary contributors" of First Light Mission feature Rev. Dr. Norwood, Rev. Bundy (before death), and Chief Mark Quiet Hawk Gould, the Principal Chief of Nanticoke Lenni-Lenape Tribal Nation and also a CoNAM member.[17] Since 2014, Bundy, Gould and Norwood have each led one or more of the Greater New Jersey Annual Conference Indigenous Welcomes that I referenced previously.

Featured on the First Light Mission website is the doctoral thesis of Rev. Dr. Norwood from 2015, entitled "The Historical Impact and Current Challenges of Christian Ministry Among the Aboriginal People of the Delaware Bay Region." In the thesis, Rev. Dr. Norwood explains that "the main aim of this study is to assess and address issues of contextualization and reconciliation through which the Church may reinforce the blessings of Christian koinonia within the context of celebrating tribal heritage and struggling for justice in such a manner that the gospel is spread afresh to the tribal people," and asserts while citing the work of other scholars:

> Contextualization of the gospel supports evangelism and spiritual development. However, contextualization can have its own thorny issues. One of the great challenges in contextualization is syncretism. Concerns over syncretism can fuel a critical and antagonistic view of contextualization... Syncretism might be said to occur when critical and basic elements of the Gospel [sic] are lost in the progress of contextualization and are replaced by religious elements from the receiving culture; there is a synthesis with this partial Gospel. In some cases syncretism reaches such portions that a totally new "gospel" appears... Scott Moreau, of Wheaton College, ... states that syncretism is "the replacement or dilution of the essential truths of the gospel through the incorporation of non-Christian elements" (2012:129). Given varying perspectives on the issue, a plausible working definition of syncretism, as pertaining to Christianity, is the blending of beliefs and practices which are incompatible with biblical teaching, thereby creating a derived false faith which claims to be either Christian, compatible with Christianity, or a superior Christianity. A typical tendency of syncretistic belief is to diminish the gospel of grace by denying the sufficiency of Christ's substitutionary atonement. Superstitious practices, rituals, and requirements are viewed as necessary for salvation and within the

capacity of the believer to provide satisfactory, or supplementary, atonement. Another tendency of syncretism is the denial of the sufficiency, and/or reliability, of Scripture.[18]

While not available in the Resource list featured on the main page of the GNJ CoNam website, a link to First Light Mission's website can be found on a separate CoNAM Resource page.[19]

Featured on the main GNJ CoNAM website as a "Resource" is, however, an "official position on full inclusion of LGBTQIAS2+ persons" adopted by The United Methodist Church Northeastern Jurisdiction Native American Ministries Committee (NEJNAMC), "unanimously" in February 2021.[20] NEJNAMC meets yearly to coordinate and support CoNAM ministries in each local annual conference. The statement includes the following:

> While we have released this statement, it is only the beginning, because the larger position paper presented during the special meeting continues to be perfected. We seek to answer a call Bishop Peggy Johnson shared during our meeting, to be in conversation and to consider the voices of those who identify as LGBTQIA, and particularly as "Two Spirit" persons, who are absent from our leadership circle as we further develop this statement and the position paper.

Bishop Peggy Johnson, then episcopal leader of both the Peninsula Delaware and Eastern Pennsylvania conferences, retired in September of 2021. Shortly after retirement, she and her husband Rev. Michael Johnson made denominational headlines as they announced that Michael had transitioned to "Mary Johnson," and they would continue their marriage with Mary now publicly identifying as a woman.[21] The Greater New Jersey CONAM main webpage also features a powerful and heart-grabbing "Litany for A Day of Remembrance for Our Children," written by, therein identified, Rev. Michael Johnson, also from 2021.

"Two Spirit" is an umbrella term created in 1990 at the Indigenous lesbian and gay international gathering in Winnipeg.[22] It is used "by some Indigenous North Americans to describe Native people in their communities who fulfill a traditional third-gender (or other gender-variant) ceremonial and social role in their cultures," as described by Wikipedia's summary of Kylan Mattias de Vries' 2009 article in the *Encyclopedia of Gender and Society*.[23] It was developed through Pan-Indianism, which, as Wikipedia summarizes from Dorothy Dobbin's 1997 article, "A short history of Pan-Indianism," "is a philosophical and political approach promoting unity, and to some extent cultural homogenization, among different Native American, First Nations, Inuit and Métis (FNIM) groups in the Americas regardless of tribal distinctions and cultural differences.[24]

According to Rev. Dr. Norwood, "two-spirit" language and the thinking behind it does not come from or represent the historical tribes of the eastern U.S., or that of many other tribes throughout the U.S.

Until February 2022, the GNJ CoNAM webpage, at the top of its page, had a video clip of Rev. Dr. Norwood and his wife, Tanya Norwood, who is an ordained deacon at the independent Ujima Village Christian Church in Ewing, NJ where her husband is the lead pastor. The clip was from the Indigenous Welcome to the 2019 GNJ Annual Conference that the two led together. At the time of the Conference, the Norwoods were no longer active with CoNAM but agreed to do the welcome. When I discovered the clip on the CoNAM webpage, I was moved by Rev. Dr. Norwood's passion in his remarks which included a wonderful witness and call to loyalty to Christ and biblically-based faith. I gave him a call to thank him for his witness. Upon learning that he and his wife were featured alongside the other content of the page, he immediately requested of CoNAM leadership that the clip be removed, as well as his name from the list of members cited. He shared with me in an email this reason for doing so:

> I am truly distressed by the CONAM's "Full Inclusion" statement and that I am included in the video on their web-page. The erroneous impression given is that I endorse the position of the UMC and CONAM, as the statement is on the same page with no disclaimer that the video was taken years prior to the writing of the statement and that not everyone in the video endorses the statement (or is even United Methodist). It is also insulting that the Act of Repentance is now being modified after the fact to include the so-called "Two Spirit" identity, which is not a traditional term or concept among Nanticoke-Lenape people and is separate issue from those addressed in the original ceremony.

His request for the clip's and his name as a member's removal was honored immediately.

Transgenderism is not directly addressed in the UMC Book of Discipline. Nor do I believe it should have to be, except as perhaps another expression of human life that needs healing and transformation through the power of Christ. My reasoning is, and I have passion about this subject, why should we regress to reinforcing patriarchal and misogynistically defined and enforced gender roles and norms that have proven to be psychologically, emotionally, spiritually and physically damaging to so many? I look back at my own life, especially childhood, when I enjoyed the smell of my own sweat as a highly kinetic and athletic rather than static and unfit person, preferred pants and sneakers to skirts and Mary Janes, hated Barbies and dolls and instead aggressively took my younger brother's Six Million Dollar Man and GI Joe for my own, was competitive not passive, detested my physical appearance because it never measured up to societally enforced standards of feminine beauty, was chastised for wanting to play the saxophone or drums instead of the flute or clarinet, was called a tomboy even by my parents and sometimes just "boy" by my grandfather. Transgenderism reinforces the rejection of who many of us know ourselves to be and locks us back into painful stereotypes. I shudder to think that instead of society working to dismantle such gender stereotypes' shackles, that I instead would have been encouraged to devalue my own body and psyche and even dismantle them instead. Yet that is what is occurring today and the mounting evidence of the negative consequences of doing so continues to grow. One example is James/Jamie Shupe, the U.S.'s first legally identified non-binary person. He criticizes his transgender treatments and surgery. He states "professional stigmatisms against 'conversion therapy' had made it impossible for the therapist to question my motives for wanting to change my sex," and "I should have been stopped, but out-of-control, transgender activism had made the nurse practitioner too scared to say no."[25] Shupe later changed his gender identity back to male and speaks out about gender dysphoria while cautioning against transgender surgeries and warning of high complication rates thereof as he details his own experience.

I have great compassion for parents struggling with children who suffer gender dysphoria. I cannot imagine the pain and suffering for all involved. However, I do not believe the answer should come at the expense of the child's fully mature and informed decision about their own bodies when psychologically and even to an extent physically do not fully mature until they are in their twenties. That transgender surgeries are offered to children with parental consent before those children are considered mature or legally old enough to make their own less life-altering and threatening choices such as consumption of alcohol, cigarettes or even driving, is deeply disturbing.

Some may say to me that, "I don't get it." But according to the life-giving Bible, that has the audacity to claim that it is God-breathed (2 Timothy 3:16-17), I do. We are all fearfully and won-derfully made (Psalm 139:14) and God created us male and female (Genesis 1:27). While there are plenty of examples of people living according to patriarchal and misogynistic gender role standards in the Bible, there are also examples of those who do not. And just as there is a positive trajectory in the Bible for the value of women as shared in my chapter "She Preaches Gospel," there is a positive tra-jectory for demolishing restrictive gender roles and norms as exem-plified by Paul's declaration that "There is neither Jew nor Greek, slave nor free, male nor female, for you are all one in Christ Jesus," (Galatians 3:28). Paul was not declaring that Jews should become Gentiles or Gentiles Jews, that those who are enslaved by humans or any other forces or free in society or in Christ are inherently loved by God more one than the other. He was also not declaring that male and females should no longer honor their physical distinctions from one another. He was enforcing a needed re-establishment that all are valued by God just as they are, not according to patriarchal and misogynistic gender roles and norms that can be harmful.

Finally, Rev. Dr. John Norwood also shared with me a concern that the Acts to Repentance by the denomination and annual conferences as originally requested and intended have become not only distorted by a progressive LGBTQIA+ agenda, but may also exhibit a tone of non-native privilege and supremacy (my words, not his).[26] In an email dated 2/14/2022, he describes this as follows:

> The "Act of Repentance" was supposed to be a "beginning" of creating understanding, correcting miseducation, and improved bridge building between Indigenous communities and non-natives all to the glory of Christ and in support of the continuing Christian mission of evangelization and reconciliation. Including a land acknowledgment during the opening of the conference sessions was a part of this initiative, along with the reaffirmation of the history of Indigenous congregations within the conference, such as Saint John Church in Fordville. It was not about repeatedly instilling a sense of non-native guilt over the sins of the past and present or characterizing all Natives as perpetual "victims," but an acknowledgement of the history and the charting of a faithful path forward, together. While the returning of land can be an important part of this, how it is returned (under what terms and conditions and for what purposes) will vary based upon the history and circumstances of its original acquisition and the contemporary situation. But, the overall aim of any action

should be the promotion of the gospel and strengthening of discipleship and not merely an attempt to "wipe hands clean" of past atrocities and then move on with business as usual.... or to simply celebrate Indigenous culture with no sense of the priority of the gospel mission. Reconciliation strategies must bear in mind the biblical mission of the church in order to ensure that they are truly God-glorifying and not merely socially satisfying. The advancement of Indigenous ministries should be part of that effort, not only to evangelize and minister to Indigenous people, but also to enhance the overall appreciation for the multi-cultural beauty of the Body of Christ and the interconnectedness of all of its constituent parts. It should be understood that Indigenous Christians have a mission to the wider world and our voices contribute to the overall mission of the church and can edify non-natives.

The problem now is that the biblical foundation that must undergird and guide the reconciliation begun in the Act of Repentance, in order for it to be Christ-centered and God-glorifying, is being abandoned. Many of the leaders and congregations involved in the "act" have embraced heresy and have become apostate. Reconciliation base upon heresy and apostasy does as much damage to the cause of Christian missions as did the atrocities of colonial imperialism. One left many tribal people hostile to Christianity because of the racist attitudes and genocidal actions of many who misidentified themselves as "Christian" and the other denies the principles of sola

scriptura and tota scriptura, abandoning the transforming power of the true Gospel of Christ – denying the very
message of salvation.

Amen and Amen. Since the time that I served as liaison to CoNAM
for the Greater New Jersey Conference, an increased unveiling
of historical and current cultural discrimination against Native
Americans Church has been occurring. I praise God for that and
those who have been involved in the apocalyptic work therein. I
also see evidence through various publications that more attention
has been given to Native Americans by the denomination, Greater
New Jersey, and other conferences. Has this Greater New Jersey
attention to Native Americans been focused on proclaiming the
traditionally interpreted Gospel, making disciples thereof, and tap-
ping the transforming power of Jesus Christ? It has not.

POLITICS OF DISCRIMINATION AND ABUSE

ODD WOMAN OUT THEOLOGY

My time on Conference staff was filled with intense learning from Bishop Schol for which I am immensely grateful. He sought to educate, shape and grow his new team to reach our potential as leaders who would lead and grow the Conference and thereby make and grow disciples of Jesus Christ according to the SMART goals that had been set. He pushed us hard to think more strategically and to be more productive. We worked long hours, as evidenced in the timestamps of the emails included in this book. He sought to build us closer as a team by having us spend much time together, including down time. I have many fond memories of that working environment as it appealed to my desire to grow, build relationships and reconnect with my business background sensibilities.

Schol's efforts were noble and of a classic successful business executive style. During the first two years especially, our biweekly extended cabinet meetings, which included the cabinet, connectional ministries team, the communications director, the conference treasurer and other key administrative personnel, frequently began with us reviewing a Ted Talk that introduced some management principle. After the viewing, Schol would be at the whiteboard reviewing and teaching the principles introduced and then leading us through discussion of how we were going to apply them. We were required to read trendy leadership and management books and articles of the time such as L. David Marquet's *Turn the Ship Around: A True Story of Turning Followers Into Leaders*, David Lencioni's *The Five Dysfunctions of a Team*, *The Advantage*, *The Ideal Team Player,* and Dan Heath's <u>*Switch: How to Change Things When Change is Hard*</u>.

Offsite retreats or the bishop conclaves that included a broader group of leaders who chaired various agencies of the conference such as the Conference trustees, Board of Ordained Ministry, Compensation and Finance, the Conference Lay Leader and more. This group was organized as the Conference Connectional Table. Those conclave meetings were centered around "balcony time," which was when we were led, either by paid consultants or Bishop Schol himself, through visioning and strategizing exercises using a broader perspective lens.

He introduced us to professional coaching training, mandating participation at least at a basic competency level, and then encouraging us to continue that training up to and including obtaining International Coaching Federation Certification. We would use those skills to coach pastors and other leaders. Other leaders in the conference were also trained as coaches. Each of us on the extended cabinet team had our own personal coach and were expected to utilize their services to aid us in our leadership decision making, action planning and execution. It was all good stuff.

This is not to say that there was not a spiritual leadership component to his style. There was. Each Monday we had a full worship service for the staff that included the serving of communion and the vast majority of the time he preached. Meetings included prayer. He even introduced a kaleidoscope bible study exercise that was used for the first twenty to thirty minutes of our extended cabinet meetings, where we would break into small groups and have a guided discussion about bible passages. There were occasional devotions.

Would I say there was travailing prayer in our meetings, an encouragement to, education of, or experience in the meetings for us as a group to engage in other traditional Wesleyan spiritual disciplines such as fasting, meditation, confession, and crying out for the Holy Spirit? No. Was there a conference prayer team? No. Were we encouraged or organized into classic Wesleyan covenant groups, known as bands? No. Were we engaged in service and celebration? No. In other words, while we were held to high standards in terms of workload and strategic leadership, spiritual accountability was not at the forefront. The sense was that those were the things that we should already know to do on our own, that our views on each discipline would vary thus corporate practice or discussion would be futile, and that precious office and other time spent together was for other things. For someone with more classic Wesleyan sensibilities, the spiritual leadership provided fell flat.

Additionally, throughout this time I was becoming increasingly disillusioned by the progressive theology of the bishop and the vast majority of leaders on Conference staff. That the theology that shaped my perspective on the decisions and products of our Conference team was different was becoming more and more evident to all and a cause of tension.

I remember poignantly an extended cabinet meeting in November 2014. The bishop had us view an excerpt of a very popular Ted Talk by leadership expert Simon Sinek. In it, Sinek explained his Golden Circle theory. The Golden Circle theory explains how leaders can inspire cooperation, trust, and change in a business based on his research into how the most successful organizations think, act and communicate if they start with asking "why," and most importantly, "why do we exist?" At the whiteboard, Schol then led a discussion regarding the concepts and language that we would use to answer that important question for the Conference. The product would head our "Conference Play Book," and also be disseminated to leaders throughout the conference. The eventual key phrase developed was, "We equip spiritual leaders to grow vital congregations and make disciples so that God's love heals and transforms the world." But there was other language that we were developing to introduce that phrase. A phrase that was on the board was, "God works through people in the world." It bothered me as being too limiting and not reflecting Wesleyan theology.

I piped up, "Shouldn't we say 'one of the ways God works in the world,' instead?"

There was a deafening silence before the Bishop spoke. "What other ways does God work, Beth?"

"Through nature, direct divine intervention, in hearts," I rattled off.

More silence. Finally, a district superintendent said in reference to my statement, "This is the UMC belief."

The communications director spoke up forcefully. "I'm no theologian, but I don't see the big deal. I don't think the statement would be read any deeper."

In an unusual move to insert herself, and I believe done more so to defend me than anything else, the bishop's executive assistant stated, "I believe the same as Beth. That God works through nature."

Deeper silence ensued as people digested her play. Another district superintendent, Rev. Dr. Andy Hoover, spoke up. "Let's address the elephant in the room. More conservative voices which are underrepresented on this team see such as statement as too humanistic." And with that, he managed to solidify for all, including the bishop, that "one of these things is not like the others."

The director of connectional ministries then offered to rework the language out of the meeting. The bishop agreed, and stated "people will always pick things apart."

I continued to believe it was important that I share my traditional theology throughout my staff ministry time and I spoke up when I thought we were missing the inclusion of traditional Christian thinking. At this particular time, I chose to steer clear of the LGBTQIA concerns and agenda that were important to most of my colleagues, but I defended traditional teaching of the bible and encouraged the transformational power of Jesus Christ in our planning and resources and seeking and discerning the Holy Spirit.

But as time went on, I felt increased tension. I will note that within the first six months of my joining the staff, the title of Director of Small Groups and Spiritual Visioning was shortened to Director of Small Groups. I had laid out and shared a considerable strategy for the Spiritual Visioning piece, but it was ignored and stopped as indicated by the title change.

I found my blog posts and other writings edited by our Conference Communications director when my theology did not meet a progressive agenda. Sometimes the editing was seemingly fueled by envy that I had hit on an important topic that would garner much attention. For example, with my most highly read blog, "50 Shades of Conversation,"[1] I had to fight to get my views clearly shared. I eventually did (mostly), yet below is the initial response I received from the Communications Director:

> Beth,
>
> I've edited your blog post quite a bit. I tried to make it more neutral of your stance and more inclusive to other opinions. Take a look.
>
> This is a provocative blog and I'm not entirely convinced we should be including it in the CMT blogs. I'm copying Hector to get his feedback.
>
> Let me know your thoughts on my edits and whether we should move forward.
>
> Thanks,
> XXX

I became more and more uncomfortable and anxious being myself as time went on. I walked a tightrope with the cabinet and other staff both because of my ministry success, popularity and their antipathy toward my theology.

It felt like all my work received extra scrutiny and efforts to squelch it were evident. Part of this was a result of the strong control requirements of the bishop. As another example, I received undue hassle whenever I or another party requested to reprint my work. However, reprinting of other staff members' work in other UMC held organizations was encouraged and more readily facilitated.

An example of this is when UMC Insight, an online publication whose content the United Methodist Church does not have any financial interest or editorial control over, would request reprints of my work. I was the only GNJ team member who received such requests. I would jump through substantial hoops to get permission for this to be done. There was always a plethora of emails that went back and forth between the director of Communications, the director of Connectional Ministries, the publication's editor, and me, as demands were made from them regarding reprint concerns. After one article was released, the communications director asserted that UMC Insight did not properly offer my article according to a new policy that the Greater New Jersey communications team had just incorporated. They now required other publications to only offer links to the original blogs and articles back on the GNJ website. This was not only different than they had required of UM Insight for my previous contributions, but was contrary to UM Insight policy at the time. The reason given by the communications director was that it was important for others to be redirected to GNJ, for the conference to receive full credit, and for the conference to gather online metrics regarding readership. It was ridiculous, embarrassing, and limiting to my ministry and work for the conference, as UM Insight never again requested to publish my work. As can be seen in the articles referenced in this link, UMC Insight always gave credit to Greater New Jersey. Again, the issue was always about control and limiting me, and not about furthering the ministry above all.[2] To solidify that point, I refer you to GNJ leadership published by UM Insight since that time. An article written by Bishop Schol, entitled "A Hard Fought Hope," was published by them on December 15, 2021. It is a reprint of a letter he posted to GNJ on December 6th, 2021, and does not offer a redirect to the Conference website.

Did I have any growing edges? Of course. Many. One was learning how to deal with those who felt threatened by my ministry. Nonetheless, my work continued to receive praise and reward. I also thoroughly enjoyed administrative ministry work at this level. I knew my ministry was making a difference and advancing the work of the Church for Christ's glory.

SEOUL MATE

With Rev. Dr. Jisun Kwak at the Delaware Bay District Gathering, Pitman UMC, 2016.

In 2014, when I joined Bishop Schol's staff, I developed a friendship with a member of his cabinet, Rev. Dr. Jisun Kwak. Rev. Dr.

Kwak was an experienced district superintendent who I found to be bright, gracious, and sacrificially ministry focused. She had been a district superintendent with Bishop Devadhar and was one of the four DS's that Schol did not replace in 2014. She was particularly adept at leading churches to grow mission work in poverty-stricken and racially diverse communities. At the local church level, she had a track record of growing churches. Her leadership skills were acknowledged by many.

She was the first district superintendent to invite me into her district to work with small group ministry. I was pleased when the bishop assigned her to the Team Vital Project Team I led. She was invaluable in her contributions, especially as she encouraged the use of technology. She also has been a leadership mentor to me. Jisun and I held our first conferencewide Zoom meetings for Team Vital leaders in 2015 and had a blast doing it, despite me being very nervous about bringing close to fifty leaders onto a virtual meeting together for the first time. We were the first on the staff to do anything even close to that. By the time the Covid-19 pandemic began in 2020 and much of the whole clergy world was scrambling to incorporate video teleconferencing technologies to their ministries, thanks to Jisun I was already comfortable with it.

Jisun and I found that our skills and personalities complimented one another and enhanced the work we did together. We also just liked each other. We saw each other as a special gift from God, given at just the right time in our lives. I liked to refer to her as my "Seoul Mate." Even though her theology is progressive and mine traditional, Jisun and I have many affinities in our understanding of ministry and spirituality. Our differences on such issues as the ordination of practicing homosexuals and marrying them within the church, while giving us much conversation and prayer for one another, have never limited our friendship.

It was wonderful to develop a close relationship with someone I worked with, as one's circle of friends tends to tighten both for professional reasons and personal ones when a person is promoted. Being on staff and, I am sure, especially on cabinet, can be a very lonely place. Jisun and I became best friends. I also want to note that even though we maintained a close friendship, she was careful to never share confidences kept at the cabinet level. I have always respected her for that.

By 2014 it was clear that Jisun was not favored by Bishop Schol. To my understanding there was never a complaint against her performance, no negative reviews, but there was a clear dislike and distrust. She has recently shared with me three situations that, based on my own experiences and observations of Schol, I believe set him against her.

Early in his appointment to Greater New Jersey in 2012, Bishop Schol brought Jisun in to assist with a conference relations problem with a large Korean church in a district different than her own. She helped Schol sit down with the leaders and have conversation after he and their DS had been rejected and prohibited from even coming into the church building. Even having no previous relationship with the leaders, she was able to convince the leaders to talk with Schol. But after the connection was made, he appeared to resent her relational effectiveness with them. At one point he even suggested that she was inappropriately sharing confidences with them, even though she was not.

Second, in 2013, Bishop Schol was already showing his long-held strategy of closing churches so that the funds could be used for other conference projects. At that time, however, Jisun did not comprehend how important this was to her new boss. So, when he wanted to close the only UMC church in Elizabeth, NJ, which is the fourth largest city in the state, she thought it would be best to develop a strategy to save the church and make it a more effective place of worship and ministry to the multicultural community around it. She worked with the mayor, other civic leaders, various multicultural church leaders, several contractors, and other conference leaders to develop a strategy for renovating and rejuvenating the church. She presented the plan to the Conference Connectional Table for approval and was met with high praise.

Bishop Schol, however, was not pleased. He scolded her in front of her colleagues and told her to close the church anyway. She followed his instructions, and the church closing was presented for a vote at the Annual Conference. However, there was a motion made from the floor to reconsider. The motion carried and the church remained open. This was an extraordinary happening.

Third, according to Jisun, Bishop Schol came to Greater New Jersey favoring disallowing international clergy candidates into the ordination process unless they already had an R-1 visa for religious workers or a "green card." He did not want the expense or administrative hassles for sponsoring such visas. Bishop Devadhar, Schol's predecessor, had sanctioned local churches to give such sponsorship. It had proven to be a burden and administrative challenge fraught with issues. Therefore, Schol wanted to alleviate the problem. Yet the reality is that our multicultural state has a dearth of qualified and called clergy to begin with, and international clergy candidates are a Godsend. Jisun lobbied to have the work of getting international candidates their R-1 visas become a conference administrative function. The cabinet agreed with her and Schol relented.

Perhaps there were more incidents, but in my thinking, these three were enough. Bishop Schol does not like being overruled or overshadowed. And, as we would soon learn, he does not let the times it happens go without punishment.

In my opinion, Bishop Schol did not replace Jisun on the cabinet in 2014 only because it would have been an unpopular decision. She was known for her good work, and he especially did not want to upset the Korean community. Korean churches were our largest churches and biggest givers to shared ministry funds. To not have a representative from that community would have been foolish, and he had not yet identified a Korean replacement for Jisun.

What he did do, however, was move her from the Gateway North District, the most urban and multicultural New York metropolitan area district, to the Delaware Bay District. The Delaware Bay District is the most rural and most white of all the districts, as well as furthest from the conference office and least active in terms of effective and growing ministry done in conjunction with the conference. To underscore the lesser amount of ministry happening, let me explain that there are more churches with part-time local licensed pastors in Delaware Bay than full-time licensed or ordained clergy combined. There, more than anywhere else in the state, churches can be found that do not support females in the role of clergy. To say that Jisun had been handed a challenge is an understatement. But she rose to it, and her ministry there was also respected and effective.

Jisun navigated difficult spiritual and political waters when she ran in 2015 to be a delegate to the 2016 General Conference. Although she had theological affinities with them, Jisun did not run with the progressive, LGBTQIA agenda focused "in" crowd. Many were jealous of her work, and she also had to navigate the more conservative Korean community of church leaders as a single, divorced female clergy.

I remember one petty incident a couple of months before the Annual Conference elections. I was in the throes of creating a video to introduce Team Vital to the conference. We had written it to feature several conference leaders and especially Bishop Schol. I had selected Jisun to be the leader explaining how Team Vital would work in hopes of attracting more Korean churches to Team Vital. I had written the script and we were set to video it with Jisun and other leaders when I was suddenly told that we were not allowed to use Jisun in the video. Baffled, I pressed for a reason why. I was told that because the video would premiere at the Annual Conference before the elections, the bishop was concerned Jisun would be given unfair advantage if she were featured in a video watched by all.

However, plenty of other candidates were featured in other ways during the conference. Nonetheless, we did not place Jisun on the screen. Instead, I had us use her unidentified voice for the part she was supposed to be in. Again, undo and unnecessary control was exerted to clamp down on a perceived threat.[3]

I helped Jisun with her initial delegate candidacy paperwork and her candidacy speech. She was incredibly diligent practicing and getting her thoughts and words as clear as possible and I learned much from her. I had a strong connection with many evangelical church leaders and laity, and I lobbied them for their vote and support for her candidacy, which they gave. Jisun was also the recipient of the COSROW Helen Alter Davidson Award for distinguished female leadership that year, which helped keep her profile raised.

Out of four clergy delegates elected, Jisun was the third across the threshold of election.

As she and I left the Convention Center floor to recess for lunch after the election, we ran into a couple of people who were not celebrating: Rev. Dr. Andy Hoover and his wife. Rev. Dr. Andy Hoover had been a General Conference delegate in 2012. This election had not gone well for him, as he was elected to the team fifth, and therefore had been relegated to serve only as a reserve delegate. The looks they gave to Jisun and I were not friendly and we moved away quickly. While not disrespectful, Bishop Schol was also quite cool to Jisun at that conference. One might have expected some encouragement from her boss for her achievement, but there was none.

FISHY ANNUAL CONFERENCE

The 2015 Greater New Jersey Annual Conference was given the theme "FISH," and we were told ahead of time that we would explore ways to "fish on the other side." That meant we would, like the disciples in John 21, follow Jesus' lead and change our strategies for accomplishing our goals. It was indeed a busy conference. Not only did we introduce Team Vital and other new conference resources, but this was the year carefully crafted petitions regarding human sexuality were introduced. We were primed to vote on six pieces of legislation: four to be sent to the 2016 General Conference in hopes of changing the language of the Book of Discipline, and two to be adopted as a conference. The entire process was carefully orchestrated to achieve the bishop's desired results.

First, the legislation was carefully scheduled not to be introduced and voted on until the last agenda item on the last day of the three-day conference. Many voting delegates leave before that time, especially laity. Progressives organized to stay and see the legislation to passed. Traditionalists were not so organized.

Second, to prepare us for voting, an exercise was staged where all members were asked to engage in conversation regarding their views on homosexuality. The exercise required partnering people who held opposing views concerning homosexuality. Each person was asked to identify themselves as a different type of "fish," building on the Annual Conference theme. Members were to select their "fish" by identifying with one of three viewpoints:

Striped Bass Fish

I am comfortable with the church's policies on homosexuality.

One or more of these statements may describe your view or belief:

Scripture is authoritative and is to be followed as it is written.

God created humanity to be heterosexual not homosexual.

Marriage should be between a man and a woman.

I want the church's policies to continue and will be concerned and may consider leaving if the church changes its policies concerning homosexuality.

Cod Fish

I have views that are moderate, not fully shaped or are in the middle of different viewpoints. I am willing to compromise so that varying views are affirmed.

One or more of these statements may describe your view or belief:

I do not feel qualified to judge any person's heart to decide whether they are good or bad in God's sight.

I understand that God's grace and love extends to all and I try to accept all people without reservation or judgment.

I am in agreement with our church's policies on homosexuality, but I experience important understandings with those who have a different view.

I am in disagreement with our church's policies on homosexuality but I experience important understandings with those who have a different view.

My view point is still being shaped about homosexuality.

I will stay within the United Methodist Church if the policies change.

I will stay within the United Methodist Church if the policies do not change.

I am still trying to understand how to interpret Scripture concerning homosexuality

Blue Fish

I am uncomfortable with the church's policies on homosexuality. *One or more of these statements may describe your view or belief:*

Scripture is the inspired word of God and is to be understood and interpreted within the culture and times of the people who lived during biblical times.

Human sexuality including homosexuality is a gift from God.

Marriage may be between two people of the same gender.

I want the church's polices to change and will be concerned and may consider leaving if the church does not change its policies.

We were warned ahead of time that this exercise would occur, and many traditionalists felt anxiety and outrage about it. Laity were uncomfortable that the topic was even being introduced to the conference. They suspected it would put them in situations with unreasonable persons with militant viewpoints who were being emboldened by the inclusion of the exercise to begin with.

For traditionalist clergy, the concern was being forced into conversation and exposed as having views that did not line up with those of conference leadership. Even in 2015, being outed in Greater New Jersey as a traditionalist on matters of human sexuality was concerning when appointments were made. It seemed obvious to many of us that traditionalists were not wanted to lead larger, active churches that could be or already were swayed to a progressive view on human sexuality. Clergy had become adept at avoiding the conversation. This "Fish"-y exercise took that option off the table.

It was therefore little surprise that when it came time for the "Fish" exercise ahead of the vote, attendance was already light. Many people got up to get a cup of coffee in the hallway with a plan to return when the exercise was over. Others chose to head home. As a member of the bishop's staff sitting right up front, leaving was not an option for me. It was time to shine as a leader whether I wanted to or not.

Ushers gave participants small banners with images of the three types of fish. We were then to find a conversation partner with an opposing view. Not surprisingly, "Striped Bass" (Traditionalists) were in high demand as there were more "Blue Fish" (Progressives) and "Cod Fish" (Moderates/Unsure) participating in the activity. I had thought and prayed about how to handle this but still was not sure what to do. I sat there praying that God would lead me to whomever I should share my views with and hear from about theirs. I opened my eyes and standing before me was the now deceased District Superintendent Rev. Myrna Bethke, a Blue Fish.

I knew that Myrna was an active proponent of Reconciling Ministries, again, an organization that states it seeks "to advance justice and inclusion for all LGBTQ people in the United Methodist Church and beyond"[4]—and used her position as a district superintendent to encourage churches to join RCM. She had led her last church, Red Bank UMC, to join Reconciling Ministries. She frequently vocalized her views on the need to affirm homosexuals. I also knew her perspective on people who held a traditional view. She did not appear to have a high opinion of us.

At the same time, I was unsure how much she knew of my own view. Thus far I had been quiet on the issue. I told people my views when asked, but otherwise I was not holding any banners. Now the banner was literally in my hand.

We sat down together to begin the exercise. Shortly thereafter, District Superintendent Rev. Dr. Steve Bechtold came by as he did not have a partner. We invited him to join us and he identified himself as a "Cod," with "moderate views not fully shaped or are in the middle of different viewpoints. I am willing to compromise so that varying views are affirmed."

We were given the following instructions:

Engage in holy conferencing with a sharing partner:

During a 20-minute period, sharing partners will introduce themselves to each other and share the answers to the following questions:

1. How has your life been touched by God, in the last year or while at Annual Conference?

2. What is your hope for the future of the church and what concerns do you have?

3. How have you personally experienced the churches struggle with homosexuality?

The sharing partner asks one question for clarification, for example: *"Share with me more about ... and why you believe this."* Or, *"How did you come to this understanding?"* Or, *"How would you see GNJ living this out?"* Or, *"What experience did you have that shaped your thinking?"*

4. What do you believe about the church's policies concerning homosexuality and what do you want others to understand?

The sharing partner asks one question for clarification, for example: *"Share with me more about ... and why you believe this."* Or, *"How did you come to this understanding?"* Or, *"How would you see GNJ living this out?"* Or, *"What experience did you have that shaped your thinking?"*

5. What is one thing that would help me know you better if I understood it about you?

Twenty minutes is not much time for three people to discuss all of the above in much depth. We spent the most time on question four and explaining why we believed what we did. I believe I ended up talking the most and being encouraged to do so. I was a curious source of information about "Striped Bass" as I was regarded as a strong female clergy leader with high potential, and at that time, probably one of the very few female clergy that either of them knew in the conference who would have such views.

I shared that my beliefs were shaped by my understanding of the Bible, the tradition that was clear on this issue and had been followed for thousands of years, and my own thoughts and experiences. I told them of my unquestioning belief that God loves all people, including those in the LGBTQIA community, and that they are as welcome at church as anyone else. I believe that we are no different in our need of the transforming savior Jesus Christ.

I shared how I had been around homosexuality first as a youth living in the San Francisco Bay area, and that the first person who had ever propositioned me sexually had been an older girl. I shared that as a college athlete I had been further exposed to and had friends who were lesbians who had found community and acceptance in the athletic world. I shared my knowledge that many of the lesbians and gay men I was friendly with came from troubled experiences that led them to question and be confused about their sexuality, their comfort level with the opposite sex and/or yearning for more attention from those of their own. I told of women I met in seminary who had come out of abusive marriages and found each other as safe havens and then moved forward into sexual relationships with one another. I told of friends, including clergy friends, who had been delivered from same-sex attractions and left homosexual lifestyles.

I told them I do not see the practice of homosexuality as a graver sin than any other, that I had homosexuals in my previous church, and that I welcome them in my future churches. I also shared that I believe it is sinister that this issue is being used to divide the Church and that it detracts from our true mission of making disciples of Jesus Christ.

I was listened to, and I also listened. I think the last statement in the paragraph above was the only one upon which we agreed in our views, but we would all make that statement in different ways. We left that conversation with two of the most powerful people in the conference being truly clear, if they had not been already, of where I stood on this issue. The conversation ended with prayer as prescribed in our instructions and that was the end of it.

The conference secretary was then called upon to set the bar to move into voting on the proposed legislation. I have heard complaints that the movement to set the bar was done too quickly, not leaving enough time for those who left because they did not want to participate in the Fish exercise to return. The lay leader to the Annual Conference that year was from a church I later pastored, and she told me that she and her husband were returning to their seats before the voting was to begin and were stopped by the bishop himself. He called out from his microphone that they needed to leave the area because the bar had already been set. I similarly know that there were a good number of people who were unhappy with how the vote was set up.

According to the Annual Conference "wrap-up" that was published soon thereafter, "At the opening of conference, we reported that 2015 was the largest Annual Conference in the history of Greater New Jersey with more than 1,500 in attendance. When we tallied the final numbers more than 1,700 people joined us during the event!"[5] Yet as you can see from the voting results detailed below, many of those in attendance were not part of this important vote. Only 749 votes were counted,[6] 44% of the total attendance as reported.

The following details the vote count for each piece of legislation:

Strike from the Book of Discipline the phrase: We do not condone the practice of homosexuality and consider the practice incompatible with Christian teaching.

410 – Yes   339 – No

Strike from the Book of Discipline the phrase: Ceremonies that celebrate homosexual unions shall not be conducted by our ministers and shall not be conducted in our churches.

396 – Yes   353 – No

Strike from the Book of Discipline that homosexuality and performing homosexual unions or weddings is a chargeable offense.

414 – Yes   336 – No

Strike from the Book of Discipline that United Methodist funds cannot support the acceptance of homosexuality or supporting homosexual ministries.

405 – Yes   344 – No

The Greater New Jersey Conference work for the full inclusion of all people including lesbian, gay, bisexual and transgendered persons and that we oppose the continued restrictions of church law that restricts the full inclusion of LGBT people.

389 – Yes   352 – No

The Greater New Jersey Conference make a public statement supporting and upholding marriage equality in civil law and that we spiritually, emotionally and prayerfully support clergy who are brought up on charges for performing homosexual unions or performing same-sex wedding ceremonies.

381 – Yes   358 – No

There is one other interesting factor that effected this vote. Two evenings earlier, during the ordination service, a widespread stomach virus began that impacted many people. I do not know how many, but it was known by all and reported and commented on for weeks thereafter. It continued to sicken participants even after the conference ended. Some therefore left early, and others were sick in their hotel rooms and not able to return to the conference for the vote. If there were spiritual factors involved in that I do not pretend to know, but I do believe this unusual illness lessened the number of people who were available to vote. Regardless, my point is that although that conference was taken as a "win" for those who wanted a change to the Book of Discipline and conference policy regarding human sexuality, the actual votes in that direction did not represent a majority of voting members. If you look at the numbers, less than 25% of the people supposedly in attendance at the conference voted the legislation through.

CUBA GOODING

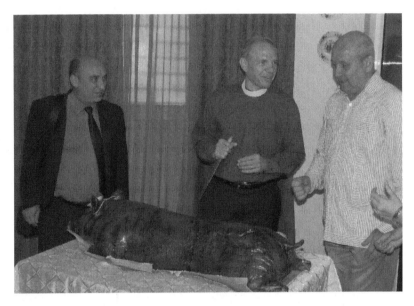

Bishop Pereira instructs Bishop Schol on roast pig carving. Seen with Council of Cuban Churches President Rev. Joel Ortega Dopico, Havana, February 11, 2016.

I include this chapter in part to draw attention to both the dire ministry needs and to the spiritual revival happening in Cuba. Partnering with the Cuban Methodists, however, is stunted if not completely halted for the United Methodist Church as it now operates through progressive leadership. The challenges, as I see it, include theological differences, power abuse, and relationship failures when bishops with similar authoritarian leadership styles clash. A trip to Cuba by leaders from the Greater New Jersey Conference that I attended in 2016 and its results bears witness to this sad reality.

Havana

The beautiful island of Cuba, located 90 miles from Florida, has eleven million people. It remains one of the few one-party socialist government bodies (communist) in the world. Living conditions for its people had been on par with European levels prior to the Cuban revolution of 1959 that was led by Fidel Castro and his socialist constituents. Following the Revolution, living conditions weakened and consequently placed the people of Cuba under enormous political and financial strain.

Baker and bakery with empty shelves in Havana

Just one example of this tight governmental reign is La Libreta, a 50-year-old food rationing system that controls the food supply for Cuba's population. This system allots a certain amount of rice, bread, milk, matches, sugar, and oil depending on the individual's age, gender, and income. While the government has put resources into education and developing advanced medical care, it has put few resources into the country's infrastructure.

In Cuba one can see an oppressed population of highly-educated people. The country boasts a 99% literacy rate and fosters a strong commitment to the arts, yet maintains a low quality of life. Additionally, the Cuban government continues to repress and punish dissent and public criticism. Punishments for infractions against the government are harsh. Short-term arbitrary arrests of human rights defenders, independent journalists, and others are common. Some accused or suspected of dissent just disappear. Many leave Cuba for a better quality of life.

Officially, Cuba was an atheist state for most of the Fidel Castro era. There was much religious persecution. For example, in 1962 the government of Fidel Castro seized and shut down more than 400 Catholic schools, charging that they spread dangerous beliefs among the people. In 1991, however, the Communist Party lifted its prohibition against religious believers seeking membership, and a year later the constitution was amended to characterize the state as secular instead of atheist.

Christianity is the prevailing stated religion on the island, and roughly of sixty percent of citizens identify as Roman Catholic. However, the vast majority of those self-identifiers are nominal in their faith (estimates range from 95-98%) and do not attend religious services.[1] Also, in a significant number of cases, Catholicism has been mixed with the African-based religion of Yorubi and other indigenous religions to form the practice of Santeria. Santeria is often described as a form of witchcraft, and unofficially it is estimated that over half the population practices it, and that its practitioners "greatly outnumber" those who practiced Roman Catholicism, Protestantism, or Judaism.[2]

It is believed that five percent of Cubans have membership in Protestant churches, and approximately 11% of the population identify as Protestant.[3] In the past twenty years they have seen impressive growth, particularly those that incorporate charismatic worship. The Cuban Methodist Church is the fastest growing protestant church in Cuba and has more than 2,000 house churches. In fact, in 2019 the Florida United Methodist Annual Conference reported that, "in the past 16 years alone, Methodist church membership has increased by 306 percent in Cuba."[4] This growth has taken place under the leadership of Bishop Ricardo Pereira.

Pereira credits the growth of churches and conversions in the Cuban Methodist Church to

> Being very committed to prayer, reading the Bible and seeking theological formation. Much of it also has to do with a modification in our liturgy. Today the liturgy of the Methodist Church de Cuba is a Caribbean liturgy that also incorporates our African roots. Before Cubans would come to church and act like they were North American or English. Now Cuban Methodists move, dance, rejoice and shout the way they normally do in

the street. I think this is one of the main things that make us attractive, especially to young people.[5]

Pereira is also the founder of the Evangelical Methodist Seminary. He took the lead in establishing an alternate seminary to the Matanzas Evangelical Theological Seminary (METS), which has served as an ecumenical training center and has been supported by various Protestant churches, including Methodists, since 1947. He says, "In the face of this growing church, we had the challenge of providing a theological formation that would eminently be Methodist and Wesleyan in the midst of so many doctrines there are in the world. The Methodist Church has taken formation in the Methodist seminary very seriously."[6]

Not only did Pereira start a new seminary, but he also withdrew his pastors from Matanzas. This move by Pereira is indicative of the challenges within the greater Methodist and Wesleyan movements as a whole, but especially within the United Methodist Church, which had been a major resource to Matanzas. Pereira and others saw the seminary becoming much more focused on social engagement and centered on progressive theology, especially liberation theology highly influenced by Marxism, rather than on classical evangelicalism.

This evolution at Matanzas is not unlike what is happening in many other United Methodist seminaries as more faculty embrace progressive theologies and become members of or pledge greater affinities with more liberal denominations and churches.

Thus, as the story goes, Pereira had had enough and started his own seminary to regain orthodox Wesleyan education for his leaders. This move caused great consternation within the United Methodist

Church through its Global Missions commission and associated seminaries that had strong connections with and offered much support to Matanzas. Matanzas was significantly challenged by the Cuban Methodist church withdrawal, including financially as it could not receive much, if any, funding from the UMC if it was not educating Methodists.

Likewise, Pereira's seminary has faced challenges receiving support from the UMC and elsewhere. Consequently, many of his faculty do not have full credentialing. Access to textbooks is limited, with many students sharing books with several classmates. Yet there is a commitment to orthodox theology and to training pastors to serve and be creative in starting the house churches that are exploding in growth through their movement. As one would guess, the friction between the Matanzas and Methodist seminaries in Cuba remains palpable.

Pereira has maintained ties with U.S.-based United Methodist traditional churches, seminaries, and other organizations, especially involving mission work, although his relations with their leaders are sometimes strained. Pereira has been especially criticized for his authoritarian style. There are numerous examples cited of him being cruel to his subordinates and abusing his power. The same concern has been expressed by progressive leaders who have interacted with him.

One incident shared with me was that Pereira had insisted that the director of his evangelical seminary grant Pereira's son advanced standing within the seminary when he had not earned such a distinction. When the Director refused, Pereira removed him from the seminary. Pereira has been characterized as vindictive and has been described as viewing anyone with power and influence beyond his as a threat. While some of those qualities I suppose could be chalked up to reflecting the communist, dictator culture of leadership within Cuba, to me, they also reflect classic narcissistic behavior, similar to many other leaders within the Church.

New Jersey has the second largest Cuban population in the U.S. behind Florida. The Greater New Jersey Conference of the United Methodist Church has several Cuban pastors, including one who served on Bishop Schol's staff as a district superintendent from 2014-2019. District Superintendent Rev. Dr. Manuel Sardinas and his wife, Pastor Elizabeth Perez Gonzalez, maintain strong hearts for their Cuban motherland and its people. It is important to note that Rev. Sardinas, like Bishop Schol and unlike most other Cuban pastors in New Jersey and elsewhere, espouses progressive theology.

When in July 2015 the U.S. government and Cuba re-established diplomatic relationships for the first time since 1961, Rev. Sardinas saw an opportunity to help his people. Despite the improved governmental relations, the challenges within the Church related to progressive verses traditional Christianity made accomplishing much in Cuba an extraordinary feat. The Obama administration's aggressive moves to re-establish ties with Cuba was a hot topic in the U.S., stirring controversy and spotlighting the human tragedy in that country. To get in on the excitement and be in the spotlight as a leader doing good, fit with Schol's style.

Working with Bishop Schol, Rev. Sardinas arranged what was billed as a "mission exploratory trip." Rather than setting up the visit in partnership with Bishop Pereira, the trip was sponsored and sanctioned through the Council of Cuban Churches as a "Cuban exchange program" in partnership with the UMC of Greater New Jersey. Our group that traveled on the trip were able to obtain religious worker visas because we were being brought in through the Council. But also, and most significantly, Bishop Pereira had minimal interest in working with the progressive Greater New Jersey bishop and his leaders, so Schol and Sardinez found another way.

The Cuban Council of Churches is a very small organization that is the Protestant umbrella body sanctioned by the communist regime. It endorses an expression of faith more in keeping with the revolutionary ideals of the government regime, including liberation theology. Critics complain that rather than addressing the real social injustices of the Cuban government, the Cuban Council of Churches merely carries out the social programs of the regime. Some even assert that the council is merely a vehicle created to keep an eye on the activities of churches for the government.[7] The Cuban Methodist Church and most other evangelical/traditional/orthodox churches are not members of the council. In fact, only a handful of churches are. Additionally, Bishop Pereira and the president of the council, Rev. Joel Ortega Dopica, do not appear to have a good relationship.

For a better appreciation of the politics that must be navigated by the churches with the government, consider the events of July 11, 2021. As documented in the media, on that date thousands of Cubans took to the streets in the biggest anti-government demonstration in decades. The protests exploded amid Cuba's worst economic crisis since the fall of the Soviet Union, and a record surge in coronavirus infections. Stronger than ever, people voiced anger over shortages of basic goods, curbs on civil liberties, and the authorities' handling of the pandemic. The response by the government was brutal, and included physical attacks, arrests, and even deaths and disappearances.

On the day of the protests, President Miguel Diaz-Canel summoned all denomination and church associated ministry leaders to his office and asked each to declare whether they supported the government or the protestors. It is documented that both Cuban Council of Churches President Rev. Joel Ortega Dopica and the current president of the Evangelical Seminary of Theology in Matanzas quickly proclaimed allegiance to the government and condemned the actions of the protestors. Bishop Pereira was visiting the U.S. at the time and did not attend the meeting. This is indicative of how these leaders roll, as well as the challenges the Church faces in government relations in Cuba.

So, when Schol and Sardinas put together the trip with Ortega, they described its stated objectives as:

- To explore experiences with the protestant churches in Cuba and identify connections for future missional possibilities.
- To identify the missional component of the Cuban church in the community and social structure.
- To learn about the expansion of the Cuban churches.

Notice none of that necessarily mentions Cuban Methodists.

The trip was officially an "initiative" of the Greater New Jersey Northern Region leadership team, of which I was a part, along with Rev. Dr. Sardinas. The reality was, however, that except for Rev. Sardinas, the rest of us were just along for the ride in most respects of planning. All details of the trip appeared to be coordinated by Bishop Schol and Rev. Sardinas.

Participants on the trip were selected by invitation, in theory prioritizing people who would be leading follow-up trips in the future. The implication was that those of us invited would be identifying opportunities for mission and partnership and establishing relationships. We ended up being fifteen people, including Bishop Schol and his wife Beverly; their adult daughter; the bishop's Executive Assistant; the Dean of Drew Theological School; the Director of Connectional Ministries and his wife; the Director of Mission; another District Superintendent of the region; two Dominican pastors who serve churches in New Jersey; Rev. Sardinas and his wife; me, and my husband, Dr. Tom Caulfield.

One reason I note the trip participant list is because it is a reminder of a repeatedly expressed concern regarding Bishop Schol and nepotism. The matter was visited last at the 2020 Greater New Jersey Annual Conference meeting held via ZOOM when Mr. Gyuchang Sim proposed nepotism legislation. A lengthy, prepared speech against the legislation was read out by the chair of the personnel committee of CF&A, Ruth London, and the legislation was defeated by a vote of 105 for to 292 against.[8]

The concerns noted have been as follows. According to Baltimore Washington cabinet members who served at that time, shortly after he was appointed Bishop of the Baltimore-Washington Conference, Bishop Schol encouraged the person who was serving in the bishop's executive assistant position to retire. She had served in the position for the three previous Episcopal leaders. Her retirement was announced at the first Annual Conference that Schol presided over.

The Conference then hired his wife, Beverly, as the new Executive Assistant to the Bishop. Beverly served throughout his remaining seven-year term in that role. Shortly after he came to Greater New Jersey, Beverly was hired into a significant leadership position as Regional Manager with the Conference's newly formed Future of Hope 501c3 initiative. She has subsequently served in other roles under his supervision including as Manager, Property at the United Methodist Church of GNJ,[9] and as a manager of Nehemiah Properties. Nehemiah Properties is a 501c3 nonprofit formed by Schol and the conference "to help turn GNJ's church buildings into financial and mission assets," through "the re-purposing, redevelopment, and or sale of properties."[10]

While Bishop Schol served in Baltimore Washington, he was Bishop in Residence and on the Board of Wesley Theological Seminary. His adult daughter, Kristin, was employed by the seminary. Kristin later obtained her International Coaching Federation Certification while training with other Greater New Jersey clergy.

Continuing the pattern, Bishop Schol's son, Rev. Mark Schol, ordained in the Northern Illinois Conference by Bishop Sally Dyck in 2018, immediately began an appointment in Jersey City, NJ in 2018. The move was in conjunction with that of his wife, Meridith Schol. Schol's daughter-in-law received her PhD in Christian Education and Congregational Studies from Garrett-Evangelical Theological Seminary in 2016. She served on the Denomination's Connectional Table from 2012 until 2018, and then was appointed as an Associate Professor and Director of Doctoral Studies at Drew Theological School, an institution for which Bishop Schol has served as a trustee since coming to New Jersey in 2012. He also chairs the

Drew Theological Advisory Committee. Finally, on February 6, 2022, it was announced by the cabinet that Rev. Mark Schol would be appointed to Madison UMC, which is a stone's throw from the Drew campus. It should be noted that Schol's children and daughter-in-law were not raised or educated in New Jersey or the Washington, D.C area.

While not saying any of Schol's family lack the gifts and grace to serve in these positions, to avoid harm to the workplace, people should be deployed in ministry settings and employed based solely on their qualifications and gifts, not nepotism or favoritism. Whether in Cuba or in the U.S., nepotism, especially when flagrantly repeated, sows seeds of distrust and resentment. Nepotism and conflict of interest assignments for staff members, as I will give further examples of in the book, continue as patterns under Schol's leadership.

Nonetheless, I was very excited to be part of the Cuban trip. I had heard from others who had done mission work in Cuba, including United Methodists, about revival and a great outpouring of the Holy Spirit that was palpable, especially in Cuban Methodist and Pentecostal churches. Reports of healings and other miracles, of a growing Church with a vast number of conversions, and the popularity of its house churches drew me to want to see how they were leading and experiencing these activities of God. I envisioned importing what they were experiencing as much as identifying mission education and opportunities. I could see how developing ties with the Cuban Church would boost connectionalism within our Northern Region of Greater New Jersey, as a good contingent of folks from our diverse region are from the Caribbean.

Additionally, I have good Cuban friends. Our neighbors across the street in Hunterdon County and a longtime friend who both came to the U.S. in the seventies as children. They both had shared stories with me of hardship under the Cuban regime and asked for prayers for their people on more than one occasion.

Access to clean water and water purification is one of Cuba's many concerns and had been identified as an area we would be exploring as mission opportunity on our trip. My husband worked for General Electric's Water and Power Division (now a part of Suez Water Technologies and Solutions) and is quite knowledgeable regarding water purification systems. Because he worked for one of the world's major producers of water purification systems, he knew where to acquire them and also had access to other technical expertise. I was excited to involve him in the trip and grateful that he was invited.

Our trip lasted eight days, February 9th thru 16th, 2016. We arrived just one week after the Obama administration loosened the U.S. trade embargo on Cuba with a new round of regulations intended to allow American companies to export products and sell to Cuba on credit. Our time in Cuba also coincided with the arrangement of a diplomatic trip to Cuba by President and Michelle Obama. It was the first time a sitting U.S. President had visited the country since the Castro regime had gone into office. We saw the team who put that together, including U.S. Cabinet members and senators at the airport. It was all very exciting.

Our guide for the trip was Dr. Ana Mayor, a close friend of Sardinas and his wife, and a very active laity for Christianity in Cuba. She took excellent care of our group and arranged some wonderful opportunities. The three nights we stayed in Havana we were housed in the central location of the Vedado neighborhood at Casa Sacerdotal. Casa Sacerdotal was built in 1918 as a convent for Carmelite nuns. It has become a cozy residence for the Archdiocese of Havana and is the venue for important events of the Catholic Church. It offers exclusive service for individuals or groups of the Catholic Church or other Churches strictly for religious activities. When Pope Frances had visited the country just a few months before us in October 2015, bishops, cardinals, and other officials from around the globe stayed at Casa Sacerdotal. The accommodations were modest by American standards, yet the courtyard and architecture were stunning.

Bed in Casa Sarcedotal.   *First night's dinner at Casa Sacerdotal.*

Our first visit was to the Council of Cuban Churches headquarters where a full presentation of their offerings and work in Cuba had been set up. We listened to presentation after presentation about the good social program work being done throughout Cuba by their members. We were given details of their strategies, locations of their presence, and the twenty-six denominations throughout the world that work with them. A particularly powerful presentation highlighted the work being done to raise awareness, prevention, and shelter for victims of domestic violence, a burgeoning problem in the country. We were all given little sock dolls with "say no to domestic violence" labels that were made by women in domestic violence shelters. The dolls were both male and female and had all different skin colors to indicate the broad spectrum of the problem.

Domestic violence awareness dolls made by victims

What struck me throughout the several hours we were there, however, was a clear distaste and even condemnation from several presenters for the Cuban churches who were not putting such social ministries in the forefront of their work. I could understand their frustration, but at the same time, I did not hear much talk from them about the need for God's work and healing miracles in Cuba, the spreading of the Gospel, or the transformation of hearts. Instead, the focus was much more about human effort to serve needy people.

The tone felt off kilter to me as if I were listening to presentations about addressing tangible needs that ignored the obvious spiritual ones. That approach is not one I advocate, either. But the sound from these progressives echoed our Greater New Jersey Annual

Conference leaders' predominant concerns. Concerns that are expressed in terms that resonate more with the stated purpose, mission, and vision of the United Way than that of the United Methodist Church that I knew and loved.[11]

In Cuba there is a growing trend toward institutionalizing the elderly. There are several reasons for this, including people living longer, more women working outside of the home or pursuing education, and as mentioned earlier, more young adults leaving Cuba, and therefore their elderly parents, behind. Over the rest of our time, we visited several church-sponsored full-time care homes for the elderly—a Methodist one and a Salvation Army one in Havana, a home run by the Gideons in Colon City, and a state-run institution called Casa de Abuelos, or Home for the Elderly, in Varadero. Casa de Abuelos provides comprehensive daytime care (eight to ten hours) to the elderly who do not have family who can attend to them during the day. We saw the dire condition of many of these homes and lack of resources for basic care.

In the rural outpost town of Placetas, we visited a Free Evangelical Church and Bishop Schol led an inauguration ceremony for the church's new dining hall. The church prepares lunches and dinners for seniors and pregnant women throughout the week, and our group participated in preparing and serving a meal for the inauguration. Nearby we visited the site where a Cuban church needed to be rebuilt and took up a collection among ourselves to contribute to the construction.

At Los Pinos Nuevos Pentecostal Church, we learned how the community has over 90% unemployment and unclean water that is fraught with disease and other problems. The church has been dedicated to social action as "Bethania en Accion" since its founding in 1951. It offers daycare, teachers for after-school care programs, and fosters special relationships with doctors for community care.

They shared extensively about how they are trying to improve the self-esteem of children and instill values such as respect for the earth, anti-violence, and health education. They have a high commitment to artistic development that includes music lessons, play, and rest for children. They also manage to partner with the schools, which is miraculous in this socialist country. They have a program for drug and alcohol abuse and plans for providing clean water to the community. It was shared that, on average, their villagers were spending 60% of their income on bottled water.

As part of our visit, Bishop Schol consecrated the ground where a water well was to be dug to supply clean drinking water for the town and my husband was asked to give a brief presentation regarding water purification and answer questions. Rev. Burgos preached for their Sunday service. A robust lunch featuring roast pig slaughtered from the pen next to the church was prepared for us in appreciation of our visit.

Traditional Cuban food is natural, healthy, and pure. A slow cooked, roasted Cuban pig is one of the most traditional Cuban foods and cooking styles you can get. There is a lot of preparation involved as well as a whole day of cooking, but roasting a pig on an outdoor fire pit is a popular way to celebrate a special occasion and feed a large group. The process of taking a whole day to prepare a natural meal, as traditional Cubans would have done hundreds of years ago, slow cooking and talking for hours over an open pit fire, can be a very meaningful experience. Rice and beans and yucca with mojo sauce (onion, garlic, lemon, and oil) are simple accompaniments, as we experienced at Los Pinos Nuevos Church.

It is no wonder that roast pig was the cuisine of choice when Bishop Pereira invited our party to have lunch at the official Cuban Methodist episcopal headquarters. The luncheon was arranged to include our party, key members of Pereira's staff, and Council of Cuban Churches President Joel Ortega Topica. We met in a large dining/meeting room. The invitation was deemed a significant bridge-building hospitality gesture, especially with the inclusion of Topica. Bishop Schol hoped to bring better relations, if not better partnering, between Pereira and Topica. The photos at the beginning and end of this chapter symbolize that effort, with Schol invited to carve, or as he put it "stab," the pig, with Topica on the left (like a communist) and Pereira on the right (a conservative Christian).

That meal was one of the most valuable times for me professionally in terms of the connections made. I found the Methodist Church ministry approach and its District Superintendents and pastors to be fascinating in their enthusiasm and distinctions from the United Methodist Church. For example, district superintendents and the bishop do not have just administrative roles, each also pastors a church. Cuban pastors also cannot be ordained unless they have planted a church.

I spent the most time conversing with my Cuban counterpart for small group formation, a young pastor and leader of their house church/small group movement, Pastor Arisbel Luna Gallardo. We connected well and have continued to stay in touch. Arisbel has a powerful call story of becoming a Christian while his family were spiritualists practicing voodoo and witchcraft. When he shared that he had become a Christian, his father and brother ridiculed and disowned him. Their relationship was non-existent for several years. But one day Arisbel took his mother, who had been paralyzed and unable to walk for eighteen years, to a church service where she was healed. She now walks, praise God! With that miracle the whole family came to Christ. Now his uncles, brother, and father all work for Christ in the Assemblies of God/Pentecostal faith.

With Pastor Arisbel Luna Gallardo, Small Group and House Church leader for Cuban Methodist Church

Other meals were shared together as opportunities to relax and experience the culture. Topica and a few other people who I did not recognize from our meetings joined us for several of these dinners. I do not believe any local church or service agency people that we encountered during the day did. Meals were late, per the culture, and we dined on more than one occasion after ten pm. Restaurants were pleased to receive Americans and were excited at the increased business that the opening up between the U.S. and Cuba might bring. We ate at some excellent private restaurants, including Los

Nardos directly across from the Capitolio (the National Capital Building) the night we roamed around Old Havana.

Sloppy Joe's Bar, Havana

Earlier that evening we had drinks at "one of the most famous bars in the world," with "almost the status of a shrine,"[12] Sloppy Joe's Bar in Old Havana. During the Prohibition era in the U.S., the bar catered to American tourists who visited Havana for the nightlife, gambling, and alcohol they could not obtain back home. American celebrities had become regular clientele back in its heyday, and it is rich in celebrity visitor lore.

Another noteworthy meal we enjoyed was at the acclaimed El Litoral, which is located along the Malecón, a broad roadway and seawall that stretches along the coast in Havana. Interestingly, "El Litoral" was closed by the government the following year after arrests were made for money laundering and drug trafficking.[13] Did

I mention that many restaurants in Cuba are government-owned and private restaurants were deemed illegal for several decades? Cuba.

Almost every one of our dinners offered wine, beer, and/or a Cuban rum drink and most if not all of us, including Bishop Schol, enjoyed the beverages. Except for perhaps the sheer amount consumed, this was not unusual for conference staff. Back in the States, especially around our conclaves and other offsite meetings, wine was offered and, in some way, expensed. This trip was a bit more than the usual, at least by my experience and apparently that of Rev. Dr. Sardinas. On more than one occasion my husband and I listened to remarks from Rev. Sardinas, including to Bishop Schol, expressing concern about how we were going to expense such large amounts of alcohol. I did hear Bishop Schol say, "don't worry about it," and, "give the receipts to Nicola." I do not know what that meant.

An absolute highlight of our time was the party Rev. Sardinas's mother-in-law hosted for our group in her lovely home. Local folk-singing sensation Trio Palabras performed for us. The hospitality was genuine and most appreciated.

The Sunday we were in Cuba we went to services at Angel E. Fuster Cuban Methodist Church in Santa Clara. The church is named in honor of the first elected bishop of the Cuban Methodist Church. He was actually elected at the Cuban Methodist Church's first General Conference posthumously, having died roughly a year before the denomination's launch in 1968.[14] We found it ironic that the church is situated just next to Communist party headquarters for the town that prominently displays the Cuban socialist flag.

But most memorable of all was the worship. It was vibrant and I felt the presence of the Holy Spirit in the packed sanctuary. I believe most in our group were impacted, but perhaps interpreted it in different ways. In an article published about the trip, the quotes attributed to Conference Director of Mission Nicole Caldwell-Gross were, "The worship was a reminder of what real love is," and, "I have always felt that in worship as we experienced in Cuba, we see how worship transcends poverty and politics. You could not leave there without feeling some resonance of joy that the world can't take away. If your life is grounded in something material, it can be taken away."[15]

The same article follows up Nicole's comment with one from Rev. Sardinas, stating "Sardinas pointed out a good church isn't defined solely by its worship." He was quoted as saying, "That church was packed and they were singing and dancing and it was great. But that doesn't necessarily translate to mission with the community. That's what Communities of Hope develops." That comment summed up the great tension that undergirded our trip's carefully planned itinerary.

Our last stop in Cuba was Varadero. We were hosted by and some of us were housed at the Social and Educational Services Centre (CESERSE), also known as Casa del Cariño, a social program and ecumenical center. CESERSE was created to provide services to children in foster care or with serious health conditions, and senior citizens living in homes for the elderly. CESERSE is located across the street from the world famous Varadero Beach and operates under the guidance of Nacyra Gomez, widow of liberation theologian Sergio Arce. CESERSE provides seaside vacations for groups of children and elders who would otherwise not have the opportunity to enjoy Cuba's beaches.

Angel E. Fuster Cuban Methodist Church in Santa Clara, Cuba.

In the winter, off season for beach vacation, the Center receives foreign groups to subsidize its social programs. They offer food and accommodation, programs to learn about history, geography, economy, religions, and Cuban culture, both traditional and contemporary. They offer "packages" of lectures and tours that include topics such as senior citizens, women, diversity and inclusion, care for people with special needs, healthy lifestyle, and more. They work closely with the Cuban Council of Churches (their President Joel Ortega Topica visited us there), the Women's Federation, and CENESEX (National Center for Sex Education). CESERSE offers tours of CENESEX and an audience with the center's director,

Mariela Castro. CESERSE coordinates opportunities to march in the CENESEX 'conga' down the streets of Havana on May 17, their National Day Against Homophobia and Transphobia. CESERSE also offers lectures on sexual and reproductive rights and transsexualism.

We ate all our meals there and listened to lectures, toured a senior center, and lodged for two nights at CESERSE. The first evening we were there, Bishop Schol, Drew Theological School Dean Javier Viera, and the Director of Connectional Ministries went to visit the leadership at the Matanzas Evangelical Theological Seminary. To my knowledge, no such visit was made to the Methodist Seminary in Havana.

I documented some of the scenes from our journey in a video,[16] set to the Cuban folk group Trio Palabras performing Popurri de Sones de Matamoros, a tribute to the works of famous Cuban folk singer Miguel Matamoros and his Trio Matamoros whose Afro-Cuban music was very popular in the 1920s, 30s, and 40s.

When we returned to the U.S., Bishop Schol gave a brief presentation about our experiences to the conference staff. Our Northern Region Team had planned to present missional partnership opportunities that we had secured during our trip at our Regional Day of Learning later that month. We held the workshop, shared about the experience, and gave a message of "stay tuned."

There was a *Relay* (our monthly Conference Communications Journal) article released in March entitled, GNJ Opens Doors with Cuba Trip.[17] The article gives a brief rundown of our activities, but highlights that "A meeting between GNJ bishop John Schol and Cuba Methodist Bishop Ricardo Pereira led to a commitment to explore partnerships between the two groups." The article lays out a commitment by the two to explore a partnership that will:

1. Participate in a pastor cultural exchange

2. Have Cuban church leaders teach GNJ how to develop and grow house churches (a growing movement in the U.S. among millennials)

3. Establish an exchange of students and professors of Drew School of Theology and the Methodist Seminary in Cuba

4. Develop and grow Communities of Hope in Cuba and GNJ

It had been my intention and hope to bring Arisbel to be a featured speaker at a Small Groups Symposium that I held at Drew Theological School the following fall. He had expressed interest in doing so. I even advertised he would be coming, as can be seen in the Small Groups Symposium promo video.[18] Bishop Schol and the Director of Connectional Ministries asked me to stop contacting Arisbel directly and required all arrangements go through them. I followed up with emails, such as the one below:

> *From Beth Caulfield*
> *To: Hector Burgos, Manuel Sardinas, John Schol*
>
> *Date: July 3, 2016, 4:53 PM*
>
> *I see from Facebook my friend Arisbel Luna Gallardo the Small Groups "Director" for the Methodist Church in Cuba is in North Carolina for the church for a few days. I sure hope we can get him to New Jersey.*

I waited patiently but was eventually told that due to visa constraints, Arisbel would not be able to attend.

As of today, I am not aware that *any* of the above four activities have been further pursued beyond my failed attempt to bring Pastor Arisbel Luna to New Jersey.

Since our time there, other Methodists have chronicled many positive happenings in the Church in Cuba.[19] Our Greater New Jersey efforts and attention were very different than what has been described by other United Methodist groups who have worked with Cuba. That includes groups who began their work in Cuba at roughly the same time that we took our trip. For example, a group out of the Midwest, along with representatives from the United Theological Seminary (UTS) and Trinity Life Center, visited Cuba just one year before the trip that we took.

I first learned of their trip from a UMC pastor in Greater New Jersey who went as a UTS student. He visited several Methodist churches in and around Havana that were spirit-filled. He saw people accepting Jesus as Savior, healings, and was asked to preach on the spot as were other pastors in the group.

When he heard about our planned trip, he reached out to me with excitement:

> *from:*   *>xxxxxxxxxxxxxxxxxxxxxxx*
> *to:*   *Bishop John Schol <bishopjohnschol@gnjumc.org>,*
>   *Hector Burgos <hburgos@gnjumc.org>,*
>   *Manuel Sardinas <msardinas@gnjumc.org>,*
>   *Beth Caulfield <bcaulfield@gnjumc.org>,*
>   *quezadae25@gmail.com*

date: Feb 6, 2016, 11:34 AM

subject: Praying for your journey

Dear Bishop & Company,

I want you to know that I will be praying for you every morning while you are in Cuba. May you be filled with countless blessings and a move of the Spirit just as I was on my recent trip to Havana. There is a special anointing there, and a deep appreciation for visitors from the United States, especially those who bring Good News.

I cannot wait to hear of all that happens!

In Christ,
XXXXX

I later learned from others that the group went in as partners with the Cuban Methodist Church and Bishop Pereira, and that they were closely attended to by then Cuban District Superintendent Guillermo Leon Mighty and his wife Adria Nunez. Their church, Havana Central Methodist, has been in spiritual revival. Since that initial visit, the academic dean at Union has led a seminary group and others on annual trips back to Havana. Several mission trips with churches have also happened, and substantial financial support has been given to Central Methodist and other associated ministries by churches associated with the trips. This support includes a large feeding program, work with the elderly and children, and donations for church construction. I am also aware of a church in Texas that raised significant funds to help buy sorely needed textbooks and other curriculum for the Cuban Methodist Seminary.

Furthermore, from that initial contact, Rev. Guillermo Leon Mighty and Adria Nunez have made ten to twelve trips back to United Seminary and to various churches that have sent folks to Cuba. They preach, pray, and share, bringing their very charismatic approach with them. One leader, an ordained deacon, shared with me how she has seen her church culture become more focused on the Holy Spirit, in part because of the experience the church has had with their Cuban partners coming to preach and pray with them.

I wish we in Greater New Jersey, home of the second largest Cuban population in the U.S., had a similar legacy story from our time in Cuba, but we do not.

My experience in Cuba further cemented to me the importance of both personal and social holiness in the lives of believers. As part of social holiness, social justice work must have an important place in our discipleship. What kind of relationship with God can one really have without concern for the needs of others and action taken on their behalf? But such work should not replace cultivating our relationship with God through acts of personal holiness, and other aspects of social holiness such as the literal sharing of the Gospel as presented in the Bible and holding one another accountable in our discipleship. I truly embrace John Wesley's theology of balance between these two concerns.

Related to this thought, during our time in Cuba, a somewhat controversial scripture continued to come to mind. It even showed up in my daily devotionals. I contemplated and prayed over it much while there. I believe it was the Lord bringing it to mind:

> While Jesus was in Bethany in the home of Simon the Leper, a woman came to him with an alabaster jar of very expensive perfume, which she poured on his head as he was reclining at the table. When the disciples saw this, they were indignant. "Why this waste?" they asked. "This perfume could have been sold at a high price and the money given to the poor." **Aware of this, Jesus said to them, "Why are you bothering this woman? She has done a beautiful thing to me. The poor you will always have with you, but you will not always have me.** When she poured this perfume on my body, she did it to prepare me for burial. Truly I tell you, wherever this gospel is preached throughout the world, what she has done will also be told, in memory of her." Matthew 26:6-13 (NIV)

There are people who rationalize the verse, "The poor you will always have with you, but you will not always have me," as Jesus asserting that poverty is a useless cause and therefore do not waste your time or money on it. That is not at all what Jesus was saying. His disciples would have been very familiar to what Jesus was referring, and therefore would have had in mind the rest of the verse from Deuteronomy that He was quoting:

> **There will always be poor people in the land. Therefore I command you to be openhanded toward your fellow Israelites who are poor and needy in your land.** Deuteronomy 15:11 (NIV)

The biblical response to poverty is openhandedness. The persistence of poverty is not a reason to ignore the plight of the poor, but instead a reason to draw near to them with generosity. This Deuteronomy verse makes that clear: Jesus says because the poor will always be with us, "therefore" we should be even more generous.

Jesus also spoke in the context of being questioned for allowing an extravagant act of devotion when the money spent on it could have been used to help the poor. Reading the account of the incident in the Gospel of John, we learn he was being questioned by Judas Iscariot, who was about to betray him. Judas was trying to find cause for criticism of Jesus and to distract from this lavish act of love shown for Him. Jesus' response was correcting the idea that any act of love for Jesus is ever wasted. He even called it "a beautiful thing!"

This passage is also testament to the fact that Jesus comes before all other people in our lives, or any of the "good works" we do, even in His name. Time and resources spent to be with Jesus in worship and adoration are not to be discounted or neglected. Doing so relinquishes needed power for God-given living and ministry with others.

I thought about this scripture in my then context. I was on a Church-sponsored mission exploration trip focused on social programs to a country experiencing spiritual revival and a growing Church. This growth contrasted in many ways to the general decline of the Church in the United States and specifically in the United Methodist Church of Greater New Jersey. To be sure, most of those in this Cuban revival were also in dire temporal need. Yet from the stories I hear from others who spent significant time in their Spirit-filled worship and prayer services, they also encountered "loaves and fishes" experiences that are extensively shared and spur faith on. Is faith in Christ not what Christianity is first and foremost? Is faith not what we are to rely on first? (Hebrews 11:6).

These thoughts continually rattled around my mind as we visited one destitute situation after another. I shared my thoughts and questions with Dean Javier Viera from Drew. We had good discussions about Jesus' statement that the poor would always be with us, its interpretations, and its application to our current context. He suggested I bring up the topic with Bishop Schol. I contemplated it and shared how I thought it better I did not. The seminary dean seemed to register my concern that it would not be a safe topic for me to bring up to Bishop Schol.

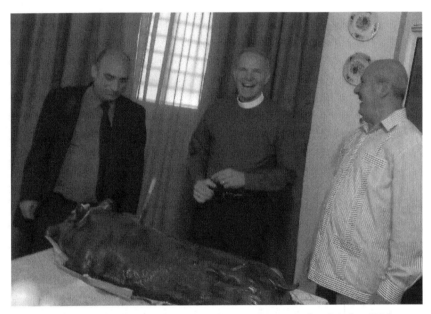

Council of Cuban Churches President Rev. Joel Ortega Dopico, Bishop Schol and Bishop Pereira, Havana, February 11, 2016.

TURNED DOWN FOR FULL ORDERS ONCE

In March of 2016, after serving on the bishop's staff for two years, I had enough full-time service as a clergy to go before the Board of Ordained Ministry to be examined for full ordination orders as an elder. I had submitted the required paperwork (roughly fifty pages), video sermon and analysis, recommendations, ministry setting interviews and all other required provisions in the fall of 2015. I had progressive clergy friends, including my assigned mentor, Rev. Dr. Vickie Brendler, review my paperwork. I was assured it was outstanding.

I had completed demonstrable work on every item of the Growth Plan I had been given three years earlier. For the item added regarding a report on itineracy because I had turned down an appointment initially, I had interviewed ten clergy, including several district superintendents on the value, challenges, and concerns regarding our UMC itineracy process. I later, by the way, gave a copy of my report[1] to all I had interviewed, including the entire cabinet. The following January, a change to our policy was announced where clergy could clearly identify limited itineracy and could apply for openings that would be posted for more transparency in the process.

From: Beth Caulfield

Sent: Tuesday, January 13, 2015 7:23 AM

To: Glenn Conaway; PastorShawnHogan@gmail.com

Cc: Myrna Bethke; Vicki M. Brendler; Andy

Hoover; checkert@morrowchurch.org; Jisun Kwak; Brian

Roberts; michael@clintonumcnj.com; lin.smallwood@gmail.com; Conference Secretary; Varlyna Wright

Subject: Itineracy Report

Hi Glen and Shawn - Happy New Year!

Attached is my report on Itineracy that is part of my growth plan required by the BOM Continuance Committee. I have copied all the folks who graciously agreed to be interviewed. It is my prayer that the report will be helpful to all. I thank you both, all who were interviewed and the rest of the BOM Continuance Committee for this opportunity to more deeply explore and reflect upon the various facets of Itineracy as seen through different lenses.

May the Lord bless you and keep you,

Beth

Rev. Beth Caulfield

Director of Small Groups Ministry & Spiritual Visioning

On a practical level, I should have had every reason to have confidence in my success at being recommended by the Board. If the Board's job was to "vote prayerfully based on personal judgment of the applicant's gifts, evidence of God's grace, and promise of future usefulness for the mission of the Church" (Para. 304, 2016 Book of Discipline), then unless I seriously bumbled more than once in the interviews, I should have had nothing to worry about. If the Board was looking to filter out non-Wesleyan theology, those who lack motivation or fruit, or those who may do harm to themselves or others through their ministry, then certainly my record stood in my favor. But then, as you know, I would not be writing this book if the board performed its function in such a way.

America's Keswick Christian Retreat Center in Whiting, New Jersey touts itself as a "place where Biblical teaching and worship lead to a deeper relationship with Jesus Christ, resulting in a transformed life."[2] The Greater New Jersey Board of Ordained Ministry Candidate Retreat was held there for many years until the Board of Ordained Ministry and other progressive UMC leaders took issue with the Keswick Center's traditional theological stance regarding human sexuality and specifically LGBTQIA issues. The ordination retreat location was eventually moved in 2019. I point this out as just another indicator of how the Greater New Jersey Board of Ordained Ministry now thinks and prioritizes its concerns and decisions. That thinking was already commanding decisions by the time I first went forward for full orders.

When I arrived at the March 2016 Board of Ordained Ministry (BOM) retreat at Keswick, the tension and treatment toward me from certain BOM members was obviously less than supportive and I immediately became uncomfortable. My clothing and appearance were clearly being dissected and judged. There was a feeling of frostiness and sense of pending doom. I told myself I was just nervous like everyone else. Looking back, however, I believe I was simply discerning the spirits present. Jealousy and resentment were at work, along with a disdain for my traditional theology.

My first interview was intended to evaluate my command of the rules, regulations, policies. and procedures at the local church and denominational level. The interview went very well. I remember even enjoying it. The letter I later received from the Board Chair confirmed the comfort I felt in that interview as it stated, "You clearly have a good understanding and working knowledge of our church's polity; you are thoughtful and reflective as you integrate your knowledge of the Book of Discipline."

My theology interview similarly seemed to go without a hitch. It is interesting to me that my theology was not even mentioned in the follow-up letter from the Board Chair. One would think that affirmation or concern about theology would be mentioned in such an assessment.

The Practice of Ministry interview results seemed to bear a good assessment of me as well, as the follow-up letter read as follows:

> Among other things, we give God thanks for your gifts with teaching and leading the groups under your care throughout the Conference, and we celebrate the commitment you have to equipping the laity. You are also careful about maintaining boundaries, which is important in the fullness of ministry. You think strategically and communicate well with the groups in your care. Your commitment to Christ and to Christ's church are evident in your ministry.

However, it was in that interview that I knew biases were at work against me. For the Practice of Ministry area of assessment, candidates are asked to write and teach a Bible study as one of the requirements. As I was serving on the bishop's staff rather than in a local church, I needed to be creative in finding a place to teach the study I had written. Thankfully, I had an easy solution. The Women's Ministries of Morrow Memorial Church had asked me to lead their annual women's retreat. I had worked with their retreat the year before, they had been pleased, and had asked me to come back.

THE SONG OF SOLOMON

I wrote a Bible Study on the Song of Solomon and taught it over the course of the retreat, giving several of its lessons and breaking the women into small groups to discuss. The study I wrote was about the intimacy we can have with and through God as demonstrated in the Song of Solomon, and that it is shown in the book as the relationship between a husband and wife. I also taught that the book is additionally interpreted as showing the relationship between Christ and the Church and God and Israel. The study was well received by the women's group leaders and retreat participants as evidenced by the email below and others I received.

Re: Thank You - Big Time!

Margaret Prentice <prentice.margaret@gmail.com>
Mon, Oct 5, 2015, 9:21 AM

to Beth, Vicki

By my third cup of coffee, the caffeine is kicking in and I'm re-entering the world of the living—and first on my agenda is to say "thank you," Beth. You took us on a wonderful journey yesterday. We had no real idea of where our theme would lead, but I can report only good things from our time together. From my own perspective, I feel some re-awakening of God's call to me. Writing the commitments empowered me—and makes me feel accountable to myself and to God.

I have a nice handful of emails from women sending their thanks for the retreat. Your testimony triggered good discussions in the groups. .... I'm looking forward to our paths crossing again. ....

M

Margaret Prentice

During my Practice of Ministry interview, however, Rev. Dr. Andy Hoover, then a district superintendent, commandeered the interview process, especially as we discussed my Bible study. A strong advocate and leader for changing the Book of Discipline regarding the marriage and ordination of LGBTQIA people, he became visibly agitated and questioned my teaching this study as a relationship between a husband and wife. I had not broached LGBTQIA concerns at all in my written study nor with the women whom I taught. I never condemned or even mentioned same sex marriages. In the interview I had to make that point very clear for Rev. Dr. Hoover as he grilled me on the topic. I repeatedly assured him that LGBTQIA issues never came up as we focused on a romantic, marital relationship as a metaphor for our personal relationships with God.

I will point out that Rev. Dr. Hoover's leading of the interview process is contrary to his role as a DS. In order to protect BOM's discernment of candidates from undue influence, many if not most

Conferences do not have DS's sit in interviews, and only a subset of DS's are to be representatives of the bishop to the board. The Global Board on Higher Education Ministry has issued directives to that effect.

Rev. Hoover did happen to be an identified cabinet representative to the GNJ BOM at that time. Such designated district superintendent representatives are to attend BOM Meetings, but have no vote, just voice. And the "voice" is limited to offering cabinet perspective on specific questions.

Yet our conference's practice with our current bishop and his cabinet is to have all DS's present for the entirety of the BOM retreat while candidates are being assessed. A district superintendent is present in every interview. As my story will demonstrate throughout the rest of this book, DS's do cross the line and control the process in Greater New Jersey. I experienced this in more than one BOM retreat and it has been the experience of other candidates as well.

I was critically examined by Dr. Hoover who specifically asked, among similar questions, if I would have taught my study on the Song of Solomon to a Reconciling Ministries Church, i.e., a church that is openly supportive of gay marriage. Another progressive clergy joined him in this line of questioning. She would later become a district superintendent. I repeated that my study was meant for any context and did not broach those issues. As the barrage went on, however, I realized I was at best being condemned because I did not make LGBTQIA issues the center of concern in my teaching, and at worst I was being condemned for a teaching that in no way challenged a traditional view of the Bible, nor did it challenge church polity on human sexuality.

175

There were only two other clergy in the interview. They both appeared extremely uncomfortable but said nothing. When I was repeatedly asked if I would teach this study to a Reconciling Ministries Church, I prayed before responding that "I always try to follow John Wesley's Three Simple Rules—do no harm, do good, stay in love with God. If my teaching were to break one of those rules, I would adjust my plan." The response was accepted, and we ended the interview. Later that day Rev. Dr. Hoover approached me and told me he appreciated that I gave that response. I naively thought that meant we had found a peace and I had passed the interview. I also felt peace in that my response did not compromise my own theology but had avoided further controversy in the interview.

What I did not know, however, was that the Cabinet had recently appointed to that church a gay male clergy who was in a same sex marriage. At that time I did not even know that pastor, as I had only interacted with the previous pastor. The new pastor and his husband would go on and serve that church for five years before moving on to another appointment after his retirement. He had also served on the BOM since 2008.

This openly practicing homosexual pastor's responsibilities were clear proof that conference leadership were not only lobbying for gay marriage and gay clergy acceptance by our Biblically-based polity, but were heavily engaged in subverting it through the appointment process and the BOM. I did not know (and still do not) if Morrow Memorial UMC had declared itself a Reconciling Ministries Church at that time. I know that the church has now done so and aggressively promotes itself as such. But at the time, such a concern was nowhere on my radar.

I now suspect that Rev. Hoover was concerned that my teaching might have caused question regarding the new, openly gay pastor's legitimacy as the pastor of the church. Or that I would have been a challenge to the signal from conference that his ministry was fully supported. Now that I look back and understand what was truly going on in the conference, I hope that my teaching did cause some, if not all, to reflect on the Biblical demonstration and definition of marriage as between a man and a woman.

What I also now understand better is that I, a traditional clergy in a leadership position whose sphere of influence had become greater than just the local church, was by then already seen as a threat to the progressive leaders of the conference who were seeking to change the United Methodist Church stance on LGBTQIA issues. Add that I was popular in the conference among clergy and laity and that I was receiving acclaim for my ministry, which also breeds jealousy, resentment, and competition, I now was a target to be shot down. I will say that other traditional candidates for ministry have received poor reception from the BOM in Greater New Jersey. I have heard many stories of sorrows, so I am not alone in my treatment.

THE HUNGER GAMES

For the preaching requirements of the Board's examination, I had preached and recorded a sermon at Clinton United Methodist Church entitled, "People with Abundant Life Plan." The crux of the sermon was that as Christians we should commit our lives to God and work under the direction of the Holy Spirit for planning, and let God transform our plans and lives to His. When we do this, we will experience abundant life even in difficult circumstances. I used several personal life experiences in the sermon to make my points. I also used the sermon as a pitch for the Team Vital Strategic Planning Church initiative I was leading for the conference. Little did I know how relevant that sermon would be for the rest of my UMC involvement as my experiences have only become more difficult, and yet I find God and God's comfort in the midst of them.

I had several clergy read over the sermon ahead of time, including my progressive clergy mentor, Rev. Dr. Vickie Brendler. With their feedback to reassure me, I felt confident in its contents. The sermon was well received by the congregation.

Yet I found the preaching interview was surprisingly difficult. My sermon was heavily criticized, specifically by the lead interviewer, who I will refer to as Rev. Saul Pawn. In the past I had always had pleasant interactions with Rev. Pawn. I find him to be very gracious. When I had come before BOM three years earlier for provisional elder status, he had pulled me aside to praise the bible study I had written on the Gospel of John. But this interaction represented a significant change. I was told by him that my sermon sounded like prosperity Gospel. I was baffled. When I asked for clarification, the concern registered was that I made it sound like every difficult situation works out miraculously if you just trust God. I reminded them as I referred to my sermon text that I addressed that concern extensively. I was making a point in the sermon that God does respond to our circumstances and sometimes our rearview of the story does indeed show miracles. Again, I thought the concerns were worked out.

Though he did not lead the interview, District Superintendent Rev. Steve Bechtold also asked questions, pointing out that my sermon was too hopeful and would not be helpful to those experiencing tough circumstances. He asked if I would preach that sermon to someone who was homeless and living under a bridge. I responded that I probably would not, but I had preached to the context of the church I was in, as the BOM had required. I reminded him and the other interviewers that the recording I submitted showed that the sermon had received a standing ovation. They acknowledged that they had seen that.

I was baffled by the line of questioning at the time. I felt a strong sense that the goal was not to support and build up someone who was called to ordained ministry, but to find any way possible to disqualify me. Months later, another BOM clergy member who was at the interview commented, "There was nothing wrong with your sermon. It was a good sermon." She said this with a look of disgust, knowing what had been done to me.

After the preaching interview, all candidates were to eat lunch with the BOM and cabinet members present. This was not a time of formal interviews, but still a time of making impressions and being evaluated. Rev. Pawn, who had just led the preaching interview, sat next to me.

Our conversation was casual and friendly. However, toward the end, he made this comment to me, "We should rename the BOM Retreat "The Hunger Games" because really, people get shot down here." He laughed. I was unnerved, to say the least. Now, I had referenced the book *The Hunger Games* in my sermon. I had talked about how Amazon had identified one line from the book as the most underlined section of any book in their Kindle product for the previous year. The line, incidentally, was this, "Because sometimes things happen to people and they're not equipped to deal with them." It gives me chills still to think about that line in the context of the story I am now telling in this book.

I tried to laugh, but the message being sent was clearly unfriendly and intended to rattle me. I told myself I was overreacting, succumbing to the normal anxieties of the interview process and that possibly he was being so crass with me because he was considering me as already "in."

In my Debrief Committee meeting, which is a final committee that reviews the results of candidate interviews and clarifies any concerns communicated to them from the interviews, little was brought up and I walked out confident that I was going to be approved. I really thought that despite what I have written above.

After the retreat I returned to the conference office for a meeting. I expected to get a call from a BOM representative sometime during the meeting telling me my results. I remember the meeting starting late as a cabinet member, Rev. Steve Bechtold (who had been in my preaching interview) and the bishop's executive assistant, Ms. Nicola Mulligan, had been in another meeting and were running late. I remember them arriving and Ms. Mulligan looking teary as I greeted her. Rev. Bechtold smiled and looked me in the eye and I remember thinking all would be well.

However, as the meeting went on and I began receiving texts from other candidates saying they had passed and were celebrating, I became more nervous. I noticed Ms. Mulligan avoided eye contact with me throughout the meeting. Rev. Bechtold just smiled whenever I looked at him. I now understand that they had come from a meeting where the BOM results, including my not passing, had been discussed.

After the meeting I left to drive home. Within five minutes I received a call from a BOM member who I will refer to as Rev. Dr. Alexa Bold, informing me that BOM had decided I was not yet ready for full orders. I was told I would receive more information in the mail, which is standard practice. Though she expressed concern for me as I was clearly surprised and upset, the entire conversation felt very cold and disingenuous in regard to care for me. Even at that time, not fully comprehending what was happening, I felt she was gloating as she gave me the news.

The experience of being told "not yet" by BOM was extremely difficult psychologically, emotionally, and for my self-esteem. These challenges felt escalated for me as my ministry had been acknowledged as bearing fruit, and I was in a high-profile position as a member of the bishop's staff. It was extremely painful because I knew that I had been treated unjustly. While lesser prepared candidates were passed, I was not.

The next day, March 17th, I received a phone call from Bishop Schol, checking how I was doing and expressing his sorrow for the difficulties I was facing. He made efforts to encourage me, saying not passing BOM the first time was not uncommon and that he highly encouraged me to apply again next year. I thanked him for his concern.

I soon learned that I was not the only candidate with a traditional theology to receive such a phone call from Bishop Schol. A long-term ministry leader with a PhD from Princeton Theological Seminary and MDIV from Duke Theological School was also not passed. She shared with me that she felt very targeted because of her traditional theology and her stated support for the UMC Book of Discipline regarding issues of human sexuality. After her experience with the BOM she immediately left the conference, taking a position as a professor at a Wesleyan college in another state.

A few days later I received the letter from the BOM Chair stating I was not yet ready to be recommended for full orders. In addition to what I shared above, the rest of the letter nebulously gave reasons I was "not yet ready to be recommended for ordination."

To: Beth Caulfield

March 18, 2016

Dear Beth;

Grace and peace be with you this day. I write to follow up on the phone call you received from the Board at the conclusion of the retreat, indicating that Board has discerned that you are not at this time ready to be ordained. We know that this is deeply disappointing and we are holding you in thought and prayer.

Please be aware that the Board lifted up numerous dimensions of your gifts and your strengths. Among other things, we give God thanks for your gifts with teaching and leading the groups under your care throughout the Conference, and we celebrate the commitment you have to equipping the laity. You are also careful about maintaining boundaries, which is important in the fullness of ministry. You clearly have a good understanding and working knowledge of our church's polity; you are thoughtful and reflective as you integrate your knowledge of the Book of Discipline. You think strategically and communicate well with the groups in your care. Your commitment to Christ and to Christ's church are evident in your ministry.

We are eager to journey with you as you attend to the areas where further strengthening is needed prior to being ready for ordination. We encourage you to explore the impact that culture and privilege have in ministry, as deepened awareness will strengthen and enrich your witness. Intercultural competency and self-awareness are essential in today's ministry. In engaging others, it is important to be attuned to how you are received, and become aware of the impact that your words and actions have on others.

While recognizing the intent of the sermon you prepared, we encourage you to deepen the level of your exegetical work in preaching, wrestle with the diverse ways in which persons in different seasons and circumstances may hear the message, and reflect on the unique nature of proclamation.

As we continue to walk together in ministry, it is appropriate to update the growth plan that assists in your ongoing development. We would like to meet with you on Friday, April 8th, at 1:45 pm at the Princeton United Methodist Church (7 Vandeventer Ave, Princeton, NJ 08542).

At that time, a handful of Board members will review the recommendations made for your ongoing strengthening in ministry, and will work with you in articulating the steps needed to support your journey toward full membership and ordination in the Greater New Jersey Conference. You might anticipate that we will spend 30-40 minutes together. Please email me to confirm your attendance (pastorshawnhogan@gmail.com).

It is my prayer that in this season you sense God's supportive and empowering presence accompanying you.

Peace;

Shawn Callender Hogan Chairperson

cc: The Rev. Andy Hoover, District Superintendent

That year a number of changes were made by Bishop Schol to the BOM, including Rev. Saul Pawn being named as the new Chair. The Board became even more progressive leaning and LGBTQIA-rights focused.

WHITE PRIVILEGE

When you are not recommended by BOM in the Greater New Jersey Conference, you are to meet with your Debrief Committee and be given a Growth Plan so that you will be better prepared for the next time you go before the Board. A meeting was set for me at Drew Theological School. Only one member of my assigned Debrief Committee was present, Rev. Alexa Bold. Instead, the people present I will refer to as Rev. Saul Pawn and Rev. Dr. Dana Harding were also present. I do not recollect at all that Dr. Harding had even been in any of my ordination interviews. Therefore, it was especially odd to me that she would be in this meeting to share my growth plan. The Chair of the Board had indicated she, too, would be at the meeting, but did not attend. The chair had also indicated that Rev. Jeff Markay would be present, but he was not. I had interacted with Rev. Markay years earlier as a student at Drew. The team present and those who were initially indicated would be present were a suspicious mix. First, the fact that only one of them was part of the assigned Debrief Team for such a task is odd. Second, present that day or not, all mentioned have long-term friendships/relationships with one another.

For example, Rev. Dr. Dana Harding and Rev. Saul Pawn grew up in Chatham together, still ministered and lived in that same basic area, and Rev. Markay was and had been for many years the senior pastor at Chatham UMC. He was also the UMC liaison for students at Drew Theological School where Dana worked, which is in Madison, the town over from Chatham. Chatham is one of the most affluent and white communities in all of New Jersey. Dr. Harding is also quite vocal about her close relationship with Rev. Dr. Andy Hoover, my then District Superintendent who I have mentioned throughout this book and will continue to do so. Rev. Dr. Alexa Bold was at that time the senior pastor at Princeton UMC, another well-known, affluent, and very white congregation. I believe she and the BOM chair of the time are good friends. I know that she is good friends with other progressive district superintendents.

But also, all present had been adamant about their disagreement with the Book of Discipline as related to issues of human sexuality. Rev. Dr. Dana Harding had been a clergy delegate to the 2012 General Conference in Tampa (as was Rev. Dr. Hoover) and has been featured in media as part of the disruptive protests that happened when yet again progressives failed to get the Book of Discipline language changed. Her efforts have, if anything, escalated on this issue since then.

At her own advice and offer, I decided to take my ordination mentor with me to the meeting. I was most appreciative of her being there for me. In spite our theological differences, Vickie was a professional who knew I was being treated unjustly. Looking back, I think she knew the players involved and that this hazing could get out of hand. She repeatedly reminded me beforehand to just "be humble."

In the meeting the issues discussed about me were quite surprising. First, my sermon was criticized for including comments about abuse of alcohol and prescription medication as a growing concern for society. The sermon clearly discussed the importance of medication and its benefits, but the criticism given was that I could make people who must take anti-anxiety medication uncomfortable. Again, I had clearly and specifically stated that such medication was important, and anxiety and depression are indeed serious medical problems.

It was repeated also that my sermon was prosperity gospel.[3] When I pressed for examples of what was meant, because I really did not know where that was coming from, I was told that not everyone has all their problems fixed by God. When I tried to mention that this very point was also central in the sermon, I was sternly warned by Rev. Pawn not to question their observations. It felt like when your dad tells you to "knock it off" or you are going to get more punishment. I then as graciously as possible stated that my sermon simply bore witness to experiences of God showing up in miraculous ways in people's lives, including mine.

Instead of discussing anything more about my interviews, the subject turned to white privilege. I was told by Rev. Dr. Dana Harding that I do not understand my white privilege and that my ministry could be offensive to minorities in our conference. This was said to me and affirmed by an all-white group who were friends with each other.

I was told that I needed to interview minority clergy, asking them their reaction to me and to write a report about what they said. I asked who they would recommend. They suggested Rev. Vanessa Wilson, Chair of GNJ Commission on Race and Religion, who is African American. I agreed and asked whom else they would recommend.

I felt they were setting me up for something. So, when they paused, I suggested District Superintendent Rev. Dr. Varlyna Wright (African American) who I worked with as part of Conference staff, and Rev. Michelle Ryoo (Korean), who I worked with in my role as staff representative on the conference agency COSROW. I later, of my own volition, added Rev. Lyssette Perez (Hispanic and president of the Hispanic/Latino caucus MARCHA of the UMC) to the people with whom I would have a discussion.

I walked out of the meeting into the parking lot with Vickie Brendler, who verbally acknowledged that I had just been put through a process designed to "humble" me. Her big hug before we departed spoke volumes.

My being turned down by BOM did not go unnoticed by others. I received many messages expressing sorrow, frustration, disgust, anger, and support. The most poignant memory I have is from the ordination ceremony at the 2016 Annual Conference when clergy were lining up to enter the ceremony. Ordinands lined up in the hallway first, the rest of us followed. When the ordinands were called to the front, a traditionalist Elder with full orders, whom I did not really know nor had I spoken to about my situation, began very loudly and repeatedly shouting, "Beth Caulfield should be at the front of this line!" I am sure there were those who thought I had somehow put him up to it, but I was as surprised as anyone else. To this day I appreciate his bold support.

Following the advice of the Debrief Committee, I met with DS Rev. Dr. Wright and Rev. Ryoo. Both spoke directly about my respect for and strong effectiveness in inter-cultural competency and cited several examples, including how I search out cross-cultural opinions before I instigate ministries, how I am approachable, and how I show comfort approaching and learning from others different from myself. They described me as having a sacrificial and compassionate heart; as being passionate, thorough, well-prepared, calm, and a good listener; and as able to bring meetings to practical conclusions. Although we really did not know each other and had not conversed before, Rev. Wilson was very pleasant and gave me pointers on inter-cultural competency.

For good measure I also reached out to Rev. Lyssette Perez (Hispanic), who I knew as the pastor of one of the churches that had benefited from my Team Vital ministry. We had good conversations and she invited me to preach at her church. It was the first time I was interpreted into Spanish. I preached on Revelation 7:9 (every tribe, tongue, and nation, worshiping before the lamb), and used Michael Jackson's song title "Can You Feel It?" as my sermon title and its lyrics to support the text. I requested that Rev. Dr. Dana Harding review this sermon and another I had written based on Peter's Restoration in John 17, entitled "Do you Love Me." I asked her opinion on which sermon I should submit to BOM for my next try. She gave support for both sermons.

Additionally, to further show my willingness to address their concerns, that summer I enrolled in a seminar led by Rev. Dr. Dana Harding on "White Privilege" and contributed robustly, sharing from my experiences as a founder of a prison ministry, a former EEO and Affirmative Action Officer, leader of multicultural Bible study programs abroad, and other life experiences.

That summer I worked hard on preparing my paperwork and meeting other requirements so that I could go before the Board again in

2017. At the same time my ministry continued to flourish, with more churches connecting to small group ministry and joining the Team Vital process under my leadership. I continued to preach the Gospel, write heavily read blogs, and take on various work, including developing Team Vital 2.0. My contributions continued to be recognized.

I do not regret the work, my contributions, or what I learned, especially about the shortcomings of the UMC system for ordination that are exploited for power abuse. I do regret the hopefulness I maintained that I would eventually be treated fairly by the corrupt and unjust power structures in place. This system is led by people not focused on empowering people to do ministry, but on political gain and achieving a focused progressive agenda fixated on achieving approval and celebration from the church for practicing LGBTQIA people.

This agenda supersedes and even replaces introducing to and discipling people through the transforming power of the Gospel of Jesus Christ. It has taken control of the Board of Ordained Ministry of Greater New Jersey and undoubtedly has in other UMC Conferences. As stated earlier, I am not alone in experiencing such sordid treatment. I would soon learn, however, that there are even larger powers at work than those that are destructive to ministry and ordination candidates exercising themselves through the Greater New Jersey Annual Conference.

RUN FOR BISHOP

Since early times, certain ordained persons have been selected and entrusted for a ministry of coordinating and leading mission within a defined geographical region of the church. In the United Methodist tradition, bishops are ordained elder who are elected and consecrated to the office of bishop. They are "set apart for a ministry of servant leadership, general oversight and supervision."

Bishops are elected by the lay and clergy delegates in each regional area (jurisdictional and central conferences) every four years following regular sessions of the General Conference...Any active ordained elder in good standing is eligible to be elected a bishop. An eligible candidate must also have at least four years (a full term) to serve before reaching the mandatory retirement age of 68.[1]

I organized my work for helping Jisun in a binder.

In fall of 2015, Rev. Dr. Jisun Kwak asked me to begin praying with her about running for bishop. She was feeling a tug at her heart but at the same time was leery. I committed to praying with her. She prayed and fasted through the fall. By January 2016 she was confident that she was discerning a call to run for bishop that quadrennium.

That January she also approached Bishop Schol out of courtesy and for his thoughts on her running. He did not offer any encouragement or help with the process and was noticeably quiet in their meeting. He only stated that she should speak with her colleagues about the idea. She says the clear signal given was, "I am not going to help you."

She asked for a sign from God about what she should do and received one. The conference secretary contacted her to tell her she had indeed been nominated. When she asked by whom, she was told by four different people. She had asked no one to nominate her. When she inquired who had nominated her, the one name she was given surprised her greatly. It was one of her clergy leaders known as circuit elders serving in the Delaware Bay District.

inside my "Run for Bishop" binder

I and others began working with her to prepare. She was my "Seoul" mate, and I was thrilled to delve into her campaign. I helped her with her candidacy paperwork, her speeches, her answers to candidacy questions, and anything else I could. We talked strategy and prayed a lot. It was an exciting time. I learned much. Working with her also was healing to me that Spring as I dealt with all that happened through the Board of Ordained Ministry experience.

There was one incident that occurred early on in her run that I see now as a valuable lesson learned and a God-protection as Jisun prepared that spring. She was to be interviewed by the other General Conference delegates (remember she was one also) to determine if they would endorse her candidacy for bishop. Nominations or endorsements of candidates by annual conferences, delegations or other groups are common but not required to be elected. Obviously, however, to be endorsed by as many groups as possible is a plus. I remember that Jisun was not overly concerned about the interview and resisted even preparing for it. I thought that was very odd and I did not like it. I knew that the delegates included some very tough opponents to Jisun, and I did not think they would let her get by them easily. But she, of course, was the boss. If there is one thing I have learned about my friend, it is that I cannot make her do *anything*.

So when she called me just after the interview, upset at how poorly it had gone, I was not surprised. She revealed that the room was very rough on her and asked voracious questions that surprised her. She had faltered as she was not at all prepared for such questions. They were on a totally different level than anything she had heard from others who had gone through these interviews before. The results were immediately reported by Conference Communications in its online Digest.[2] My attitude was one of "I told you so." However, in the end, I believe what happened was the best that could have happened to my friend.

For starters, I do not believe all those questions were solely the products of that team. I believe their genesis was from elsewhere, and my money is on them being encouraged by Bishop Schol. I believe he wanted to help those who opposed Jisun and ensure that others did not vote for her. It worked, as even staunch Jisun's allies on the team were hesitant to vote to endorse her with the poor performance she gave.

But what I later saw as good about this was that Rev. Dr. Jisun Kwak never allowed herself to be unprepared for such questioning again. I had the privilege of working with and learning from her during the long hours we spent preparing for the Jurisdictional Conference episcopal candidate interviews. Those early questions helped prime her. Also, as I learned later, it is not uncommon for strong Episcopal candidates to not be endorsed by General Conference delegations. Many clergy delegates have political aspirations themselves, and sadly are more interested in those than backing another rising leader. In the end, I think it was good Jisun said very little in that interview that could tip her hand regarding her campaign and the strength that she would have as she went on. After that interview, I think people were satisfied that she would not perform well as a candidate in the future.

Before the 2016 General Conference, when Legislative Committee assignments for delegates were given, Jisun chose the Ministry and Higher Education/Superintendency Committee. Soon after the General Conference began that May in Portland, Oregon, she was elected by her committee colleagues to chair a significant subcommittee: The Episcopacy and District Superintending Committee. This role represented a huge volume of work as that group considered over two hundred-fifty petitions at the time.

But most significantly, Jisun led this committee in crafting legislation for term limits for bishops. In the United Methodist system, bishops are elected for life. They serve in that capacity until retirement. They have a mandatory retirement age of 68 to 72, depending on when their birthday falls (the goal is to avoid bishops reaching the mandatory clergy retirement age of 72 in the middle of their four-year terms). But bishops can serve in a variety of capacities post-retirement, and retired bishops have voice (but not vote) at Council of Bishops meetings. This means that when you are elected bishop, not only do you retain the title for life, but also retain other significant benefits.

Under Jisun's leadership, a committee with strongly voiced differences and keen interest from the Council of Bishops managed to draft and approve a resolution that would limit bishops' terms to eight years. Thereafter bishops would be appointed back to serve in a local church and their benefits and salaries would be commensurate with their level of serving. The vote on the committee to endorse the petition was 56 for and 30 against.

Jisun spoke to the resolution at the plenary session. This was a brave act, especially for someone who was seeking endorsements to run for bishop herself in just a couple of months. This was not the first General Conference that such legislation was introduced, but it was the General Conference when such legislation came the closest to being passed. To pass it needed a two-thirds majority vote. It received well over a majority vote and just barely missed the two-thirds (67%) threshold with 493 votes for and 312 votes against, which was 61% of the vote for the motion. There was a subsequent motion to reconsider the legislation again in 2020 that did pass (needing only a majority vote), with a 482-382 result.[3] Jisun's strong leadership for that committee was acknowledged by many leaders across the denomination.

Jisun and the rest of the Greater New Jersey delegation headed home from Portland and straight to the 2016 Greater New Jersey Annual Conference Session. There she would seek endorsement by the Annual Conference for her Episcopal candidacy. We created a campaign and a campaign speech around her beliefs that we needed to "get back to basics" in our approach as a denomination, focusing on spiritual matters, Wesleyan holiness, rich prayer, and cultural competency to best reach a world in need of Jesus.

Her challenge was quite daunting as it was clear that Bishop Schol was not supportive of her ministry nor her candidacy for bishop. His efforts to derail her endorsement were obvious at the Annual Conference. For example, there was only one other candidate seeking endorsement from Greater New Jersey that quadrennium, Rev. Heseun Kim. Before the two candidates went before the Body to give their speeches, Bishop Schol got up and spoke ad nauseum to make a point that neither candidate had to be voted for and that neither had been endorsed by the General Conference delegation. He repeated those statements. It was evident that he knew he had power to influence people's thinking and he was very clearly abusing it at that time. I contrast his speech and action in that moment to the previous year when I was told not to feature Jisun in a promotional video that ran during the conference because it might give her unfair advantage when running to be a General Conference delegate. The double-standard is again obvious.

There was also a little power play made with where he stood and spoke and where Jisun was invited to stand (behind him) when she came to give her speech. She had to intentionally move to a more central place on the stage to be better viewed and heard. You cannot make these things up. He was brazen in how he did everything in his power to stop her being endorsed.

But he failed. Jisun's speech was well received. During it I sat on the edge of my seat, saying every word with her in my head. I think I was more nervous than she was. Her confidence amazed me.

Shortly after Jisun's endorsement for bishop at the Greater New Jersey Annual conference, May, 2016.

After the vote was tallied, it was reported that she had been endorsed as an Episcopal candidate by the Greater New Jersey Annual Conference with a 65% vote. That is outstanding. She was also endorsed later that week by the New Federation of Asian-American United Methodists.

According to Jisun, Bishop Schol did not congratulate her. Not that day and not ever. Instead, later that day, he had someone summon her. When she responded and walked to the staging area known as "the green room," she was confronted by Bishop Schol the moment she entered. This was done in front of other district superintendents, conference staff, laity, and Convention Center employees. Schol began accusing her of causing a problem he was having with a lay person who she had put on her Delaware Bay District Superintendency Committee.

That person was the infamous Mr. Creed Pogue. Creed is notorious within our conference and jurisdiction for his careful examination and challenging of conference and jurisdictional decisions and legislation. His heart is for justice and the appropriate handling of the Book of Discipline, which he knows very well.

Creed had challenged Bishop Schol in front of the body on a matter and so Schol accused Jisun of having given him access to too much information by putting him on her team. Rather than welcoming Creed's input, Bishop Schol preferring to limit Creed's voice. Schol, on numerous occasions that I have witnessed, has privately and publicly ridiculed Creed in clear attempts to discredit him. It should be noted that Mr. Pogue, well before Jisun was the DS for Delaware Bay, had been examining and, often challenging, conference and jurisdictional edicts and decisions. Jisun had nothing to do with his efforts.

Instead of being cheered for her endorsement, Jisun found herself in a ludicrous confrontation initiated by her boss just hours after her victory. She ended up raising her voice back at Schol in defense of Mr. Pogue. If only more people had the courage to stand up to church leaders when they are out of line. But voices are stifled by leaders who construct insular bubbles where they must always be right and anyone who challenges them is likely to be struck down or isolated.

It is noteworthy that the report from the conference given by UMC News does not even mention the endorsement that Jisun received.[4] By comparison, the Baltimore-Washington Annual Conference did report their endorsed episcopal candidate, Rev. Cynthia Moore-Koikoi.

Bishop Schol was on the Board of the United Methodist Communications agency from 2013-2016, while his close friend Bishop Sally Dyck was chair of UMCOM. So, it would not be out of character in my opinion for Schol to have used his influence to squelch the announcement.

I believe all that happened next was as much related to Schol's desire to ensure Rev. Moore Koikoi was elected as it had to do with his apparent disdain for Jisun. That year, 2016, in the Northeast Jurisdiction of the UMC, which is made up of ten Annual Conferences from New England to West Virginia, the only two African American bishops in the Jurisdiction were to be replaced. Bishop Marcus Mathews was retiring, and Bishop Martin McLee had died. There had also been a great deal of concern raised that there had not been any African American female bishops elected in the denomination since the year 2000. Therefore, it was important to the Northeast Jurisdictional bishops, who were feeling the pressure, that African American female bishops were elected that year.

There were three running: Rev. Estelle Easterling from the New England Conference, Rev. Adrienne Brewington from New York, and Rev. Cynthia Moore-Koikoi from Baltimore-Washington. Schol had ordained Moore-Koikoi in 2010, while he had been bishop of the Baltimore-Washington area. Seeing her elected bishop would be a feather in his cap. Bishop Mathews had discouraged his cabinet in Baltimore-Washington from running for bishop that year except for Moore-Koikoi. If Rev. Dr. Jisun Kwak was elected instead, it may have been seen as an embarrassment in front of his colleagues.

If she had succeeded, Jisun would have become the first female Asian UMC bishop of all time in the entire world.

However, that was not to be.

DIRTY POOL

I will never forget the chilling phone conversation I had with Jisun on the evening of June 6, 2016. I was out watering and deadheading the red geraniums I kept in large cement planters on the front steps of my home. My body was tending the plants and blossoms, but my mind was cultivating Jisun's election. I had an idea for sharing her platform and decided to give her a call about it while tending the blooms. She was driving when she picked up but listened to me quietly as I energetically went on about my idea. After a bit, I could tell she was not really listening to me. I asked if something was wrong.

In an initial calmness that I could never have mustered, she shared that she had just had a devastating experience in a meeting with Bishop Schol. It was a meeting that had been arranged only through email initiated by Bishop Schol. The email message in no way prepared her for what was going to happen in that meeting. The email stated:

Bishop John Schol   *Jun 1, 2016, at 2:22 PM*

Jisun,

A concern has come to my attention about a complaint that was filed back in 2010 and if it was properly followed up with. The request has come to my office to follow up on this matter. I have reviewed the file. There is not a lot in the file but it did indicate that you received $13,000 and you were treating this as a loan and would repay it. I trust we can clear this up.

I would like to meet with you on Sunday evening following a meeting I have in the South at 7:00 PM. I will provide a more precise location and time by Friday. What I want to see is any documents you have about money you have received and payments that have been made. I will also want to learn more about what occurred and your understanding. Because this involves a complaint that was filed in 2010, and I have been asked to follow up on it, you are welcome to bring another clergy person with you if you desire.

Keep the faith!

John

John Schol, Bishop

Although reading the contents of his initial email appear concerning to me as written, I did not have the background on the subject matter that my friend did upon receiving it. Jisun, of course, knew exactly to what he was referring. While she had been a pastor at the Mendham, NJ UMC for twelve years between 1995 and 2007, there had been a faithful, retired couple who were members of the church, John and Julie Patchin. The two were part of a tightly knit group at the church that Jisun affectionately refers to as the "Mendham gang." It was well known that the Patchins, who had no grandchildren of their own and a strained relationship with their only daughter who was significantly older than Jisun, informally acted as surrogate grandparents to Jisun's daughter Lydia and were close to Jisun. For example, beginning when Lydia was five years old, to aid Jisun while she worked late afternoon and evening hours, Julie and John would walk Lydia from school to the Patchin's home, and even take her to after school activities on occasion. The Patchins lived walking distance from both the school and parsonage. Jisun and Lydia frequently ate meals with the Patchins in each other's homes. They attended social activities together.

The Patchins were financially well off as John had enjoyed a long career with many business successes. As Christians who thanked God for their blessings, they were faithful stewards and generous givers. Over the years the Patchins gave big-heartedly to the church. Their offerings included gifts to maintain the church parsonage. They also gave abundantly to Jisun and her daughter personally. Their actions, including the gifts to Jisun and her daughter, were known by many at the church. The Patchins recognized that Jisun was raising her daughter alone, pastoring a church and at the same time working on her PhD, all on a minimal salary of under $25,000 a year. The Patchins knew they were able to help and gladly did so. Over the years, the Patchins began repeatedly offering that they wanted to help pay for Lydia's college and wedding someday.

While Jisun stayed in Mendham until 2007, the Patchins moved from there in 2003 to Maine. They continued their relationships with the "Mendham gang," including Jisun and Lydia, returning to Mendham for visits and special occasions. By 2006 the Patchins determined that Julie needed nursing home care, so the couple left Maine for Lenox, Massachusetts, to be closer to their daughter. The "Mendham gang," including Jisun, traveled together to visit Julie in the nursing home.

In 2007, Jisun received a new appointment to a church in Rockland County, NY. John continued visiting not only Mendham, but would stop in New York to visit Jisun and Lydia as well. When Julie died in 2008, the funeral was held at Mendham and John requested Jisun perform the funeral, which of course, she did. After a thirteen-year relationship, the Patchins were not just former parishioners, but had long been family to her and Lydia.

When Lydia went off to Boston University in 2007, her expenses were mostly covered with financial assistance and scholarship. She did not request any help from the Patchins. John, on occasion, visited Lydia at college, maintaining the close ties. For the school year beginning fall of 2008, Lydia wanted to move off campus but her scholarship would not cover the cost and neither could Jisun. John insisted on helping, reminding the family that it had been his wife's wishes that they help. He gave $1000 per month to Jisun to cover the costs.

In 2010, upon learning of these payments, the Patchins' daughter, rather than approaching Jisun, sent a letter to the denomination's United Methodist Women's office asking for intervention by the Church and that Jisun be sent back to her own country. She also specifically asked that her father not be informed that she was intervening. The letter was then passed on to Jisun's superior, the then bishop of Greater New Jersey, Sudarshanna Devhadar.

Bishop Devhadar consulted with Jisun and the conference chancellor. Given the delicacy of the situation with the daughter and the father's relationship, the chancellor advised the bishop to tell Jisun to treat the money as a loan and that is what he did, even though the money had not been given as a loan. Jisun agreed to go to John and pay the money back, thanking him for a loan. The amount she had received over the previous two years for Lydia was $13,000.

Jisun did as agreed. She told Mr. Padgin, who at that time was in his eighties, that she had been grateful for his help, appreciated the loan, but now wanted to pay him back. She handed him a check for $13,000. Mr. Padgin expressed hurt and confusion. He repeatedly told her the money had not been given as a loan, was a gift from him and Julie, and that he did not want "a penny back." Jisun honored the daughter's request not to tell him about her letter. She just continued to insist on paying the money back. At one point Mr. Padgin became upset and tore up the check. He also added that he wanted to pay off Jisun's education debt. She again refused the offer, but he insisted the refusal was a rejection of what he and his wife had always intended to do and thereby a rejection of their relationship. He thereby convinced Jisun to allow him to pay off the debt. Based on his firmness on the matter, Jisun felt the concern was resolved.

Now, six years later, upon receiving the email from Bishop Schol, Jisun was surprised to hear the occurrence was being revisited but was prepared to explain the situation. Unclear as to how the matter had come to Schol's attention, Jisun hoped that Mr. Patchin's daughter had not somehow caused him more grief. Perhaps Schol had simply been reviewing her file in which Bishop Devhadar had placed a note and had questions on the matter. Aside from the obviously strained relationship she had with Schol and the unusualness of the requested meeting rather than a phone call, she was not concerned about clearing up any concern. She responded via email and they agreed upon a meeting to discuss the matter directly after the next Cabinet meeting to be held on the afternoon of June 6th.

Schol had written, "because this involves a complaint that was filed in 2010, and I have been asked to follow up on it, you are welcome to bring another clergy person with you if you desire." In no way was the fuller, grave agenda of the meeting made known further to her beforehand. But given his repeated behavior toward her in the past, she decided it was not a bad idea to have someone else present in the meeting as he had suggested. Rather than thinking about the need for an advocate for the meeting, she naively and unwisely asked one of her district superintendent colleagues if he would be willing to stay after the Cabinet meeting with her to meet with Schol. She chose him as someone who was fair-minded, wise and with a good head for tactful conversation. He was also a good choice as the matter could have been kept confidential within the Cabinet. She shared with him about the email she had received. He agreed to attend.

Little did Jisun know, she was walking into a carefully orchestrated meeting that would last well over two hours and would be full of shocking revelations. The first surprise she experienced was that two other district superintendents were also present, invited by Bishop Schol, without her knowledge.

In the meeting, Schol was in control; the others, besides Jisun, said little. He asked Jisun to explain about what had happened in 2010. For some time Jisun went on in explanation, answering questions about her relationship, actions, the money, if and why she did not pay it back and so forth. Jisun shared freely, and looking back, I would say she did so unwisely, as it now is clear that Schol was shifting her words to the worst light possible. For example, her description of the relationship she had with John Patchin construed by Schol to be an inappropriate sexual one and even predatory on her part.

After thoroughly examining her, Schol delivered the second surprise. He told Jisun that in late May (after her endorsements for bishop by the Annual Conference), he had received a letter from John Patchin's daughter stating that Jisun had never repaid her father. Additionally, he said there were receipts, cancelled checks and so forth that gave evidence that over the years the Patchins had either given to churches Jisun had pastored for parsonage expenses, donations to the church, or given directly to Jisun gifts and money that totaled up to $110,000, including the original $13,000 previously mentioned.

He asked her if this was true. Head spinning, Jisun readily agreed that the Patchins had been generous to her and that it could be possible that there had been that amount given on her behalf, but she did not know, especially for gifts and money given to the church and not to her directly. As a reasonable request, Jisun asked to see the letter. Even though they were meeting within the Bishop's office suite, feet from where his executive assistant was seated in her office and also a short distance from his own desk, the Bishop stated that he did not have the letter. It would take several requests from Jisun for her to receive a copy more than a week later.

I do not believe that Patchin's daughter had a direct relationship with the United Methodist Church (and it can be reasonably assumed that she was not a follower of the denomination or Jisun's bishop candidacy). Yet, uncannily, she had revisited the 2010 complaint at this time, six years later, sending a letter to Bishop Schol personally. Then, not only had he not shared the letter with Jisun ahead of time, it was not until far into the meeting that he informed her of it. Instead, he opted to have her tell her story first, answering only according to the information she had been given, without knowing where the bishop was going with his questions.

As he asked further questions that became very pointed, she continued to answer honestly. He outright asked if she and Mr. Patchin had been having a sexual relationship. The accusation was revolting to Jisun. She explained that Patchin, who was ten years older than her own father and she years younger than Patchin's daughter, had become a father and grandfather figure in their lives. She became further upset that Schol was disrespecting Mr. Patchin with his accusations. Schol continued to ask her to agree that the relationship could be seen by others as having "red flags." Not agreeing that there had ever been anything inappropriate, she did acknowledge that receiving monetary gifts could be perceived the wrong way if others did not know the familiar relationship between her and the Patchins. Schol asserted she had not been forthcoming about the circumstances surrounding the complaint and its resolution, and that her relationship with John Patchin in particular had been immoral. He even shouted at her, saying, "John Patchin is not your father!"

Given the seriousness of the assertions against her, Jisun suggested that Patchin be contacted to corroborate her story. Then came the next surprise. Schol informed Jisun that John Patchin was now deceased, having passed several months earlier. Shocked, Jisun began to cry. Not only was she feeling the sudden loss of her friend and the reality that she had not even been informed, but also was dismayed that the information had not been shared with his many friends at the Mendham Church. Otherwise, she would have known, too. The realization of personal loss and the neglect towards her and the "Mendham gang" was too much.

Her weeping continued as she realized that the loving relationship she and her daughter had with the Patchins for many years was now being portrayed as a seedy one, and that rather than trying to help her, the bishop and others present were, in her words, "trying to kill me." Schol and the others present indicated that her crying was evidence of her remorse for being caught manipulating her friends and not paying the money back.

She then asked Schol, "What's next?"

He answered, "It depends on how you respond. If you do not cooperate, a complaint will be filed against you."
Then came the biggest surprise of all: the bishop's ultimatum. He stated that the matter could be handled and remain at the supervisory level. In which case she needed to do the following:

- Resign her position as a district superintendent and take an unpaid leave of absence effective immediately for three years.

- Abandon her candidacy for bishop.

- Go into counseling for maintaining appropriate relational boundaries

- Issue a public statement/apology for her alleged immoral behavior and reason for withdrawing her episcopal candidacy.

If she did not comply, the Cabinet would file a formal complaint against her. He said he needed to confer alone with the two district superintendents he had brought to the meeting, and that she could take that time to think about her decision. They gave her twenty minutes to consider Schol's ultimatum.

To be clear: Jisun had been told to surrender her job, income, hopes for the future of her calling and career, and humiliate herself publicly. She was given twenty minutes to make that decision, with the threat of disciplinary action against her if she did not do so. Her twenty minutes to decide were spent with someone whose own career was also at the whim of the bishop.

The friend Jisun had brought with her to the meeting began, in a gentle way, to tell her that this was very serious and that she should do what the bishop instructed. Never did he encourage her to ask for more time to think about her decision, to ask deeper questions, or push back in any way. He repeatedly encouraged her to comply. So the fuller picture is that Bishop Schol, in this meeting, had initiated a complaint about Jisun to and for three district superintendents who he directly supervised, meaning their lucrative jobs by conference standards, were at his discretion. She was informed that the matter was now suddenly being revisited because of a request to follow up on the 2010 agreement had suddenly been given to Bishop Schol personally, just before the episcopal election. The line, tone and avenue of the questioning Jisun endured was intimidating and wrought with coercive power. Jisun's head spun as her integrity was not only called into question, but tried before her.

When the group returned to Jisun and her friend, Schol produced a prepared document for Jisun to sign that stated she was complying with his requests to resign immediately, give up her candidacy and issue a public apology. They even had drafted the statement to be sent out to the public and asked her to agree to it. She has shared with me that what went through her mind at that time, was "Who would win fighting the Bishop?" At this point, she actually held the pen in her hand and almost signed.

But God. She came to her senses as everything in her screamed, "do *NOT* sign that document." And so, she did not. Instead, she told the group, "I need to think about it."

Clearly disappointed, Bishop Schol informed her that he would give her three days and set a meeting with her for June 9th. She was reminded that if she did not sign the document, a complaint would be filed against her by the district superintendents. In other words, his hands would be washed, as they would carry out the rest of the actions from a public perspective. The meeting ended.

As she bore her soul to me about all that had just transpired, Jisun cried. I was quite concerned for her, as she was driving as she spoke. I was also in shock myself. All I was being told about the original complaint was a surprise, as I did not know Jisun in 2010 and therefore had been completely unaware about the gifts from the Patchins or that a complaint had ever occurred. But mostly I was appalled regarding the treatment she had described as occurring in the meeting with Schol. Still, I asked my best friend very pointed questions about the meeting, the circumstances around the original complaint, and her relationship with the Patchins. By this point, I had to work hard to understand my friend for several reasons. One, because in her distress, her English, which is her second language, began to fail her. Second, I found the treatment she described coming from these church leaders to be beyond anything that I had ever fathomed. The more we talked, the more disturbed I, too, became.

My head spun as I tried to figure out how to help my friend. I had just a few days earlier reached out to and begun consulting with former District Superintendent Rev. Bob Costello for help with Jisun's run for bishop. He had worked on episcopal runs in the past, had been on cabinet and understood the political situation Jisun was navigating. He had processed complaints as a cabinet member and helped others through the process, had a keen understanding of the Book of Discipline, and was trained as a lawyer in addition to being a pastor.

"Call Bob," I encouraged. Later that night, she did.

Jisun did not eat or sleep much for the next few days. On June 8th, Schol emailed Jisun an agenda for the meeting to be held the next day, a copy of the agreement he was urging her to sign, and an explanation that it needed to be signed in time for a Board of Ordained Ministry meeting scheduled for June 13th. The push for a signed document to be given to the Board by June 13th was an unwarranted pressure; it was not necessary for the entire Board to accept her resignation and request for leave of absence. Only the Executive Committee would need to approve it and, as a smaller group, especially for such a serious matter, could meet at an alternate time. That night, Jisun again requested a copy of the letter from Patchin's daughter. Schol responded the next morning that she could review the letter right before the "supervisory meeting."

There was no meeting on June 9th because Jisun was in the hospital. At around 6am she had called the pastor of Elmer UMC to take her to the emergency room. He literally had to carry her to his car. After a full examination, the diagnosis she received was low potassium, dehydration and exhaustion. She stayed in the hospital for two nights.

Jisun chose to not sign the document Schol had crafted. Therefore, his public slights of her hit a new peak on June 24, 2016, just three weeks before the elections, when the Greater New Jersey Cabinet, under his power and influence, very publicly filed a complaint against her. Per church law, the Board of Ordained Ministry Executive Committee had been consulted for a recommendation to suspend her from her duties, and also under his undue influence, made the recommendation. With the needed blessing secured, he suspended her from her duties as a district superintendent. I remember the turn of events well, as it coincided with other interesting ironies to my clergy journey with the UMC: a visit to Glide Memorial UMC in San Francisco.

GLIDE MEMORIAL UMC

My husband and I were planning a special trip for our twenty-fifth wedding anniversary to San Francisco and the Nappa Valley. Upon hearing that I would be in San Francisco, Bishop Schol had encouraged me to visit his friend and her church service. His friend was Rev. Dr. Karen Olivetto, then lead pastor of the famous Glide Memorial UMC church. He had connected us via email and text. She gave Tom and me pointers of places to visit in San Francisco, including the Mission neighborhood and the famous La Taqueria taco bar therein.

Glide Memorial opened in 1930 and "although conservative until the 1960s, since then it has served as a counter-culture rallying point and has been one of the most prominently liberal churches in the United States."[5] Glide's membership of 13,000+ represented twenty percent of the entire California-Nevada Annual Conference. Its 3600 attendees made it the UMC's only megachurch in the western U.S.[6] On its website it shares that:

> Glide is a nationally recognized center for social justice, dedicated to fighting systemic injustices, creating pathways out of poverty and crisis, and transforming lives. Through our integrated comprehensive services, advocacy initiatives, and inclusive community, we empower individuals, families and children to achieve stability and thrive.[7]

June 26, 2016, outside Glide Memorial UMC, San Francisco.

If you have seen the Will Smith movie *The Pursuit of Happyness* (2006), then you may remember that the church shelter that Smith's character and his son stayed in was Glide Memorial. I will tell you there are no bibles, crosses, or other references to Jesus in the Glide Sanctuary. The incredible band, dubbed a Gospel band, features prominent jazz musicians from the Bay area and more, but I would challenge that any of the songs, at least the day we were present, had any origins or claims to Christianity. The music was incredible in its effect, however, caused by the talent performing it and the upbeat, festive air it conjured.

Rev. Dr. Oliveto was open about her lesbian marriage to UMC deaconess Robin Ridenour, and the annual conference in which she served did not enforce the Book of Discipline and instead encouraged her by ordaining her ministry. As fate would have it, Tom and I ended up in the worship service at Glide on a momentous day for the congregation for two reasons. First, it was the morning of the San Francisco Gay Pride parade, the largest LGBTQ community celebration in the U.S. The church was preparing to participate in the parade later that day. Many in the pews were already in parade costume and the service was cut short so that people could leave to participate. It was also the day that Rev. Dr. Oliveto announced to her congregation that she had been nominated for bishop by their annual conference, Cal-Nevada. And there I sat. You cannot make this stuff up.

This was a new level of dissidence by UMC progressives, as she was nominated and within weeks became the first elected openly practicing homosexual bishop. That election fueled the next step, and I believe the largest move toward schism in the denomination.[8] I can tell you that day, as she had just been endorsed for bishop the week before, she looked to me like a deer caught in headlights. I did not see her as the leader of a firestorm, but someone caught up in it and put on display.

Also, and not surprisingly, less than two years later, Oliveto's replacement at Glide, the Rev. Jay Williams, resigned his appointment, alleging that the church's leadership refused to allow him to set direction for the church's ministries. "While I love Glide, I do not love its organizational structure," he said. "Dynamics in the current configuration prohibited me from leading fully as a trained Christian theologian called to ordained ministry as an elder in the United Methodist church."[9] There had been stirring that the Glide Foundation was "attempting to sever ties with the UMC and wrongfully assert control over the trust property."[10] Shortly thereafter, according to Jay Barmann in his November 2020 article for hoodline.com, progressive leaning Cal-Nevada Bishop Minerva Carcaño accused the foundation's board of "corruption" in its leadership and, in an email to Methodist pastors, derided the fact that the "great majority of the participants at Glide's Sunday Celebrations claim other faiths, such as Jewish, Buddhist, Muslim, and Wiccan."[11]

And this was shocking revelation to the bishop? Even I had been sharing my own observations for two years. Many others had done so way before me. But with the threat of Glide parting ways with the UMC and thereby taking valuable resources away from the denomination, the California-Nevada Annual Conference, along with Bishop Carcaño, filed a lawsuit against the Glide Foundation (also known as Glide Memorial United Methodist Church) in the Superior Court for the County of San Francisco. The suit sought a court order preserving the UMC's control over trust property in accordance with the original intent of Lizzie Glide, a devout

Methodist who established a trust in 1929 for the express purpose of building a Methodist church for Christian witness and service in honor of her late husband. The suit also asked the court to enforce the UMC's long-standing rule that all property of each local United Methodist church is held in trust exclusively for the benefit of the UMC. In 2020 the lawsuit was settled, with Glide allowed to proceed as an independent entity and retain full ownership of the multi-million dollar property at 330 Ellis Street. The United Methodist Church received a onetime payment of $1.5 million to the Conference, as well as a $4.5 million fund which had grown out of Ms. Glide's original donation.[12]

BIG NEWS

But while I was flabbergasted by what I was witnessing in San Francisco on June 26, 2016, UM News associate editor Heather Hahn was publishing an article that featured a prominent photo of the Book of Discipline that was entitled "District Superintendent Suspended." In it she reported on the complaint filed two days earlier against Jisun by the Greater New Jersey cabinet:

> The conference's cabinet in June filed the complaint under church law against the Rev. Jisun Kwak. According to the conference, the case is related to issues in a 2010 complaint that resurfaced in May this year. The conference did not disclose any further details.[13]

Bishop Schol was quoted as saying:

> Because this is part of a complaint process, I will not respond to any questions at this time. ... I am very sad

that these measures had to be taken and I call each of us to pray for Rev. Kwak, the Delaware Bay District and all involved. … I have complete confidence in the cabinet's work and discernment and in those who will be leading the complaint process.[14]

He shared with the world what he had done to Jisun Kwak while at the same time cloaked and protected his action with the loyalty and disciplinary role of his cabinet, all without having to include any details as to what she was accused of having done. He pivoted attention from his broader actions to a myopic one by touting how he was following the Book of Discipline's complaint process. The UM News article helped punctuate that diversion by featuring the prominent photo of the Book of Discipline just above the article title.[15]

Jisun, herself operating under the constraints of church policy, could not share the details of the accusations against her. All the world received from her came through the voice of Rev. Bob Costello. Bob, acting as Kwak's advocate, did the best he could to aid her by sharing with Hahn that:

> Kwak is not accused of abuse, harassment, sexual misconduct or conviction of crimes. She also is not accused of issues related to ministry with lesbian, gay, bisexual and transgender individuals. … It is worth noting that she is not involved in any cases in the civil or criminal court systems.[16]

Thus, two weeks before the election, while Karen Oliveto's Discipline-breaking candidacy was being heralded, Jisun's candidacy for bishop was effectively sabotaged. Still, she decided to persist in her pursuit of obedience to God's call to run. I continued to aid her through the election process, working on her candidacy, profile and preparation for the interviews she would face. Along with her newly formed team of advocates for the trial she would eventually face, I helped her snap out of despair long enough to give it her all for the Jurisdictional Conference. That was a tall order at first, but she got there.

2016 NORTHEASTERN JURISDICTIONAL CONFERENCE

The Northeast Jurisdictional Conference was held July 11- 15, 2016 in Lancaster, PA. – UMC Communications gives the following description of Jurisdictional Conferences:

> In the United States of America, The United Methodist Church is divided into five areas known as jurisdictions: Northeastern, Southeastern, North Central, South Central and Western. These provide some program and leadership training events to support the annual conferences. Every four years the jurisdictional confer- ences meet to elect new bishops and select members of general boards and agencies.[17]

The Northeast Jurisdictional Conference Rules Committee had to meet and decide if Jisun was still eligible to still be considered for election. An episcopal candidate under suspension and the subject of an active complaint was an interesting twist for them. They decided she was still a viable candidate based on the Book of Discipline and their rule.

So, late in the afternoon of my birthday, July 10th, after a sweet luncheon in Lambertville, NJ, I left my family and drove two hours to Lancaster to join Jisun at the Conference. Because we were afraid of repercussions against me from Bishop Schol for continuing to assist her, I was very careful not to be seen coming and going from the Lancaster Marriott that hosted the conference. I purposefully drove my husband's car there rather than my own, so it would not be recognized. Texting with Jisun from a discreet parking space in the hotel garage, we anxiously planned the right timing that I could enter the hotel from the garage, make my way to the lobby, take an elevator from the lobby to her room floor, and then walk three hallways with my wheeled luggage to her room without being recognized. Getting from the garage to her room took more than thirty minutes because there were so many people moving about and the chances of being seen was high. There was even one point when I was halfway down a corridor to enter the lobby from the parking garage, when Jisun urgently phoned to tell me to halt and go back to my car because the bishop and several of his cabinet members had suddenly appeared in the lobby. As one can imagine, our hearts were racing through this whole ordeal.

Once I made it to her room, I remained there for almost forty-eight hours without leaving. She and I stayed up through much of the two nights I was there, as I helped her prep for interviews with the jurisdictional delegates. When she was at the many conference meetings, meals and other activities, I was ordering room service, showering, watching the conference online and catching up on sleep. I was most certainly more rested than she.

The specific questions to be asked in the interviews we prepped for were given to the candidates the night before the interviews. We had, of course, anticipated the basic flow of the questions, but spent the night before the interview polishing her answers to be as specific to the questions asked as possible. Of interest is that we carefully crafted her responses to make clear that she would never intentionally break the Book of Discipline, and certainly not with the intent of changing church policy with such action. She would uphold it as the role of bishop requires. This was an important question to both progressives and traditional church members in the debates regarding overturning the Book of Discipline's language on the ordaining and marrying of practicing homosexuals. Additionally, Jisun and her team of advocates had prepared a statement for her to make at the beginning of each of her interviews addressing the suspension and complaint that she was now facing, and reassuring them that she was following church law and expected full exoneration from the complaint.

I stayed until the late morning of July 12th, which was the full day of her interviews. That day candidates were given six rigorous interviews by different delegate panels from the various annual conferences of the jurisdiction between the hours of 8:15am and 9:15pm. We planned that it would be safest for me to leave without being seen in the middle of the first session of interviews, when most conference participants would be occupied and all of the bishops would be in their own jurisdictional meeting, the College of Bishops meeting. When I left, I rode an elevator down to the lobby in a baseball cap, my head down so far that I could barely see. I prayed no one would notice me. When we stopped at a floor and Rev. Tom Lank, head of the a Greater New Jersey delegate delegation got on, my heart raced even faster as I lowered my head further and held my breath. To this day I do not know if he recognized me. I got off on the next elevator stop, not caring where it lead as long as it was out of that elevator. Walking as rapidly as I could while dragging my wheeled luggage, I then found my way from there to the hotel kitchen. I asked a hotel employee to show me a back exit and how to get to the parking garage from there. It felt silly and stressful, yet very necessary.

Jisun on episcopal election interview day

Several friends of Jisun went to the conference that day to observe the interviews. As I drove home, I received phone reports of how she was performing and the treatment she received. The reports' consensuses were that she was doing well, considering.

There was still evidently a concern that she might be elected, as during the session the next day before the voting began, a progressive, ordained clergy delegate from Eastern Pennsylvania gave a speech stating that it had been improper and unfair for Jisun to be allowed to give her short statement at the beginning of her interviews regarding her suspension and the complaint filed against her. She stated that the complainants had not been given the same opportunity to share. After reading the statement, she walked away from the microphone and over to Greater New Jersey's own District Superintendent Andy Hoover and handed the pre-written speech (apparently) back to him as the owner of it. As a member of the cabinet, he, of course, was one of those complainants.

To be elected, an eligible person needs to receive sixty (60) percent or more of the valid ballots cast. Votes are taken in consecutive ballots until the threshold for election is reached and a candidate is elected. The process continues until the total number of bishops needed for that jurisdiction or central conference is elected. In the U.S., bishops are elected for life.

Unfortunately, and of course not surprisingly, under the dark cloud of the complaint filed against her, Jisun lost the election. Her results, however, were better than to be expected given the tragic circumstances. On the first legal ballot, she was in fourth place out of eleven candidates. Her results steadily declined for each ballot thereafter.

When she stood to concede the election, as is customarily done by all the candidates, Jisun gave a brief speech. Like everyone else, she thanked all for the opportunity, shared a little of her call and background, and graciously bowed out. She added, however, that just as she has fought for for others, she intended to fight for full justice to be served in the face of the injustices that were being thrust upon her. Despite an exhausted and weak bodily appearance, her words and demeanor were strong. There was a respectful and resounding applause for her.

The other significant event of that Jurisdictional Conference was that Schol received an additional four-year appointment to Greater New Jersey Conference. The Episcopal Committee, along with serving as the personnel care committee for bishops and their families, makes the determination every four years at Jurisdictional Conference as to where in the jurisdiction each bishop will be appointed. After the Episcopal Committee made its appointments in 2012, it was leaked from the Committee that the committee, because of concerns expressed regarding John Schol's leadership at the Baltimore-Washington Conference, had seriously debated not giving him an episcopal appointment in 2012. Their deliberations went through the night and on well into the wee hours of the morning. Finally, a concession was made and Schol was appointed to Greater New Jersey. It was when that appointment was announced the next day that Baltimore-Washington delegates cheered openly that he would not come back to them.

In 2016, concerning the Episcopal Committee itself, legislation was introduced from the Baltimore-Washington Conference to the Jurisdiction, that:

> Whereas, it is important for the church to have confidence and trust in leadership at all levels, And Whereas, supervision of those at the highest levels of authority in the church can be problematic for many reasons, And Whereas, our Discipline currently calls for greater protection from even the appearance of impropriety of church pastors than it does for Episcopal leaders, And Whereas, our Episcopal leaders actually carry greater burdens of responsibility, both temporal and spiritual than their local church colleagues, Be it Resolved that: The Northeast Jurisdiction of the United Methodist Church shall amend their rules regarding the Committee on Episcopacy to conform more closely to the rules regarding the Committee on Staff Parish Relations in the Discipline as follows: 1. (Paragraph 258 a) No (Conference) staff member or immediate family member of a (bishop) may serve on the committee. Only one person from an immediate family residing in the same household shall

serve on the committee. The desired outcome is that this change will eliminate even the appearance of conflicts of interest in the critical area of supervision of the highest levels of leadership in the church and provide for stronger and more independent support for Episcopal leaders, and create greater transparency.[18]

As mentioned in my discussion of nepotism in the Cuba Gooding chapter, both District Superintendent Andy Hoover and Conference Chancellor Lynn Caterson were the GNJ representatives on the Episcopal committee for the Jurisdiction in 2016. Both were conference staff members that would have been disallowed if the above resolution had been adopted. However, when the resolution report was given to the conference, the Jurisdictional Rules Committee announced that their decision had been against adopting it. Who was representing Greater New Jersey on that Rules Committee? District Superintendent Varlyna Wright, herself on conference staff to Bishop Schol. After the announcement, a motion was made from the floor to refer "all of this resolution to the Rules Committee for their consideration and report in 2020."[19] As the 2020 Jurisdictional Conference has been delayed as of this writing due to the pandemic, it is my sincere hope that the Rules Committee will give due diligence to this serious topic before the next Jurisdictional Conference occurs.

Bishop Schol was visibly relieved that he would remain in Greater New Jersey. A celebration was held with Greater New Jersey members there in Lancaster and with the staff later back at our new conference office building. Schol released a statement of gratitude to Greater New Jersey the next day.[20] Others were not celebrating his continued appointment, however.

NOWHERE TO HIDE

COMPLETELY DISILLUSIONED

By the end of the summer of 2016, I was very down. It was the culmination of my Board of Ordained Ministry experience, the continued lack of adherence to or support for traditional Wesleyan Christian theology by leadership, Bishop Schol's strong focus on advancing LGBTQIA interests in our Conference churches and the entire denomination, the abysmal display of denominational dysfunction at the 2016 General Conference because of the LGBTQIA focus, and persecution of my best friend. I had lost respect for the leadership of the denomination and felt at odds with what I now understood to be their number one concern: advancing an LGBTQIA agenda.

Finding connection with other like-minded, Holy Spirit-filled Christians within the conference was difficult, especially given my connection to the bishop as a member of his staff. Finding female pastors with traditional views in our conference was even more difficult. I had in 2014 joined a small consortium in the conference that was dubbed the Evangelical Network for Growth and Renewal (ENRG), but they were low functioning, rarely meeting and with few goals or action items. I had been asked to lead the group, but as a still not ordained clergy in a hostile, progressive environment, we all agreed that was not a good idea because it would be held against me in the ordination process. Other than that, I felt very isolated in my theology, especially as a woman.

Then, in late summer of 2016, two meetings gave me hope. First, I attended the World Methodist Conference in Houston, Texas as a conference representative. There I regained connection with world-wide Christianity, the vast majority of which still adheres to traditional teachings. I came to better appreciate that over 80 different Wesleyan denominations exist, not just the one, highly dysfunctional United Methodist Church. The Holy Spirit began reviving me through that conference.

Next, as I had heard rumblings of a new movement intent on revival in the UMC, the Wesleyan Covenant Association (WCA), I attended its first Global Gathering in Chicago that fall. Before attending, however, I thought long and hard about the implications of my attendance. In the end, I decided I would not try to hide it. Before going, I met with Bishop Schol intentionally to tell him I was going and to make a point of telling him I would be taking vacation time to do so. He told me he was glad I was going and asked for me to give him a report of what I experienced.

What I experienced was Holy Spirit-filled worship, teachings, preaching, and fellowship with 2000 people like I had never experienced before in the United Methodist Church. At the end of the conference, I joined and became a Founding Member of the WCA. In an email I gave Bishop Schol a summary of my experience and he thanked me for it.

A third occurrence that season was a nomination to serve on the Board of Trustees of the Ocean Grove Camp Meeting Association.

Ocean Grove is an organization that operates outside of Bishop Schol's control. While all parties work to maintain a good relationship, they have had conflicts over various issues. Me joining their Board of Trustees presented an opportunity to strengthen the relationship between the two, as I was the only staff member (including Cabinet) included on the Board at that time.

Ocean Grove has been another of God's great gifts to my family and me. We discovered it the first year we moved to New Jersey. One of the women in my Community Bible Study class was a tenter there,[1] and she introduced me to this Christian Seaside resort. I even brought the CBS group to Grove Hall, the Retreat Center, in 2006, and had my mentor/friend Joan Minor from Paris come and speak at the retreat. It was our preferred destination for beach trips as a family, and my husband and I regularly attended programs in the beautiful six-thousand seat Great Auditorium. I had also taken our youth group from North Hunterdon Church there for an outing. Again, it has been a special place for our family.

Being a Trustee has been a great honor and blessing as our family has become even more involved in "God's Square Mile" and all of its Christian and beach community offerings. It is a place where we can relax and connect with God. It was through a UMC clergy that I was nominated to join the trustees, so I see it as a blessing related to my UMC journey.

WITCH HUNT

Beginning three weeks before the election, Jisun earnestly entered a journey through the very emotionally devastating, financially destructive, and socially isolating process of being subject to a complaint, then waited two years for charges to even be filed, then waited almost another year for the trial to occur. She then had to endure the trial itself and its aftermath.

Meanwhile a true witch hunt began. At least two superintendents, the clergy prosecutor for the trial, and the bishop's executive assistant began researching, looking through files and bank accounts, and interviewing people to find any impropriety from my friend over her more than twenty years of ministry with the UMC. People began whispering about phone calls they received, questions they were asked, documents they were required to produce, and agreements they felt forced to sign.

As he handled this Jisun complaint situation, Schol left a trail of fear and question marks behind him. For example, he began calling groups of leaders together to apprise them of the situation regarding her. He required that they sign non-disclosure agreements as he shared with them details of why he had suspended her and that he had other concerns about her leadership.

One such meeting was with the Delaware Bay district leadership team Jisun supervised. They were called together for a meeting with Schol and all were required to sign a non-disclosure agreement regarding what they were about to hear. The agreements were signed and collected by the bishop personally. When asked if they could have a copy, he responded that he would "see." No copies were ever given. As stated previously, non-disclosure agreements have many negative effects, like silencing victims or witnesses of harassment and discrimination. In the real world they are designed to protect trade secrets and, except in very limited circumstances, they have no place in ministry. Similar meetings were held with Korean leaders and others. If transition plans were needed for the group to function without her, Schol discussed them as well. There were people who left those meetings with newfound negative impressions of Jisun and/or questions of her leadership competency.

In one case, a Greater New Jersey elder who was serving as a missionary in Bolivia was interviewed by Bishop Schol over Zoom. When the interview concluded, he was sent a document to sign that was supposedly a summary of his own statements regarding work he had done with Jisun when she was his district superintendent in the Gateway North district. The statements as written would be damaging to Jisun's case and did not accurately reflect his comments. The elder refused to sign the document. He later came to New Jersey to testify on Jisun's behalf at the trial. Curiously, when it was time for his three-year missionary contract in Bolivia to be renewed, the General Board of Global Mission refused to do so. He was sent back to New Jersey.

Additionally, as the clergy prosecutor and the district superintendents conducted their investigations, they would sometimes ask pointed questions that twisted facts. Like Schol, they would produce their own notes of what was said by those interviewed and require that those notes be signed by the interviewees. Some felt coerced to verify different versions of the truth. Some signed out of fear and some did not. Those who did not sometimes faced appalling consequences. One example of this is of a certified local pastor in the Delaware Bay District at the time. He refused to sign a statement that he disagreed with, saying, "This is not what I said." He was told, "but this is what we heard." He still refused to sign. His district superintendent then said, "even with your DS, you will not sign?"

He refused. Later his certification was discontinued by the district committee. The less skeptical would regard this as coincidence, but to most it was seen as punishment for not signing the statement. He then requested to transfer to the New York annual conference. This became a challenge to accomplish, with the district superintendent putting roadblocks in his way that extended the process substantially. He did eventually get the transfer.

Numerous attempts were also made by Schol to find a "just resolution" as urged in the Book of Discipline for avoiding a trial. However, his offers continued to require Jisun admit wrong-doing and suffer other penalties and consequences. Jisun and her team always countered that Jisun should be declared innocent of any and all allegations and claims against her, and that demands to provide restitution and protect others from retribution for supporting her be met. Over the two-and-a-half-year period leading up to her trial, Jisun received phone calls from other clergy pressuring her to consent to the bishop's just resolution requests.

Jisun moved out of the parsonage in Elmer, NJ in October 2016 when placed on an interim, involuntary and unpaid leave of absence by the Board of Ordained Ministry. She moved in with her brother and sister-in-law in Landsdale, PA. She purged a significant amount of her belongings, giving what she could away to needy people and friends and storing the rest in a bedroom at her brother's house and in a corner of his basement. She began staying with our family frequently, hoping to give her brother and sister-in-law breaks.

Other friends were generous as well, but in general, she began receiving much less frequent calls, texts and emails. People were afraid to be associated with her for fear of retaliation. Others thought the worst of her. Still others kept quietly away while covering her with prayer. I was proud of my friend as she faced such losses with strength that she continued to credit to the Lord. She repeatedly would say to me, "I've been lower than this and God has pulled me out. I am not afraid to lose everything."

INTIMIDATED

Soon after the WCA gathering and joining the Ocean Grove trustees, I began to notice Bishop Schol and the rest of the staff being distant toward me. I was not being included in meetings, conversations, or projects as before. This was concurrent with a heightened tension related to the continued persecution of Rev. Dr. Kwak. While Schol and cabinet members focused on investigating ad nauseum every nook and cranny of her ministry to find any chargeable offense, she was placed on an involuntary leave of absence. I was even advised not to mention her name. This was difficult not only on a personal level, but professional as well, as she had been integral to the work I was doing with Team Vital to get training materials translated into Korean and encouraging Korean congregations to participate in Team Vital.

I remember two separate occasions that were very odd in this regard. While in the Director of Communications' office, I brought up Jisun as someone who could access information we needed for getting materials translated. The Director quickly motioned for me to silence myself. On another occasion, I asked the Director of Connectional Ministries what was going on and why we were walking on eggshells around Rev. Kwak, and he put his finger to his lips telling me to be quiet. At the time I thought perhaps their offices were being bugged or somehow otherwise recorded. I told myself that was crazy. Whatever the case, what was clear was that there was fear. This is classic evidence of the toxic environment of narcissistic and tyrannical leadership.

On December 12, 2016, I received a phone call from Bishop Schol's executive assistant stating that the bishop wanted to set up a meeting with me. I was told that she would clear a couple of hours on his schedule for the meeting. I was not given an agenda. We set the meeting for Friday, December 16 at 2:30pm. Via email I inquired about the meeting's purpose because it was unusual for the bishop to request a meeting with me alone and to give me no agenda.

From: *Nicola Mulligan*

Sent: *Tuesday, December 13, 2016 9:56 AM*

To: *Beth Caulfield*

Subject: RE: Meeting with John on Friday

Good morning Beth,

I don't think there is any special preparation needed.

Blessings,

Nicola

Nicola Mulligan

Executive Assistant to the Bishop

The United Methodist Church of Greater New Jersey

The day before I was to meet with the bishop, I attended the staff Christmas party/luncheon at the conference office that began with team development exercises and discussion pertaining to our Annual Roll-Up Goals as a staff. The staff were pre-assigned seating at round tables in groups of 5-6 people per table. For the first exercise I was assigned to Table #1. After I sat down the bishop came and sat with me. We had what seemed like normal discussion through the activity, but I did feel that he was listening carefully to me, which seemed unusual. At the conclusion of the exercise, additional invited guests came to the room and everyone again was shuffled in their seating arrangements to pre-assigned tables. I was surprised to find that I had again been assigned to Table #1, along with the bishop's wife, Beverly Schol. I greeted her and then intentionally sat across the table from her, thinking it would be better for someone else to sit next to the bishop given that I had just spent time with him. Beverly very determinedly got up and moved her purse and seat so that the bishop would be sitting between me and her. I was surprised by this. I assumed that when he came to the table he would still take a different seat. He did not. We conversed more through the entire meal and party exercises. Again, this was very unusual and felt very premeditated.

We had a normal discussion regarding family and holiday plans. We talked about my professional background. I told him more about my hopes for working with COSROW and BOM in getting sexual ethics training into the conference on a mandatory basis. I told him we really need to have performance appraisals for clergy. We also discussed my leadership. He told me that I exemplified the top qualities of leadership—I was presidential, entrepreneurial, a risk-taker, disciplined, and possessed other characteristics of an athlete. He made additional positive comments, including telling me that I had a bright future. I kept wondering where he was going with all this. Was this my official performance appraisal? All he said was positive, but it felt awkward. Beverly listened in on much of the conversation but was quiet.

At the end of the party, Schol said we could have our previously scheduled meeting then so I would not have to drive back to the office the next day. I agreed. He waved me into the Ruby Room. He told Ms. Mulligan that we were going to have our meeting then. I waited in the room for him a few minutes.

When he arrived, the bishop sat down across from me and very directly said, "I feel there is tension from you toward me." I was caught off guard and asked him what he meant. He simply said that he felt tension. I stated that there were some projects that I was frustrated were not moving forward, and shared that I was hoping for more responsibility, which is something I had said to him before. I didn't feel either of these resulted in tension between us, and I asked him to clarify what he meant.

He very calmly stated that he felt there was tension "because of Jisun." I threw up a bullet prayer and chose my response carefully. To the best of my remembrance, I said, "Oh that ... I *have* been sad about Jisun. I enjoyed working with her very much. We were working on things with Team Vital and had some cultural competency training planned for the Northern Region that had to stop. I had hoped her issues would be resolved in the Fall and she would be back. I had planned accordingly. But it doesn't seem to be happening that way. I'll have to figure something else out. So yes, I have been sad about Jisun." He nodded and made facial and vocal expressions indicating that he understood.

The scary part, though, is he looked me directly in the eye and moved his face closer and stated, "Jisun is never coming back. Never." I responded by looking him very purposefully in the eye and saying, "I get that." He then changed his demeanor completely and said he, too, was very sad about Jisun and that he prays for her. He said in a sad voice that there will be a hearing and a trial. I purposefully told him I was aware of what had been written. He emphatically stated that he was very disturbed by the whole thing. I nodded in agreement.

He registered my response and then turned his eyes and mumbled something like, "I didn't believe there was a problem here. I don't want you to worry about this. Let's just forget about this, OK?" I agreed.

I instinctively reached out and hugged him and we said goodbye. I think I hugged him because I felt desperate about what was happening. The entire meeting was less than 15 minutes. I went to my car and vomited in the parking lot. I knew that I had just been threatened about my relationship with Jisun Kwak.

There was never any other meeting set up between us to discuss any other topic. In fact, from then on while I remained on staff, the bishop clearly avoided eye contact with me.

Others gave indications that they knew something was going on that was harmful to me. After a Special Clergy Session called by the bishop in January 2017 that I firmly believe was held and orchestrated simply to slander and prejudice potential jurors in a trial against Rev. Dr. Jisun Kwak, I received an unexpected text from an elder serving in a large church. Again, he is a colleague (and progressive in his theological views), but no one with whom I have ever had more than professional interactions.

Facebook message I received

A MANDATORY CLERGY MEETING

On January 11, 2017, Bishop Schol held a special, "mandatory" clergy session. A "mandatory" special session was unusual during that era, so people's radars were up. Two days before the meeting, at an extended cabinet meeting, highlights were shared from the bishop and cabinet regarding a new and first-time effort at rolling out performance expectations for clergy and consequences for not meeting those expectations. The information was shared to get our feedback to help in tweaking their coming presentation. These were going to be challenging subjects for some clergy, we all knew. I was in favor of much of what I heard and wanted to share my perspective on outlining the direction we were going in more of the business terms I had learned to use in years past. This was also just a few weeks after I was threatened. So, looking back, I can see that at that time I was again trying to show my value to the bishop. Both points are highlighted in the email exchange below:

From: Beth Caulfield

Sent: Monday, January 9, 2017 4:42 PM

To: John Schol

Subject: Word of Encouragement

Hi John,

Just wanted to affirm the direction you are taking with the clergy, including with this bold meeting on Wednesday. As a former HR professional, I have a strong appreciation for

- *the importance of setting clear expectations for employee performance*
- *spelling out clear consequences for continued failure at meeting such standards*
- *giving honest, direct and documented feedback on performance against such standards*
- *providing them with remedial growth plans when necessary to help them achieve stated standards and then*
- *being consistent on how we take action on those who do not respond to such measures.*

Its fair, honest and legal. But most important I think it is the best way to grow people in their gifts, talents and calls.

Thank you for your leadership.

May our whole beings bless the Lord,

Beth

Rev. Beth Caulfield

Bishop John Schol   *Jan 9th, 2017, 5:07 pm*

To Beth

Thanks Beth. Your words are an encouragement and your experience in the area gives me confidence.

John

John Schol, Bishop

The United Methodist Church

of Greater New Jersey

I was not privy to the full agenda of the upcoming meeting, however. Other than our Director of Worship leading a brief worship session to kick-off the meeting, the Connectional Ministries Team that I was on was given no role for the session other than to be greeters along with the rest of the administrative staff. But somehow, I did not want to sit up front with the rest of the staff for the meeting. We had not been required to do so, so I did not. I felt in my gut that something was going on and I did not want to be seen as a part of it. I sat with other clergy I was working with out in the local churches instead. I now have a fuller appreciation of how that meeting was being set up to go.

The agenda for the morning included two presentations by cabinet members that had been partially flushed out after our discussion two days earlier. The first shared that based on a combination of factors that include position availability and clergy performance, some clergy would be moved to part-time. As you can imagine, this was a very somber prospect for clergy, so a tone was set. The other presentation outlined a narrative standard for the kind of leadership the conference was looking for from clergy: a move from a "shepherd" leadership model to an "apostolic" leadership model. These were concepts we had all discussed at the conference office previously. This for many, was, indeed, a radical shift. I still, by the way, endorse that shift for many settings and talk about those models in the chapter "Go Ahead and Shine Anyway." But when the encouragement to shift styles was offered alongside a presentation about people losing full-time positions, it sounded more threatening than encouraging. The undergirding message for those with ears to hear was the conference is in control and we will be making some changes for those who do not play along.

But then the real bombs, in my opinion, went off in the meeting. As detailed in a letter to all clergy that was released just after the meeting, the cabinet gave a presentation on the complaint process as outlined in the Book of Discipline ¶2702. The cabinet's comments that day and written in the letter included the following statement:

> For much of the recent history of the United Methodist Church, complaints were to be confidential. In the 2012 Book of Discipline, the phrase about confidentiality was removed. Best practices today indicates sharing complaints and details of the complaint are appropriate in some cases to actually vindicate and/or protect victims or potential future victims. It can also lead to healing. For instance, if a clergy person has harmed an individual or the church by crossing a boundary, the victim or leaders may want this to be shared to protect potential future victims or to allow other victims to come forward. The Book of Discipline does warn the cabinet not to share alleged facts until after the complaint is fully resolved so

as not to compromise any pending judicial or administrative process.[2]

Then, after that set up, a case from several years earlier of a clergy
who had complaints against him for sexual misconduct with minors
was shared in detail before the group. It was a situation and a clergy
I had never heard anything about. We were given explicit details
of this clergyperson's inappropriate contacts with youths, and, to
everyone's bewilderment, even handed copies of text messages
between the clergy and a youth that were lewd and egregious on the
clergy's part. We were instructed to not take photos of the copies of
the texts that were passed among us and the papers they were on
were then collected.

It was shared that when the offending clergy was confronted, he
turned in his credentials and left the United Methodist Church. In
telling the story, the bishop shared that by turning in his credentials,
the clergy did not go through the trial process. The bishop explained,
further, that the reason he was bringing this matter before all clergy
now was because there had been evidence that some churches have
continued to work with this former clergy via youth retreats and/or
camps not sponsored through the UMC. He said he wanted to make
sure people understood this situation and that we should not be
working with this former clergy. The entire presentation, of course,
caused much emotion to rise within the room and much discussion.
There were those who felt more penalties for the clergy should have
been given. If what was alleged was true, a crime had been committed. But the bishop's comments were confusing at the time about
whether the allegation had been taken to the police. I later learned
there were also those who felt accurate details about more recent

contact with the former clergy member were not fully presented by the bishop. As I said, the room became extremely charged.

The complaint against Jisun was, of course, then brought up. The bishop shared that charges were still pending and that no further details could be shared at that time, per the Book of Discipline. There was some discussion, and Jisun's advocate, Rev. Bob Costello, stood and pointed out that Jisun's case was in no way comparable to the situation that had just been described and discussed by the bishop. Bob kept in control as he encouraged the bishop to help people understand that point. He asserted that people could be confused by both cases being discussed together.

After all that transpired in the meeting, I and many other people present that day believe that a motive for the meeting was to raise doubt and fear about supporting Jisun and to justify the cabinet's actions against her so that, 1) she would feel pressured to accept the bishop and cabinet's terms of a just resolution rather than go to a trial, and 2) clergy would be predisposed against Jisun. This would be helpful for any clergy voting about her situation in the future, including the voting of jurors at a trial.

NOWHERE TO RUN (EITHER)

The last phase of a power-based and fear-inducing culture is—no surprise—removal from the circle entirely. Banishment is the ultimate form of the power pastor's disapproval. It is experienced as total rejection, and often feels like disapproval by God himself. Once removed from the circle, people who have lived in a fear-inducing culture can lose their faith; more often, they need some form of mental health therapy. It takes years for some people to trust pastors and leaders again, and many develop a keen eye for the signs of a fear culture.

— *A Church Called Tov: Forming a Goodness Culture That Resists Abuses of Power and Promotes Healing* by Laura McKnight Barringer

I knew that I needed to leave staff before more harm was done to me and/or my ministry. As I prayed with my husband, I knew I was still called to the United Methodist Church. But my options were few.

Because the bishop had changed the Conference policy, church job openings were posted and clergy were allowed to apply. Clergy are given less than 24 hours from the posting to email their district superintendent asking to be considered for the opening. That was really my only option unless I chose to quit, even though I knew some sort of retaliatory plan for removing me from conference staff was probably in the works.

In February, the Princeton United Methodist Church became open, as Rev. Dr. Alexa Bold (mentioned earlier) was appointed to a conference staff position. I had worked with the Princeton UMC on revitalizing their small groups and was aware of several issues the church was facing. I also had many contacts with the community and university that would be valuable to the church and in doing mission work with the nearby Trenton community. I contacted my district superintendent, Rev. Dr. Andy Hoover, via phone and text, and asked to be considered for the position. He told me to send an email so I laid out a plan in my email to him for revitalizing ministry there. He acknowledged this email:

> **Beth Caulfield** *<bcaulfield710@gmail.com>*
>
> *Dear Andy,*
>
> *As I have mentioned to you recently, I have felt a stirring in my spirit for a few months now that God might be calling me to contribute in new ways. This has been challenging for me because I am content in my current role with GNJ and know that I continue to make a positive difference for God's Kingdom in it.*
>
> *In just the past few days I have grappled with a realization that my unique gifts and graces would be very beneficial to Princeton UMC and the unique Princeton community specifically. For a variety of reasons, including my ties within the community, my spirit has become enlivened at the thought of serving there and a confidence in what it would bring has welled up within me.*
>
> *Last night (or actually in the wee hours of the morning) as I was praying fervently about this, what came to me was that not only could I grow the church, but I could lead the church along with partners and resources from the university, seminary and elsewhere to extend the church's current Community Kitchen ministry to start a Hope Center in the Princeton/Trenton area. This realization has emboldened me to pursue this appointment.*
>
> *So I am applying for this specific local church appointment opportunity and no other. I welcome the Bishop and Cabinet's discernment. I welcome conversation about this and will be in the MRC early tomorrow morning.*
>
> *Thank you very much for the opportunity to apply.*

The next morning, I walked into the bishop's office and told him of the email I had sent. His response was merely an acknowledgement of my comments to him. He was clearly staying removed and avoiding eye contact. Rev. Dr. Hoover did not make himself available to me that morning.

Another clergy was chosen for the position and I never heard more about it. I did in subsequent years, however, see a plan enacted for partnering ministries in the Princeton area, very similar to what I had proposed. I celebrate that at least the idea took hold.

SQUASHED

In March of 2017 I again went to the BOM's Retreat in hopes of being recommended for full elder orders. Although I knew my paperwork, onsite interviews, and sermon were all in the best order ever, I was extremely stressed. This turned out to be for good reason.

When I arrived at my theology interview, I was met by what can only be called a stacked team. The Dean of the Cabinet, and several other progressive female ministers who are part of her "flock" were on the team. They were all advocates for changing the Book of Discipline regarding LGBTQIA issues. The Dean of the Cabinet commandeered the interview from start to finish, disregarding the separation of cabinet and BOM required. Others predominately stayed quiet or asked follow-up questions.

The Dean of the Cabinet quickly zeroed in on my paperwork, specifically part of my response regarding how my practice of ministry had affected my theological understanding and experience of humanity. In that question I shared that I had become more aware of the challenges of breaking cycles of sin, in particular those of addiction and abuse that are often passed from generation to generation. I detailed how I had become more appreciative of and empathetic to those bound by such chains, and more believing that God's grace is needed, available, and can overcome even the most difficult situations.[3]

Her first question was, "So you would tell the mother of an alcoholic that it is her fault that he is an alcoholic?" I of course said no and clarified that my point or ministry approach was nothing of the sort. The interview continued along that line of questioning. The Dean of the Cabinet used a bullying tone and demeanor as she continued to try to put words in my mouth. I still get nauseous and teary when I think of that interview. I was not alone in that feeling.

That afternoon I received a text from a terribly upset BOM clergy member. That person was aware of how I had been treated in the theology interview. That person took the risk of inviting me to meet and discuss a strategy for recovering from the damage of it being said that I failed that interview. The person is progressive in theology, by the way. I was advised to be prepared to explain my answers to the theology questions to my assigned Debrief Team.

That Debrief Team did ask me extensively about my theology and it was clear that they were disturbed it was being questioned as my answers were quite clear. I was asked to clarify a couple of simple polity questions as well. I left that meeting feeling that the team was satisfied and any concerns were cleared up.

Before I left the retreat, however, another Board member, who was also progressive in her theology, came to me with concern in her eyes and stated, "You better pray and pray real hard." She then walked abruptly away. It was late in the evening before I received a phone call from a distraught traditional clergy BOM member sharing that I had again not been approved. We spoke for several minutes, with much of the conversation coming from him decompressing and apologizing profusely to me for the board's actions. His comments included, "May God have mercy on the United Methodist Church," and "The verse God is giving me for you is Psalm 126:5: 'Those who sow in tears will reap with shouts of joy.'" He stated that several fought for me and that an injustice had been done.

What I now know, as several from the board and their friends have relayed to me, is there was an unusually lengthy discussion regarding me when the board met to vote. There were very vocal LGBTQIA-focused and progressive theology individuals who were not even in my interviews who spoke against me. My district superintendent, Rev. Dr. Andy Hoover, was the cabinet representative to BOM who stated that he did not recommend me for ordination. The discussion and debate regarding me went close to an hour. More than half voted for ordaining me, but I did not receive the required ¾ majority vote.

That week I sought out and began seeing a therapist to deal with my distress and emerging depression due to the hostility directed toward me over a lengthy period.

When I received the letter from Rev. Saul Pawn that I was not being recommended, it stated:

March 17, 2017

Dear Beth:

Grace and peace to you in the name of our Lord and Savior, Jesus Christ.

This letter is to confirm the notification you received on March 15th following the Board of Ordained Ministry Full Members Retreat. As you know, the Board determined during its time of discernment that you are not yet ready to be recommended for ordination. We know that this is deeply disappointing and we are holding you in prayer at this time.

Please know, however, that the Board recognizes the many gifts that you have for ministry. Among these include: your pulpit presence and effective homiletical skills which were evidenced by your passion for the sermon topic, your clear communication to the congregation, and your strong exegetic work; your commitment to the covenantal connection, as well as your gifts for program development and administration; and your high performance standards and strong work ethic which make you an effective teacher and leader.

The Board has also discerned that additional work is needed in certain growth areas prior to your being approved for ordination. In the area of theology, it was noted that while you were able to use stories in answering the questions that were asked, you struggled at times to reflect theologically upon them. In addition, the personal reflections you offered sometimes lacked significant depth and insight. In the area of polity, while you had a firm grasp of this topic in a general sense, it was suggested that further work might be needed to enhance your understanding of the use polity at the local church level. In the area of practice of ministry, there were some concerns expressed about your level of connection with your audience and a perceived "presumptuous" attitude. There was also a concern about your willingness to itinerate.

It is my understanding that a designated person from your debriefing team has contacted you about arranging for a date when your growth plan can be discussed and updated. If this has not yet occurred, please let me know. The purpose of this meeting is to assess the recommendations that were made for your continuing development in ministry as you work toward the goal of full membership and ordination. A "Provisional Growth Plan Information" form was attached to this letter that I initially sent to you via e-mail.

It is my sincere prayer for you, Beth, that this process will enable you to grow even further into your calling and assist you on the path toward ordination in the United Methodist Church.

Blessings to you,

Rev. Saul Pawn

Chair, GNJ Board of Ordained Ministry

Cc: Rev. Andy Hoover, District Superintendent

I immediately compared it to the letter I had received the year before and noted it said almost exactly the opposite about my gifts, graces and needs to improve. The inconsistency was glaring. Additionally, the letter stated blatant inaccuracies about my willingness to itinerate. I wrote to Rev. Pawn and asked for reconsideration:

Dear Tom,

First, I would like to say that I appreciate your time, grace and candor with me today. Thank you for your care.

As I stated on the phone, I approached you only after long, careful and prayerful reflection. As I have considered all that

I have experienced through the entire ordination process this year, the BOM retreat, the contents of the letter you sent me post-retreat, and my conversation with my Debrief Committee, I am respectfully requesting that the decision regarding my Full Member ordination be reconsidered by BOM before this 2017 Annual Conference.

While I understand that the GNJ BOM may never have been requested to reconsider its decision in the past, I am humbly asking the Board to do so in part to offer consistency and fair mindedness with other BOMs throughout the denomination. I am doing so in this manner as GNJ does not offer a formal appeal process, unlike other Conferences such as New England and others in Florida, California and elsewhere.

I am requesting reconsideration because of uncommon circumstances. I understand that BOMs are organic and while consistency in considering candidates is an utmost goal, it can be challenging. Given my current role as Conference Staff and its many implications, I am questioning if the process has indeed treated me fairly. For example, as my duties and responsibilities have been focused at the Conference level (and all that implies) rather than locally, assessing my qualifications, performance and interactions may require broader reflection. I specifically question if all information shared at my Onsight interview was fully considered at the retreat. The folks present at that onsite meeting included several District Superintendents, my supervisor, other staff colleagues, administrators, local church clergy and laity from throughout the Conference. I also had letters of recommendation from a variety of other sources throughout the Conference attesting to my effectiveness as well that may not have been fully considered.

Your letter stated that BOM questioned my willingness to itinerate. This perception concerns me in that I had been in conversations with Cabinet (especially my District Superintendent) about a potential new appointment well before the retreat. I had approached them sharing that as my daughter is now graduating high school I would like to be considered for an appointment back in the local church. During the retreat on more than one occasion I volunteered that I am willing to itinerate and that I was in conversation with the Cabinet about a potential appointment. As you are aware, I have indeed been reappointed to a local church and am going to my new assignment which is over two hours away from my current home. I believe this important factor for ordination was somehow lost in the consideration process given that it was brought up as a concern in your letter.

As I shared with my Debrief Team, I was uncomfortable during and upon further reflection afterwards with how my Theology interview was handled. The best I can say was that the vibe in the room was confusing. When I was given questions from that interview by the Debrief Team, I answered fully.

Finally, I ask for consideration given the disconnect between the letter I received last year and the letter from this year. For example, polity, connection and communication were all mentioned as strengths last year yet were listed as growth areas this year. None of the growth areas mentioned this year were mentioned last year. The area listed for growth last year (preaching) was listed as a strength this year.

It is with these questions in mind that I humbly request reconsideration from BOM. This is challenging for me to do. At the same time, I believe given the circumstances it is appropriate to do and may be helpful to more folks than just me. Again, I appreciate your care.

Sincerely,

Beth Caulfield

My request was turned down, I was told, because they had no appeal procedure in place to even consider it.

From: *Saul Pawn*

Sent: *Tuesday, May 16, 2017 12:05 PM*

To: *Beth Caulfield*

Subject: *Request for Reconsideration*

Good Afternoon, Beth:

As we discussed, I forwarded your request and concerns to the Executive Committee of the Board of Ordained Ministry. I wanted to allow enough time for members of the committee to process what they were being asked to consider before responding back to you.

The committee were all in agreement that since there is no current procedure in place to consider appeals from candidates who were not approved at the Board retreats, and since there is not sufficient time to put such a procedure in place should the Board decide that one is needed, your request for reconsideration cannot be honored at this time.

I know that this is disappointing to you - but please also know that your request has started a conversation among Board members as to whether such a procedure should be discussed for the future.

I pray good things for you in your new appointment. I'm sure you will be a blessing to those who will be in your care.

Grace and peace,

Rev. Saul Pawn

More heartache and disenchantment. But God said continue. That included my therapy sessions.

CONSERVATIVE SINKHOLE

Yes, I received a new appointment. On the surface, it did not appear to be a bad one. I was offered a position as an associate pastor at one of the conference's largest churches. The church had a satellite "church plant," that would be my primary responsibility.

The church is located in the Delaware Bay District (the same District Jisun had been sent to three years earlier), in one of the most rural counties of the state. The satellite church plant was located 15 minutes away in a relatively new community of mostly suburban Philadelphia professionals. The church was known as a highly successful evangelical church that had grown exponentially under the Senior Pastor's leadership. Three years prior I had visited the church and videoed an interview with several members of the church and the Associate Pastor I was now to replace about their thriving small group ministry. Ironically, I had also been the Conference coach to the Associate Pastor as he had transitioned over to leading the church plant in the summer of 2015, so I knew a bit about the church.

The church in its heyday had roughly 600 attendees each Sunday, but in recent years had declined to just under 500. On paper, the satellite church plant boasted to be attracting 100+ attendees at the time. But when support from people attending from the Main Campus withdrew,[4] the numbers were significantly less.

My compensation:

Salary $45,000

Housing Allowance $22,000

Health Insurance $14,000 (less 2% of pastoral salary)

Pension Yes

Expense account $2,500

The pay, of course, was substantially less (39%) than my Conference staff compensation, but slightly above guidelines for my level. I point it out, however, because that is one of the problems of ministry in the UMC. Not only is there no consistency in income, but it can fluctuate greatly at the whims of the bishop and his appointments. Thus, salary and benefits can be used as a retaliatory weapon. Because the church was over two hours away from my then primary residence, it also meant selling my home with all the expenses and logistical burdens that entails. We had expected moving expenses with a new appointment and were committed to them as part of being in an itinerate system that really does not afford or make provisions for moving homeowners who must sell their primary residence.

When I was to meet with the church's Staff Parish Relations Committee for them to review and accept the appointment as is standard procedure, a whole additional story regarding this appointment surfaced. First, I arrived to find that they and other members of the church had been praying in the sanctuary for thirty minutes before the meeting.

I initially took that as a signal of a wonderfully discipled and disciplined church, and it was. But what I soon discovered as the meeting unfolded was a very upset committee and pastor.

One upset was that their Associate Pastor had suddenly been informed of a new appointment without any request by or consultation with him or the SPRC. The UMC Book of Discipline calls for a consultative process that involves the church, clergy, and district superintendent before an appointment change:

> Consultation is the process whereby the bishop and/or district superintendent confer with the pastor and committee on pastor-parish relations, taking into consideration the criteria of ¶ 427, a performance evaluation, needs of the appointment under consideration, and mission of the Church. Consultation is not merely notification. Consultation is not committee selection or call of a pastor. The role of the committee on pastor-parish relations is advisory. Consultation is both a continuing process and a more intense involvement during the period of change in appointment.
>
> 1. The process of consultation shall be mandatory in every annual conference.
>
> 2. The Council of Bishops shall inquire annually of their colleagues about the implementation of the process of consultation in appointment-making in their respective areas. ¶ 426

Also, the Senior Pastor had not been informed before Pastor Bill received the appointment change phone call, which is standard practice and courtesy. Instead, the Associate Pastor received a blind call while on vacation and he himself was the one who informed the Senior Pastor of the appointment change. The Senior Pastor and church felt slighted by the bishop in this process and were livid with the district superintendent charged with handling the appointment. The animosity was such that the bishop had sent not only the offending DS to handle the meeting, but also an incoming district superintendent who was from the area and respected by the senior pastor and church so that he could smooth out the situation.

I soon learned the Associate Pastor had been prepared by the church even as a lay member of the congregation, through seminary, through ordination, and through the appointment to be the successor to the Senior Pastor. He had never been appointed anywhere else and had been ingrained in the community for over twenty years. While the church knew that they were subject to the appointment system, they had not received a new appointment in over 20 years. Evidently, because the Senior Pastor had been their pastor since 1993, their expectation was they would also keep the Associate Pastor. Losing him was losing family for all involved. Surely a sensitive bishop and cabinet would have consulted with them per church regulations prior to making such a drastic move. But they did not.

Furthermore, the church had resentment toward the bishop because of his stance and actions promoting changes to the Book of Discipline regarding LGBTQIA marriage and ordination. In fact, after the 2015 "FISH" Annual Conference where legislation on this matter was passed to be sent to the 2016 General Conference, the church's laity had invited Bishop Schol to speak to the church and explain his position. The meeting was hostile, and all reported to me from the church with satisfaction that the bishop looked very uncomfortable the entire time he was there. I am sure he was. Many felt that this appointment change was retribution for their behavior and intentions for that meeting. I can see their point.

Part of Schol's vengeance, some believed, was to send them a female minister from his staff. As I quickly learned, many in the congregation and on staff did not believe in or support female pastors. They believed it was non-biblical.[5] There also was a strong suspicion that my theology would be pushing either overtly or covertly a progressive LGBTQIA-centered agenda given my role as staff in the bishop's office.

The church is very insular, invested whole-heartedly in the white, evangelical members of the surrounding Salem County. It boasted not only working-class families, but many industrial farmers, local politicians, heads of local banks, and lots of homeschooling moms and Christian school families as its members and leaders. As I got to know the congregation, I would best describe it as cultish, fully invested in and devoted to its senior pastor. I point this out to say that outsiders to the community, like myself, have had a very hard time being accepted.

Additionally, the satellite church plant in the neighboring county had its own challenges. It had been placed in an ideal community for a church plant, a growing young professional suburb of Philadelphia (at one point deemed the fasting growing community in America) and had been started with between a quarter and a half a million dollars given to the main campus by the Conference. Yet in its 6th year of existence, I would be its third pastor.

A tremendous effort had been made by the main campus folks to start the church, with families committing to attend there instead of the home church for several years, but the commitment had been fulfilled and was growing thin, especially now that one of their own was not going to be the pastor. The grant money had run out and they had no building, thus they had already been setting up and tearing down for worship every week for six years with limited volunteers and no strategic plan or capital campaign to facilitate doing otherwise any time in the foreseeable future.

The satellite church plant was far from self-sustaining and had already become seen as a financial, pastoral, and volunteer resource burden to leadership at the main campus church. Their ministry model was to mirror the main campus's, and there had been tension because of this as the communities they were to reach were vastly different. Finally, I would learn the challenge would be even greater because the satellite church plant's leadership was not included in any of the major committees of the church, including SPRC and Church Council.

So, there I sat, shell-shocked and being introduced in a very hostile meeting. I was grilled extensively on my theology and ministry approach. Unlike with the Board of Ordained Ministry, however, my honest answers were appreciated and approved. As the SPRC was as satisfied as they could be given their lack of alternatives in the UMC appointment system, leaders from the satellite church plant and other church staff were then invited into the meeting and questioning continued.

As I was walked out of the meeting by the incoming district superintendent, he was grinning and told me I did a great job. I felt it too, but also realized I was heading into a very difficult situation. Ever trusting God, however, I told myself that this might turn out to be a beautiful story if I could lead in turning the satellite church plant around and teach this church that God does indeed call women to be pastors.

In mid-May 2017, before my appointment was to begin in July, I was informed by the Senior Pastor that over twenty families had already left the church because of the change of appointment and me being a woman. These included the leader of the satellite church plant's Praise Band and his wife, who was also an instrumental leader to that campus. He said I needed to do something quickly to help stop the mass exit.

GCOSROW and UMW

Although I had been warned by other female clergy that I would not receive much support and that the politics involved may work against me, I reached out to the General Secretary of the General Commission on the Status and Role of Women (GCOSROW) for advice.

> *From:*   *Beth Caulfield*
>
> *Sent:*   *Friday, May 19, 2017 3:13:58 PM*
>
> *To:*   *dhare@gcsrw.org*
>
> *Cc:*   *Leigh Goodrich*
>
> *Subject: Need GCOSROW Consult*

Dear Dawn,

I hope this finds you well. I am Rev. Beth Caulfield, Director of Small Groups of the Greater New Jersey Conference (John Schol is our Bishop) and Staff Liason for COSROW. We have not met but I have met and worked some with Leigh Goodrich who I am copying on this email. I am writing to you because:

1) Effective July 1st I have been reappointed to serve as an Associate Pastor at one of our largest churches in NJ (Sharptown), leading its new, young and growing satellite campus as well as maintaining pastoral responsibilities at the main campus. The church is also one of our most conservative/evangelical churches in New Jersey. Sharptown did not request an appointment change, has not had a new appointment in over 20 years and I will be their first female pastor ever. I have already been told that several families are leaving because they do not agree with/support women as clergy. I am looking for advice and savvy approaches for such situations.

2) I will be in Birmingham next week picking up my son from Birmingham Southern where he is a sophomore and bringing my daughter to freshman orientation at UAB. I will be free late Thursday afternoon or anytime on Friday. Would it be possible to meet with you?

May our whole beings bless the Lord,

Beth

Rev. Beth Caulfield

Director of Small Groups Ministry /TEAM VITAL Champion

The United Methodist Church of Greater New Jersey

We ended up having a lengthy phone conversation. Regarding my concern about serving my new church appointment and its negative response to a female pastor, she referred me to another GCOSROW representative who followed up with me in friendly consult and gave me several resources to prepare for the appointment. That consultation was reassuring and helpful, but at the same time, it was clear the representative was very busy. I was left feeling that if I could not win the congregation over it would be because of my own shortcomings, not the congregation's. Looking back, I do not think that was intended, but as my challenges with this congregation escalated, I did not reach out again to GCOSROW as I did not feel they would be very responsive.

My conversation with the general secretary, however, turned mostly to how I ended up in the appointment, my concerns about treatment from Bishop John Schol, and even more about the handling of Rev. Dr. Jisun Kwak. I believe the GCOSROW General Secretary was taking notes. She stated that they had been following Bishop Schol's handling of women for quite some time and they were "monitoring the Jisun Kwak case closely." She indicated that there was an understanding that Schol's treatment of women had been a concern.

However, I never heard more from her and to my knowledge she had no interaction with Rev. Dr. Kwak. For all the interest displayed in that phone conversation, I had expected more follow up with both of us. The week of Rev. Dr. Kwak's trial, almost two years later, I emailed the GCOSROW General Secretary:

RE: FYI on Jisun Kwak

Hi Dawn,

I hope this finds you well. We have not spoken in a while. I just want to make you aware that there will be a trial for Jisun Kwak next week. It is scheduled for February 5, 6 and 7 beginning at 8:30 a.m. each day at St. Andrews United Methodist Church, Toms River, NJ.

Peace,

Beth

She never responded to me and there was no follow through with Rev. Dr. Kwak, either.

Certainly GCOSROW can claim to be understaffed for the great task they have. I believe that to be true. But the lack of attention given to me and Rev. Dr. Kwak could be reflective of the fact GCOSGOW is financially tethered to the denomination. While I doubt Schol had knowledge of my inquiry for assistance, it could very well has been a case of not wanting to bite the hand that feeds you, plus institutional reluctance to aggressively follow-up with complaints made about mistreatment by bishops and other high-level officials within the UMC. If true, it is tragic.

On December 15, 2016, I had taken a trip to the United Methodist Women's office in Manhattan to meet with its General Secretary and Chief Executive Officer. She had graciously invited me to tour the facilities and meet her staff.

We discussed the challenge of getting traditional Methodist women involved with the United Methodist Women. We talked about growing awareness of traditional ministry opportunities that already existed through UMW and ways to add more. We conversed on how we could better educate traditionalists about the agency. Our discussions were good and led to me bringing in a member of her staff to do an information session about UMW for the 2017 Greater New Jersey Annual Conference. I also planned a workshop with them in the southern region of the state where many of our traditional women laity reside.

As UMW's General Secretary and Chief Executive Officer, a Harvard Law graduate who is also a member of the Greater New Jersey Annual Conference, is in one of the most powerful advocates for women positions in our denomination and elsewhere, I ventured to briefly mention the problems that were happening with Rev. Dr. Jisun Kwak. I was disappointed that she expressed little interest in the subject. She simply told me she knew nothing about it and, in a way that felt very purposeful, moved on to a different topic.

with former NJ governor Christie Todd Whitman, May, 2016

These experiences with GCOSROW and UMW's top executives punctuated points I had already been pondering. The year before, I had attended a special forum sponsored by New Jersey Women

Leaders of Tomorrow that featured female panelists, including Governor Christie Todd Whitman. Whitman had been the only female governor of New Jersey. At the event I queried Whitman and other panelists regarding glass ceiling issues and how women could better work together to overcome them on the immediate level. The importance of senior level female advocacy was affirmed. It was also mentioned that senior women often are not very good advocates because they become risk averse, which points to their continued perception of themselves as vulnerable.

During the forum, there was also conversation regarding female competitiveness with one another. It was asserted that women often relied upon stepping on other women to move up to the few positions still allotted them at the top. I remember someone quipping, "There is a special place in hell for women who hold other women back in leadership."[6] Given my experiences in Greater New Jersey, I say to that comment, "preach it." We have got to do better. We are the church, for goodness' sake.

FASTING FOR FREEDOM

In May 2017, at the Greater New Jersey Annual Conference, eight months after being placed on involuntary leave, charges still had not been filed against Jisun Kwak nor the circumstances warranting the complaint against her and the involuntary leave of absence released. Per the Book of Discipline, an involuntary leave of absence recommendation by the Board of Ordained Ministry must be approved by the clergy session of members in full connection with the annual conference and done so by a two-thirds vote. (¶354.4). The session voted to turn down the recommendation. This did not happen without drama, however. First, for the first time any of us could remember, the cabinet led efforts to ensure that during the clergy session, any non-eligible voters, meaning those who were not elders or deacons with full orders, were sequestered outside of the main voting area and told to sit at tables on the edges of the room. In the past, it had simply been understood and trusted that those of us who were provisional elders, provisional deacons and local licensed pastors were not to raise our hands or in any other way vote. Clearly there was tension from the bishop and cabinet regarding the vote that would be taken about reinstating Jisun. This suddenly new concern about the voting arrangements unsettled many.

I remember being watched closely by district superintendents as I arrived early to the session and sat down in the designated fringe area. A clergy colleague on extension ministry for the denomination in Nashville, whom I had begun working with, sat down next to me to continue a previous conversation. At some point he shifted the topic to asking me what was going on with all this "Jisun Kwak stuff" we were about to vote on. He did not know my relationship with her. He probably asked me both as a friend and as a conference representative. Suddenly two district superintendents rushed over and told him to move into the voting area immediately, one even reaching for his arm. This was done with an unwarranted urgency that caught the clergy in question's attention as well as my own. It was like they had read his lips or were eavesdropping our conversation.

Once the session began, it was charged with speeches for keeping Jisun on a leave of absence that were given by the district superintendents leading the investigation against her. The clergy advocate chosen to act as lead prosecutor for the conference for the coming trial also gave a speech against Jisun. Accusations of further wrong-doing by Jisun were made, such as that she had made decisions over the course of her ministry that had not been forthcoming to the bishop. However, those claims were clearly not at a point that they could be substantiated as the conference, now eleven months after the suspension of her duties began, had not yet filed any charges. Still their accusations were stinging. I could hardly sit through them and could not imagine how my friend did so herself, as she sat up at an elevated table facing her peers. Jisun was also allotted a time for a speech, in which she declared her innocence of all wrong-doing and implored all for justice, including that she be re-instated to do the ministry that she loved and was her only source of income.

Bob Costello spoke as her advocate, pointing to the cruel treatment of Jisun and other tragedies about what was happening. He did so carefully without violating any confidentiality rules that would prejudice a potential juror, as the people in the room all represented potential jurors for Jisun's coming trial. Someone requested that a written ballot be taken for the vote, rather than people revealing their votes by raising their hands in front of the bishop and others. People were uncomfortable being seen casting votes that might cause retaliation against them or ill feelings from their peers. A written ballot would also ensure accuracy in the counting. The request for a paper ballot was voted on and carried. When the written ballot was taken, the vote failed by 122-137. Less than half the votes were to keep her on leave of absence, well under the required two-thirds needed. The Board of Ordained Ministry's decision to place Jisun on an unpaid, involuntary leave of absence was thereby reversed. This meant that Jisun should receive an appointed position immediately. Bob Costello asked that she receive backpay for the eight months she had been unpaid and that the pay be at her full, district superintendent level. This request was denied by Bishop Schol and a question for a ruling by the Judicial Council for the denomination (our Supreme Court) was called by Rev. Bob Costello.[7]

At the end of the clergy session, I watched as few had the courage to even speak to Jisun. The room of several hundred clergy cleared out quickly. I watched as she stood alone, uncontrollably crying. One district superintendent, a Korean female who had been serving in the role for about a year, was watching Jisun cry. I saw her hesitate, unsure what to do, then slowly walk over to Jisun and put her arm around her. You could tell she was stuck between compassion and fear. I made my way over to the two and when the other Korean woman saw me, relief crossed her face as she released Jisun, knowing she could leave Jisun to me and exit the situation as soon as possible. I put my arm around my friend and walked her out of the room and building. We skipped the ordination service scheduled for the evening and I took her out to a restaurant instead, as she had fasted food for some time and was famished and exhausted.

A few weeks after that clergy session, it was announced that the conference clergy advocate for the case against Jisun was being replaced by a different clergy. I do not know the details of why that occurred. But it did not exude certainty that the conference's case against Jisun was strong.

Bishop Schol reinstated Jisun as pastor of an eleven-member church and paid the lowest clergy salary allowable under conference compensation guidelines for an elder with as many years' service as she had. When the backpay issue was later taken up by the Judicial Council, the determination was that Jisun was to be given backpay, but only at the minimum pay level, not at her former District Superintendent level. (Decision Number 1355)

The Judicial Council ruling, as John Lomperis noted in his November 2017 *Juicy Ecumenism* article, "Is UMC Bishop Schol Now in Favor of Church Trials After He was Against Them?" was

> ...as about extreme a demotion as Bishop Schol could have possibly imposed without unilaterally defrocking her. The conference's aforementioned minimum salary for full-time elders is less than half of the salary of district superintendents, albeit still much less than Bishop Schol's own six-figure salary (meaning that even with the mandate for Kwak's retroactive compensation, she has lost over half of her income for over nine months).[8]

The suspiciousness of the complaint and its reflection of Schol's pattern with others was also detailed by John Lomperis in that article. His comments included that

> The cabinet did not file charges against Jisun for more than another year after the May 2017 clergy session. That meant that she had to wait roughly two years for those charges, with a cloud over her head, questions lingering at the small church she was now assigned to and people throughout the denomination continuing to avoid her. When the charges finally came, there were three: 1) immorality, 2) undermining the ministry of another clergy person, and 3) disobedience to the order and discipline of the church. Within the three charges, there were 8 counts. She then had to wait another roughly

six months for the trial date that was set in February 2019. The pressure and stress of the entire twenty-eight months before she could be exonerated through a trial process was only bearable through the grace of God.

SALT IN THE WOUNDS

Customarily, when leaving staff positions for whatever reason, staff are recognized at Annual Conference and their ministry achievements are celebrated. When we got to that May 2017 Greater New Jersey Annual Conference, where I officially left staff and received my new appointment to the church in South Jersey, my conference staff ministry, which had exceeded all measurable/metric goals set and done so ahead of schedule, was not even acknowledged. I was instead shunned. During the appointment reception ceremony, clergy queue up to be handed an appointment letter, have their name and new church announced to the conference, and then shake hands and have a photo with the bishop. When it came my turn, rather than shake my hand and have a photo, Bishop Schol stepped away. This was done just for me, it would appear, because he was there for the person in line ahead of me and again for the person directly behind me. It felt petty and purposeful.

More bizarrely, when I was to be photographed by Conference Communications with my new church leadership, a standard practice that was done for all new appointments, the bishop stepped in front of the camera and shouted, "Photo Bomb!" and made a silly face. It was completely unprofessional and disrespectful. His actions did not go unnoticed by others. The Senior Pastor of my new church, who was in the photo with me, asked, "What was that?" I received several comments, including this text from a pastor I only knew as a member of a PACE group (Peer Learning Group) I led for the conference:

MAY 23, 2017, 1:48 PM

Beth, I couldn't help but notice the slight paid to you by the Bishop by not acknowledging your service and transition. I'm sorry. Please know that you and your family are in my prayers as you go forward. Enjoy Alabama. That will be a nice change of pace and scenery. God bless you

Facebook message sent to me

My therapist told me to decline the farewell luncheon that conference administrative staff wanted to set up for me in June 2017. She was concerned that the pain and anxiety it would cause me would be harmful. But in interest of being polite to kind administrative staff members, I decided I could handle the very awkward situation. The luncheon was not attended by any district superintendents and was sparsely attended overall. In fairness, however, it was held at a time when many on staff take vacations before summer workloads begin. I was given cards of appreciation and gifts from the bishop's office and from the connectional ministries team.

When the bishop stood up to speak briefly about me, the main, final, and lasting comment he made regarding my leadership was, "Beth has proven to have a real way with certain male clergy and other male leaders in the southern part of the conference." This was a classic Schol comment. He takes liberty to make comments right up to the edge of appropriateness to sting his victims. I saw him do it at other times publicly with Rev. Dr. Kwak. In this case, the comment could be, and most likely was, interpreted as meaning I had inappropriate relationships with men (untrue and never alleged before), and/or it could have been taken to mean I had developed alliances with the mainly male clergy and other male leaders who at that time made up the Evangelical Network for Renewal and Growth and were mostly from the southern part of the conference (true).

I felt violated and sick. Given the comment's understated nature, I had no recourse. I wish I had been more quick-witted and less intimidated by the comment and challenged it. But I just didn't have the strength left. I also did not feel the comment would be taken seriously if I reported it. I had been in human resources management for large corporations and investigated and resolved many complaints regarding hostile work environments and more for others. But because I was now in a church system that was immune to most state and federal anti-discrimination laws under the U.S. legal doctrine known as the Ministerial Exception, and because I did not have the protection of full clergy orders, I felt trapped with no recourse. Yet as I prayed, I still did not sense God's call to leave the United Methodist Church.

COWTOWN[1]

In late June, before my new appointment started, I attended a ladies small group home gathering for mainly the satellite church plant women, led by the main church Director of Ministries.

The women present from the satellite church plant congregation were very welcoming. The Director of Ministries much less so. Over casual conversation as all were getting acquainted, she abruptly asked me in front of the group, "What makes you think it is OK for women to be pastors?" While my response to her hostile comment led to good conversation with the rest of the group, she remained silent. I now believe that there was a hope of affirmation for her own sense of calling in that question, even though it was offered to me in such an unfriendly way. I also do not know if there was a resentment that I was living out my calling that perhaps she felt herself denied because of the theology she had been taught and embraced.

I would come to understand that this person had worked hard as a leader in the initial startup of the satellite church plant and was leaned heavily upon by its first pastor. Her salary came from the conference grant that provided for the new campus, so it was understandable that she felt very invested in it. When that original pastor stepped down from the satellite church plant lead position, the Associate Pastor I was replacing was moved over from the main campus to replace him. Not her. The Director of Ministry maintained heavy involvement in the satellite church plant campus at that time, but a more local team was being groomed and so there had been some friction.

As it has been explained to me, when the Associate Pastor I was replacing was then reappointed elsewhere, the Director of Ministry had expected and hoped to become its pastor or in some other fashion be placed in charge of the campus herself.

That hope had been kindled during the week between the news that the Associate Pastor was leaving and the news of my appointment, when church leadership had apparently discussed having a local hire lead the church rather than receiving an appointed pastor. I am unclear whether she had been told that local hire would be her or not, but I do know that I would have been resentful if I were her and not placed in charge of the church.

If this expectation from her were true, it certainly showed conflict within her between the theology she embraced and perhaps the calling she was discerning. As detailed in the chapter "She Preaches Gospel," I understand women being conflicted on this issue. I do remember being approached shortly after coming to the church by a male leader within the church asking me to encourage her to pursue ordination and to assure her that women can be pastors in the sight of God. I offered such conversation to her at various times. One of the contributions I celebrate giving to that church community is the example of a traditional Wesleyan female pastor who reassured men, women and youth that we exist and fulfilling our calling is possible. Also knowing that I inspired other females at both campuses is a blessing. Not long after I left that church, the Director of Ministries began continuing education to become a pastor. She was named Associate Pastor there in 2021 as a local hire.

But when my appointment was announced, I think in part to make amends and assure her that she was highly valued, leadership gave her more responsibility at the main campus. This shift in responsibilities was perhaps intended to help alleviate ongoing conflicts between her and the satellite church plant Children's Director and the potential for such conflicts with me. The shift in responsibilities also served to take responsibility that had previously belonged to the former pastor and kept it with insiders, thus protecting the main campus from the unknown female pastor outsider—me. Nonetheless, the point is there was significant change being made and accommodated because of my abrupt appointment into an already tenuous and even toxic environment.

To make matters worse, a month after I arrived, the senior pastor's troubled adult son, who lived with him, went missing. There was darkness surrounding the circumstances. Seven months later his body was found in a field in Maryland. To this day, the family continues to lobby law enforcement for justice and during my entire tenure at the church remained fixated on this pursuit.

From the moment it was learned their son was missing, the family understandably dove into crisis mode. The mistake, however, was that the Senior Pastor was allowed by the church and the Conference to stay at the reigns of the church. He should have been put on a leave of absence to focus on receiving the help he needed. That did not happen.

This horrific occurrence and much of the details around it with police investigations, lack of satisfaction with the police effort, and general distress consumed much church leadership energy throughout my time there, including energy that could have been used in aiding my acceptance onto the church ministry team. The church leadership circled around the Senior Pastor and my energies toward aiding them met with resistance as they were seen as unwelcomed outsider threats that would somehow undermine the church and its leadership. The troops circled and more opportunity was given for those who sought to push me out.

About a year into my appointment, my district superintendent said to me that if he had been me, he would have just taken over the situation. The comment was astonishing to me. He was the Senior Pastor's boss and he was not taking over the situation, not insisting the Senior Pastor go on leave, not becoming interim leader himself, or naming me or anyone else interim leader. The Senior Pastor was my boss, and yet he was now suggesting I should have done further relationship damage at the church by insisting everyone follow me when I was given no authority by him or the church to do so.

The week before it was announced that the pastor's son had gone missing, I was asked to preach my first sermon at the main campus. The sermon went over very well, and I received positive feedback from the Senior Pastor. However, I never again was asked to preach at the Main Campus. I was relegated to the satellite church plant from then on. I was never given an explanation as to why. I asked many questions during my time at the church, which were often rudely ignored or evaded.

One demand that the church Staff Parish Relations Committee put on me was that I must reside within Woolwich Township, where the satellite church plant was planted. They were adamant that not doing so would be a deal breaker for being able to serve the church effectively. I knew the church had no grounds to require this of me. I also knew that they had not required the Associate Pastor before me to move to the area when he began serving the church. Yet I really wanted to do everything possible to make this church successful. Therefore, even though my husband worked over an hour and a half away in Trevose, PA and the district superintendents had suggested I live somewhere that could split our commutes more evenly, like Cherry Hill, NJ, I made every effort to move to Woolwich Township.

The conference allowed me to live in another church's vacant parsonage while I worked to sell my house in Clinton Township and find a new home in Woolwich Township. Vacant homes are never good situations, so the conference and the church were eager to have a pastor tennant. We found a buyer for our home in August 2017. We made an offer and got a contract on a house in Woolwich Township immediately. We began the necessary inspection process for the new home. We enrolled my daughter in the second grade at Woolwich public schools. But the plan wasn't to be.

The septic system for the house we were buying failed inspection miserably. The seller was not willing to negotiate for the $40,000 new system. Having invested significant time, energy, and several thousand dollars in the home inspection and legal process, we had to walk away.

We found another house. This one's yard backed up to the school, was five minutes from the satellite church plant campus, and was in the midst of the prime neighborhood that the church targeted to attract new members. It was empty and thus could have a quick settlement. My daughter started school while we were beginning the inspection process. Each day I was driving her from our parsonage twenty minutes away to the driveway of the new home and walking her to school with the other neighborhood kids. I picked her up the same way each day as we wanted to get her acclimated as best possible. Suddenly the seller changed their mind and backed out of selling the property. No reason was given.

That second house contract fell through in mid-September 2017, and our home sale up north was about to close. We had a house full of belongings and nowhere to go. We decided to move everything into our temporary parsonage until we found our new home. This would necessitate two moves, but we had no choice. Thankfully the parsonage had a HUGE finished basement that we had been using as a roller rink for my daughter to learn how to skate. We quickly filled it with all our belongings.

In the midst of the move, literally while we were instructing movers at our old house, on the day we were saying goodbye to fourteen years of living space, my husband received a phone call. It was the urologist he had been referred to after bloodwork at an annual physical had come back with abnormal results. The doctor was calling to confirm that test results showed that, at 54-years-old, he had prostate cancer and the number of cells already affected were significant and demanded immediate treatment.

We stopped looking for a new house. After three weeks in the Woolwich Township school, we withdrew our daughter and placed her in yet another new school in the school district of the temporary parsonage in which we were living. My husband underwent surgery the week of Thanksgiving 2017. He spent several weeks on a medical leave of absence and further months in recovery. We thank God for his healing.

GO AHEAD AND SHINE ANYWAY

The entirety of my situation now included hostility from Sharptown leadership, Bishop Schol, and the conference; no funding, strategy, or support for the Sharptown North Campus; the crisis surrounding the disappearance of the Senior Pastor's son; and now my own personal challenges. Given all of this, I knew I would have little time or support to do effective ministry at the church. My choices were to 1) quit (which would be just fine with conference and the church leadership), 2) keep my head down and just focus on and be blamed for the satellite campus sinking due to my leadership ineffectiveness (also fine with all other parties), or 3) rock the ship by doing what I thought was needed to introduce new kinds of ministry and thinking. This would require finding new leaders and facing the consequences of stepping on toes. No choice would go well in terms of my acceptance and treatment. I prayed hard. In a leap of faith, I chose option 3 and leaned into my apostolic style of leadership.

In July 2017 I rallied and engaged a new worship and praise band team as the leaders and several other members of the previous one had left upon news of a new female clergy appointment.[2] I spent much time with our youth and youth director. I attracted new families to the church as word spread and I engaged local media to share the news that a new pastor was in town.

Eight months into my tenure I raised up a new leadership team to engage in a spiritual strategic planning process to lay out our ministry plans. Based on the gifts and graces present and the plans that came out of our process, my efforts at the satellite church plant then focused on better connecting the church with the local community through community service. I saw this as a growing edge for this conservative leadership team as well as a clear connection to those who might be attracted to the church. I also saw this as important to developing new leaders who needed the opportunity to grow and mature their gifts. In other words, the church had young families who were interested in community service and at the same time, service needs in the area would be a strong way to connect people to Christ.

I personally spent significant time developing relationships with local officials, including the mayor and other local government leaders, the superintendent of schools, the local Young Life leadership, local business owners, and service organization leaders. Building better and further reaching relationships with the community was key to any hopes of growing and sustaining this church.

In that short time, we rallied and introduced new partnerships and activities with the local Kiwanis chapter, Head Start, the Faith on the Field Sports Radio team, an African American Baptist Church, a Christian thrift store, and a local yet nationally renowned ER doctor with a ministry around substance abuse. We also began laying groundwork toward ministry with those suffering from domestic violence and homelessness. We established a new presence at local community events. I was the first pastor from that church invited to preach at the community's 9/11 memorial service.

We engaged in community prayer walks and I honed my preaching skills as I was free to give the thoroughly traditional, Holy Spirit-induced evangelical sermons that were in my heart. I baptized youth and adults who proclaimed their faith. I contended against other staff and church leaders to have our youth director develop and lead a confirmation class. We prevailed and the first class in the church's memory was initiated and completed. We built and trained a tech team of youth. We started a Men's Ministry, a new, rich adult small group, a new children's program, and nursery. We served as race officials for the community "08085" 5k-race, and our praise band was invited to play and did an excellent job at the Woolwich Township FUN DAY. We took church outings to Longwood Gardens to discuss baptism, and to the historic St. George's Church in Philadelphia, which is the oldest Methodist church in America.

I encouraged members to dream big and present ideas and they did. We worked together to bring them into fruition. We also labored with joy to maintain ministry that had been established by previous pastors, including putting on two Christmas "Eve Eve" services under a large tent in Lockwood Park that drew several hundred attendees, a Halloween event, a community Thanksgiving parade, a Christmas parade float, and so much more.

Without a doubt there was very rewarding local ministry during my time there. When I step back and remember this period in the context of the lives affected and changed and thus ministry achieved, I can see my dance with God and I celebrate.

The satellite church plant Service July 9, 2017. Christmas "Eve Eve" Service, Locke Ave. Park, Swedesboro December 23, 2017.

I joined the Kiwanis club and our church partnered with

Youth Haunted Hayride 11/2017 them for several community service activities. Photo 11/2017.

Organized Community Prayer Gathering September 2017

Trip to Longwood Gardens Fountain Show to discuss the meaning of Baptism. September 2017

Praise Band I loved so much. 2018   We were a Portable Church. 2018

Serving at the Ronald McDonald House.   *July 2018 Serving as Race Officials for the Community Annual 5 and 8k races. We did this partnering with Kiwanis*

I still believe this!

Satellite church Men's Group Gathering April 2018

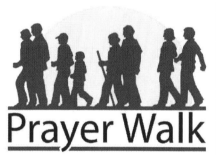

Organized several of these around town.

Outing to understand the caves in the Bible.

When another church in the area sponsored this, we helped out.

We established a team to read to the local Head Start Program, monthly.

They wanted an Easter Bunny for the egg hunt, so I agreed.

I enjoyed organizing field trips to historic and sacred religious sites.

But it was also a very brutal time given the open hostility toward and resentment of me. Ministry successes under my leadership were at best ignored, but usually criticized. I personally was attacked often. I was accused by existing church Main Campus focused leadership for everything from spending too much time in the bathroom before services to supposedly not being willing to do the physical labor myself to set up and tear down the temporary sanctuary each week. Although the work we were doing for the Lord was invigorating, the constant battles caused much exhaustion as well.

Under great pressure, I became challenged to quickly recall names. I would never say that remembering names has been a strength of mine, but I would not say it had been one of my major challenges. Yet at this time I became worse at it than I have ever been. I would regularly struggle to conjure names both in discussing people or even to their faces. I developed anxiety over contemplating remembering a name. It was very upsetting as I wondered what was happening to me.

Now I recognize it was the stress. Yet I was shown little grace. My challenge with names was snarkily and repeatedly mentioned by leadership (which caused me to get worse, I believe), and I was accused of being so uncaring that I did not even bother to get to know people's names.

I was lectured by the Senior Pastor on more than one occasion that shepherding is the only effective style of leadership and that my apostolic style with its many changes and outward focus was ineffective. At the same time, I was told I could not take my time on turning the satellite church plant around and that I was not making enough change. The messages were contradictory. I was told I needed to take decisive actions and yet when I did, my efforts were resented and criticized.

I was repeatedly not invited to staff meetings. I remember one staff meeting that I was actually invited to where everyone was prayed for, except me. I was deliberately kept out of leadership of outreach events that were to involve both campuses. I never received any positive encouragement from the Staff Parish Relations Committee. When and if an acknowledgement had to be made of ministry success, it was quickly followed by a criticism. But I pressed on, remembering whose I was and whose approval I sought. Galatians 1:10, Psalm 118:6-9.

By February 2018, about eight months in, I recognized several things about the area and communities we served. First, having searched for months with a team and a couple of realtors, I knew it had no space or building available then or in the foreseeable future that we could afford to purchase or even rent. Woolwich Township was stagnating and not growing at the rate it once had as its taxes were high, and it was known for the many septic system failures in the area.

Encouraging, however, was what was happening fifteen minutes north of the Woolwich Township building, in East Greenwich Township where I was residing. That community was growing much more and enjoying lower taxes. We had families from that community as members of the congregation and we were receiving visitors from there. Because of the parsonage I was living in, I also developed a relationship with the temporary, retired pastor and lay leadership at Evangelical United Methodist Church of Clarksboro (East Greenwich Township). This was a struggling congregation with one traditional worship service. They had ample space in their church and large grounds that could be built upon. They had allowed our satellite church plant Leadership Team to have our strategic planning sessions there. An idea came to mind.

I thought, what if we moved the satellite church plant congregation there as a second, contemporary service option? If I was appointed to both churches, preaching both services, they could split my salary. The satellite church plant would no longer have to pay rent and both churches could save money for future endeavors. For the satellite church plant that could mean affording a building of their own. The drive there was not far from Woolwich and volunteers would no longer be needed for setting up and tearing down, an issue that was continuing to cause problems in the church.

It was appointment season, and I knew it was a good time for the idea to go to the Cabinet. I knew I could not present this idea to the district superintendent myself. First, I would be accused of going around the Senior Pastor. I also knew ideas from me were not going to be supported by the cabinet given their treatment of me. There would have to be support from the Senior Pastor. I prayed hard, trying to think of a way for him to discover the idea himself or for someone to take the idea to him from the laity or for it to be presented by the Clarksboro church. No clear direction or opportunity arose.

I knew the clock was ticking with the cabinet, so I went to the Senior Pastor with the idea. He listened and expressed support. He said he would discuss it with the district superintendent. I doubt he ever did. Another pastor was appointed to the church and a different plan enacted.

What I was reminded of from the experience was that when you are asking the Holy Spirit's intervention and are willing to accept it, no matter what, the Holy Spirit's wisdom will prevail. If the Spirit is not with something, no matter how good the idea or its intentions, it will not move forward. Acts 16:6-7

THE WESLEYAN CHURCH AND CONNECTIONALISM

with Rev. Dr. JoAnn Lyon

Also in February 2018, I received an opportunity to get out of the whole mess. But first, a little backstory:

At the end of April 2017, while still on Bishop Schol's staff, I had attended a wonderful conference in Alexandria, Virginia, *Awakenings*, offered by Missio Alliance and sponsored by my friends at Fresh Expressions U.S. There I met and was encouraged by Rev. Dr. JoAnn Lyon, General Superintendent Emerita and Ambassador of The Wesleyan Church. I had previously seen her speak when she received the World Methodist Peace Award in at the World Methodist Conference Houston in 2016 and was drawn to her spirit. Her words of encouragement and acknowledgment of the treatment I and others were receiving at the hands of the United Methodist Church did much to comfort me.

I was inspired so much by this strong traditional female Wesleyan that the following weekend, for Mother's Day, I brought our family to a little Wesleyan Church near our home in Hunterdon County for worship. There I met the pastor, Bonnie Eastlach, who became a friend. We soon discovered that I was in the midst of moving to the very area of South Jersey she had recently left to serve in Hunterdon County. We shared much in common in our thoughts toward ministry.

Even more amazing was that when I started at the church I was serving, I discovered that the Women's Ministries team was looking at Pastor Bonnie as a possible women's retreat leader for 2018. I was able to vouch for and encourage Bonnie's selection for that retreat. We both saw that ours was totally a God connection and timing. I love how when we walk with God, we experience these divine connections.

Bonnie's family was extensively involved and had been for more than a generation in the leadership of the Wesleyan Church. Her brother, Dr. Karl Eastlach, is its Northeast district superintendent and his wife, Dr. Anita Eastlach, serves as the Executive Director of Church Multiplication and Discipleship for the denomination. I was introduced to both.

So by February 2018, at my request, Karl was talking to me about an opportunity as the lead pastor of a Wesleyan Church in nearby Aston, PA. It was a great opportunity with a denomination whose polity and practices were congruent with each other and with my own beliefs. I knew that Dr. Eastlach would be a supportive and role model leader for me. I even went and sat in the Aston church sanctuary and parking lot and prayed over the decision. Yet when it came time to meet with the church leadership, I knew in my spirit that this was not the path that the Lord was leading me to take. It would have solved many issues for me. But as I wrestled with God over this decision, I knew that it was not my call at that time.

I have been extremely grateful, however, for the continued prayers, connection, and support of the Eastlachs and Dr. Lyon. It was difficult to say no to them after having pursued the position at my own initiation. But they were very gracious.

ASIAN PREPARATION

I had wanted to visit South Korea for some time because of the great connection with its people through Methodism. It had been Methodists and Presbyterians primarily that had brought Christianity to South Korea in the late nineteenth Century. One of the great Methodist missionaries, Henry Appenzeller, had been a leader in that movement, and he also was a celebrated student and leader at Drew University, where I had gone to seminary. Due much to his initial influence, there is a strong tie between Drew Theological School and Korean Methodists, universities, and churches. While I attended seminary, for instance, a major source of our students, I guestimate at least thirty percent of the student body, was South Korean. Koreans are known for being passionate in their faith, having incredible discipline that includes daily early morning prayer and Bible reading rituals, and fervor in their prayer lives. Their faith also, as developed in South Korea, is, in general, very traditional.

Add to that much innovative ministry coming out of South Korea, a beautiful country with warm people and incredible technology, culture, and cuisine, and one can understand why it would be on a minister's bucket list. Having a best friend from there of course topped it off for me. I really wanted to go.

Early in 2018, my friend Rev. Jisun Kwak arranged the opportunity. I received an invitation from several Korean ministers to go to South Korea in early March for ten days to do ministry, learn from ministers there, and experience the culture. I visited Seoul and Jeju Island. I will always be grateful for Jisun's support and the incredible hospitality I received on that trip because of her influence. I also believe the Lord wanted me to have that experience, as it prepared me for better work in the future with South Koreans and it was a much-needed reprieve from the hostile environment and treatment I had been experiencing.

Myongi University, Seoul, Korea, March 2018

First, I was invited to speak to the student body at Myongi University by the chaplain's office and Dean Jeehong Koo. I gave the first address of the school year to the several hundred students who were attending chapel as a mandatory requirement. This was a wonderful opportunity as Myongi is a secular university with only 30-40% of the students being Christian. Many of them are evening students working to make a change in career with a new degree. I spoke to them about my experiences following the Lord's lead through career change and different phases and challenges of life. My presentation was well received.[3]

Yongsei University, Seoul, Korea

Second, I went to Yongsei University, one of the two most esteemed universities in Korea (think Harvard and Yale). This is Jisun's alma mater. I met with Dr. Soo-Yoon Kwon, Dean of the College and Graduate Schools of Theology and Hyun-Sook Kim, the Associate Dean at the college of Theology. Dean Kwon also directs Yongsei's Center for Counseling and Coaching, one of the finest and most innovative pastoral care centers in the world. He gave me a tour of their facilities and we all discussed pastoring as part of a multi-site, portable church, the WCA, and the conflict and challenges occurring in the United Methodist Church.[4]

I had the honor and privilege as well to meet with Rev. Younghoon Lee, Sr. Pastor of Yoido Full Gospel Church, the world's largest church with 875,000 members and an annual budget of $120 million. At the main campus they have seven services on Sundays. He has 440 pastors serving under his leadership and 1200+ elders. The very morning we met, he had just returned from the US where he had attended Billy Graham's funeral and then his own mother's funeral in Ft. Lee, New Jersey. That he kept our meeting showed what a special person he is. He shared with me that he was spending much time those days assisting with U.S. and the new South Korean government's relations. He spoke about how his predecessor, Rev. Cho, was called to focus the church on personal salvation while he has been called to focus also on serving the poor throughout the world. He shared they spend $38 million a year on serving the poor. He said that *true* prosperity gospel leads its followers to focus on giving and it is the giving of themselves that causes them to become prosperous within. He said ministry success starts with a church focused on prayer, then evangelism, then service and healing. I was privileged to pray with him at the end of our time together. I was very affected by this meeting and our conversation. Also, the tour of the church's facilities was spectacular.[5]

With Rev. Younghoon Lee at Yoido Full Gospel Church, largest church in the world, Seoul

I visited the EWHA Girls School in Seoul and learned of its impact up close. In 1886 Methodist Missionary Mary Scranton started the school as the first ever for educating girls in Korea. That first class of girls included Esther Kim Pak who grew up to become the first female medical doctor in Korea. I enjoyed touring their new school museum, the school itself, and the amazing stories of this historic school's beginnings. I also enjoyed watching the girls at the EHWA high school that still exists today walking to and fro at the new campus. As I recorded, the whole thing gave me goose bumps.[6]

I met with representatives of the United Methodists' General Commission on Global Ministries at their Seoul office and took a tour of the facility, learning of their ministry work, challenges, and successes. I traveled to Suwon, a suburb of Seoul, and met with Dr. Tongmin Chang, a Presbyterian minister and church history professor at Baekseok University. I especially enjoyed discussing missional theology, Tim Keller's ministry (who he follows closely), and multisite churches. On Jeju Island, which is like the Hawaii of Korea, I visited a Presbyterian Church service and found familiar hymns being sung, including Blessed Assurance and others most American Methodists would know. The liturgy/order of worship was familiar as well, just all in Korean. We recited the Nicene Creed (not the shorter Apostle's Creed). The message was on Philippians 2:1-10, imitating Christ's humility.

One interesting aspect of the JeJu Island service was that a brochure was distributed from an organization educating on the concerns of homosexuality. It was advocating that the Korean Government/National Assembly not approve of homosexual marriage. South Korea does not recognize same-sex marriage nor any other form of legal union for same-sex couples. The brochure gave many statistics regarding the higher number of homosexuals in large city vs rural and small city environments, college vs high school educated, and treatment for mental issues such as depression, etc. It was announced that this brochure was distributed to all churches (not just Presbyterian) on Jeju Island that morning. Support for homosexual unions is growing in South Korea, but it still receives minority support.[7] Furthermore, LGBTQIA practices are recognized as spiritual and emotional health issues from the vast majority of Christian churches and leaders in this highly concerned country.

Seeing the brochure distributed and discussed in the service brought two thoughts to mind. First, it often seems I personally can never get a break from this issue, even half-way around the world. This testifies to me the importance of the concern and my call to pay attention, educate myself, and speak into it, as tiring as it may seem at times. I have often prayed to God to search my heart on this issue and, if it needs to change, I am open to it. Sometimes, I confess, I have even prayed to be released from even dealing with this issue as it is such a difficult topic that divides. Yet the Lord has not seen fit to change my perspective from a traditional view on matters of human sexuality, but to instead broaden my understanding of this view. Likewise, I seem to rarely get a day when this topic is not broached in some fashion that I cannot ignore.

Second, I was impressed that the traditional church was discussing the subject. I believe part of the problem for traditional Methodist churches in the U.S. is that we do not discuss matters of human sexuality enough from the pulpit. Too many are often intimidated, uneducated on how to share our views and concerns, and outright afraid that we will say the wrong thing and end up being misinterpreted or even attacked. The concern today for American traditional United Methodist ministers is often that the attack will not necessarily be launched from the congregation, but could instead come from or go to the conference and be detrimental to one's ministry and vocation.

This trip was a highlight during my tenure with the United Methodist Church. Even though I asked for and received approval to take the time away from the church I was serving, I went knowing that I would be criticized for going by that very same leadership. I knew that choosing not to go would not really make a difference in the way they were choosing to view me as a contributor to their team. I did not ask for, nor was my trip paid for, out of educational funds from the church or any other resource than myself. I used vacation time to take advantage of this incredible educational and ministry opportunity. I only missed one Sunday from the pulpit because of the trip.

Yet, as no surprise, instead of support, the church leadership refused to ask me about the trip, did not encourage me to share what I had learned with the congregations, or find ways to capitalize on the relationships I had established for the church. I brought back gifts for staff members and presented a pearl-inlaid Bible stand for the office that was given by Myongi University. The stand was ignored by church leaders, so I also presented it to the satellite church plant and tried to display it at our portable church. I shared much about what I had experienced and learned in my sermons and conversation with laity.

The trip was later brought up by SPRC as an example of my lack of commitment to their church. Their willful ignorance and weaponizing of my short absence, though at that point expected, still stung. I chalk it up as another rock thrown. I never used up all my vacation time at the church. Looking back at the time, I know that was a real mistake. My family and I sure could have used more Sabbath.

SUCK IT UP

Yet I chose to keep up good ministry at the church in spite of the roadblocks and lack of support. Just a few weeks after my trip, the satellite church plant's Easter 2018 services boasted the highest attendance of the church plant's history. Each spring there had also been a tradition at the church of collecting money for capital projects such as paying off mortgages of buildings and parsonages. The campaigns were called "Joash drops," in reference to King Joash in 2 Chronicles 24, who paid for repairs to the temple by asking citizens to place donations in a trunk outside the temple. The people gave freely and enough for the needed work. The satellite church plant had participated in such campaigns to raise funds for future building needs as well. This year, however, I was told by the Senior Pastor, without opportunity for me or the satellite church plant leadership team to give input, that we were to have a Joash drop campaign to raise money for a Vacation Bible School program for the satellite church plant. My leadership team and I questioned why this would make sense as we clearly needed money for a building or some other arrangement to continue the church. Nonetheless, we did as told and the money was raised.[8]

I made efforts to talk to the SPRC chair on several occasions regarding moving forward with various leadership and staffing ideas and issues at the satellite church plant, and about my continued exclusion from ministry at the main church and staff meetings, but she avoided me. It was clear to me that they were not going to help me with my outside ideas and they were not going to include me as a leader as part of their home-grown team. What was also becoming clear, but still felt unfathomable to me given the strides we were making, was that they were withdrawing the needed support for sustaining the campus.

FAMILY LIFESTYLE CHALLENGES

In late March 2018, I was informed that we would need to be out of the temporary parsonage we had occupied since July by early June as its church was receiving a newly appointed pastor who would need it. We began actively searching for a new home and trying to decide whether we should just rent something or go ahead and purchase. On the surface, there really seemed to be no reason to buy a home. I would clearly not be at the church and probably not with the United Methodist Church much longer. My husband's commute to work continued to be lengthy. Yet buying a home felt right to both my husband and me.

We decided that we were not going to require our daughter to make another school change just so that we could live in Woolwich Township as the church leadership demanded. It was a difficult decision. We continued to look at home after home and nothing felt right. Time was ticking.

Finally in May, we decided to build a home in a new development in East Greenwich Township. I saw potential as the neighborhood was made up of diverse, young couples just beginning to start families. It would be a great place to share the Gospel. It felt right. But building a home meant we would have to move two more times— first into a temporary apartment while waiting for the house to be built and so that we would be out of the way of the new occupants of the parsonage we were then in, then into the home we purchased. And, of course, the moves were completely at our own expense.

In June 2018 we moved most of our belongings into two large PODS and the rest into a furnished apartment in Woolwich Township. The apartment was roughly a mile from the satellite church plant campus. I began having leadership meetings and a small group Bible study in the lovely apartment complex clubhouse. I met people at the community pool and invited them to church. My husband was extensively involved with the labors of the church, building relationships and participating in small group ministry. My two older children came home from college and helped us move and do ministry that summer. My daughter worked for the ENT physician who, along with her family, was attending our church and really supporting us. Our family was doing the best it could.

SPRC ABUSE

The actual first meeting I had with the SPRC after starting at the church was roughly 11 months into my tenure in late May 2018. It was then when I was handed without any warning a "Benchmark Growth Plan," similar to a secular, corporate performance improvement plan. The meeting lasted three hours (no exaggeration) and solely consisted of raking me over the coals. For some reason the district superintendent did not attend the meeting.

I cried in the meeting and was criticized in front of all by the Senior Pastor for doing so. This benchmark plan was devised without a single person from the satellite church plant campus even being on the committee. The number one issue listed on the plan was "perceived absence." I was instructed to devise a weekly schedule with specific, Salem County, main campus (not Woolwich Community where I was still only assigned to serve) office hours, and I was to give a detailed accounting for every hour I spent in ministry.

I was also raked over the coals for having bought a house outside of Woolwich Township. In fact, that seemed to be the issue they were most upset about. Again, I laboriously explained my situation and reasoning that I could no longer honor their request after much pain and financial stress for my family in having tried to do so. Again, the house we were building was less than twenty minutes from where the church was meeting and was in a community that several of our members lived in and was a growing, young community. It appeared few on the committee cared.

The benchmark plan did not include me being invited to partake in any ministry at the Main campus, yet I was to spend the bulk of my time there. The plan was also devised without any SPRC committee members, to my knowledge, having visited the satellite church plant campus worship service. I pointed this out and the SPRC Chair then did visit in June. Her comment to me was, "The Spirit is not here."

What she really meant was that the church leadership had decided it would no longer support the campus nor my salary, ministry, or presence. The end was coming.

My family went further into disgust with the United Methodist Church. My older children continued with what they had been requesting for months: repeatedly asking me to quit because they saw me being abused. My husband continued to remind me that he would support whatever I chose, but he could not understand why I would allow the treatment that I was receiving when I could follow many different options.

I engaged a therapist, a coach, and a spiritual director during that time. All helped me develop an understanding of my call to apostleship, the true growing edges I needed to hone, and strategies for coping with grace and perseverance, especially in my current position. Those resources helped me to stay close to the Lord, not give up, and see past the situation.

WCA

It was during my time at this church that I also began feeling the tug of a greater ministry calling. I had been following the progression of the Wesleyan Covenant Association and its continued efforts to renew the United Methodist Church, provide connection for traditional Methodists, and uphold the UMC Book of Discipline's teachings regarding human sexuality. I saw that it had elected Rev. Keith Boyette out of the Virginia Conference as its President. In the summer of 2017, he had retired from the UMC to take up this calling when it had become clear that his efforts to lead the WCA would be met with much resistance by the denomination.

I knew those in the Greater New Jersey Conference within the traditional ranks, both clergy and laity, were an incohesive group that sorely needed and desired leadership. Our team at the Evangelical Network for Renewal and Growth was inconsistent and needed more direction. I had been asked to lead this group in the past but had declined because of potentially perceived conflict of interest with my conference staff duties and vulnerability as a clergy without full orders to those who would use this involvement against me in the ordination process.

I knew in my heart that my leadership would be welcomed by the WCA. Yet I did not want to pursue greater involvement with them if it was not of the Lord. I spent several months praying about what to do. As I prayed, the Lord began showing me something special. I have always been a connector, and I began to see how I was uniquely positioned to not only lead in New Jersey, but to connect several groups of traditional Methodists who otherwise were not connected.

In Greater New Jersey, even though conference leadership and the majority of clergy considered themselves progressives, the largest churches boast a large percentage of laity and clergy that are traditional, orthodox, evangelical Christians. Korean churches, who are by and large very traditional in their theology, at that time comprised close to 5% of all our churches and they also included five of the top ten largest churches in the conference. In my time on conference staff, I had cultivated relationships with several of these churches and their senior pastors, especially the largest three in our conference.

Of the other largest churches in the conference, the vast majority were white, traditional churches, and most located in the southern region of the state where I now was a pastor. I had grown relationships with many of these churches through my work on conference staff, my involvement with ENRG, and now as a pastor at one of the largest traditional churches.

Additionally, I had strong relationships with leadership of the three largest Methodist Camp Meeting Associations in the state. All three have strong traditional Christian ties and leadership. I was a trustee at Ocean Grove, had a good relationship with the Malaga Camp President, Rev. Dan Amey, who was also the President of ENRG, and I had worked with Rev. Steve Elliot and other leaders at South Seaville Camp Meeting.

I recognized that these four entities—Korean churches, large evangelical churches, the Camp Meetings and ENRG—had, at best, very minimal connection with one another. If they joined forces, they would enjoy connection and be better able to assert their influence and interests within the conference. I was the best connector to make this happen.

In October of 2017, I placed a call to Keith Boyette. We had a wonderful conversation. By its end I invited Rev. Boyette to Greater New Jersey to share more with me and others about the Wesleyan Covenant Association. Within a week I received a phone call from Rev. Walter Fenton, who was to soon become the second hire to the WCA (he called on 10/26/17, I know because I kept the voicemail as I knew it was significant). We, too, had good conversation and began to formulate a plan for Keith and Walter to visit Greater New Jersey.

In February 2018 I offered four meetings with Walter and Keith across the state. We met with large church pastors in the southern region, held an open meeting at Ocean Grove, met with the largest Korean church pastors, held another open meeting in the southern region of the state at an American Legion facility, and Keith preached at both Sharptown and Sharptown North campuses. We were one of the first conferences that Keith and Walter visited in such fashion. The meetings were well attended and there was much enthusiasm for the work of the WCA shown.

Word got back to Bishop Schol that Keith and Walter would be in Greater New Jersey and he requested a meeting with them. They obliged. To my knowledge my name did not come up in their meeting, as both sides opted to keep my leadership quiet. Keith and Walter did not want to cause me any trouble with Schol. Schol, I believe, did not want to give credence to my influence in the conference.

Three months later I orchestrated with our ENRG team for Rev. Dr. Carolyn Moore, at that time a WCA Global Council member (later the Council's Chair), to speak at our ENRG dinner during the GNJ Annual Conference in May 2018. Although our presence was growing and increasing in momentum, the conference was not about to acknowledge us. There were beginning signs of their hostility toward our efforts, however. During the 2018 Annual Conference in Wildwood, for example, there was a time when I was in the back of the main convention center auditorium where I had been chatting with various other conference attendees. We were outside of the perimeters of the set Conference Legislative Bar and were not conducting any business, just engaging in the usual socializing that takes place during breaks or on the sidelines of the conference proceedings. For those who know the venue as it is set up for the meeting, I was next to the main entrance, by the bleachers set up for guests. It is a large, noisy venue with many people milling about.

As I was speaking to another clergy (and certainly not loudly), a clergy serving as a conference page approached us and told us that it had been requested by conference leadership that I move my conversation outside as I was being disruptive. We were both shocked. The messenger obviously felt uncomfortable as well. We complied but it was evident that I was being bullied. Clearly, I was being watched and undoubtedly my WCA connectivity was not welcomed.

That summer and fall I organized a series of prayer meetings at each of the three largest Methodist Camp Meeting Association sites in the state: Ocean Grove, Malaga, and South Seaville.

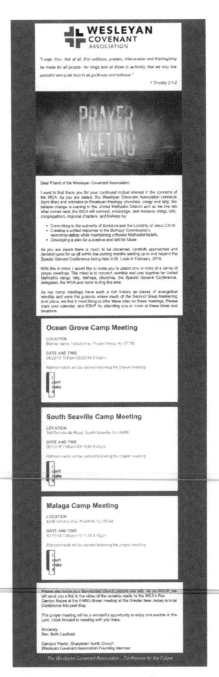

Prayer meetings organized in 2018

We also established the Wesleyan Covenant Association Greater New Jersey Chapter as a legal entity. I was elected its President, Rev. Dave Werhle its Vice President, Mr. Creed Pogue its Secretary/ Treasurer, and Rev. Dan Amey as an Executive Committee Member. We disbanded the Evangelical Network for Renewal and Growth and imported its email contact list into our own, new Constant Contact account. We transferred its bank account over to our own. Creed and I also were elected as delegates to the first WCA Global Legislative Assembly that was held in Atlanta, Georgia in early November 2018. Literally, a new chapter for traditional Methodists had begun in Greater New Jersey.

NOW SHOOT HER DEAD

But as matters were taking off for me with the WCA, they were only getting worse at the church I was assigned. Not only had I been put on a Benchmark Plan, but a deliberate further withdrawal of resources to the satellite church plant escalated. The Children's Program Director announced she would move her ministry back to the main campus. She took a few young families with her. I also began to recognize and see that not only she, but the Senior Pastor and other leaders were actively recruiting such families to the main campus. Families began to leave the satellite church plant altogether for a variety of reasons. Most of these left because of the incessant demands of a church that for a long time required most everyone to be involved in set/up tear/down each Sunday. People began to recognize I did not have support from the main campus and we were probably not going to make it for much longer as a church. Some perhaps left because of my leadership style.

I gave one more big event opportunity to rally the troops. I had developed a relationship with two local Christian celebrity-types—Doug Horton and Rob Maaddi. Doug and Rob, among other endeavors, hosted Philadelphia 610 AM Radio's "Faith on the Field" show that featured interviews with Christian professional athletes. I had in March brought Doug in to speak at the satellite church plant as part of a sermon series. He had been well received as his ministry is inspiring and the testimonies he shares are powerful.

with Doug Horton

Rob, who is also a bestselling author, radio, and television personality was about to release his book on the Philadelphia Eagles football team, entitled *"Birds of Pray."* The Philadelphia Eagles had just won their first Super Bowl ever after a seemingly miraculous season. The entire Philadelphia region, including where both the main and satellite churches were located, was still full of excitement over the Eagles and sharing about their many players and leaders who have Christian faith was an excellent ministry opportunity. I arranged for Rob to speak at a book signing party that also featured our praise band. and donated Philadelphia soft pretzels, cupcakes, and other snacks from local businesses directly after the service on a weekend that the Eagles had a bye in their schedule and would therefore not be playing.

Rob, Dave, and the satellite church plant members advertised the event heavily for over a month throughout the area. I asked our DS to advertise it in the district newsletter and he did. I also asked the Senior Pastor and the main church leadership team to advertise at that campus as there was a huge Eagles fan base there. He did not, and it was clear at the leadership meetings that these efforts were not going to be supported. There was no interest expressed either in bringing the book signing to the main campus. Instead, the exciting endeavor was met with clear resentment.

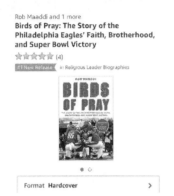

Rob Maaddi and 1 more
Birds of Pray: The Story of the Philadelphia Eagles' Faith, Brotherhood, and Super Bowl Victory
⭐⭐⭐⭐⭐ (4)
#1 New Release in Religious Leader Biographies

Format **Hardcover** >

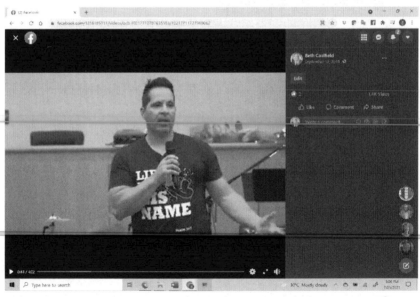

Rob Maaddi's book signing at our church was a blessing to all. His book is even better.

The event was enjoyed by all, and Rob gave a wonderful testimony. There were a few people who made their way over from the Sharptown campus. Several stated that it should have been advertised during the service over there and they were surprised more people did not come. I, of course, said nothing.[1]

Abuse by the staff and leadership continued. I was frequently fed inappropriate jokes about female leaders. One clergy colleague on staff emailed me an incredibly offensive video entitled "Who Needs Feminism" "as a joke." He knew I would not find it funny. I am baffled anyone with good intentions would send to a colleague, especially a female one, a video that goes on for five and a half minutes with the commentator declaring that he is an "anti-feminist," who egregiously stereotypes women and bullishly asserts "feminism has made both men and women less happy and less free." Watch the video at:

https://www.youtube.com/watch?v=In8jWBlc8xo[2]

At the same time, there were some real troopers who had the vision for what we were trying to achieve at the satellite church plant and they stayed solid through the end. I will be forever grateful and indebted to their ministry, prayers, and personal support.

In October 2018, the very week we were settling the purchase of and moving into our new home, as we were unpacking, I received an email from the bishop's executive assistant, Nicola Mulligan:

Dear Rev. Caulfield,

It has been brought to the Bishop's Office by the pastor and SPRC that there are issues and conflicts that has affected the present, short term and long term health of the congregation.

It has been requested that there be an immediate appointment change. Bishop Schol wants to hear your perspective and discuss next steps with you. You are welcome to bring someone with you, not a lawyer and preferably a clergy person. You do not have to, it is a courtesy Bishop Schol provides.

A meeting is scheduled for Wednesday, October 31, at 8:30AM, here at the Mission and Resource Center, 205 Jumping Brook Road, Neptune, NJ 07753.

Please confirm you have received this email.

Thank you.

Blessings,

Nicola

Nicola Mulligan

Assistant to the Bishop

I had not received any communication from the Senior Pastor or the SPRC about their request or that such a letter was being sent.

The evening I received that email, after leading a small group with our strongest satellite church plant leaders, I broke down and shared with one of our new Co-Children's Directors, Grace Ellis, about my experiences with the satellite church plant leadership. I told her about the letter and showed her the anti-feminism video that had been emailed to me. I told her how I had been treated. Grace, a former Air Force Academy cadet, someone whose mom had been killed on 9/11 while serving in the Pentagon, did not take the matter lightly. She was appalled by the behavior of church leadership, but stated she was not surprised. Many knew I was being treated unfairly.

Without my knowledge, she began contacting members of the satellite church plant, apprising them of the situation and soliciting their assistance. What I know is that a variety of laity from very different professional, ethnic, age, and so forth backgrounds began contacting the bishop on my behalf, stating that I was the victim of injustice, saying very nice things about my leadership and that they wanted me to continue as their pastor.

Some later forwarded me copies of their emails. They came from youth, a disabled individual, retirees, teachers, doctors, lawyers, small business owners, a decorated female Naval Officer, young adults, police officers, a Girl Scout executive, and more. They were African Americans, Asians, and Caucasians, male and female. I tear up when I think of how they stood up for me. At the same time, it makes me sad that people who just wanted to worship and serve God together and believed in the ministry we were doing would have to be effected by and learn about such internal strife among church leadership.

When I contacted my district superintendent, he told me he had not been informed that the church was contacting the bishop with a request for a change. He said he had not seen the letter they had sent to the bishop, either.

The day before I was to meet with the bishop, I approached the Senior Pastor in his office. I remember being so calm, despite everything. I told him of the letter I had received. He stated he had heard a letter was sent but that he had not seen it. Given the way the church operated and what had been written to me from the bishop's assistant saying that he as the pastor had requested my removal along with the SPRC, I found this hard to believe. I told him so.

I also said to him that I knew he knew my history with the bishop. He nodded in agreement. I said I knew he and I were in agreement that this appointment was not handled well or even with good intention by the bishop. He again nodded. I said I knew he knew all the work I was now doing with the WCA, and that the bishop was hostile to it, so that this complaint letter from the church was giving the bishop opportunity to squelch me. He nodded. I said I knew that he knew that my support of Rev. Jisun Kwak was also being held against me, even though we knew she had done nothing wrong. He nodded again in agreement, still giving no words. I said I knew he knew that I was just this very week settling on and moving into a new home so that I could be near this satellite church plant appointment. He again nodded. I said, "You know this is an exhausting, stressful endeavor, right?" He agreed. I said I knew he knew that my goal was simply to grow the satellite church plant into a relevant ministry that would attract the Woolwich Township community. He nodded again.

I then said very specifically, "So rather than figuring out some way we could work this out, you have now chosen to handle me this way without any warning and without even acknowledging that you are leading it?" He stayed silent. I did not. I said, "Shame on you. What is meant for evil, God will use for good." I rose and departed, shaking the dust off my feet.

When I met with Bishop Schol, my district superintendent and the bishop's executive assistant were present. I brought Rev. Dan Amey with me to be my advocate. Dan is a long-term and well-respected traditional clergy known by the bishop.

The meeting began with the bishop informing me of all the communications he had received of support for me. He stated that in just a couple of days he had received somewhere between 14 and 20 such communications. A significant number of those were later sent to me by their writers and/or their phone calls to the bishop's office were detailed to me. The bishop said he also had received communication that was not supportive of me but would not elaborate or show me such emails. He said all would be kept in my file.

He then asked me to share all that had happened. When I finished, he said, "I believe you, Beth." He then asked me what I would like to do.

I told him that I, too, did not want to stay at the church. I told him my mental health was at stake. I told him my first preference would be to take the satellite church plant as a separate, standalone church or one yoked to another and move it forward. It would take resources to do that, but otherwise the church was going to collapse as the main church had already pulled the vast majority of its resourcing from the campus. I still believed, however, that we had begun attracting the right leadership to move the church forward. I still believe that to this day. Bishop Schol committed to discussing this option with the Senior Pastor at Sharptown, but also stated that I should not be hopeful this would happen.

Our meeting lasted just over two hours. I point this out as I was surprised that I would be allotted this much of the bishop's time. Clearly the situation was deemed important.

I do believe the bishop could have made what I proposed happen, but he was again not supportive. I knew I was being handled as someone who could cause problems and who was already viewed by the bishop as a problem, given all I had experienced through him, the cabinet, the Board of Ordained Ministry, and my being President of the Greater New Jersey Chapter of the WCA.

Bishop Schol, I am certain, recognized that the mishandling of the previous Associate Pastor being moved from the church without proper consultation and my subsequent appointment to it was a violation of the Book of Discipline, and could be seen as bumbled at best and as retaliation toward me and the church at worst. Retaliation toward me for my traditional ministry and relationship with Rev. Dr. Jisun Kwak, and against the church for their public questioning and embarrassing of Bishop Schol regarding his stance and proposed changes to the Book of Discipline regarding matters of human sexuality. Yet, within the United Methodist polity and operating system, there is no real recourse for me or anyone else who suffers such injustices. Schol did not have to do a thing. While violating UMC policy on handling appointments and undermining the ministry of another pastor is a chargeable offense for bishops according to the United Methodist Church, BOD ¶ 2702.1(f), the repercussions for filing a charge outweigh the reward for many. The emotional toll, energy and time involved (years) are great. The chances of winning case when the deck is stacked against you are great. Even when you do win, there is no restitution for you or corrective penalty for the bishop worth your efforts. And if you win, you still are subject to the same bishop unless you leave your conference or the denomination entirely.

I suspect that what Schol had not anticipated was finding out that a roughly four hundred thousand dollar investment by the conference's church planting and grant teams had been poorly managed by both the conference and the church. Although personally painful as I had been handed the reigns of an empty cart with the wheels already falling off, I learned much from seeing the fruits of such management. In my later roles within WCA leadership, I became a very vocal advocate that efforts for church planting should be initiated by the local church rather than a conference team so that responsible ownership would be better fostered. I also have been adamant that there needs to be much more accountability required for any conference funds given to a local church for church-planting. Finally, as with other denominations, I believe raising a substantial amount of local own funds should be required before conference funds are given. That church is not the first church I have seen simply handed money by the conference with minimal accountability.

Bishop Schol told me he could give me another appointment, but it would be far away from where I live. My other choice was to take an unpaid leave of absence until the next appointment season and then I would receive a new appointment. I told him I wanted an appointment and I wanted the inappropriate behavior to me from the church leadership to be addressed.

Within a day I received this follow-up email:

> **From:** *Bishop John Schol <bishopjohnschol@gnjumc.org>*
>
> **Date:** *November 1, 2018 at 11:51:18 PM EDT*
>
> **To:** *Beth*
>
> **Cc:** *Nicola Mulligan <nmulligan@gnjumc.org>, Glenn Conaway <gconaway@gnjumc.org>*

Subject: Follow up from meeting and phone call

Good evening Beth,

Thank you for meeting with me on Wednesday and your phone call today for clarification. I am grateful for you and your gifts and your desire to improve. I have heard from several people at Sharptown North of how you have helped them and their families. They spoke well of you. I have also heard from others that you have not led well in some instances. I know you encountered some very difficult and unresolved issues.

I affirm your ability to move projects forward, connect with a variety of people, engage with passion and that you have strong leadership skills and potential. I also have concerns about your pacesetting and commanding style at times and the need to grow in emotional intelligence. I offer the upcoming Bishop's Convocation as an opportunity to start understanding emotional intelligence.

In a phone message you left for me, you asked for the names of the people who have emailed me. I have decided that I will not be sharing them with you, ___ or the SPRC. These are emails written to me. I think you can bring down the anxiety of others by lowering your anxiety. I recognize this is difficult at this time but has we talked about, you leadership is key to help the mission and ministry move forward.

I committed yesterday, Wednesday to talk with ___ about your being the senior pastor of ___ and seeing ___ as a standalone new faith community. ___ spent time considering this idea but he and I agreed that it would not be healthy for the overall ministry of ___ church. I do not believe it would be good for you to continue in the same community.

I also asked ___ to have the church continue your salary and benefits through December 31, 2018. He will talk with his leadership about this.

As I mentioned in our meeting, I am prepared to appoint you to a new appointment. You will be able to continue to live in your home although it will be a significant commute.. You will receive an appointment letter on Friday for this appointment which will begin on November 26, 2018.. As is our practice, you will have 24 hours to indicate that you would like to move forward or ask for reconsideration. Because we do not have any other appointments at this time, the only other option is to request a leave of absence. We will also consider you for other appointments during the upcoming appointment season. If you were to receive a new appointment, it would begin July 1, 2019.

Your final Sunday with ____ will be November 11, 2018.

The salary and benefits for the new appointment will be outlined in the appointment letter you will receive on Friday. As you have questions about the appointment or next steps, you are welcome to contact me.

I know this is a difficult time for you and your family. My prayers continue with you during this time of transition.

Blessings

John

Bishop John Schol

His "pace-setting" comment stung in that I had been in a situation where the SPRC and senior pastor insisted I do something quickly, criticized me for not doing enough, and, although I knew they really did not want me to do anything, I had made bold moves to lead ministry despite them. I was going to be criticized for not making bold moves as well. In fact, the district superintendent had already said I made a mistake by not going in and taking more charge. So, although I like to learn from mistakes, this was not a valid criticism given the situation. I do agree that relationship-building is the first and most important part of one's initial ministry with a congregation. But with that church, there was a strong force against that being possible with critical people in its leadership.

More troubling, however, was the bishop's statement regarding my commanding style and need for growth in emotional intelligence. This is classic lingo used against strong female leaders. They are broad statements that can be interpreted as helpful, but in the end are used to take power and influence away from women. Men are rarely saddled with complaints about their "commanding style at times," and while emotional intelligence is something that we all need to grow in, it is an easy, lingo-du-jour-shot to be thrown at assertive female leadership. Emotional intelligence was also the theme of his upcoming convocation so it was an easy area to mention and pitch as a growing edge.

It was clear to me that he had not and would not address the distressing and demeaning behavior and actions the church leadership had exhibited toward me, but instead was mapping a course that would appease them and not jeopardize their significant apportionment contributions to the conference.

After meeting with the bishop on October 31, 2018, I boarded a plane for Atlanta on Nov. 1st to attend as a delegate the First Global Assembly of the Wesleyan Covenant Association and their third

Global Gathering. It was a bit surreal, as I was literally voting on efforts for the WCA to move forward to uphold the traditional theology and the Book of Discipline of the UMC, and having a testimonial video[3] about me being shown at the "unashamed" Global Gathering while at the same time dealing with my own dismissal from local ministry leadership.

Within 24 hours I was told of an appointment to two small, struggling churches over an hour away. I sent this response:

> *On Nov 3, 2018, at 7:45 AM, Beth Caulfield wrote:*
>
> *Hi John,*
>
> *I just left you a voicemail. I am at this point most interested in pursuing some kind of study and renewal leave rather than accepting the appointment that was sent to me yesterday. I think I can better serve the Church by recharging my health and spending some time preparing myself for my next appointment/ ministry through study and reflection.*
>
> *Thank you for ensuring my current salary and benefits through December.*
>
> *Please advise next steps.*
>
> *Beth*

The response:

> *Hi Beth,*
>
> *Paragraph 351 is the paragraph about sabbaticals. You must be a full member or associate member to go on sabbatical. The only leaves available for you are voluntary leave of absence in*

paragraph 353 which can be personal, family and transitional. It sounds as though you are looking to take time away for a period of time. This can be achieve under voluntary leave. I would ensure salary and benefits through the end of the year as in the appointment change.

Keep the faith!

John

Bishop John Schol

This meshing of events felt even more dramatic as there were some problems with emails from and to Bishop Schol. I literally was walking out of the WCA Legislative Assembly session repeatedly to receive phone calls from his assistant who was trying to ensure I was receiving appointment and other information from him. This was very stressful as I experienced the resolution that my then local ministry efforts were coming to an end as well as my future paychecks.

Having no real choice, I opted to take the unpaid leave of absence beginning January 1, 2019. The bishop gave me instruction on how to handle it with the Board of Ordained Ministry and with the congregation. I followed his instruction. I was to announce my leave to the congregation on Sunday, November 4th, and Sunday, November 11th would be my last day.

I was sitting in the Atlanta airport waiting to board my flight back home late Saturday night, polishing my sermon and writing my words for announcing my leave of absence, when my phone rang. It was roughly 9pm. It was the Senior Pastor calling. The first I had heard from him since I spoke and he refused to speak in his office about all that was happening. He simply asked if I needed anything. This time I was speechless. I did not know what he meant nor why he was reaching out. The call lasted less than a minute.

The next morning there were a couple of Staff Parish Relations Committee members who attended the worship service, including its chair. Neither spoke to me, they just sat in the back. Neither the Senior Pastor nor any other main campus leadership attended.

At the end of the service I read out the following:

> I have requested and plan to take a leave from serving in ministry in the United Methodist Church here in Greater New Jersey for renewal and study. I will be taking this leave for several months, up to a year. My last Sunday with you will be November 11. In The United Methodist System, pastors are appointed by the bishop. My bishop, John Schol and I along with the district superintendent have been in conversation about this and together we believe it is the right step for me and my ministry and the church. This congregation has meant a great deal to me and I have learned much at Sharptown. I have also grown and learned from serving on _____'s staff. I will look back on my short time with you and recognize how valuable this time has been to shape and form me as a leader. During the next months I will be caring for my physical, emotional and spiritual health and that of my family. I will spend time reflecting on my learnings from my time at _____ and how I can apply them to my next ministry. I ask for your prayers in this continued work. Thank you for your support and

work with me. You all have been a blessing to me more than you will ever know. I celebrate much about our time together and the relationships that have been built. While this announcement is challenging to make and hear, I am confident it is the Lord's leading at this time.

You could have heard a pin drop as I read it. Then there were gasps, shaking of heads, and also tears. But no one from SPRC did anything. I just stood there, waiting for some kind of announcement or acknowledgement or something that is normally done in these situations by the church leadership. So did the congregation. When it became clear that there was no plan for anything to be said, our praise band leader, himself in shock, stepped forward and led the congregation in prayer for me. We then dismissed.

My nine-year old daughter, who had not been in the worship service but instead with the children's program and therefore did not hear my words, saw as people left upset that something was wrong. She asked, "Mommy, what's happening?" My husband and I just led her to the car in silence.

Later that day, the bishop called me and asked how things had gone. I told him that there had been no pastor present and no SPRC comments to me or the congregation and that our worship leader had done the right thing. His response was "thank God for that Worship Leader."

In the midst of this entire situation there were several phone calls from Bishop Schol. I will say that I knew I was being carefully handled and that pressure was being applied to speed along this process of getting my agreement to go on leave. Trying to protect myself, I asked him for something in writing regarding receiving a new appointment for the following July. I know I asked for clarification of his plans for me more than once. At one point, on the phone, the bishop said to me, "Beth, if you are receiving advice from someone with a legal mind on this matter, it is not going to go well for you." Another threat.

On my last Sunday, November 11th, the district superintendent, the senior pastor, the Director of Ministries, and the SPRC chair and other Main campus leaders were all present for the service at the satellite church plant. There was a small celebration, gifts, cards, and a couple of speeches on my behalf from satellite church plant members. I was proud of my sermon; I felt God's grace in preparing its content and tone. After I preached, the district superintendent led a prayer and told the congregation that there would be more to come regarding what would be happening with the church.

I remember the Senior Pastor coming up to me and forcefully hugging me as people were dismissing themselves. If he said anything, I do not remember what it was. The hug shocked me and felt like one last assault. My husband later said that if he had seen it, he might have punched the Senior Pastor. Anyone who knows my gentle husband knows that something like that is a big deal for him to say. We were all so very hurt.

I look back on the sixteen months I spent in that appointment with feelings of satisfaction in ministry well done, ministry learning experiences, and some cherished relationships built that continue, but also with tears of agony over the cruel, petty, and unfair treatments I received from much of the church's staff and leadership team, including its pastors. I felt no real assistance was available or offered to me from a bishop and cabinet that had, in effect, thrown me away and a GCOSROW that was at best disinterested.

SUNSHINE THROUGH THE CLOUDS

NEXT STEPS WORKING GROUP

I was emotionally damaged and exhausted for quite a while from the combination of the conference and then Sharptown experiences. But God's grace and mercy abound. I am astounded at His ways and timing which are always there for healing me. God never leaves me alone nor forsakes me. Many friends rallied around me and my family. Even though so much inside me wanted to just give up and see myself as a colossal ministry failure, God and the angels he sent to me, including my family, would not let me wallow in such misery and lies.

On October 31st, the same day I had met with the bishop about the letter he had received from the church requesting I be removed from them, I received a call from Rev. Keith Boyette, President of the Wesleyan Covenant Association. He asked if I would be part of a new and highly confidential Next Steps Working Group.

The group was being tasked with drafting a Book of Doctrines and Disciplines for a new Methodist denomination. Approval for formation of the group was to be voted on at the Legislative Assembly that I was attending in Atlanta, just two days later. I prayed and said yes. In Atlanta the group's formation was approved by the legislative body, but the names of its participants were withheld. All that people knew was that we were a group of only sixteen diverse voices from across the connection.

We held our first meeting on November 12th in Reynoldsburg, Ohio, at the taskforce's leader's home church, Reynoldsburg UMC. The meeting began at 1pm that day and ended on November 14th at noon. This meant that I was on a very early 6am flight out of Philadelphia to Columbus, Ohio, less than twenty-four hours after saying goodbye to Sharptown. Again, that is God's timing. My ministry changed course, but it did not skip a beat.

The taskforce was led by the Global WCA Council Chair Rev. Dr. Jeff Greenway. Keith and Rev. Walter Fenton were also present to guide our proceedings. Many of the rest of us had never met as we were local church pastors, laity, district superintendents, deacons, and academics from across the connection. We were tasked to have a draft document completed by mid-February 2019. This would be an extraordinary accomplishment if achieved.

That initial meeting, we worked each of the first days up until 9pm as a group and some worked even later. We then met weekly for one hour (only) via video conference up until Christmas week. I recall that we did take that week off. In addition to those weekly meetings, we were all involved in subtask groups and held our own meetings, phone calls, and emails. We met as a group again in Atlanta, January 7-9, 2019, with a schedule that went into the night just as it had in Ohio. We then continued meeting through February 11th, when our draft was done.

This time and work were some of the most exhilarating I have had in ministry. First, I was introduced to and worked with a group of extraordinary leaders who were dedicated to traditional Methodism in their own faith. Every one of us was on the same page in terms of our Wesleyan understanding of the primacy of

Scripture, the lordship of Jesus Christ and his transforming power, and the Holy Spirit's importance in guiding us as the foundation for our faith.

We were consistent in our understanding that the United Methodist Church no longer holds to the basic principles of traditional Methodist faith nor do its leaders intend to comply with a Book of Discipline that supports them. We were all in agreement that the issues that divide the United Methodist Church are truly around those concerns.

Progressives define the issue as one of disagreement over human sexuality and full inclusion of LGBTQIA identifying people within the church. Their concerns for social justice, especially around that issue, seem to usually trump all other faith concerns. There is a strongly held belief that unless churches are willing to perform same-sex weddings and ordain actively practicing homosexuals, they are being unjust and exclusive to people.

We all recognized the LGBTQIA concerns to only be a present- ing symptom of a deeper disagreement. Recently one progressive leader stated that the Bible "is a human-written document, proba- bly inspired by an encounter with the divine."[1] That statement is a good indicator of our disagreement with progressives. We believe that the Bible is the Word of God for the people of God and is inter- preted through over two thousand years of tradition along with reason and experience. Through that lens, the Bible is clear on its definition of sexual sin, which includes homosexuality. It is also clear on the divinity, resurrection, and transforming power of Jesus Christ, which are also often called into question by progressives within the United Methodist Church.

It was such a breath of fresh air to not even have to discuss those issues. That we were all on the same page was a given. We had immediate trust and ease with one another as we understood that we all had the same aspiration: to bring traditional Wesleyanism as an expression of Christianity back to Methodism, whether through revitalization of the United Methodist Church or by creating a new denomination.

There also was agreement that the United Methodist Church had become an ineffective, bureaucratic institution that had lost its emphasis on its primary mission of spreading the Gospel and making disciples. The UMC system had also grown to include loopholes that were being exploited by corrupt forces that are unjustly robbing the faithful of resources and opportunity to do good ministry for the Lord. There was much discussion around that common understanding as we learned from one another's experience.

Our work was not centered on revising the current UMC Book of Discipline. Our work was focused on building a simple-to-understand document that contained fresh ways for guiding a modern church into Wesleyan faith. We built on new ideas, Wesleyan doctrine exercised in the past, lessons learned from UMC experience, and from other traditions.

The subcommittee I worked on was "Deployment," which focused on the system of moving clergy to churches in the best ways that would best match the growing gifts and graces of the clergy with the needs of the local church and the greater denomination. We started with a blank slate and held robust discussion regarding call systems, appointment systems, and hybrid models of deployment. We talked much about the guaranteed appointment policy of the UMC and how to best achieve the original intent of that policy, which was to ensure equal opportunity and fair treatment of women and minority clergy within the deployment system.

Out of our work grew a model of deployment that offers more input from the local church and clergy. We created a Hosier Rule, inspired by the NFL's Rooney Rule that requires interview slates to include at least one female and one minority candidate. I decided to contact the NFL and connected through their leadership with the civil rights attorney Cyrus Mehri, who along with attorney Johnnie Cochran created the infamous Rooney Rule. I picked Cyrus's brain extensively and learned from his firm, Working Ideal, a consulting company that provides thought leadership on diversity, equity, and inclusion.

I also drafted and championed the inclusion of a Just Ministries Commission that will challenge, lead, and equip the people of the Global Methodist Church to become interculturally competent to share the gospel and grow disciples of all people with gracious confidence, and to ensure equal and just opportunities at all levels of clergy and lay leadership for such ministry. The commission would function as an advocate with and on behalf of women ministry leaders, ministry leaders with disabilities, and anyone serving in cross-cultural settings, individually and collectively within the Global Methodist Church. My initial draft was embraced and later perfected by first the Next Steps Working Group and then the WCA Global Council.

Those Next Step colleagues remain my friends and were supportive of me during a time that I had been so deflated by the United Methodist Church.

REV. DR. JISUN KWAK'S TRIAL

The UMC trial process can be confusing. The first concept to comprehend is that the denomination's Judicial Council does NOT conduct our clergy trials. There is a different process outlined by our Book of Discipline and that is the process that Jisun was subjected to. It is outlined from ¶2707 - ¶2714.[2]

In short, the Bishop of the Annual Conference where the complaint is filed selects the presiding officer for the trial. So, in Jisun's case, Schol chose a retired bishop from another conference per ¶2713.2. When the clergy is tried, the district superintendents provide the pool of 35 jurors who are to be clergy in full connection (ordained) in that annual conference. (¶2713.3). In the presence of the respondent, their counsel and the counsel for the Church, the pool is whittled down to 13 clergy, (¶2709.2). So, to be clear, Bishop Schol chose the judge (another bishop), and Schol's cabinet (de facto him), chose the jury pool exclusively from a group of people who report to them for a trial that was being held based on a complaint that was also filed by the cabinet (de facto Schol). This was all legal under the UMC process. As this Greater New Jersey application of the legalities of the process demonstrates, conflict of interest opportunities are made legal through naïve regulations that need to be rectified.

The trial took place February 5-7, 2019. Jisun's advocacy team consisted of four retired elders who serve as part of the Association in Advocacy, which helps clergy and churches resolve disputes. They included Rev. Bob Costello, Rev. Scott Campbell, Rev. Elizabeth (Betzy) Mowry, Rev. Peter Millow, and Rev. Jerry Eckert. Not being experienced in these matters, I was not an official member of Jisun's advocacy team. It also would have been too dangerous for me given Bishop Schol's retaliatory patterns toward anything to do with her. However, I did give significant input and worked with Jisun throughout the over two and a half years they prepared for trial.

When it was time for the trial, I made hotel reservations for the team. I also independently decided to contact Rev. Laura Blauvelt of the Baltimore Washington Conference. I established a relationship with her and invited her to the trial. Laura had at one time been a cabinet member (district superintendent) of the Baltimore Washington Conference, had her own run-ins with Schol, and was aware of other female and minority clergy who had undergone similar unjust treatment by him. Laura accepted the invitation and was also prepared to testify if necessary. This began what many would see as an unlikely friendship. I am a leader in the WCA, Laura at that time was a leader in the Reconciling Ministries Network, serving on their National Board. Again, the Reconciling Ministries Network is an organization seeking the inclusion of people of all sexual orientations and gender identities in both the policy and practices of United Methodist Church, including ordaining practicing homosexuals and marrying LGBTQ couples.[3] Despite our theological differences, we hit it off instantly and the friendship has lasted.

The bishop did not officially attend the trial, but did make his presence known. He showed up at the beginning, saying that he "just came to say hello," and to open the day. He stayed outside the trial meeting room for quite some time, at least during the first day, even though the location of the trial was more than thirty minutes from the conference office and from his own residence. He had staff members in the courtroom who were not part of the trial, including his executive assistant, the Director of Connectional Ministries, and the DCM's wife. His staff were clearly communicating with him the play by play of all that was transpiring and reporting who was there, as they were texting during the trial and making phone calls during breaks. These were additional abusive pressures for anyone attending or involved in the trial to navigate. He was clearly very invested in the trial's outcome, having spent countless staff hours preparing for it and spending over $79,000 of church money on it.[4]

I attended the entire trial, sitting directly behind Jisun's team. While there was a good contingent of faithful supporters that I know Jisun is incredibly grateful for, I personally was saddened to see how many did not attend the trial given the amount of support she received when she ran for bishop and was endorsed by 65% of the conference. Some did not attend out of fear of retribution from Schol. Others, sad to say, were being more political in their choice not to attend. Others had believed the lies spread about her and no longer supported her.

The entire event was an incredibly tense and draining experience for all involved. It certainly was for me. It lasted three days and included two late night court sessions, extending to nearly 9pm. Jisun and her team worked much later into the night after the sessions ended. On the last day, the jury went out to deliberate before lunch and the verdict was not announced until past dinner time.

I was amazed at how well my friend stood up to scrutiny on the stand and to misrepresentation of the facts. The rigor in which she and her team had previously prepared and continued to do so throughout the trial was extensive. Their work paid off, despite a deck that was strongly stacked against them. I was incredibly impressed by Jisun's advocacy team's performance, especially Rev. Bob Costello. I also applaud all who testified in her defense. Great bravery was shown, especially by currently serving clergy.

During the trial, Rev. Costello told the jury, "This has been perhaps the greatest example of prosecution overreacting and overreaching in my 54 years of ministry in the United Methodist Church."[5] Yet, despite Schol's considerable control and abuse of power over the process, at the conclusion of the trial, Jisun was "acquitted" or "found not guilty" on all three charges and all eight counts.[6] I find this result especially poignant in demonstrating Jisun's clearly unjust treatment by Schol and his cabinet. Still, given how Bishop Schol and his cabinet operate, I applaud those jurors' courage to vote as they did. I also believe I witnessed God vindicating the righteous.

As recorded by UM News, Jisun "said she feels deep gratitude to fellow clergy, who at great sacrifice, proclaimed her innocence. 'I felt a holy duty and obligation to make justice served,' she said. 'And here I am. Again, I am so thankful for God's caring hands.'"[7]

Here are photos taken at the end of the trial. You can see the elation and also exhaustion of the team. I was so happy for all.

At the conclusion of Jisun's trial. A relieved and happy, but exhausted group.

GRACE?

Schol gave Jisun a new appointment at a larger church, but her pay remained at the minimum level required of a clergy with her years of service. The previous pastor of the church had been paid more, but the conference set hers at the minimum salary level. The church, of course, had no reason to disagree with the lower amount of salary from the conference. I talk more about these realities in the chapter "A Word About Pay."

Yet even after the trial, Schol continued to slander Jisun's name and undermine her ministry and health. She still is not fully recovered in many ways. The day after the trial, Conference Communications issued the following statement. Notice it is NOT an apology. Nor to this day has one ever been given by him to Jisun:

> By a jury of her peers, the Rev. Dr. Jisun Kwak was found not guilty of three charges: immorality, undermining the ministry of another clergy person and disobedience to the order and discipline of the church.
>
> The cabinet filed a complaint against Rev. Kwak in June of 2016. The United Methodist Church has processes when charges are made against a clergy person and the trial was the result of a two and a half year process.
>
> Bishop John Schol is grateful for all of those who participated in the trial. "Our system works because people give of their time, wisdom and experience," said Schol. "While these experiences are very difficult for everyone, I will work toward healing and reconciliation among those involved and within the conference."
>
> "I recognize the pain for everyone involved. It will be my commitment to create opportunities for healing and reconciliation. I have offered to meet with Rev. Kwak to hear what she needs moving forward."[8]

In reality, however, according to Jisun, Schol did not offer to meet with her when the above notice went out. He did not do so for more than a year, and then it was only done after a new Korean District Superintendent encouraged him to meet with her.

An FAQ document about the trial was released the following week. In it, although I am not a lawyer or expert, I believe Bishop Schol portrayed Jisun in a false light, a civil offense in the state of New Jersey. The way much of the FAQ is worded makes Jisun sound sneaky at best and twists the events of the trial. The wording used disseminates a sense of controversy over the trial results. Just one of several offending statements in the document given by Schol to the entire conference and available online is as follows:

> **Was Rev. Kwak acquitted of all charges, "I heard the jury believed she was guilty of one charge."**
>
> Rev. Kwak was acquitted of all charges. The jury returned a majority vote to convict on a count of immorality, but the presiding bishop ruled the jury did not have enough votes to convict.

The inclusion and wording of both the question and answer above gives the impression that the trial's result was not supported by the jury's decisions, that some injustice in not convicting Jisun may have occurred. Again, the truth is that Jisun was acquitted of all charges and specifications/counts according to The Book of Discipline requirements found in ¶2711.2.[9] The judge ruled completely in line with the Book of Discipline.

The document is riddled with other statements that raise doubt about Jisun. I share the entire document here for your conclusion. Notice it is signed by Bishop Schol and raises many questions about Jisun's ministry and integrity by cleverly using the appearance that the document was only generated as a good-faith effort to respond to much concern, and that to respond appropriately requires Schol to share carefully chosen and worded details so that he can justify the conference's actions against Jisun. Like his previous statement, this document offers no apology.

Dear Clergy Colleagues,

As most of you are aware, GNJ had a church trial recently and Rev. Jisun Kwak was acquitted of all charges. Our Book of Discipline describes trials as a means of last resort and all efforts were made to avert a trial. Trials are a fundamental right of clergy within the church.

I invite each of you to remain prayerful and to assist in the healing process. The support and care of individuals and our GNJ mission should always be of utmost importance.

In my letter to you following the trial, I indicated that conversation is appropriate to help clarify matters and begin the healing process. Some of you have asked for more clarification about things you are wondering, reading and hearing.

To provide clarity, below is a response to some of the questions. I hope that we can move forward together to continue God's call for us to make disciples of Christ for the transformation of the world.

Why did it take more than 2 ½ years to complete the process?

This was a complex case that involved five bishops, five lawyers, two counsels for the church, four just resolution conferences, a suspension, two requests to the Judicial Council, investigation into four different bank accounts, two votes by the board of ordained ministry, two pretrial hearings, more than 1,500 pages of material, 14 motions to dismiss the case, a review of four charges and 23 counts by the committee on investigation, three charges and six counts sent for trial, and a three-day trial. In all, I estimate well over 2,000 human hours were invested for a fair process and resolution. The process and work on the case was led and carried out by lay and clergy volunteers and each step of the process was guided by prayer, done with great care and included significant research and deliberation.

It is most unfortunate that the case took so long, particularly for Rev. Kwak. Our volunteers dedicated a significant amount of their time as well. Time into a matter like this is essential to clergy rights and to our ministry and mission together.

How much did the trial cost GNJ?

The trial and the activities leading up to the trial cost GNJ $79,128. This can be divided into three main categories.

1. Investigation – The committee on investigation is a group of laity and clergy elected by the clergy session that acts as a grand jury. They review evidence, call witnesses and deliberate to determine if there is evidence of wrongdoing. The Book of Discipline permits the committee on investigation to hire an attorney to work with the committee. The committee did hire a lawyer, a chancellor from another conference, who worked with the committee over a year-long process. Costs also include a court reporter for a hearing in which witnesses testified. The total cost for the year long process was $34,754.

2. Preparation for and conducting of the trial – These costs involve a year-long investigation by the counsel for the church, an auditor's review of several bank accounts controlled by Rev. Kwak, the cost of a bishop from outside of GNJ to preside over the trial, accommodations and meals for the jurors and other officers of the court, a court reporter and legal fees. $42,424.
3. Miscellaneous administrative costs - $1,950.

The funds for the process came from the reserves from three different budget years. The funding was not taken from any program spending. Nor did our reserves slip below annual conference policy.

How does this compare to the cost of trials in other conferences?

Trials generally cost a minimum of $50,000 and can be more than $200,000. These costs are an important part of any fair judicial process, ensuring effective due diligence, guidance and judicial fairness to all parties involved.

The following are quotes and questions resulting from information about the trial including statements made on social media.

What was Bishop Schol's involvement in the trial?

A bishop from outside the conference, Bishop Alfred Gwinn presided during the trial. The resident bishop, a bishop from the conference where the trial is conducted, is only asked to open the trial with prayer. It is not recommended for the resident bishop to testify or even attend the trial so that the bishop can continue to lead following the trial. My goal is to continue to lead GNJ forward as we seek to transform the world by making disciples and transforming the world.

There was "a certain degree of racism and chauvinism (in this case) and self-righteousness has no place in the board of ordained ministry."

The board of ordained ministry and others who led the process engaged with integrity, sensitivity, professionalism and concern for everyone involved. The board of ordained ministry had to make two decisions: one, whether to suspend Rev. Kwak and the second, whether to place Rev. Kwak on involuntary leave of absence.

The board suspended Rev. Kwak with full pay and benefits because potential evidence was being deleted from the GNJ server and clergy on her district raised important concerns about Rev. Kwak's leadership. The suspension provided an opportunity to research these concerns.

The board also voted to place Rev. Kwak on involuntary leave after a fair process hearing based on written evidence. Rev. Kwak reserved her right not to talk about the allegations and evidence or offer a defense prior to a trial so that the case would be heard by a jury of her clergy peers.

This was an "overreach" by those responsible for this case.

This claim is in relationship to the number of charges and counts made by the counsel for the church.

Over a year-long investigation, the counsel for the church with support from the conference chancellor, reviewed hundreds of emails, conducted or supervised more than 20 interviews with individuals with information about the case, researched four different bank accounts controlled by Rev. Kwak, reviewed several immigration issues handled by Rev. Kwak and researched several other issues. The counsel for the church referred four charges and 23 counts. This is a lot. A count is an instance in which there is evidence that a disciplinary matter had been violated. A number of the counts sent to the committee on investigation were related to a separate administrative complaint and not handled through judicial procedures. The committee referred three of the four charges for trial and five of the counts. The committee on investigation also added an additional count of immorality based on their own investigation.

In six other counts, it was recommended that GNJ develop clearly delineated policies to govern the conduct of superintendents. These recommendations have been referred to the council of finance and administration for their review and decision.

In summary, the committee reviewed four charges and 23 counts. Based on the committee's hearing and deliberations, it sent three charges and six counts for trial and requested that policies be developed based on administrative issues arising from this case.

Was Rev. Kwak acquitted of all charges, "I heard the jury believed she was guilty of one charge."

Rev. Kwak was acquitted of all charges. The jury returned a majority vote to convict on a count of immorality, but the presiding bishop ruled the jury did not have enough votes to convict.

Those responsible for this case "played a game of gotcha."

The phrase, "gotcha" refers to the defense's argument of entrapment in relationship to a meeting held in early June of 2016. The meeting was called to understand both the 2010 complaint filed against her and the just resolution that she, Bishop Devadhar and the complainant agreed to. It was not called to trap Rev. Kwak.

This was a "hit job" by the person who filed the 2010 complaint.

This phrase is referring to the individual who filed the 2010 complaint which resulted in a just resolution. The 2010 complainant sent me a letter in early May of 2016 alleging that the 2010 just resolution had not been completed and that new documents emerged in 2016 indicating the 2010 issues were more serious than she originally understood. I communicated several times with the complainant throughout the process who was deeply concerned about how the church handled and oversaw the 2010 just resolution and how she and her mother were harmed. I never felt the 2010 complainant sought revenge or to hurt anyone. She wanted the matter addressed. In fact, the complainant had been satisfied with the original just resolution in 2010. When she learned the just resolution was not fulfilled, and that the matter was far worse than she realized in 2010, she sought the church's help in resolving the matter.

The jury prayerfully and wisely weighed the evidence. I am grateful for their service. They served the church well. I am grateful for the defense team and their service to Rev. Kwak and the church. A rigorous defense serves the church and process well. Rev. Kwak was acquitted by a jury of her peers and is an elder in good standing in the church. I am also grateful for those who felt compelled to bring and advance these charges on behalf of the church. They acted out of their conviction and their commitment to the church and to our clergy covenant. They too served the church well. Thank you.

Ephesians 4:32

Be kind to one another, tender-hearted, forgiving each other, just as God in Christ also forgave you.

I pray that we all can find forgiveness, healing and reconciliation. It is what the church and world needs within the body of Christ and what Christ has called us to. I call each of you to respectful conversation and not to use words that harm but heal.

I have deep faith and belief in God and in our clergy. In very challenging times, you continue to serve faithfully and seek to do the right thing. Thank you for your leadership, integrity and service to the church and the world. Let's continue to serve together to be hope and healing in a challenging season.

Keep the faith!

John

John Schol, Bishop

United Methodists of Greater New Jersey[10]

The false light portrayal of Jisun by Schol escalated further. In the chapter "March 2019 Greater New Jersey Special Annual Conference," I detail happenings with its announcement of a "Way Forward" committee. But that conference was also called in part to encourage Greater New Jersey to quickly adopt new Committee on Finance and Administration policies developed by CF&A and the cabinet "based on recommendations from the Committee on Investigations after review of the financial management issues in the recent 2019 clergy trial."[11] The implication was that Jisun had somehow wrongly gotten away with being acquitted because the conference was negligent in not having such policies in place. When the proposed new policies were presented to the Conference, there were many questions asked, including if other Conferences had such policies. No clear answer was ever given. The body did not vote to pass the policies suggested and instead they were deferred to the May 2017 Annual Conference. From there they were lost, and never followed up on or passed as legislation. In other words, they were not pushed as important once their utility for making public implications about Jisun was realized.

Additionally, that March session was called to amend the conference budget to "resolve a complaint resolution" for $110,000. The money was the amount calculated to have been given either monetarily or in gifts by the Patchins to Jisun or to the churches that Jisun served for her benefit over the years. During this debate, Schol's portrayal of Jisun was most misleading. When the proposed payoff was called into question from the floor, Bishop Schol used it as an opportunity to give lengthy unsubstantiated claims against Jisun that, again, portrayed her poorly in front of her colleagues and lay people she was called to lead. The following is a transcript of a recording of what transpired that day.

Bob Costello: I would like to make a motion to amend this budget that was presented to us by deleting $110,000 and if I have a second, I would be happy to speak to that.

Bishop Schol: There is a Second

Bob Costello: What we are attempting to do here today, between you and me we shouldn't do in my opinion, we had too many years getting ready for trial in our conference … Bishop Schol and I agree on one thing that it ought to be over and we should be moving on. I have complete disagreement with what we are doing here today with this money. As we went through the trial, those of you who were there, know there was information submitted whereby what happened is a gentleman named, John Patchin, and his wife Julie were friendly with Rev. Jisun Kwak and her daughter Lydia. The time came when they became generous to her and gave gifts to her, their daughter Carol Neuman who is dentist in MA, and her husband also dentist, wrote letters to Bishop Devadhar to complain. The combination of Bishop Devadhar, Lyn Caterson (conference chancellor) and Jisun tried to resolve the thing by writing some letters to have Jisun begin to repay the money. We need to recognize that it was never promised to Carol Neuman to repay anything. She's owed nothing. Jisun began to pay John Patchin back and he got upset. He tore up the check. During the trial we brought her old checks, check registers, and check books that showed that he rejected that. There is no contract between Jisun and John Patchin. There is no contract between conference and John Patchin...

She is basically saying the United Methodist church has to pay her back. But she is owed absolutely nothing. She couldn't even come to the trial and show up. She's never shown up. I am the one who said she has made a hit and run. Two bishops, two sets of letters, we are on the track again. It's time for us to recognize that our bishops are doing their best they can, they don't owe anything to Carol Neuman. Neither does Jisun. That was the result of the trial where was found Jisun was exonerated on every single charge. We've already spent $79,200 and some dollars on that process. We don't throw good money after bad. If Carol Neuman wants to sue us, turn it over to the insurance company. Let's not turn it over to churches and burden them.

Bishop Schol: That was a speech against.

CF&A chair, Bob Dietz tried to speak. Bishop Schol said that he would have a final say later.

Bishop Schol: So folks, this is a very difficult time in the life of the church. And I often do not like to weigh in on matters like this. But I think information is important. I was not at the trial. I did not testify at the trial. I am actually sorry that you had to go into this much depth. There are two stories. One is just as Rev. Costello has shared that a family wanted to share $110,000* with a pastor. With their former pastor. And did that on their own and on their own account. And that Rev Kwak was not found guilty of any disciplinary charges. That is all fact. It also was stated that Rev Kwak attempted to pay back and that Mr. Patchin would not receive the money. This is a very complicated matter. But in 2010 as complaints were shared, that a letter written to the complainant every cent would be paid back. Later on, they became aware that none of

345

the money was paid back. What Dr Neuman shared is that a pastor became very friendly with her father and spent a lot of time with her father, an elderly gentleman 82 years old, that caused disruption in the family that the mother,

Bob Costello: Point of order, Bishop!

Bishop Schol: No, let me finish it

Bob Costello: One of the logical point of order is that it has to be accurate information. That charge was brought and Jisun was exonerated from it, and I believe you are out of order giving that speech and contradicting what happened at the trial.

Bishop Schol: All I am saying is from when I talked to both parties in this matter. I am just giving more details. That Dr Neuman says the pastor got close to her father and that created disruption in the family. The mother asked to move away from this area to Maine to get out of the situation. The father reluctantly came. It created great division in the family. And that she was looking for the money that it was said would be paid back. Two sides. Two different stories. What we are being asked to do today is to help all of this to move forward. There is no dispute that Rev Kwak was not found guilty. There is no dispute about that. And there is no dispute that she received $110,000. There is no dispute that there is a complaint that was filed in 2010. There is no dispute that Bishop Devadhar wrote that every cent will be paid back. That's where we are. Just trying to move all this off the plate so that we can move forward. It's not costing you any more apportionment money. It's all being absorbed within the budget as just described here...

Again, this played out in front of hundreds of people. The motion to amend the budget and pay the $110,000 passed. I really do not believe that most of the body who voted to authorize the payment to the complainant comprehended all that was happening.

Jisun should have sought counsel from a defamation lawyer, and I pleaded with her to do so. I even took her to an employment lawyer I was working with on a different matter for the new denomination, Cyrus Mehri. Cyrus suggested she see a defamation attorney. I tried to get her to do so right away. She was mentally exhausted, though, and did not act upon the suggestion. Also, unbeknownst to me, she had been given poor legal advice that said she had three years from the incident to rase it with the state of New Jersey. When she was healthy enough to deal with filing a suit in the Spring of 2021 and began to pursue the matter, she was told the legal time limit for filing a lawsuit had expired.

ST. LOUIS

Two weeks later we were in St. Louis for the 2019 Special Session of the UMC General Conference. The purpose was to act on a report from the Commission on a Way Forward, authorized to examine paragraphs in The Book of Discipline concerning human sexuality and to explore options to strengthen church unity.

I was not a delegate, of course, but attended as an observer and WCA leader. I communicated back to traditionalists on our team in New Jersey and other interested parties. I was featured in a WCA video report on the conference that aired during it as well. This was my first General Conference to attend in person, and what a conference to learn from.

Shortly thereafter, Walter Fenton summarized the results as follows:

> Despite the strong support of the majority of U.S. bishops the General Conference delegates declined to endorse the One Church Plan (OCP), a plan that would have liberalized the UM Church's sexual ethics, teachings on marriage, and ordination standards.
>
> On three separate occasions the plan failed to gain support from the majority of delegates. During a prioritization phase, when delegates were given the opportunity to categorize as "high priority" as many plans and petitions as they liked, the OCP ranked fifth receiving support from 49 percent of the delegates. When it came to actually voting the plan up or down, it was defeated 53 percent to 47. And in response to a last ditch effort to resurrect it: the delegates opposed it by a margin of 55 percent to 45.
>
> Instead, the delegates steadily if narrowly supported the Traditional Plan, a proposal calling on the church to reaffirm its teachings on the matters before it and to enhance its accountability standards. During the prioritization phase, 56 percent supported the plan. And in two more votes it received 56 and 53 percent respectively on its way to becoming the church's officially endorsed plan.[12]

The controversy, hostility and tactics demonstrated by bishops and other progressives astounded me. They have been highly reported on and recounted. The accusations made regarding the WCA and other traditionalists floored me as I knew them to be false.

Even as I left for the airport to go to the conference, I was already receiving texts regarding accusations by progressives. They claimed that traditionalists were buying off African delegate votes through the Missouri Conference team providing many of them with needed coats to stay warm in a brutal climate that they were not prepared for. From the first I heard it, that made no sense to me as Missouri was the host Annual Conference and thus charged with hospitality. It also made no sense given that the majority of African delegates had already been clear that they were going to be upholding the UMC's Book of Discipline in their voting and therefore such votes would not need to be "bought off" at the conference.

For the most part, GNJ progressive delegates and attendees avoided me at the conference. After a vote sealing the fate of the One Church Plan, I came across Rev. Dr. Dana Harding (a reserve delegate) in the hallways. She had clearly been crying. I honestly would have preferred to have avoided contact with her, but we were directly in front of one another. I awkwardly said hello. She glared at me and made no audible response. I had a similar experience with another conference staff member who was at the conference to participate in some sort of prayer circle offerings. I ran into the Chair of the Board of Ordination, Rev. Saul Pawn, there as a supporter of the One Church Plan, who stumbled through talking to me.

I spent most of my time with WCA leadership, developing new relationships as well as enjoying previously established ones with members of the Next Steps working group and others I had previously met at WCA events. Again, I felt I had found my tribe. Not a tribe bound together through ill-considered loyalty, but one with theological and spiritual experience affinity.

I have three specific personal experiences from that General Conference that made distinct impressions on me regarding the UMC and all that was transpiring.

The first was that day-by-day I would see retired bishops, their wives, and the wives of current bishops gathered in the hotel lobby to board shuttle buses paid for by the denomination to take them to the conference center, while I and other attendees walked there in the brutal St. Louis cold. I would leave before them and see them arriving at a private entry point to the Convention Center while others stood in long lines to get in.

I thought about how church money was spent to fly them there, pay for their hotels, meals, and other expenses. I thought about how these were perks, among other similar ones, offered to them for life. I pondered the value of such perks. I pondered the conscious of those who accepted them, especially during a time that was already being revealed to be one of financial crisis for the denomination. I was greatly disturbed to be part of a system that supported this.

Each day I entered the Convention Center and every time I left, I was assaulted by the chants and signs of members of the Westboro Baptist Church[13] who were demonstrating outside. According to Wikipedia, "Westboro Baptist Church is an American hyper-Calvinist hate group. It is known for engaging in inflammatory homophobic and anti-American pickets, as well as hate speech against atheists, Jews, Muslims, transgender people, and numerous Christian denominations." I saw them receiving much media attention. I remember being very careful not to go near them for fear I would be photographed or filmed and thereby be associated with their beliefs and cause, which in no way reflect my own or the

Wesleyan Covenant Association or the Global Methodist Church we were building.

But what that experience also solidified for me was how the narrative of the beliefs traditional Methodists, including my own, had been seized and falsely represented by progressives to match the hate-filled attitudes, tactics, theology, and goals that Westboro Baptist, led by Pastor Fred Waldron Phelps, represents. I thought about how we traditionalists had allowed that false narrative to grow, and about our failings to counter it. I decided then that I would do my part to reframe and reclaim our narrative. Yes, we unapologetically follow the Bible's clear teachings on human sexuality. But we also follow its teaching on love and the transforming power of Christ that can and desires to overcome all sin and heal its victims.

Thirdly, as the conference was ending, my Reconciling Ministries leader friend from the Baltimore Washington Conference, Rev. Laura Blauvelt, and I walked out and met up at a nearby restaurant/bar. We both were in tears regarding all that we witnessed during the conference. While we disagreed regarding the legislative results, we both comprehended a more disturbing storyline than would be emphasized within both our circles, the general UMC population of clergy and laity, and the outside press. We saw the entire conference as a very expensive and deliberate attempt at deflection from the underlying bureaucratic, hypocritical, corrupt, and power abuse-filled Episcopal leadership of the UMC. In the end, we saw LGBTQIA people and their concerns used as pawns to fuel fires that would fill discussion and debate and distract from serious analysis of Episcopal leadership failings and misdeeds. All of this played out through a charade of an expensive conference and high-powered

SUNSHINE THROUGH THE CLOUDS

Way Forward Task Team. Money, people, and effective ministry for sharing the Gospel were sacrificed for this aim.

With no accountability built into our doctrines and disciplines for bishops except through each other, nothing could be done within this system. We both agreed that although we knew that God can do anything and we would try on our ends, we personally could not see how the United Methodist Church could survive without a split and that it needed to happen. The theological differences are insurmountable. But even more so, we agreed that the current Episcopal system needs to end and never be replicated in any denomination.

My time spent with Laura was documented in comments I gave regarding the 2019 Special General Conference to the Philadelphia Inquirer and the New Jersey Star Ledger, in which I was quoted as saying, "The effort to resolve the differences of opinion within the wider denomination have left members feeling 'wounded' by the General Conference process, which has not ended the debate,"[14] and that my friend and I "held each other and cried together," as "our theological and experiential differences on this issue have not stopped us from being not only civil, but loving and encouraging of one another. Regardless of whether our denomination splits, we, like countless other Christians, will be able to continue in relationship and work tirelessly for the sake of the Gospel and mission to the world."[15]

Two months later, Laura and I worked together to facilitate an introductory conversation between Keith Boyette, President of the Wesleyan Covenant Association, and Jan Lawrence, Executive Director of Reconciling Ministries Network, about finding ways to end the conflict within the UMC. We both felt pretty good about that.

KOREAN GIFT

Although the Special General Conference was in itself an abysmal experience, the connections and learnings were invaluable. God also had a special surprise for me. During the conference, Rev. Will Kim, a friend and senior pastor of First Korean UMC of Cherry Hill, NJ, approached me about an opportunity. His church, with over 800 members, had a strong youth program with 100 youth, but their youth pastor had just accepted an offer to return to Korea to be a senior pastor. He would be leaving in less than a month. The position would not be replaced by the conference until an appointment beginning in July was announced.

Will asked if I would be willing, while on leave of absence and awaiting a new appointment myself in July, to lead the youth ministry. My responsibilities would be leading and preaching a Sunday morning service and leading a Saturday evening Youth Fellowship time each week. Me, lead at a Korean church? My spirit was stirred immediately, and I told him I would pray about it. Upon returning from St. Louis, I accepted the position.

SPRING 2019 GNJ SPECIAL ANNUAL CONFERENCE

Soon after returning home, Bishop Schol invited me to share the following letter for the Pre-Conference Journal to a Special Annual Conference he called on March 16, 2019, for Greater New Jersey:

A STATEMENT FROM THE WESLEYAN COVENANT ASSOCIATION OF GREATER NEW JERSEY

Thank you Bishop Schol for your invitation to address this conference. We welcome this opportunity to mend relationships within GNJ in the aftermath of General Conference. We believe the world is watching, and opportunity exists to model working through strongly held disagreements respectfully. Perhaps given the many divides that distress our world today, we have been called for such a time as this.

The WCA of GNJ is a connection of orthodox churches, clergy and laity who adhere to Wesleyan theology. We prioritize Scripture's authority, Jesus Christ's Lordship, personal and social holiness and reformation in the UMC that will strengthen the effectiveness of our witness. We delight in the diversity of our GNJ connection that represents a microcosm of the growing global nature of our denomination. With women and men representing every district, our membership reflects that although the current leadership of GNJ evidences a strong progressive theological stance, many in our conference do not.

We are Wesleyans who strive to love all people. We acknowledge our own need for deeper reflection and repentance. While our movement is not centered on the topic of human sexuality, we have a strong sense of accountability for what we affirm and teach (Mark 9:42). We strive to carefully consider *all* matters related to healthy expression of human sexuality. We regard entering covenant with false pretenses and breaking covenants as heart-breaking and dishonoring to all. We welcome good faith conversation on all these matters.

Regarding General Conference:

We encourage all to read the WCA Council statement https:// wesleyancovenant.org/2019/02/28/statement-of-the-wes- leyan-covenant-association-council-on-next-steps/ and the blog by WCA Council member Cara Nicklas, who served as a delegate https://peopleneedjesus.net/2019/03/04/cara-nick- las-a-lay-delegate-perspective-on-gc2019/ .

We are thankful the UMC has reaffirmed its sexual ethics, teachings on marriage and its ordination standards.

We are surprised that progressives/centrists were shocked by the defeat of the One Church Plan. As UMCOM reported, the UMC's largest U.S. segment identifies as conservative/ traditional. Delegate representation trends reflect that we are an increasingly globally connected denomination. Therefore, more universal church and thus orthodox conforming legislation should be expected, now and into the future.

We hope to work together to remedy factors that lead to the under representation of orthodox evangelicals on GNJ's General Conference delegation.

We hope GNJ leadership will provide an environment that orthodox churches and pastors can feel comfortable to be themselves.

While we acknowledge Bishop Schol's letter of February 27th was released during a highly emotional time, many regard it as dishonoring to General Conference's work, counterproductive to many local church ministries, and contrary to the good order and unity of the whole church. Given that the One Church Plan was not adopted, we trust Bishop Schol will provide further clarification of his stated intention to lead GNJ as if it did.

We hope all will practice good ministry stewardship so that valuable time and resources will not continue to be used to intensify our deep division.

More WCA of GNJ connectional opportunities affirming and equipping those with our beliefs and educating others are forthcoming.

Rev. Beth Caulfield

WCA of Greater New Jersey Chapter President

The conference was the first time the bishop had openly acknowledged the existence of the WCA without calling us a fringe group. I also received the following invitation to be part of the bishop's Way Forward Team:

Mon March 11, 2019, 2:25 pm

CONFIDENTIAL

Dear Beth,

May the grace of God be with you in this Lenten season.

The GNJ Connectional Table (CT) met last week to debrief and discern next steps after the Special General Conference session that took place in St. Louis. After prayerful consideration, the CT decided to present legislation to the Special Session of Annual Conference on March 16th, 2019, to create a GNJ Way Forward team that will identify and propose a plan to the Annual Conference Session by or before the May 2020 Annual Conference Session.

The proposal coming from the team shall include, but not be limited to, how GNJ will 1) support congregations in different contexts to be in ministry with the LGBTQI+ community per paragraph 161.G of The Book of Discipline, 2) respect and honor one another based on our theological and cultural differences, 3) and share our hopes and concerns with our United Methodist sisters and brothers around the world.

The GNJ Way Forward team will be comprised of a group of GNJ clergy and congregational leaders that represent the rich diversity of our Conference.

On behalf of Bishop John Schol & Rev. Sang Won Doh, chairperson of the GNJ Connectional Table, I invite you to be part of this team which will be doing missional critical work on behalf of the Connectional Table and GNJ.

*Click here, to fill an online form with your response to this invitation by **12:00PM on Wednesday March 13, 2019**.*

......

So, we were given two days to respond to being on a taskforce that was very clearly designed not to determine how we were going to work within the upheld legislation of General Conference, but to show to the world that leaders in the conference wanted a way around it. Having worked with Schol long enough, I and others knew that the task force already had a pre-destined work product, and it would be created by Schol. We would not truly be working from a clean slate but instead be used as pawns for endorsing the plan Schol had already decided upon for how he would take the conference around the requirements of the Discipline.

When I did not respond within twenty-four hours, I received a call from an administrative assistant on March 12 asking me to do so. I told her the letter stated I had another twenty-four hours to respond and I had not yet made up my mind. She accepted the answer.

Yet that evening, a Pre-Conference Journal was released putting the formation of the team on the legislative agenda and my name was listed as one of the seventeen team members.

2019 Special Sessions of the Annual Conference Agenda and Pre Conference Journal

March 23, 2019, 5:58 PM

Dear Bishop,

I was very surprised to see my name listed on the proposed Way Forward Team. When I was contacted this morning by Ashley Wilson asking if I had made a decision, I was very clear that I have not made a decision.

I have not made such a decision and request that my name be removed from that list. I'm sure you understand.

Beth

Bishop John Schol bishopjohnschol@gnjumc.org

To: Ashley, Hector, Carolyn, me

Sorry for the confusion. We will remove your name and identify someone else.

John

Bishop John Schol

The rush put on this further indicated to me that the plan had already been devised and our jobs as team participants were simply to comply. I did not want to waste my time in being such a puppet.

When the list was published in the Pre-Conference Journal, it showed that then WCA of Greater New Jersey Vice President, Rev. Dave Werhle, was also named on the taskforce. As we reviewed the list of participants together, we were confident that out of the possibly four, at best, traditionalists invited to the team, we were the only two that would not simply capitulate to the bishop's plan. While I did not want to waste time and risk my views being misrepresented as agreement with the bishop's plan, Dave was more open to the possibility that the team could be swayed to at least listen to conservative thought and incorporate it into their actions. He joined the team with that aspiration. I was replaced by an institutionalist and other progressives were slowly added to the team.

The lingo around the GNJ Way Forward Team (named after the General Conference Way Forward Task Force whose work led to the legislation put forth at the St. Louis Special General Conference) made it clear that Schol's intent was to create his own version of the One Church Plan, the failed legislation at General Conference that progressives and institutionalists had pushed for changing the Book of Discipline's policies on the ordination of homosexual clergy and performing gay marriages. The plan offers churches the right to comply with the Book of Disciple or not comply with the Book of Discipline. Their choice. It is really that simple. In other words, the guiding principle is we no longer follow the Book of Discipline as a denomination. Since the One Church Plan had failed at General Conference, Schol would now implement it at least in Greater New Jersey.

That implementing the One Church Plan on his own was indeed one part of Schol's agenda was emphasized at that March 16, 2019, Special Annual Conference at Brookdale Community College by the fact that everyone who attended was greeted at the door by people who were handing out a One Church Plan Button left over from the previous month's Special General Conference in St. Louis.

Rev. Dr. Ginny Samuel-Cetuk of the Board of Ordained Ministry attempted to hand me a button. I refused to take it. I was not the only one. I felt Rev. Dr. Ginny Samuel-Cetuk's disapproval of my action and her taking note of me.

FIRST BOM DISCONTINUATION LETTER

The week after that Spring Special Annual Conference, on Thursday, March 21, I had driven to Newark to visit a woman I used to minister to when I had started a prison ministry Bible study some ten years earlier. I had been told that she was now out of prison and in poor health. I went to her acute care facility to visit.[1]

Afterward, I stopped to spend the afternoon with a friend. While there I received a phone call from Rev. Saul Pawn, the Chair of the Board of Ordination. I was informed that I was being discontinued as a provisional member. The reason given was that I had not been attending required Residence in Ministry (RIM) meetings. Incidentally, Rev. Dr. Ginny Samuel-Cetuk, who tried to hand me the OCP button five days earlier, oversaw the RIM program for the Board of Ordination. Rev. Dr. Dana Harding, who had angrily refused my greeting after the OCP plan failed to pass in St. Louis, ran the program. The follow up letter I received was as follows:

March 25, 2019

Dear Rev. Caulfield:

Grace and peace to you in the name of our Lord and Savior, Jesus Christ.

I am writing to you as a follow-up to our phone conversation following the conclusion of the recent Board of Ordained

Ministry meeting of March 21. As I communicated to you, it is the Board's discernment that your provisional membership be discontinued. I understand that this decision is deeply disappointing and painful. Please know that I continue to hold you in prayer during this difficult time.

During our time of discernment, it came to the attention of the Board that you have not been a regular participant in the Residency in Ministry (RIM) program for two years. Paragraph 326 of The United Methodist Book of Discipline outlines the need for "all provisional members to be involved in a residency curriculum." This information was also confirmed by the Reverend Dana Harding, one of the facilitators of the RIM program.

Moreover, Section 2.10 of the Greater New Jersey Board of Ordained Ministry Policy Manual indicates the following: "Provisional Members are required to participate in the Residency in Ministry program as outlined by the Board for the full length of her/his provisional period." This requirement is shared with candidates for full membership and ordination verbally and in written form during the candidacy orientation meeting that is held each year.

Thus, given this information, it was the discernment of the Board that your provisional membership be discontinued. As you are aware, this process is held by the Board and its sub-committees in confidence. Should you decide that you would want to, or do, make anything public, please just let me know.

2. I would also like to inform you of your rights and options following the Board's decision.

Paragraph 327.6 of the 2016 Book of Discipline specifies that, prior to any final recommendation for discontinuance, you have a right to a hearing before the Conference Relations Committee of the Board of Ordained Ministry. For this purpose, a hearing date has been set for Wednesday, April 3, 2019, at 1:30 PM at the United Methodist Church of Red Bank (247 Broad St, Red Bank, NJ).

If you wish to avail yourself of this right, you will need to contact me in writing by Monday, April 1, 2019.

Under the provisions for Fair Process as outlined in ¶361.2c, at the hearing you have a right to be accompanied by a clergyperson in full connection who shall have the right to speak on your behalf. The purpose of the hearing is to determine if there is sufficient cause to request a reconsideration of the vote of the full Board of Ordained Ministry.

Please consult ¶327.6 and ¶361.2 for your information and review.

Following this hearing, the Conference Relations Committee shall report its decision to the Board of Ordained Ministry, which may affirm or reverse the decision of the committee.

Should you have further questions about the process, I would be glad to discuss them with you. However, under the fair process provisions, I am required to limit my conversations to be about process only.

I pray God's blessings upon you, Beth, as you enter into this difficult time of challenge and discernment.

Peace,

Rev. Saul Pawn

Chair, GNJ Board of Ordained Ministry

Cc: Bishop John Schol, Resident Bishop, GNJAC

Rev. Glenn Conaway, District Superintendent

Rev. Jessica Naulty, Conference Relations Committee

Rev. Beth Whalley Mitchell, Administrative Review Committee

And BOOM! BOM had apparently fixed me.

While I attended RIM meetings from 2013 to February 2017, since being appointed to the church down in southern New Jersey in 2017 I stopped attending. I don't recall receiving any communications about RIM meetings, although they may have been posted online. Dr. Dana Harding, Dr. Samuel-Cetuk, Rev. Saul Pawn nor anyone else expressed any concern regarding my absence in the two years since I had stopped attending.

Additionally, the Growth Plan that I had been given in 2017 when I was turned down for approval by the Board for the second time did not mention that I was required to attend RIM meetings. The first Growth Plan from 2016 had clearly included RIM. This, and the fact that I never received any communication regarding RIM over the past two years, had indicated to me that I was not requested or expected to be at these meetings.

The Board of Ordained Ministry, fraught with progressives supporting the One Church Plan and/or Reconciling Ministries, had voted to discontinue me as a candidate for ordination (after turning me down for full orders twice before), not because of my ministry fruit, but because I had not attended RIM meetings that prior to my becoming the President of the GNJ Chapter of the WCA had not been an issue.

The whole thing smelled fishy. I received a phone call from my district superintendent encouraging me to go to the hearing the Conference Relations Board offered and plead my case.

I once again brought Rev. Dan Amey as my advocate. The tone of most in the meeting, led by Rev. Jessica Brendler-Naulty, a vocal OCP and Reconciling Ministries advocate, was one of resentful resolve that they were going to have to recommend overturning the discontinuation decision. Rev. Dr. Ginny Samuel-Cetuk was noticeably silent in the meeting. I told them I would be willing to attend the RIM meetings if I were informed of them in the future. My record from 2013 to spring 2017 showed I had faithfully attended in the past when aware of the meetings.

They claimed that information had been sent to me about the meetings. However, the only evidence they produced to corroborate that assertion was an email sent to an email address that I had not used in many years. The Board of Ordained Ministry had been using my new email for roughly five years.

The Residence in Ministry program is, among other functions, designed as a support group. If they had reached out, they might have found out I was going through a lot that I needed support for, including my husband's battle with cancer and mistreatment as a female minister.

April 27, 2019

Dear Rev. Caulfield:

Grace and peace to you in the name of our Lord and Savior, Jesus Christ.

I am writing regarding the Conference Relations Committee's Administrative Fair Process Hearing that addressed the Board of Ordained Ministry's recommendation for discontinuance of your provisional membership. As I mentioned when we spoke on the phone, the CRC has voted to overturn the Board's recommendation for discontinuance, and the Board affirmed the CRC's recommendation. This means that you will be continued as a provisional member at the clergy session of the Annual Conference on May 19th, 2019.

Blessings to you,

Rev. Saul Pawn

Chair, GNJ Board of Ordained Ministry

Cc:

Bishop John Schol, Resident Bishop, GNJAC

Rev. Glenn Conaway, District Superintendent

Rev. Jessica Brendler Naulty, Chair, Conference Relations Committee

Rev. Beth Whalley Mitchell, Administrative Review Committee

Rev. Dan Amey, Clergy Advocate present at the hearing

KOREAN CROSS-CULTURAL MINISTRY EXPERIENCE

In late March 2019, I began my work with the youth of First Korean UMC of Cherry Hill. This was a wonderful cross-cultural experience for not only me, but for my entire family. In addition to my leading the youth program on Saturday nights and for their own service and small group meetings on Sundays, my daughter, Camille, attended the Children's Sunday School class every week. My husband, Camille, and I joined the satellite multicultural church service on the Cherry Hill campus.

Mother's Day, 2019 with First Korean UMC of Cherry Hill youth.

We participated in many events at the church and felt fully embraced. My older two children, TJ and Amber, upon their returns from college, also joined the services and events. We learned about Korean culture, including lots of great food, a tiny bit of Korean language, and a love for K-Pop music.

My ministry was appreciated. I was asked to preach the main Easter service for the entire congregation and was translated into Korean. I also preached the graduation day sermon for the congregation.

I regularly was a communion steward for the main services and learned how to say "the body of Christ" and "the blood of Christ" in Korean.

But what was most poignant about this time for me was a growing confidence that youth not only could still be fully engaged in their relationship with Christ, but also could be filled with passion for such relationship and welcome the Holy Spirit's lead. Many times, I filled with tears as I watched youth worship with abandon, pray fervently alone, with, and for one another (even in Holy Spirit-filled tongues), and fellowship with one another with an eye to growing in discipleship.

The program I briefly oversaw included much discipline and accountability for youth and they were responding. I also watched as my daughter was part of an "old-fashioned" Sunday School program that required her to be engaged with the Bible and actually memorize scripture. The programs did not pander to concerns of overtaxing or turning kids off because they were being asked to engage more fully, but instead offered educational and worship experience substance that attracted both youth and children.

This reinforced in me the importance of accountable discipleship beginning at an early age. Many churches have lost this priority. I believe it is critical and yearned for by children, youth, and adults alike.

My family and I will forever be grateful to Rev. Will Kim and this congregation for their welcoming of us into this experience. Many of the relationships continue to last. Are Korean American churches perfect? Of course not. I learned a good bit about their challenges, and those challenges also inform my leadership.

NAVIGATING THE MAY 2019 GNJ ANNUAL CONFERENCE

As the May regularly scheduled Annual Conference was approaching, our WCA team had several agenda items. We wanted to host our WCA dinner again in a way that we would show that we were not simply being led by a bunch of out of touch, aged, homophobic white men as was continually being asserted about us. The previous year we had brought Rev. Dr. Carolyn Moore of our WCA Global Council to speak. For 2019 we secured Rev. Dr. Joy Moore to speak.

Our GNJ WCA chapter leaders with Rev. Dr. Joy Moore

We also had concluded that we wanted to elect delegates for the 2020 General Conference who would vote for any kind of separation legislation for the UMC. In the aftermath of the 2019 St. Louis Special General Conference, anarchy from adhering to its reaffirmed Disciplinary Language regarding human sexuality not only became clear, but was being endorsed throughout the denomination and its affiliate and partners. Schol is not a leader in breaking his vows to uphold the Discipline. He is one of many.

For example, theological schools and seminaries, including Drew Theological School, the primary source of MDIVs to clergy in our conference (and from where I received my MDIV) began to publicly denounce the United Methodist Church for the results of the General Conference and disaffiliate with us. I suspect those decisions were aided by the fact that UMC financial support for such institutions had drastically changed over recent years.

In the past, financial resources had been evenly divided up between ten or so UMC feeder schools. However, in 2013 the denomination made a shift and began reallocating its financial support based on actual UMC membership of the students/graduates at its traditional feeder schools. This meant schools like Drew, that had for years been attracting students and producing graduates that were mostly going to other denominations like the Church of Christ and the Universalist Unitarian Church whose progressive theology and doctrine bear little resemblance to traditional Methodism, would now have roughly 75% of their funding cut. Drew had been maneuvering around that major funding problem for the past five to six years. Therefore, making a public statement that they were leaving the UMC was a bit ironic, as truthfully, financially the UMC had decided to leave them already.

Thus, given anarchy and continuing hostility and harassment of traditionalists and most importantly the harm being done to ministry and our witness, we wanted to separate. The WCA was sadly becoming clearer about the need for changing its focus to pursuing separation.

In Greater New Jersey we knew that the chance of electing conservative delegates to General Conference was next to zero. We had not had a conservative elected to General Conference in several sessions.[2] In addition, there was a huge push by progressives across the denomination to ensure that more progressive delegates were elected for 2020 in hopes of overturning the 2019 decisions.

In our conference, upon returning from St. Louis, a decision was suddenly made by Schol to reopen and extend the application deadline for running as a delegate to "ensure more diversity of delegates." I am not alone in believing that this deadline extension had to do more with achieving delegates that would not only support but advocate for a progressive agenda than it had to do with any concerns about racial, ethnic, or gender diversity.

I prayed a lot about what, if anything, to do as the WCA Chapter leader. One morning I woke up and knew that the Lord was putting a plan in my brain. It was clear and precise. I would contact every candidate for delegate and ask them if they would support legislation for separating the denomination. I would tell them I was going to share their answers as it would be helpful to many as separation of the UMC was now front and center to many.

My email to each candidate was:

> *Sent: Wed, May 15, 2019 6:18 pm*
>
> *Subject: Thank you and clarifying question*
>
> *Dear Clergy/Lay Delegate Candidate for Greater New Jersey,*
>
> *Thank you for offering yourself as a candidate to represent Greater New Jersey as a delegate to the 2020 General and*

Northeast Jurisdictional Conference. Your discernment to enter this process is not only appreciated, but is admirable.

While the Wesleyan Covenant Association will continue to strive for renewal and reform, we recognize that the United Methodist Church is now irreconcilably broken. We are committed to finding a way forward through amicable separation. We trust centrists and progressives will also see the wisdom of working for this goal, rather than spending their time and energy in futile and destructive attempts at changing or overturning the will of the General Conference.

To help the WCA of Greater New Jersey members and all in GNJ evaluate your delegate candidacy in relation to the above stated mission and thoughts, please answer the following question and return your response to me no later than midnight, Friday, May 17.

Do you believe the differences between progressives/centrists and conservatives are irreconcilable, and will you as a delegate put priority on working for a fair and equitable plan of separation to allow new Methodist expressions or churches to come into existence?

Your response (or lack there of) will be shared within GNJ and possibly the denomination. Please respond directly to this email.

Thank you for your cooperation and blessings to you and your candidacy journey.

Sincerely,

Rev. Beth Caulfield

President, Wesleyan Covenant Association of Greater New Jersey

The responses arrived. I told our team that I wanted to publish the results to every voting member of the Annual Conference and asked how we could do it. We agreed that every name needed was published in the Pre-Conference Journal. Those names and email addresses were public information. Rev. Dave Werhle, our Vice President, was confident he had access to resources that could extract those emails for us and upload them to our pre-existing Constant Contact email account that we had been using for communications already. He did exactly that. We had a list of roughly 1500 additional names and emails to add to our pre-existing lists.

The day before Annual Conference, May 18th, at 2:15pm, I pushed send on the following email:

> Dear fellow members of the United Methodist Church of Greater New Jersey,
>
> Greetings in the name of our precious Lord and Savior Jesus Christ. I write on the eve of our 2019 Annual Conference in Wildwood to share hopefully helpful information with you. As you are probably aware, an important part of our agenda in Wildwood will be to select clergy and lay delegates for the 2020 General Conference.
>
> The combative display at this past February's Special General Conference in St. Louis cost upwards of $5 million dollars of money intended to further the mission of Christ. The cost to our witness for Christ cannot be measured in dollars. The many challenges that the United Methodist Church is currently facing as significant voices within our denomination have expressed their unwillingness to abide by the legislation

passed at that Conference and are thwarting ministry to express their displeasure, call to question more than ever the future viability of the United Methodist Church. Our witness is being further invalidated as continued attempts at carrying out the One Church Plan at Conference levels cause further pain and disillusionment (see this blog post from Robert Schotter, who openly identifies as gay, was a 2020 delegate candidate from GNJ, but has very recently withdrawn from the UMC related to the efforts around the GNJ Way Forward team https://robdeanblog.wordpress.com/ .)

It is not an exaggeration to say that what gets accomplished at the 2020 General Conference is crucial to our witness to the world. I believe souls are at stake.

As President of the Wesleyan Covenant Association of Greater New Jersey, I want to share with you that while the WCA will continue to strive for renewal and reform, we recognize that the United Methodist Church is now irreconcilably broken. We are committed to finding a way forward through amicable separation. We trust centrists and progressives will also see the wisdom of working for this goal, rather than spending their time and energy in futile and destructive attempts at changing or overturning the will of the General Conference.

To help us all better understand the delegate candidates*, we asked each candidate to answer the following question per the email copied at the end of this one.*

Do you believe the differences between progressives/centrists and conservatives are irreconcilable, and will you as a delegate put priority on working for a fair and equitable plan of

separation to allow new Methodist expressions or churches to come into existence?

All candidates were made aware that their responses (or lack thereof) would be shared within GNJ and potentially elsewhere in the denomination.

*Below are the **answers received VERBATIM**, simply copied from their email responses.*

*Regardless of your personal sentiments on this issue, I trust that this information will be helpful, and that you will use it either for your own vote or to encourage your clergy and lay delegates on their voting. I also **hope that those who declined to respond will address this issue in their one minute speeches** during the Conference.*

May God bless you, and I hope to see you all in Wildwood,

Rev. Beth Caulfield

President, Wesleyan Covenant Association of Greater New Jersey

The responses shared can be found here for the e-book, or at the link below.[3]

By the time I arrived at the Wildwood Convention Center for the Annual Conference, roughly twenty-four hours later, Constant Contact was reporting that 64% of recipients had opened the email. That was God. Since then, we have sent emails that have received higher open rates, but that was an astounding result to us at that time.

You can imagine the response in general. I got a lot of grins, high-fives, "thank yous," and prayers. I also received hostile emails, glares, stares, and comments of disapproval. During the clergy session there was discussion regarding an apparent attempt to file a complaint against me. As we had done nothing against the Book of Discipline, this action was dissuaded and even mentioned by Bishop Schol openly as not a good option.

The most disappointing rumor I heard, however, was that I or our team could not have come up with this exercise on my or our own. That the wording and concept must have come from a lawyer. It was speculated that Rev. Dr. Bob Costello had done this for me. Or Rev. Keith Boyette. Those assertions were dead wrong.

We celebrated that of the eight delegates elected for General Conference 2020, one laity was openly traditional and there were three to four traditionalists among the rest, including jurisdictional and reserve delegates that we had hopes would vote for a separation. While most conferences suffered a decrease in traditional theology delegates for the coming year, we, a progressively led conference, achieved an increase. This along with the notice and respect we received made this Annual Conference our biggest success of that era of our local chapter's existence.

Our membership and "WCA Friends" email list began to grow significantly. My phone rang regularly with traditionalists calling to express support, frustrations regarding the direction conference leadership was taking, and looking for answers for how to combat such direction. I remember one call in particular. It was from Rev. James Lee, pastor of the largest church in the conference, Bethany UMC, a Korean church of roughly 2000 members in Wayne, NJ. James and I had conversed over the past few years regarding several ministry opportunities. Now he was calling very upset about the direction and steps the conference was taking with its theology and revealing of its plan at the Annual Conference. Bethany UMC and Rev. Lee were already following our WCA work in Greater New Jersey, but at this point they became closer with us.

NO TIME FOR ORDINATION

I thought briefly about going before the Board of Ordained Ministry again to attempt receiving my full orders during the summer of 2019. I contacted a couple of Board members I trusted and asked if they thought I would have a chance at being approved. No surprise to me, both told me they did not see me being given a fair assessment at this time and that I should wait. I had one more year to apply before the Book of Discipline required that I be discontinued due to an eight-year time limit. I decided to wait.

FRESH EXPRESSIONS US

As I was navigating the difficult UMC waters, the Lord was offering me other opportunities to learn, grow, and contribute through connections I had previously cultivated. One such blessing was through Fresh Expressions US.[1]

Back in August 2016, while on conference staff, I had attended the UMC School of Congregational Development held that year in Evanston, Illinois, just on the edge of Northwestern University's campus and Garrett-Evangelical Theological Seminary. A seminar that made a strong impression on me was given by Fresh Expressions UK. The seminar introduced a way to cultivate new forms of church alongside existing congregations to better reach a changing world. I listened to stories of fresh expressions of church founded through skateboarding communities, dinner churches, homeless shelters, and more in London and other areas of the UK and US. The emphasis was on listening to the Holy Spirit about where to reach people and forming church around new or even existing affinity communities. The idea was not to lead their communities to replicate church as we know it, but to find ways to share the Gospel and incorporate the basic elements of church that are life changing into their contexts and thus form new ways of doing church that reach them effectively.

The seminar impressed me so much that I researched and contacted Gannon Sims and Chris Backert of Fresh Expressions US. I began a professional relationship with them that started with bringing Shannon Kiser, their Director of Training, to an event I led for the northern New Jersey region in March 2017, _Outbound - A Day on Evangelism_.[2]

with Cheryl McCarthy of Fresh Expressions US. A real prayer warrior! Arlington, VA, April, 2017.

I also was introduced to Cheryl McCarthy, Director of the Ananias Project for Fresh Expressions U.S. She began working with me in the Spring of 2017 as I envisioned incorporating Intercessory Prayer Team Training as part of the Team Vital 2.0 resource that I was developing for the conference. Although my appointment changed and Team Vital 2.0 never made it past a workshop stage,[3] I maintained my relationship with Fresh Expressions after leaving conference staff, while the conference chose a different direction.

During the Spring of 2019, Shannon Kiser contacted me and invited me to join the Fresh Expressions training team and I accepted. I joined the staff and team at a planning retreat in Harrisburg, PA to get to know the team and join their visioning work. This is a dynamic ministry group that getting to know, learning from, and working with has been a real privilege.

I was trained as a trainer for their Pioneering Learning Communities track and did work in Indiana. I also had developed and was set to lead with Dr. Dee Stokes and Rev. Dr. Eliseo Mejia a workshop entitled Rev 7:9 Glory: Multiethnic/Multicultural Fresh Expressions at the Fresh Expressions National Gathering in Reston, Virginia in April 2020, but that and much other work with them has been postponed due to the current Covid-19 pandemic.

I continue to contribute and interact with this dynamic ministry and mention them as one of the many blessings God has shown me through my time with the UMC. I thank God for Fresh Expressions and the ministry they offer to church leaders.

with Rev. Matt Lake and Shannon Kiser of Fresh Expressions, Indianapolis, September 2019.

SUMMER OF PRAISE – REV. LEO PARK

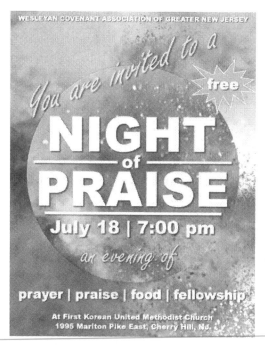

Advertising our GNJ WCA praise event

Also that summer of 2019, our WCA of GNJ team decided to offer a praise and worship event at First Korean UMC Cherry Hill. We secured a young adult Korean praise band through the church, an African American pastor from a UMC church in Trenton to preach, and WCA member, Rev. Leo Park, to lead us in worship to include Tong Song Keedo style prayer, which is when all voices simultaneously pray out loud as led by the Holy Spirit. We were excited to offer a Spirit-filled, multicultural worship event.

We also wanted to use the event to take up a collection for the WCA's Central Conference Fund which had in May been created to support African and other central conference ministries. Not long after the 2019 special General Conference had ended, a number of leading moderate and progressive pastors and organizations either announced suspension of financial support for ministry initiatives in the central conferences of The United Methodist Church, or expressed reservations about continuing with such support. This was because African votes had been instrumental to passing the Traditional Plan for maintaining the Book of Discipline's language on human sexuality. I know here in Greater New Jersey, Morrow Church, while not explicitly cancelling funding for the central conferences, chose to withhold funds to the Annual Conference and General Church[1] in protest.

We had asked the Greater New Jersey Conference Communications Team to promote the event weekly from mid-June until July 18th in their digital news source, *The Digest*, but they were unresponsive. After several attempts, Creed Pogue was able to get them to commit to advertise the event one time. They included a small blurb toward the bottom of their paper on June 26th only. Our further requests were denied.

Our planned Agenda had been as follows:

Night of Praise 7-9pm

7-8 Worship

8-9 Fellowship

7:00 Welcome and Call to Worship (5-10 minutes)	Rev. Will Kim and Rev. Beth Caulfield
Songs of Praise (around 20 minutes)	Dan Park and Praise Band
Words of Encouragement (10 minutes)	Rev. XXXXX
Songs of Praise and Encouragement (2 songs)	Dan Park and Praise Band
Tong Song Keedo Prayer for HS Power	Rev. Leo Park
Offering for WCA and Central Conference Fund	Creed Pogue
Offertory song	Rev. Dan Amey
Fellowship Time Introduction and Parting Prayer	Rev. Dave Werhle

At first it seemed that if anything could come against that time of worship and praise happening, it did. Not only were we challenged with promotion of the event, but the day of the event, just before noon, I received the following email from our planned preacher/ main speaker for the evening:

to David, Dan, Creed, Leo, pastor, me

Good Morning Beth

Unfortunately I will not be in attendance tonight. As Caucus Chair of Black Methodist For Church Renewal for GNJ, I have been called to a planned nationwide conference call this evening to explore the basis for our denomination's lack of response both to the most recent racists tweets and comments of President Trump and the Attorney general's decision not to bring "murder" charges against Eric Garner's killer. Racism has been and still remains an issue in our Society and in our denomination.

Peace

I let the pastor know we understood and would pray for him if he would pray for us. I quickly put together a sermon of my own. We also added the following words and a prayer that were said by Creed Pogue before he introduced me that night:

Rev. ___ is not able to be with us tonight. He is the Caucus Chair of Black Methodists for Church Renewal in Greater New Jersey. He is participating in a nationwide conference call to explore the basis of the lack of response by denominational leaders to the recent racist tweets and comments by President Donald Trump as well as the decision of the Attorney General of the United States not to bring murder charges against the officer who choked Eric Garner to death despite chokeholds being against New York Police Department procedures. Racism and how we treat our fellow human beings sadly has been and remains an issue here in America as well as in our denomination. While we try to continue to walk toward perfection, sometimes that walk includes stumbles. We pray for our brothers and sisters in Christ.

Arriving at the church, we discovered that on that sweltering 90-plus-degree day, the church's air conditioning had failed. The

Grace Ministries sanctuary where we were to meet, was on the second floor, i.e., where all the heat was gathering. Church leaders were working to repair the unit, but the chances of having a cool sanctuary were looking slim. We began collecting electric fans from around the church facilities to add to the sanctuary, but as time grew closer to our event, it was clear that we were not going to have a comfortable place for people to gather. We were praying hard.

We decided to move the event to the Youth Sanctuary across the campus, which did have air conditioning. It just needed to be turned on to cool it down. This was not ideal either, as it was a second-floor room and, unlike Grace Ministries, there was no elevator to transport people there. But it was all we had. As people had already arrived, we decided to have our food and fellowship time first in a lobby area that was not ideal but could do. This would allow time for the sanctuary area to cool off.

Despite the heat, we had a good crowd, close to one hundred people who stuck with us through all the mishaps. When the service began, however, all went really well. The praise band led us into solid worship. I felt God gave me just the right words for the message and when Rev. Leo Park led us in Tong Song Keedo prayer (which is when all voices simultaneously pray out loud as led by the Holy Spirit), it was POWERFUL.

The energy was strong, Rev. Park's prayer leadership gift was so anointed. In fact, in the height of our prayers, there was a surge of energy and all electricity in the building suddenly shut down! We finished the service in the dark and I know that many who were present felt they had experienced God's power in that place. We agreed that none of us had experienced such power in conference-led gatherings. Later, my twenty-two-year-old son, TJ, who attended that night, said, "That was awesome! That Leo guy is so all in! That was the best praying I ever was part of!" I believe my son was fore-telling events that would transpire in a few months.

The electricity exploded as Rev. Leo Park prayed at our Praise Gathering, July, 2019.

THE LAST STAND

FRANKLINVILLE AND NEWFIELD UMCs

Roughly two weeks after I had returned from the St. Louis Special General Conference, the first week of March 2019, I was contacted about serving in a full-time appointment from Bishop Schol as the pastor of Franklinville United Methodist Church, beginning July 1st, 2019. The appointment was only twenty-five minutes away from my home, meaning I would not need to move. That, of course, was a positive for which I was grateful.

When I originally received the appointment, I was to be paid the conference minimum salary by Franklinville. I would not receive a housing allowance, as the church offered a parsonage only. I was told I could use the parsonage, but as I did not plan to move my family for such a short commute, I chose not to do so. I would be required to participate in, and the church and I would need to contribute to, the conference-sponsored healthcare plan again, even though I retained healthcare benefits through my husband. I point these matters out, again, to highlight the fluctuations in compensation packages for pastors over our careers as we are subject to the appointment system.

The congregation had once been robust, enjoyed rich ministry history with two worship services and over one hundred and fifty regular worshippers, a choir, praise band, Sunday school, and other ministries. But in just a few short years there had been discord in the church and many had left. I was told the church had roughly forty regular worshippers at the time I was notified of the appointment. I was told by the district superintendent there also were major financial concerns, but the conference was working with the church to overcome them. When I met with the SPRC they were clearly enthusiastic about my appointment, wanted to do good ministry to attract new people, and were hopeful about a project they were planning for the summer for remodeling the church's sanctuary. They wanted to attract new people and wanted new ideas for how to do so. The church sits at the center of town, next to the beautiful Franklin Lake. We all welcomed the appointment.

Franklinville UMC

Those conversations were held in March. The last week of April, however, at the end of the appointment season, I was again contacted by our district superintendent and told that the appointment was going to be changed. Upon further review, the district superintendent and church leadership had determined that Franklinville could not afford a pastor full-time. Therefore, I would be receiving a two-point charge. Suddenly a plan that was to give full-time attention to a church in trouble needed to be modified by me. I would need to balance their needs with the needs of another church.

Prayer Walk at Newfield UMC

The second church, Newfield United Methodist Church, was only ten minutes away from Franklinville, but offered a very different ministry setting. It also unfortunately has a reputation among pastors as a difficult place to minister as its demands were truly full-time, with a regular worshipping congregation of seventy or more and an additional long list (twenty when I arrived) of shut-ins whose needs the congregation expected to be supported mainly by the pastor alone. The only other paid staff are a custodian and pianist.

In Greater New Jersey, and I suspect in many other conferences, a seventy-person congregation usually supports a full-time pastor. I certainly know many pastors who enjoy those sized full-time appointments. I am not aware of other half-time appointments of that size. Newfield, however, has declared that it could not support paying a pastor anything more than part-time since 1972.

They also expect pastors to serve them in a full-time capacity despite the part-time support. They had experienced and favored pastors who were later in life, retired from other careers, and had leaned in to having more free time to spend on pastoral care, especially to shut-ins, as lead ministries to the church. Additionally, when I arrived, they were not accustomed to sharing a pastor with another church.

Both churches were ninety-nine percent white, but in communities with growing minority populations.

It was clear that my work would be extremely difficult and time consuming, as one church needed full-time attention if it hoped to be revived and survive, and another demanded full-time attention for its pastor to be accepted by them. Knowing I would not likely receive support, I asked the cabinet to reconsider the appointment and if there were any other appointments available to me that might better meet my ministry gifts. I was denied.

Friends speculated that this appointment was once again a punishment to me for my theology, WCA leadership, and support of Jisun Kwak. Others said I had once again been set up to fail. Whether these thoughts were true or not, I do know that neither I nor my gifts were being shown any favor. Yet I knew God could use me even in these situations.

I accepted the appointment, trusting God. But I did have many doubts and concerns about the workload and uphill battle apparent for the two churches, and about the increasing knowledge in my heart that I would never receive a good opportunity to lead a church utilizing my full gifting within the United Methodist Church. I would probably never be ordained by them and the outcome of these two churches could very well be that I would be the last pastor before their doors were closed for good. In other words, this was yet another opportunity to fall in love with some people and lead some good ministry with them and into their communities while at the same time fail in terms of growing their ministry to survive. Again I was discouraged, but believed God had a plan.

ASSEMBLIES OF GOD CONFIRMATION

As I prepared for the Franklinville/Newfield appointment to begin, what really kept my spirit up was the ministry I was leading at First Korean that spring and the ministry work I was doing within the WCA. Yet I decided to explore more for the future. I thought about returning to my Wesleyan Church friends and asking if I could still join them, but felt awkward having just in February turned down an opportunity far into the process. I did not have any greater sense that joining them was what I was called to be doing. A friend in the Assemblies of God had been talking to me about joining their flock, and possibly planting a church with them. She put me in contact with a couple of female AG pastors and the sectional presbyter (similar to a district superintendent) for the area of New Jersey where I lived.

Rev. Arlene Corzine, who is the executive pastor at Kingsway Assembly of God in Cherry Hill, and Rev. Jamie Morgan, the Senior pastor at Life Church in Williamstown shared about their experiences and vison as pastors in the Assemblies. Rev. Kurt Kinney, the sectional presbyter and senior pastor at Bethel Church in Blackwood were all very helpful and supportive. As I spoke to all three, however, it was clear to all that no matter how difficult, I had work in the Wesleyan Covenant Association that I was called to that still needed to be finished. The work was hard and going to get harder, but God would see me through. I did not know how I would accomplish this work while taking care of my family and two very needy churches, but this was indeed my call.

Rev. Kinney left me with the understanding that if I felt called to join the AG's in October 2019, I could come back to him. I really thought I would be doing so. Yet I never did.

In September, I held a well-attended simulcast meeting for clergy friends of the GNJ WCA in both Cherry Hill, where I was in the southern part of the state just outside of Philadelphia, and in Leonia with Rev. Dave Werhle, in the northern part of the state just outside of New York City. In that meeting I shared about the various separation plans that were being introduced to the upcoming General Conference that included the Indianapolis Plan that at that time we were supporting, as it was previous to the Protocol that was later introduced and the work and direction of the WCA both in GNJ and globally.

We also shared the exciting news that the leadership team of the Korean Association, a national UMC organization of traditional Korean churches, had all joined the WCA. This was a huge encouragement for our Greater New Jersey friends. So events were moving well within my WCA responsibilities and this boosted me for continuing in my challenges within the United Methodist Church.

Although I never contacted Rev. Kinney again about joining the AG, I do stay in touch with Assembly of God leaders who have been very helpful in resourcing my local WCA chapter with various ideas and materials for church planting efforts, connectional funding, and so forth. Their willingness to partner and support has been a gift. It is a model I try to replicate.

ANOTHER DISTURBING 2019 GNJ SPECIAL ANNUAL CONFERENCE

In October 2019 yet another wedge in the divide between traditional and centrist/progressive Methodists in Greater New Jersey was added by Bishop Schol and the conference. The GNJ Way Forward Team that I had declined to join but of which our WCA Chapter Vice President Rev. Dave Werhle had become a member, had prepared a report and was presenting it to be voted on at a Special Annual Conference Session on October 26, 2019.

Dave had been careful to keep the work the GNJ Way Forward Team were doing confidential, as instructed by the bishop. Our WCA team was not privy to their meeting contents or to the plan being developed. But by mid-September Dave shared with our leadership team that he had become extremely uncomfortable with the Way Forward Team's final product and in good conscious he could not support the plan that had been devised.

What we soon would learn with the publication of the pre-Special Conference Journal was that the plan was simply to introduce a localized version of the One Church Plan that had been voted down in St. Louis. This was no surprise. Yet the brazenness of the plan to subvert the work of the General Conference was shocking and saddening.

According to the GNJ Way Forward Plan, churches and the Board of Ordained Ministry would not be held accountable to following the Book of Discipline on matters of human sexuality, the bishop would not support any complaints filed for breaches to such matters, and churches would be encouraged to develop their own internal covenants for how they would like to approach gay marriage and the acceptance of openly practicing homosexual clergy. Furthermore, the language used in the Plan and by the bishop and others at the Special Annual Conference clearly encouraged ignoring the Book of Discipline on these matters.

Our WCA team supported Dave as he decided to write a letter of dissent to the bishop from the team's recommendations. As you can see in the letter below, when he emailed his concern to the bishop, Dave requested that his dissent also be published in the Pre-Conference Journal along with the team's plan. Dave was contacted by Bishop Schol and the team's leader, District Superintendent Sang Won Doh, and strongly encouraged to change his mind. He was told that his dissent could not be published in the Pre-Conference Journal because materials had already been sent to press and therefore they could not be changed. I will say that I find this response to Dave's request to be questionable in its representation of what could have been done.

As a result, relying on prayer and his good conscious, Dave sent out an email to all voting members of the Conference detailing his dissent a full two weeks before the Special Session.

October 16, 2019

Dear Friends in Jesus Christ:

Many of you have asked me about the work of the Way Forward Team and my feelings about that work. Thank you for allowing me to keep the work and recommendations of the team in confidence until now per our team's covenant. Many of you have prayed for me and the team as we have gone about our work. Thank you, and please continue to pray.

On October 2, I wrote to Bishop Schol to register my dissent from the recommendations of the Way Forward Team presented in the report you have received. Unfortunately, it was not possible to include my dissent in the materials mailed to you by the conference office.

Now that the report has been published and my name appears in the report, I feel it is important that I share with you the letter that I sent Bishop Schol. It is included in unedited form below.

Grace and peace in Jesus Christ,

David

Rev. David Wehrle, Pastor

Leonia United Methodist Church

396 Broad Ave.

Leonia, NJ 07605

October 2, 2019

Dear Bishop Schol,

Thank you for the opportunity to serve on the Way Forward Team; I consider it an honor and a privilege. I feel loved and respected by all the team members and feel nothing but love and respect for them.

I trust you know I have made a good faith effort to work with the team toward our established goals. I have been willing to speak and write publicly and positively about my experience while serving. At the same time, I have attempted to represent the views of Traditionalist United Methodists in our annual conference. I have done my best to engage in the process with an open heart and an open mind.

As the work of the Way Forward Team is about to be shared with our annual conference delegates prior to our October special session, I think it is important that I register my dissent from its recommendations.

I had hoped our team would find a way forward that would allow us to maintain conference unity and honor the will of the general conference. Unfortunately, I think we have failed to discern that way forward. Instead, at a minimum, the team calls for tolerating defiance of The Book of Discipline and even moves toward encouraging defiance. The Way Forward Team would have you, your cabinet, and the connectional table allow local churches to make covenant with their clergy, the cabinet, and with you to defy our church's sexual ethics, teachings on marriage, and its ordination standards.

Our teachings and standards regarding these matters have been discussed, debated, refined, and reaffirmed by 13 General Conferences over 47 years. To recommend that some United Methodists in the Greater New Jersey Annual Conference are somehow exempt from those teachings and standards would imperil our unity with the rest of our global church and set a divisive precedent for other annual conferences who might disagree with other portions of our Discipline.

I believe the proposal that the Way Forward Team will present to the special session, and will be included in the pre-conference material, works toward division in our annual conference and our global United Methodist Church. As an ordained elder and a member of the Greater New Jersey Annual Conference, I have vowed to uphold the Discipline and therefore I cannot in good conscience endorse the product of the Way Forward Team. I respectfully ask that you publish my dissent in the pre-conference materials.

If you have any questions or concerns regarding my dissent, I would of course be more than happy to meet or speak with you.

Grace and peace in Jesus Christ,

David

Rev. David Wehrle, Pastor

Leonia United Methodist Church

396 Broad Ave.

Leonia, NJ 07605

After Dave's email was sent, I was contacted by our friends at the GNJ Korean Association, which is made up of all Korean churches in the conference, and asked for help in publishing their own letter of dissent. I agreed to help, and the following was sent.

October 25, 2019

Dear Friends in Jesus Christ:

On October 23rd, we, The Association of Korean United Methodist Church of GNJ, wrote to Bishop Schol and the Way Forward Team our response to the GNJ Way Forward Team's Report and Recommendation for the upcoming Special Session.

We feel that it is important to share with you the letter that we sent to convey our concerns and to let you know where we, all Korean churches in GNJ, stand.

It is included in unedited form below. Please continue to pray with us. Thank you.

In prayers,

The Association of Korean United Methodist Church of GNJ

October 23, 2019

RE: Our Response to the GNJ Way Forward Team's Report and Recommendation for the Upcoming Special Session

Dear Bishop Schol and Way Forward Team:

Thank you for your diligent leadership in this great annual conference. We are grateful for the opportunity to serve the Lord under your leadership. We acknowledge the receipt of the report and recommendation of the Way Forward Team for the upcoming special session of 2019.

It was our understanding that GNJ's Way Forward Team would allow us to maintain conference unity and honor the decision and will of General Conference while working under the parameters of its guidance. The Book of Discipline 2016 stipulates in page 27 (Section II General Conference article 16) that the General Conference shall have full legislative power over all matters distinctively connectional, and in the exercise of this power shall have authority ......to define and fix the powers and duties of annual conferences.

Unfortunately, we believe that GNJ's Way Forward Team has failed to discern and follow the Discipline to make a way forward. There is no doubt that the recommendation of the Way Forward Team appears to be allowing GNJ to make its own decision rather than following the law determined at the Special General Conference in St. Louis that took place Feb. 23-26, 2019. In addition, the team calls for tolerating defiance of the Book of Discipline and even encourages defiance. We want you, Bishop Schol, the Connectional Table members and the Way Forward Team to keep the accountability to the Book of Discipline and the decision and will of GC 2019.

It seems to us that GNJ is taking a pro-active way even before 2020 General Conference decision and it already defies 2020 General Conference's way forward under the name of GNJ's Way Forward. We are not sure of its legality because GNJ's Way Forward attempts to override the upcoming 2020 GC's resolution. We also want you, Bishop Schol, the Connectional Table members and the Way Forward Team to wait until GC 2020's way forward. We hope that nothing will be acted upon until the decision of GC 2020.

It is our understanding that we, as clergy members of the Greater New Jersey Annual Conference, have been ordained under covenant to uphold the Book of Discipline. Now we are being asked to defy the same discipline if we accept and approve GNJ's Way Forward Team's recommendation. We resolve to keep our covenant to uphold the Book of Discipline.

We, as clergy of Association of Korean United Methodist Churches in GNJ, hereby register our dissent from the recommendation of GNJ's Way Forward Team.

In prayers,

The Association of Korean United Methodist Churches of GNJ

Bountiful UMC of Martinsville

Calvary Korean UMC

Grace-Bethel UMC

Korean UMC of SJ

Glory Korean UMC

Korean Community Church of New Jersey

Livingston Korean UMC

Ridgewood UMC

Monmouth Grace UMC

Morristown KUMC

Bethany UMC

Arcola Korean UMC

Appenzeller Nari UMC

Disciple Church

Lord's Grace Church

First Korean UMC of Cherry Hill

Teaneck Korean UMC

The introduction of the Greater New Jersey Way Forward Plan was carefully crafted so that only an innocuous portion of it that did not break the Discipline[1] would be voted on at the special session. At the special session, the whole plan to break the Discipline was discussed and encouraged, but not during the legislative portion of the conference. Much strategic energy had been given to accomplishing the bishop's desire of openly breaking his vows of upholding the Book of Discipline and giving a green light to others to also do so.

Our WCA of GNJ leadership team met several times before the conference to discuss strategy for standing up against the plan and its legislation. We crafted questions, including Questions of Law, and a strategy for getting all to the floor, which we knew would be actively fought against by progressives including the bishop. In the end, we had a strong showing, with several of our leaders making speeches.

I introduced two Questions of Law regarding the legality of the actions approved. Creed Pogue and Gyuchang Sim also submitted Questions. There was drama involved in our submissions, however. After being told that I raised a question while the voting assembly was technically not in session, Rev. Beth Ealie, Gyuchang Sim, and I ended up walking up and handing written copies of the questions to the bishop and to the conference chancellor to ensure they were acknowledged while we were in session. They were accepted and the bishop announced his responsibility according to the Book of Discipline to rule on them within 30 days. (*BOD Paragraph 2609.6*)

The Conference itself was extremely uncomfortable to Traditionalists for several more reasons that day. As stated previously, Bishop Schol announced he would not be keeping his vows to uphold the Book of Discipline on matters related to human sexuality, and that he would not hold churches, clergy, or the Board of Ordained Ministry accountable to do so either. He stated that trials around these matters were extremely painful to all involved. I, and I am sure many others, found this comment extremely hypocritical after the trial he had less than a year earlier dragged Rev. Dr. Jisun Kwak and the conference through. Later, when I spoke from the floor, I reminded him that all trials are extremely painful for those involved, not just those related to human sexuality. He acknowledged and agreed with my comment.

A certified ministry candidate, whose pronouns we were informed are she/her/hers, was brought to the podium and lectured on transgenderism and on the various choices one can make for identifying your own gender or sexuality, and on the proper use of pronouns based on how people choose to identify their gender. We were encouraged to name our preferred pronouns each time we addressed the gathered body and this was modeled by several conference leaders throughout the session. We were instructed by her to not use the Bible in arguments for legislation affirmation or dissent because the Bible can be interpreted in many ways. This presenter was commissioned as a provisional elder the following year by the Board of Ordained Ministry. She then began her PhD studies at Princeton rather than serving a church and was supported by the Board of Ordained Ministry in doing so. I point this out to highlight the apparent priorities of the board. The priority seems to be more on making a statement on matters of human sexuality than on ministry to the local church.

Little was mentioned by conference leadership or presenters about the transforming power of Jesus Christ – a power that can heal us from brokenness and confusion about any issues.

When the Way Forward Team introduced themselves, a carefully crafted story about the team was shared regarding how a "businesswoman" and a "tech wiz" were on a crashing plane and jumped off early. The businesswoman jumped "right away," unlike a youth and elderly pastor who cared more about each other and the plane and decided to stay with it. The tech wiz was depicted as a fool for when he jumped at the end, he grabbed the youth's backpack instead of a parachute. The story was a clear mocking of Dave Werhle and me. We had both dissented from the team. Me by refusing to join, and Dave, the now infamous techy enabler of our ability to email a long list of Conference members, for having dissented at the end.

Furthermore, when Rev. Leo Park stood to make a speech against the adoption of the Way Forward Report, a Point of Order was raised against his comments. He had referred to the Bible as the Word of God and the Truth and that the Book of Discipline follows the teachings of the Bible and therefore its contents should not be violated. He stated that the issue at hand was not about culture, humanity, or even sexuality, but about upholding the Bible. The person who made the point of order reminded all that he had inappropriately asserted a view of the Bible that was not supported by all. You can view the exchange and the response (or lack thereof) by Bishop Schol here or at the link given in the footnote below.[2]

Despite our efforts, the GNJ Way Forward Report and Plan was overwhelmingly adopted. Its approval was celebrated through various media and reported on in UM News. UM News, did however, at the very end of its lengthy article, report that at least one question of law[3] had been raised. Traditionalists lamented that our conference was in open rebellion to the Law of the Church and was using slick handling of the legislative process to ensure they could get away with it.

ELECTED TO THE WCA GLOBAL COUNCIL

More calls and support for the WCA came to our team as a result of our vocal dissent before and at the Special Session.

Two weeks later, on November 9th, 2019, at our Global Legislative Assembly in Tulsa, Oklahoma, I was elected to the WCA Global Council along with Rev. Dr. Jorge Acevado of Ft. Meyers, Florida, and Rev. TJ Kim of Chicago, IL. I was surprised and humbled to be elected to this thirty-five-person council that, working with the WCA staff leadership of Keith Boyette and Walter Fenton, drives the work of the WCA. I have worked with the council faithfully since that time.

I also continued in my role as the WCA of Greater New Jersey President, and still do today, having been elected in Greater New Jersey in three separate elections: 2018, 2019, and 2020.

A BRIEF FOR JUDICIAL COUNCIL

Thirty days after our Special Annual Conference, Bishop Schol announced his rulings that upheld the GNJ Way Forward Plan as presented on all of our Questions of Law (reproduced later in this chapter), except for one. This was a seemingly minor exception that no doubt had been strategically crafted to be ruled null and void. It was, in fact, NOT minor. That null and void ruling emphasized that the cabinet has appointment-making authority that supersedes any covenant made by a congregation. It thereby flagrantly touts that they have the right (and, in my opinion, will no doubt exercise it) to appoint an openly practicing homosexual clergy to a congregation even if that congregation has adopted a Way Forward Covenant that states they will not accept such an appointment because they choose to uphold the Book of Discipline law.

I began working on interested party briefs in response to the bishop's ruling. This was a new experience for me. I pulled together a team of six people for a conference call to aid me by discussing the best approach for the briefs. All were from Greater New Jersey except for two. One was a WCA-affiliated pastor/lawyer in Indiana whose wife I had worked with on another project. I also had contacted Tom Lambrecht whom I had been working with. He gave me a wonderful tutorial and supplied me with a copy of a brief he had previously submitted to Judicial Council on another matter so that I could learn how to approach stating arguments for and formatting briefs to Judicial Council.

I actually enjoyed developing the arguments, working with others to find evidence to support them, and then writing the briefs. I enjoyed learning more about Judicial Council, their work, and interacting (appropriately) with them. I have great respect for them and the incredible challenges they face, especially given the very broken environment of the United Methodist Church. God bless them.

The first question of law I had raised was:

Do the provisions of the Greater New Jersey Way Forward Report, as presented to or modified by this special session of the Greater New Jersey Annual Conference, negate, ignore, and/or violate provisions of the Book of Discipline, including those provisions which take effect on January 1, 2020, including, but not limited, to paragraphs 161G, 304.3, 304.5, 341.6, 362.1(c), 362.1e), 413.3c, 413.3d(i), 415.6, 613.19, 635.1(a), 806.9, 2701.5, 2702.1b, 2706.5.c.3, 2711.3, 2715.10, and thus are the provisions of the Greater New Jersey Way

Forward Report, as presented to or modified by this special session of the Greater New Jersey Annual Conference, null and void pursuant to Judicial Council Decision 886?

In my brief, the first point I argued was that Bishop Schol's ruling did not take into account that the session was not called properly to take *any* action during the session. The Call only stated that the GNJ Way Forward Team would present their report. There was *no mention of voting* presented. Forty-eight hours before the special session the bishop held a series of conference calls with all Clergy where he reiterated in response to numerous questions that there would be *no voting* at the session. *Less than 24-hours* before the special session, however, all voting members were notified via email that a subset of the report would be voted on. This voting was not mentioned in the call and the proper 30-day notice of the voting action was not given. Therefore, I argued, the session was null and void.

Unfortunately, because I did not explicitly ask if the session had been properly called in my submitted question, the point I made here, was not addressed by Judicial Council. I emphasize that is part of the challenge when someone knowingly calculated to suddenly change direction and call a vote within 24-hours of it happening. The full implications of what was being done did not sink in in time for me or anyone else to realize we should have called them to question on their illegal procedure for calling the vote during the session. *Lesson learned*. It would have been good to see how Judicial Council would have ruled if they had actually addressed that question.

I also argued that his ruling did not regard the implicit and explicit direction given to the conference in the substance and presentation of the Way Forward Report. This had immediately led to the widespread understanding that the session authorized local churches to adopt local policies in direct disobedience to the Book of Discipline. In fact, the very day after the session, such policies began to be implemented within the Greater New Jersey Annual Conference, citing the actions of the special session as giving authority to do so. Those local policies and their rationale have been widely distributed. I included in my brief exhibits from church websites, social media, and other communications revealing their new policies as a result of Annual Conference. Such as:

MORROW
MEMORIAL UNITED METHODIST
CHURCH

Monday October 28, 2019

To Members, friends, and others who have a connection to Morrow Church:

On Sunday October 27, 2019, at a special meeting of church council, the council discussed and passed a resolution in response to the actions of the October 26, 2019 Special Session of the Greater New Jersey Annual Conference.

Morrow Church Council Resolution:

Whereas, Morrow Church is a reconciling congregation that recognizes that all people are children of God, and that specifically the LGBTQ+ community is welcome to full participation in the life of the church, including ministry and marriage,

Whereas, the bishop of GNJ clearly stated that there would be no trials or punitive action taken against clergy or churches that break ranks with The Book of Discipline in regards to LGBTQ+ issues;

Whereas, the gathered body affirmed the work of the The Way Forward Team that creates a plan that allows more churches to join Morrow's example of an inclusive community- ministry by, with and for the LGBTQ+ community;

Whereas, the gathered body affirmed that the Board of Ordained Ministry would not take into account issues of sexuality or gender in recommending persons for ordination;

Be it resolved that Morrow Church restores its commitment of payment of apportionments to the Greater New Jersey Annual Conference.
10/27/19

When Morrow Church began withholding apportionments, it was decided to continue to do so until a time when LGBTQ+ persons in the Greater New Jersey Annual Conference have the same privileges as all members, including marriage and ordination. Morrow Church is uplifted by the actions of Bishop Schol and the decisive legislation of inclusion and affirmation that are both in alignment with providing those privileges to all members.

At Morrow Church, we firmly believe in the sacred worth of all people and are grateful for this movement of the Holy Spirit in GNJ. There is still work to do. As we continue our work in the United Methodist Church, we desire to be an example. We also hope to be a model and resource to assist our peer churches. By taking this action we can do, and be, all of these things and so much more. Thank you for agreeing to support this action.

I am grateful to be with you in ministry,

Rev. Janice Lynn

Waterloo Village United Methodist Church

November 17, 2019·6

Waterloo Covenant - On 11/17/19, at our all church meeting we unanimously passed the following covenant to be in ministry with and for the LGBTQ+ community:

Waterloo United Methodist Church affirms the following:

1. Scripture, Tradition, Reason, and Experience reveal to us that all human beings are of sacred worth, and LGBTQ+ people are not (and never have been) incompatible with Christian teaching.

2. Our present and future pastors are permitted to perform weddings for same-gender couples.

3. Our church is permitted to continue to host weddings for same-gender couples.

4. As a church who has in our past been blessed by the ministry of LGBTQ+ clergy persons, we affirm the ordination, licensing, and appointment of LGBTQ+ candidates on the basis of their gifts for ministry. We have been and remain open to receiving appointments of LGBTQ+ clergy.

5. Our church is permitted to utilize financial resources for social justice, advocacy, and ministry with all persons, including LGBTQ+ persons.

6. Waterloo United Methodist Church understands that we are free to carry out our ministry without the threat of formal charges and/or other punitive measures, recognizing that United Methodists in Greater New Jersey are

not punitive but a body of believers who choose to live in grace and unity.

This covenant was allowed by the Bishop and the Greater NJ Annual Conference of the UMC at a 10/26/19 special session during which Bishop John Schol said the following in his episcopal address: "Today as a bishop who humbly claims his first call as a pastor, I share with you that I will not forward complaints to trial against LGBTQ people who serve the church or those who bless lesbians and gays in marriage."

On 10/26/19, the Greater NJ Annual Conference of the UMC also overwhelmingly affirmed the following:

A) Bishop Schol's prayerful declaration that he will not forward for trial any charges arising out of the ministry of LGBTQ+ clergy or any clergyperson's ministry with the LGBTQ+ community,

B) the principled decision of the Board of Ordained Ministry to disregard sexual orientation or gender identity as a basis for recommending candidates for ministry, and

C) the Spirit-led witness of local churches and clergy who will create covenants for ministry with the LGBTQ+ community, while recognizing the courageous leadership of churches and pastors who have been engaged in this ministry for years.

If you have any questions re: this information, please feel free to reach out to Pastor Tim.[4]

A Way Forward Covenant

The United Methodist Church of Red Bank

A Way Forward Covenant

The United Methodist Church of Red Bank, as a reconciling congregation (church), seeks to transform our Church and world into the full expression of Christ's inclusive love. We celebrate our human family's diversity of sexual orientation, gender identity, gender expression, race, ethnicity, age, faith, history, economic status, marital status, physical and mental ability, and education.

We affirm that all people are created in the image of God and as beloved children of God, all are worthy of God's love and grace.

We welcome the full equality and full inclusion of all people in the life and ministries of The United Methodist Church of Red Bank as we journey toward reconciliation through Christ.

We affirm the same rights and privileges of marriage for all individuals. Our present and future pastors will work with all couples seeking marriage with the same respect, dignity and preparation, regardless of sexual orientation or gender identity. Our pastors and our church are open to performing wedding ceremonies for all same- and other-gender loving couples.

We affirm the candidacy, licensing, ordination, and appointment of ALL persons, including LGBTQ+ persons, regardless of marital status, on the basis of their gifts for ministry. We have been and remain open to receiving appointments of LGBTQ+ clergy. (emphasis added)

Our church is permitted to utilize financial resources for social justice, advocacy, and ministry with all people, including LGBTQ+ persons.

We work diligently to make the larger United Methodist Church inclusive and welcoming of all. We proclaim this statement of welcome to all who have known the pain of exclusion or discrimination in church and society. We invite all people to join us in our faith journey toward greater love, understanding and mutual respect.[5]

Greater NJ Annual Conference Approves "A Way Forward" Plan

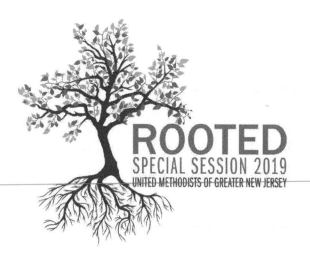

The United Methodists of Greater New Jersey leadership, meeting on Oct. 26, voted to help all churches thrive and to assist congregations to be in ministry with the LGBTQ+ community including performing weddings for same gender couples, said the Bishop of Greater New Jersey John Schol.

Separately, the Board of Ordained Ministries affirmed that it would examine candidates based on their gifts for ministry, not on their sexual orientation.

Quoting from his address, the Bishop said: "I will not forward complaints for trial against LGBTQ+ people who serve the church or those who bless gays and lesbians in marriage. I believe it is the pastoral action to take. The LGBTQ community should not live in fear of what the church will do to them because they pursue their calling, because they want to serve people, or because they seek God's blessing, because all people are of sacred worth."

Read the Bishop's full address.

The Greater New Jersey Annual Conference created a commission on A Way Forward, in response to the global UMC decision earlier this year, with respect to inclusion of LGBTQ persons in ministry and performance of same-sex weddings. Yesterday at a special meeting of the Greater New Jersey group, the report of the Commission on a Way Forward was approved.

See pdf for full report.

The plan provides a mechanism for churches to create a covenant to govern how they will operate with respect to LQBTQ+ pastors and same-sex weddings. We invite your prayers for all New Jersey congregations.[6]

These statements and social media posts had not been corrected by the leadership of the Annual Conference in the then 100+ days since the session occurred and the five questions of law were raised. Thus, I argued that the GNJ Way Forward Report was illegally enacted according to Judicial Council Decision No. 886 with its many violations of the Book of Discipline.

In my second question I asked:

> Can the provisions of the Greater New Jersey Way Forward Report, as presented to or modified by this special session of the Greater New Jersey Annual Conference, which have not been nor will be voted on at this special session be implemented without those provisions having been affirmed by the vote of delegates to a meeting of the Greater New Jersey Annual Conference? See paragraph 604 of the Book of Discipline.

The analysis given by the Judicial Council, however, as no doubt in my mind had been expected by Schol and Caterson, was superficial. Despite my asking them to do so, they did not consider the context of the entire report as presented in ruling on the ten recommendations. This is the Decision given:

Decision: No action was taken concerning the report called The Way Forward and the request for a ruling of law is moot and hypothetical. The bishop's Decision of Law is affirmed. May 5, 2021

There was a Dissenting Opinion published along with their Ruling that was issued by Beth Capen and joined by Kabamba Kiboko:

> I must dissent from the majority's holding. The majority affirms the bishop's ruling while simultaneously rejecting and modifying the bishop's ruling. The question posed is whether

the proposals contained in the report (that was presented to the special session of the annual conference for informational purposes and was not subject to the action of the special session of annual conference) could be implemented prior to the report being acted upon by the annual conference. The presiding bishop provides a direct answer to the question: "All parts of the GNJ Way Forward report which were not acted on, in order to be implemented must be affirmed by members of GNJAC at a duly called conference session." I do note that this question appears to be quasi-parliamentary, or as stated in Memorandum 546, a question of parliamentary interpretation. The inherent issue in the inquiry is a concern which appears to be shared by others who also submitted questions of law at the conclusion of the annual conference special session. This issue is evidenced in the response of the presiding bishop when he prefaces this question's answer with the sentence: "It was simply presented as a report and so there was no action that was or could be taken as to whether the report negated, ignored and/or violated The Book of Discipline (2016) as amended at the February 2019 Special Session of the General Conference." However, my dissent is premised upon the inconsistencies within the majority's analysis and decision. They have two separate holdings which cannot coexist. In the analysis the first sentence is from the bishop's answer, although it is not a direct quote and it differs from the bishop's statement. The majority set forth: "any item in a report...must be specifically voted upon." It's helpful to note that action on a report by an annual conference can take various forms. There may be circumstances which warrant an annual conference voting upon each individual item separately, but there are many situations wherein an Annual Conferences may also vote to adopt a report as a whole or by sections. In any event, in the first sentence of the analysis the majority appears to affirm the presiding bishop's response to the question by somewhat restating the essential element of the answer. In order to be implemented, any item in a report that has been presented to the members of an annual conference at its session, must be specifically voted upon. However, the second and third sentences of the analysis appear non-responsive to the immediate question of whether the un-adopted provisions of the report can be implemented without first being subject to action and approval by the annual conference. In the situation herein, the only part of the GNJ Way Forward report which was presented for a vote was the 10 recommended items which, after modification, were approved. Nothing else in the report was approved for implementation. The last sentence of the analysis [The question of law is moot and hypothetical] is confusing because the majority has affirmed the bishop's ruling that the report cannot be implemented without the prior approval of the annual conference during a duly called session. Stating in the very next sentence that the question of law is moot and hypothetical is not what the bishop ruled nor is it contained in the episcopal ruling that the majority affirmed in the preceding sentences. Holding that "the question of law is moot and hypothetical" is contrary to the bishop's ruling on this particular question and is in direct conflict with the majority decision's second sentence, "The bishop's Decision of Law is affirmed." These two particular holdings cannot coexist. Without consistency or clarity in the analysis and decision, I must respectfully dissent. I further dissent because I believe

the release and publication of this decision was premature.
May 5, 2021

They also ruled superficially as follows, taking and agreeing with
Schol's argument that only ten points were voted on and only the
one, number seven, regarded requiring cabinet honoring congregation's covenants in their appointment processes as being illegal and
therefore null and void.

> **Decision** The Judicial Council affirms the bishop's
> Decision of Law that recommendation #7 is null and
> void because it removes the discretion of the cabinet to
> carry out their mandated responsibilities.

In her concurring opinion, Beth Capen did mention the "obvious
concerns" we had in the first place about how this report was implemented intentionally to circumvent the law.

> Concurring Opinion: An annual conference resolution
> or statement cannot prevent or impede the Cabinet's
> Disciplinary mandates related to the appointment of
> clergy and I thus concur with that aspect of the major-
> ity's holding regarding the bishop's ruling, although
> the analysis of the legality of other nine items should
> include the context of the nine points, pursuant to
> Judicial Council precedents. That being said, absent
> context the nine points on their face, limited to the
> written words on paper, do not in and of themselves
> appear to violate the Discipline. **There are obvious
> concerns that some members of the annual con-
> ference had pursuant to the content of this annual**

conference special session (some of which is referenced in the dissents to JCD 1413 and 1414). Beth
Capen May 5, 2021

I believe the bishop hid behind the fact that the only action the
conference took was on the ten recommendations. As Capen
said in her dissent, on their face, the ten recommendations do
not appear to contradict the Discipline. The closest is #10, which
advocates for full inclusion. Since that term is undefined in the
action item, the Judicial Council chose to interpret it considering General Conference actions rather than reading it in the
context of the debate advocating full inclusion as supporting
same-sex marriage and LGBTQIA ordination. So the message is
that the GNJ AC is expected to operate within the parameters
of the Book of Discipline, and the Judicial Council believes that
the ten recommendations (absent #7) are in line with the Book
Of Discipline.

I had hoped Judicial Council would rule regarding the clear direction given by the bishop and the clear direction that the Board of
Ordained Ministry stated they would now take with clergy candidates. Instead, just as the bishop and his legal team had anticipated,
Judicial Council chose not to rule on those statements that did not
constitute voted on legislation adopted by annual conference. Their
rationale apparently being that intended violations are not subject
to church law in general, because the person or body might not
carry through with the intention. Never mind the evidence I had
presented that clearly showed violating the Discipline was now
being adopted as policy for churches. The bishop had found a loop-
hole and Judicial Council allowed him to exploit it.

The bottom line is that none of these decisions change the fact that GNJ continues to be accountable to the Book of Discipline and is expected to operate within its parameters. Where GNJ transgresses those parameters, a complaint could be filed. If GNJ adopted a policy that transgressed those parameters, it would be subject to a question of law. But there has to be an official action. In other words, the outcome is kind of nebulous.

My two major takeaways from this experience were that, 1) How the question of law is asked influences the decision that the Judicial Council makes; and 2) As carefully calculated, this report and special session did not present a situation where a question of law would work properly. Nonetheless, I am grateful for the experience of learning about how United Methodist bishops and conference lawyers can and do put energy into working around the Legislative and Judicial branches of the United Methodist Church.

I find it important that as we build a new denomination, The Global Methodist Church, such loopholes be examined carefully. Bishops should be given authority mainly as spiritual leaders and we should hold them accountable if their actions subvert the Book of Discipline. Enacted properly, unethical actions such as the way the GNJ Way Forward Report was implemented, could be avoided.

If anyone is ever interested in the full content of my briefs and those of Bishop Schol's regarding the Questions of Law I raised, they are available. I am happy to share them. Likewise, I am certain that, although I do not discuss them in detail in this book, Creed Pogue would be happy to share his briefs and subsequent analysis.

SHINE BABY SHINE

Franklinville UMC sanctuary, September 2019

The twenty months I spent ministering at Franklinville and Newfield churches were filled again, with much to celebrate, especially the forming of some wonderful relationships, great ministry, and the opportunity to succeed in introducing new modes of ministry and connection with the community. At Franklinville in particular, we tried a number of new ministry ideas and I celebrate the members' and leaders' willingness to step up and do so. I spent much time improving the administrative processes and rebuilding leadership teams at Franklinville. What I felt most was the love of this congregation. I felt appreciated and cared for by all. I knew they understood my love for them as well. They had some of the biggest challenges to overcome yet were committed that God would find a way and they were willing to trust. That is what following Jesus is all about.

At Newfield I learned appreciation for some ministry that was ingrained in their DNA and that they led well. Their VBS and children's program were well done and well attended. They even ran an adult VBS program that I led during my first month there that I thought was innovative and fun. They had a good adult and children's Sunday school program. Their choir and music ministry, though growing outdated in its music in some ways, was strong. In fact, I believe that Newfield is a strong model in lay leadership in terms of their desire to make a difference and ability to mobilize and get things done.

Newfield's location is a difficult one for attracting visitors, being buried in a neighborhood in a small town nestled in a rural area. Their outreach to the immediate community had been minimal. Even their many service activities tended to reach outside their immediate community rather than to those in close proximity. Yet the congregation is vibrant in terms of its support for one another and many service and social activities.

Newfield UMC Sanctuary, August, 2019.

The Spirit continued to lead me into apostolic ministry that looked strategically at how we could better reach the local community for Christ, offer a welcoming place for them to worship, and provide discipling resourcing that was relevant for the place and time (context). It was clear that neither church was yet in a relational or strategic mindset that would be amenable to consolidating too many efforts with each other, or with any of the other smaller churches in our area that we were yoked to as part of a co-operative parish. This would take some time. But the possibilities were there.

The challenges, however, were as expected. The workload was tremendous, especially with the frequent pastoral care needs and shut-in visits demanded by Newfield. Newfield's unwillingness to bend, try new ways to meet those needs, and resentment of my inability to keep up with their expectations caused unnecessary tension. Some might say the issue was a mismatch between their needs and my gifts, but I do not believe this was the real challenge. This was a challenge of a church whose leadership was having a hard time catching the vision for the future of effective, sustainable church. I do have confidence, however, that we made some real progress.

Friends and family knew that I was working over 70 hours a week on average and that this was rough for our family, but all stepped up and I am proud of them. Not only was the time spent in this particular two-point charge excessive, as others who have been in two-point charges with very needy churches know, the constant pressure of racing from meeting to meeting between the churches and arriving fully prepared and nonplussed was tough.

Joint church trip to the Museum of the Bible, Washington, DC, February 2020.

Add to that very vocal dissatisfaction from some Newfield leadership that I was not spending enough time with them and their open resentment of Franklinville and the time I spent their members, there was unnecessary pressure put on me as their pastor. Finding Sabbath was difficult. I have always been one who needed to learn to slow down more than I do and have taken pride in my ability to produce much and work hard, but at this appointment the toil became clear, even to me, to be beyond God-honoring.

I had just begun encouraging the churches to engage in some ministry together, hoping this would expand and thus have greater impact and lighten my load, when the pandemic hit. For example, I led a weekly Confirmation class with six students, three from each church. I used that class to encourage both churches to take a bus road trip together to the Museum of the Bible (50 people participated) to Washington, DC in February 2020. The class took a trip to read books to the children of displaced families at the Cumberland County Shelter, went roller skating together, and did other activities that were helping bond some of the younger families in the churches. I brought in young adult community leaders to speak to the class and to the church to expand our presence in the community. We were making some progress in what I hoped would be more shared ministry and vision someday.

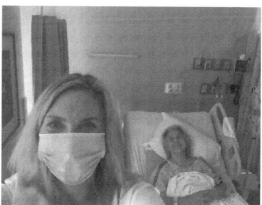

Busy and fulfilling ministry times at Franklinville and Newfield UMCs.

Christmas Eve after church with my family, 2019.

RIM AGAIN

During my time there I also attended the Board of Ordained Ministry RIM meetings that had been clarified I was required to attend as a provisional elder, submitted mandatory reports, and participated in group activities. I note that all the meetings, as had predominantly occurred in the past, were held far north of the location of most (if not all) traditional theology identifying candidates. We had been relegated to appointments in the southern region of the conference. My commute, though long, however, was by far not the worst of those affected.

In the summer and fall of 2019, we were called to meetings at Princeton UMC, Drew University, Neptune Township, and Demarest, NJ, all locations in the northern part of a very congested-to-drive-in state. We were requested to make this journey during the worst possible time, rush hour. Demarest was especially painful as it is a northern suburb of New York City. Pretty much everyone from around the state had a terrible commute there. It was conveniently, however, held at the church of one of the RIM leaders. It wasn't the first time we had been asked to travel to this location, and it had been registered previously that this was extremely inconvenient, but nonetheless we were again required to go there. That November day I spent over four hours commuting to this location. I am aware of others whose commutes were six hours. Some have small children, most had other church responsibilities to attend to those days as well. I must emphasize that the commutes we were required to take were not leisurely and peaceful countryside jaunts, but solid and congested travels, with bad weather to boot. Nonetheless, we went.

Every subsequent meeting for the 2020/2021 season had also been scheduled to take place in the northern half of the conference:

1/6-8: Sabbath Retreat Devotion: Philippians Place: Grove Hall, Ocean Grove, NJ

2/11 Devotion: Corinthians Place: Conference Center (MRC)

3/17 Devotion: Ephesians Place: Drew University

4/21 Devotion: Galatians Place: Christ UMC in Piscataway, NJ

No May Session—Annual Conference

6/16 Devotion: Romans Place: Drew University

I really do not know whether these location picks which had been consistently difficult for those in the South over the seven years that I was associated with RIM, were just being inconsiderately chosen, or if they were done so deliberately to discourage more traditional Methodist candidates. I know I am not alone in this question.

At the meeting in Demarest in November 2020, a district superintendent was present as a guest speaker. I shared with him my and other's dissatisfaction with the discourteous locations. He listened and seemed to indicate that changes were about to be made to the RIM program anyway, but he did not elaborate. The following year new leaders were brought in and the format of the meetings was drastically changed. The meetings have thus far all been on Zoom because of the pandemic. I hope that as the Covid-19 pandemic ends, the RIM meetings for others will be consistently more courteous by at least continuing Zoom options and offering gatherings spread out across the state rather than causing hardships for the same people each time.

THE PROTOCOL

In January 2020, a plan known as the Protocol of Reconciliation & Grace Through Separation Agreement was introduced by an impressive list of denominational leaders that include representatives of advocacy groups with contrasting views and bishops from around the world. This group, with the help of a well-known and respected outside mediator, collaborated on and unanimously supported a compromise proposal for the separation of The United Methodist Church. The Protocol lays out an eight-page plan that would allow conferences and churches to leave the United Methodist church—with their assets and liabilities—and join a newly formed "traditional" Methodist denomination, or perhaps another Methodist denomination that could be created. More specific information about it can be found at the footnoted links.[7]

The Protocol signers include two other progressive-leaning bishops from the northeast jurisdiction: Bishop Thomas Bickerton of New York, and Bishop Estelle Easterling of the Baltimore-Washington Annual Conference. When it was made public on January 3, 2020, Bishop Schol shortly thereafter admitted on a call to all Conference clergy that he had been caught off guard. On that call he made clear that he was not supportive and downplayed the significance of the Protocol and those who had been involved.

The Wesleyan Covenant Association fully supports the Protocol and has a detailed statement regarding it on its website.[8] As a WCA leader, I immediately began an information campaign for my own churches and for others regarding the contents of the Protocol. I created a presentation that I gave in numerous settings and released to members of our "WCA Friends" email list. I subsequently released much more info from other leaders as well as from myself, utilizing various forms of media.

The Protocol gained much support around the denomination and appeared to be heading for adoption as legislation at the 2020 General Conference to be held in May in Minneapolis. Many saw the light coming at the end of a tunnel that had been very long. Others were in denial, still clueless about its existence or contents, or were actively campaigning and otherwise working against it.

For me personally, I really thought my painful journey with the United Methodist Church was about to end. I thought I had managed to hold on through difficult circumstances, was completing ministry with them that made a difference according to God's economy, and had helped others prepare for a change that would happen in the coming summer. I would not have to deal with the Board of Ordained Ministry anymore beyond attending a couple more RIM meetings. I would simply be contacting them for transferring my provisional elder credentials/status over to the new denomination.

The Covid-19 pandemic changed all that.

COVID-19 PANDEMIC

The specific-to-ministry hardships throughout the world caused by the Covid-19 pandemic have certainly been acknowledged by many. The challenges I had in my ministry at Franklinville and Newfield, my WCA work, and my RIM participation were all also exacerbated by it. Yet I believe God has been using this time as one that is refining us all.

I learned much from both churches as they rallied in their own ways to take on the challenges of the pandemic and to care for one another and the community. I celebrate also that my apostolic gifts put new ministry and vision into both churches and that my shepherding gifts were pushed to grow during this time. I do believe Newfield's priorities on shepherding helped me become better with those skills as well.

One of the priorities I had guided each church to in the early months of our ministry together was upgrading their internet presence and technology for their sanctuaries. Once the pandemic hit, at least we had those pieces in place. We did end up having a mostly online worship service and other activities for roughly a year (with few exceptions), but it again became an opportunity to combine ministries of both churches and increase their reach. Our online following between the two churches averaged throughout the time over 425 views per week, far outpacing our pre-pandemic regular attendance. I was able to incorporate more youth and other families into leadership roles as they became part of leading the weekly online service from the comfort of their own homes, or by pre-recording segments of scripture reading or singing and other elements with me at the churches or other locations. While producing an online service was extremely time consuming, I enjoyed learning new skills and that the platform lent itself to much creativity and opportunity to reach more people.

We began other new ministries related to the pandemic, with making masks, initiating phone chains, and enhancing our food pantry at Franklinville. Newfield also stepped up its giving to other local food pantries. I was particularly blessed by how we completely revamped and increased the Franklinville food pantry and those doing ministry through it and receiving from it. The food pantry became a central way the church stayed together through the pandemic. It also helped rejuvenate our connection with the community and other civic leaders who began partnering with us.

BLACK LIVES MATTER, FOX NEWS, AND ANOTHER CONFERENCE SNUB

Perhaps the most important ministry I led during this appointment, however, began with the Holy Spirit tugging on me when during the aftermath and rising protests regarding the killings of George Floyd, Breonna Taylor, and Ahmaud Arbery, Franklinville, New Jersey made international headlines for all the wrong reasons. On June 8th, 2020, during a peaceful Black Lives Matter protest organized by Franklin Township high school students, two white men acted out the killing of George Floyd in their yard as protestors, including small children, walked by on the road. Their actions were accompanied by offensive and hurtful language. Video was captured of their antics and given to the press. Franklinville quickly gained a reputation around the world as a bastion for racist hate.

I knew, as a community leader, I was called to do something. We clearly had significant racism problems in Franklinville if anyone felt comfortable acting out in such a way as these two men had. At the same time, we were being demonized beyond what was warranted through the press and by others. We were cast as an entire community that was overtly and aggressively racist.

My first response was to contact members of the church to hear their reactions. Most were disgusted and embarrassed by the antics that had been displayed. All condemned the actions and racism itself. There was a clear sentiment that racism exists, but "I personally am not racist and neither is my town." I also learned that because many in our church had ties to the local police (either having served themselves or their spouses, parents, children, or other family members, often several generations), many were skeptical of the Black Lives Matter (BLM) movement itself and resentful of its actions. Many interpreted BLM as making unwarranted attacks on the police that were both putting police in harm's way and disrespecting police for the sacrifices that they make. They also wanted their town to not be painted as blatantly racist as they believed whole-heartedly that it was not. I also learned that there were relatives to the two men who had acted out so hatefully in our church who were very embarrassed and saddened by their actions.

I contacted other pastors in town to see what they were doing regarding these events. I learned that there was another Black Lives Matter protest scheduled for the coming Saturday, but all pastors I interacted with had decided to stay away from it and were skeptical of its intent and leaders. None seemed interested in doing any ministry beyond prayer and discussion in their own local churches regarding this issue.

So, I called the mayor, Jake Bruno. He answered my call right away. He told me it was his hope to begin building a coalition to better unify our community and address tensions once we got past the upcoming protest, which would be the third in two weeks in Franklinville. He had attended the first protest at the local high school (Delsea Regional) in support. He had not been present at the second, but was providing police support at the third one coming up. He told me the third one was scheduled before the second protest occurred and was not planned in response to the problems that had occurred. He gave me the phone number for the woman who was organizing it.

When I called Beverly Merrit, I identified myself as a pastor who wanted to help but that I would be coming at this from the lens of faith and I did not know if that was a lens she welcomed. She started to cry. She said she had been praying that God would send her an ally with faith from the community. She thanked Jesus.

She said she could not get any ministers from the area to support her and she was stunned that the mayor gave me her number. She said she had simply planned a small demonstration, thinking maybe fifty people would attend. She had planned it a couple of weeks earlier after having attended a wonderful, multicultural, peaceful protest in Vineland. Now her plans were being overtaken. She had been told there were ANTIFA representatives coming that she did not want, protestors from as far away as Chicago and there would be a media frenzy. She was admittedly rattled.

We prayed. We talked about the importance of this being a peaceful demonstration that was not taken over by outside interests. I was very impressed with her faith and desires for this event to glorify God. At the same time, she was also very understandably wounded, stung hard by the sin of racism and perceived wrongs by the local government, including the current mayor. She was a life-long resident of Franklinville and described many injustices done to her and children that, in her opinion, should have been corrected by local authorities, including the schools, but had not been. I believe she spoke truth.

She was far from anti-police, however, and was genuinely concerned that message be given. She had support from black ministers from outside the community who planned to attend the event. She asked if I would speak at the protest. I accepted.

I contacted a relative of the two brothers who had committed the heinous acting out of the killing of George Floyd. I told her to relay the message that I was available to them and their mother for prayer support. She was doubtful they would be interested in my support, but she gave the mother my phone number and the message anyway. I was never contacted.

The event was planned to begin in the parking lot of the Franklin Township Public Library just a block from our church. I organized church leaders to offer a prayer service in our parking lot and open the lot to those who would like to park and walk over to the event. Our soon to be Staff Parish Relations Committee Chair, Nicole Cliver, led the Prayer Vigil while I spoke and walked at the demonstration.

Church members had a variety of responses. Some attended the event and marched in it. Some went to the prayer vigil. Some committed to pray from the safety of their own homes because of Covid and concern for possible violence. Others literally boarded up their windows and left town for the day. Some contacted me in support, some contacted me in fear for me, and some expressed disagreement and resentment that I was getting involved in what they perceived as an anti-police event.

I also asked the Newfield Church leadership to get involved as they were in the same township and only ten minutes away, but I received no support from them. I did receive a couple of angry emails from a some of their church members and a couple of emails expressing support but declining to be there because of previous commitments. I also reached out several other UMC pastors in the area, but none chose to get involved. My friend Rev. Dr. Jisun Kwak from Audubon UMC committed to attend and did. I had a good conversation about the event with a black UMC pastor who lives in Franklinville but pastors a UMC church elsewhere. He was not available to attend but promised to send some people our way. Personal friends, my daughter, and her college-aged friends attended and of course my amazing husband.

Beverly and I called and texted one another frequently that week to pray. The day of the event, June 13th, was incredibly Spirit-filled. It was a beautiful day, not a cloud in the sky and a perfect temperature in the low seventies and no humidity. Over five hundred people attended. Our church parking lot was filled with cars, and Nicole led a wonderful prayer vigil.

The township had prepared for us, setting up a podium and offering a sound system for our use. There was police assistance along the entire route from the public library to the police station, a two-mile walk.

When we arrived for the event thirty minutes ahead of the planned start, however, the parking lot was filled with people. There were already media everywhere, including in helicopters. ANTIFA representatives were parked in front of the Community Center where they had set up a sound system and were spewing their messages to much attention.

When Beverly arrived, she stood up and denounced the ANTIFA representatives as not part of the leadership of this protest. She was filled with the Spirit and they were quieted. I and a couple of black ministers from outside Franklin Township gave speeches. You can read mine here or at the link in the footnote.[9] It is heavily lifted with permission from Rev. Dr. Jeff Greenway, then chair of the WCA Global Council who had spoken previously in Ohio at a similar event. I then led the entire crowd in the Lord's Prayer. It was beautiful.

When Beverly spoke, her words were firm. She repeatedly stated that she thanked God for the police and that she was not antipolice.

But she also held her ground that actions had occurred because local government, including the police and mayor, were not doing a good enough job to stop them. She then shared her vision about the order for the day and <u>directed the crowd to march not with loud shouts</u>,[10] but instead in complete silence as Dr. Martin Luther King had also directed in Selma. To many people's amazement, <u>as CBS 3 Philly News and others documented, the crowd complied</u>.[11] I was very proud to be part of this God and people-honoring event.

Black Lives Matter Peaceful Protest, Franklinville, NJ, June 2019.

I gave one of the opening speeches at the BLM Protest in Frankliville.

Beverly Merrit, who organized the event, delivered a powerful speech.

When I was interviewed by NJ.com that day, I told them what I really believe, that the church needs to step up and be leaders in these matters.[12] But what I really wanted to explore was how we could do so by actually engaging people in interactions that would lead to better understanding and thus better relationships. I prayed about this.

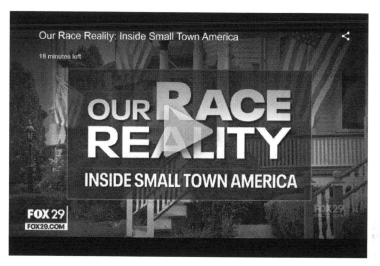

FOX NEWS made a thirty-minute documentary about Franklinville.

Within a couple days Beverly and I were contacted by Philadelphia FOX NEWS affiliate's Bill Anderson. He wanted to do a thirty-minute documentary about what had happened in Franklinville and the town's response to it for a new regular series entitled "Our Race Reality: Inside Small Town America." At first I was skeptical, but as I listened to him and remembered him from his regular program, "For Goodness Sake," which highlights positive activities in the Philadelphia area, I agreed to the interview. Bill told me he was trying to get the mayor of Franklinville to agree to an interview as well, but was having no luck. I told him I would do what I could.

Meanwhile, Mayor Bruno invited me to a Community Roundtable discussion and luncheon to discuss the problems around race and how to better achieve unification. I agreed to attend. I also encouraged the mayor to accept the interview with Bill Anderson via text:

> Hi Mayor Bruno, I so apologize for reaching out to you so late. This is Rev. Beth Caulfield from Franklinville UMC.

I am trying to reach you about what appears to me to be a very good opportunity- Bill Anderson, who hosts the Fox 29 series "For Goodness' Sake" is doing a documentary on the good things that are happening in Franklinville after the Monday June 8 protest incident. He contacted me this evening and I do believe this is an opportunity to talk about community leadership's desire to improve relationships and educate in the community. I have agreed to speak with him on camera tomorrow. I think it would be a good for you as well. This is a standup reporter whose work I have admired on very different subjects in the past. Thoughts? I have his cell if you need it.

Sent from my iPhone

The Mayor's Roundtable was attended by roughly forty people, including the town council, high school principal, chief of police, other community leaders, a police chaplain, and roughly twenty black members of the community. The luncheon was excellent and the mayor's agenda even better.

We opened with prayer. Mayor Bruno said he did not have much to say that day but instead wanted to listen to the community and turned the floor over to us. For over two hours there were story after story from people who felt they had experienced unjust treatment and felt black citizens were left out of local community. There were comments of desires to improve relationships and agreement that if we could try as a community, we could make inroads into this major problem. Suggestions for what could be done were recorded by the Town Council. The mayor and Council listened. There was a spirit of enthusiasm as we ended the meeting.

During the meeting I received a text from Bill Anderson thanking me for contacting the mayor as the mayor had agreed to be interviewed directly after the roundtable.

The **Fox 29 Philadelphia documentary**[13] was completed and aired four times over the weekend of July 9-11 in the nation's fourth largest media market. It was a nice birthday weekend present for me.

I shared about the documentary with the bishop, my DS, and the Conference Communications Director. All three responded. They acknowledged this was "well done," "wonderful," and "great" ministry, respectively. My DS even said he saw the documentary on TV.

Yet only a one sentence blurb was included in the Conference Digital Digest two days later. It was directly under praising that UM News had covered the bishop when he had spoken at a small church/district-sponsored event entitled, "Silence is Not an Option."

We at Franklinville were not contacted by Conference Communications or anyone in the Religion and Race Commission, including those who organized the rally where the bishop spoke. Our accomplishments in Franklinville were not covered any further. Given the secular attention we were receiving and the conference's long pattern under Bishop Schol's leadership of promoting GNJ local church ministries that receive media attention, it seemed an odd omission. Many could celebrate and learn from what other United Methodists were doing to work with local community leaders. But they were not going to celebrate.

Franklin Township Unity Committee, September 2020

Just a couple months later, in September 2020, Mayor Bruno went on to appoint a Franklin Township Unity Committee and I was asked to serve on this fifteen-member team. In spite of many Covid restrictions, we began meeting monthly, put together a strong vision and mission statement, formed subcommittees on Intercultural Competency, Community Events, Community and Police Relations, and Media/Web/Information. I was to chair the Intercultural Competency group.

We sponsored several events including a community Halloween event, a craft fair at the Newfield New Terrace Community Center that serves the local black community, and offered Thanksgiving and Christmas meal delivery through the Franklinville UMC Food Pantry (white church) and New Life Ministries Church (black church). This was the first time these churches had partnered together and that all these groups had come together as one. We also coordinated a Martin Luther King Day community cleanup with Delsea Regional High School.

Additionally, in November 2020, I invited our police in to be prayed over at both the Franklinville and Newfield churches. This was a special opportunity for our police and our church families to pray and honor their own family members who have and are serving in law enforcement. Both services were beautiful.

I led our Franklinville and Newfield congregations in prayer for our local police.

Bill Anderson contacted me in January 2021 and asked if he could come back and do a second documentary about how we were doing as a community six months later. He featured our work at the church, the Community Unity Advisory Committee, and Mayor Bruno along with other concerned citizens. Our church was featured even stronger in <u>Race Reality in America: Revisiting Small Town America</u>.[14] It was even better coverage of our church's involvement in the community than the first documentary.

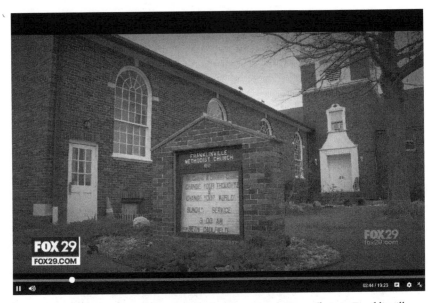

FOX News produced a second documentary on our race relations efforts in Franklinville, January 2021.

Again, I reached out to the conference and shared what we were doing and included the link to the second documentary. Again, there was no follow up or coverage by Conference Communications. Instead, the final rocks were about to be thrown.

SHAKE THE DUST OFF

MY UMC ORDINATION DECISION

From the moment it was announced in April 2020 that the General Conference would be delayed because of the pandemic, I dreaded June 2020. That was when I needed to make a decision that I thought would never be needed if the General Conference had occurred and the Protocol passed. I knew that I was entering the last year that I could go forward to be examined by the Board of Ordained Ministry to be approved for full ordination orders. If I did not receive approval that year, following the stipulations of the Book of Discipline, my candidacy would be discontinued.

My first option was to declare that I would go forward and proceed for the third time in my experience through the rigors of preparing paperwork, obtaining written references, scheduling ministry visits and projects and Bible studies to be turned in by November 1, 2020. I would then be examined and go through the interview process at the retreat, or "Hunger Games" as the BOM Chair had referred to them to me previously. I could do all this with absolutely no confidence that I would be treated fairly.

I thought about all the tears, humiliation, anxiety, and therapy I had experienced in the past. I knew that I would receive another letter declining to recommend me for ordination and it would have nothing to do with my readiness for ministry or even the fruits of my ministry. It would have to do with my theology, my leadership in the WCA, and general resentment and jealousy toward me.

My only other option was to not do it. To not go forward and then have the Board declare me discontinued because my time had run out according to the Book of Discipline. Neither option was appealing.

I prayed a lot about it. I consulted many friends and family. I waited, hoping, something might happen to change me needing to make such a decision. I thought much about the reasons not to go forward beyond the inevitable conclusion that I would be denied anyway. I thought about that I could not ethically take vows to a denomination whose leaders openly ignored and disavowed its doctrines and regulations. I thought about giving vows to a denomination whose leaders predominantly espoused a very different theology and understanding of the Gospel than I do. I thought about vowing to stay in communion with people who were doing me harm. I wondered if it was ethical for me to take such vows when I was resolved to leave the denomination to be part of a new one that more closely aligns with my theology and ethos.

But then I realized this: If recommended for ordination, the vows I would be taking would be to uphold the Book of Discipline, with all its doctrines and disciplines. When I realized that, it occurred to me that those were vows that indeed were important to me. They were vows I wanted to take. Even though I was confident I would be denied, I had more peace that attempting to do so would be most honoring to God.

Resolved, I contacted Rev. Saul Pawn to declare my intent to go forward and completed the necessary paperwork to make that intent official.

On August 31st, I received an email stating that the Board of Ordained Ministry registrar needed an updated physical for me and a copy of my Master of Divinity transcript. Updating the physical made sense as it had been several years since I had submitted one. They had already required in the past a second psychological exam, second credit and background/criminal history reports, and other redundancies, so I was not surprised.

But the request for my transcript was a different matter. I had gone before the board three times in the past eight years (once to be commissioned in 2013, and twice for full orders, 2016 and 2017). All three times, my transcripts (undergraduate and graduate schools) had been in my records. I would not have been allowed to move forward in the process if they had not been included. Now I was being told that they did not have my official transcript. This had never come up before. I contacted the Board, and they confirmed that they did not have one.

Although incredulous, I politely responded that I would get it and the physical, but, quite bluntly, I felt like I was being harassed. I prayed for several days. One evening I clearly understood the Holy Spirit speaking to me. "It is now time to stop casting your pearls before swine."

So I did. From there on out I made no attempt to complete any paperwork required to go before the Board. Instead, I began thinking about a future beyond the United Methodist Church that was coming, and I had peace.

WESLEYAN COVENANT BAND

For a while I had been feeling a need to have a deeper connection with other traditional female church leaders that would be moving with me to the Global Methodist Church. I wanted to be in an accountability group of my own where theological affinities would be a given, spirits would be mature, and understanding about what was taking place with the birth of a new denomination would give common ground for conversation. I wanted to be in what John Wesley had originally intended as the core disciplining mechanism for Methodists: a band. Yes, I had friends I prayed with, had been in peer learning groups and small groups, but a Wesleyan band brings you even closer to one another and the Lord. I had reached out to a couple of women about this in 2018, but never followed through. The timing was now right.

I contacted the following three women and they all readily agreed. Rev. Nako Kellum, Rev. Dr. Kim Reisman, and Rev. Janet Lord.

Rev. Nako Kellum is an Elder serving a local church in Tarpon Springs, Florida with whom I had become friends with while serving on the WCA Next Steps Working Group. Nako is on the WCA Global Council and serves as Secretary of the Florida WCA Chapter. She also serves on the Board of Ordained Ministry for the Florida Annual Conference. Her non-anxious presence and big heart inspire and comfort me.

Rev. Dr. Kim Reisman serves as the Executive Director of World Methodist Evangelism and thus is connected beyond the United Methodist World, as she works with a number of Wesleyan-based denominations. Kim is based in West Lafayette, Indiana. She has served as a General Conference delegate for Indiana. I had met Kim on several occasions, beginning in 2016 at the initial WCA Global Gathering in Chicago where she presented, and at a gathering of leaders in Pensacola, Florida in 2018. Kim's energy, creativity and love of all people add fuel to my fire.

Rev. Janet Lord is a UMC Deacon whom I met as part of the Next Steps Working Group in 2018. She serves as the Board of Ordained

Ministry registrar/Ministerial Coordinator in the Western Pennsylvania Conference and hails from Creighton, PA, which is just outside of Pittsburgh. She has been a General Conference delegate in the past and is one for 2022 as well. Janet is incredibly resourceful, keeps me laughing, and has a heart of gold.

We began our band in October 2020 and what a blessing it has been. In May 2021, we unanimously agreed to add Cara Nicklas to our group. Cara is UMC laity and when not serving the church directly, is a partner at a law firm in Tulsa, Oklahoma. She has served as a UMC General Conference Delegate and currently serves on both the WCA Global Council and the Transitional Leadership Team for the Global Methodist Church. Cara keeps us hungry for the Lord and rounds us out nicely. I give thanks for her and all in this group.

We meet weekly for an hour via Zoom. We try to follow the traditional questions offered by Wesley as captured below. This is from an app we use, *Discipleship Bands*, by Seedbed, which has been very helpful as it offers tools, devotions, prayers, etc.

questions

Each person takes 15–20 minutes to share around the questions below.

1. How is it with your **soul**?

2. What are your **struggles** and **successes**?

3. How might the **Spirit** and **Scriptures** be speaking in your life?

WHEN YOU ARE READY TO GO DEEPER...

4. Do you have any **sin** that you want to confess?

5. Are there any **secrets** or hidden things you would like to share?

When each person has finished sharing, allow time for prayer.

This group has indeed been a blessing and Godsend! They have been walking with me through this transition and the writing of this memoir, encouraging me with prayer and wisdom. God is good and so are these friends!

ENDING WITH THE UMC

As the November 1, 2020 deadline for the Board of Ordained Ministry paperwork being turned in came closer, friends attempted to sway me to submit something. "Just submit anything," they told me. Others suggested that I request an extension due to the challenges of the pandemic or the uncertainty of the direction of the denomination with the impending split. I considered their suggestions. I prayed with my Band. But I had a peace about my decision. A sadness, but a peace.

On October 28, I received the following email and responded as directed.

Hello,

Since I have not received any paperwork for you or from you, I would like you to please respond to me asking to be deferred from being a candidate for Full Membership this year.

Waiting for your response,

Beverly Karlovich| Connectional Ministries Administrative Assistant

O: 732.359.1086 | E: bkarlovich@gnjumc.org

Beth Caulfield

Nov. 1, 2020 5:59 pm

Dear Beverly,

I ask to be deferred from being a Candidate for Full Membership this year.

Bless you,

Beth

I did not receive any further communication until February 1, 2021. At that time, the new chair of the Board of Ordained Ministry, Rev. Michelle Ryoo, contacted me by phone to tell me I would be discontinued effective 6/30/2021 because I had reached the eight-year maximum time in the process. I asked if the Board was willing to rethink this given the extraordinary circumstances with the pandemic and within the denomination at this time.

She responded by reading the paragraph in the Discipline that stated I had maxed out the time allotted. She said she was sorry and appeared to be sad. I believe she was. I felt nothing. I told her that clearly, I had a different path. She suggested that I contact my District Committee on Ministry and apply to become a licensed local pastor as it would be a way to have some credentialling to stay in ministry during these turbulent times.

Within a few days I received the following letter:

February 5, 2021

Dear Rev. Caulfield:

Grace and peace to you in the name of our Lord and Savior, Jesus Christ.

I am writing to inform you that your provisional membership will be discontinued on June 30, 2021. We give thanks to God and you for your faithful ministry as a provisional member since commissioned in 2013.

The Book of Discipline clearly specifies that, "No member shall be continued on provisional membership beyond the eighth regular session following their admission to provisional membership." (Par. 327)

Furthermore, it states, "After discontinuance, provisional members may be classified and approved as local pastors." (Par. 327.7) If you would like to pursue this direction, please consult with your district superintendent and the District Committee on Ministry.

I pray God's blessings upon you, Beth. You are in my thoughts and prayers during this season of discernment. May God continue to light your path with grace and mercy.

Grace and Peace,

Rev. Michelle Ryoo

Chair, GNJ Board of Ordained Ministry

Cc: Bishop John Schol, Resident Bishop, GNJAC

Rev. Glenn Conaway, District Superintendent

Rev. Jessica Naulty, Conference Relations Committee

The Global Board of Higher Education for the United Methodist Church states the following about local licensed pastors:

If God is calling you to become a pastor, but you do not see seminary as the best path for you, then you may want to consider becoming a local pastor. When appointed, a local pastor performs the usual duties of a pastor, including:

Preaching and teaching.

Leading in worship and liturgy.

Receiving new members.

Performing the sacraments of Baptism and Holy Communion in their appointment setting.

Performing the services of marriage (where state laws allow), burial and confirmation.

A local pastor answers God's call to serve the mission of Jesus Christ typically by serving a local congregation in The United Methodist Church. They need not make themselves available as itinerant ministers and are not ordained or elected into full membership of the annual conference. Additionally, a local pastor's authority is only within their appointment setting and does not extend beyond it. Local pastors serve under the authority of a license for pastoral ministry after completing the steps outlined in ¶ 315 of The Book of Discipline (2016) and meeting any annual conference requirements.

I would be considered in normal circumstances amply qualified for this role, given my educational credentialing alone. I did not want to disappoint my current churches and I did believe we had good ministry ahead of us. I thought and prayed hard about what to do. I decided to follow Michelle's advice. I contacted our District Committee Chair, Rev. Jim Bolton, and District Superintendent.

The following emails occurred beginning the next day.

RE: Obtaining Local Pastor Licensing

Feb. 2, 2021, 9:55 AM

Hi Glenn,

As you are aware I am being discontinued by BOOM. I am interested in pursuing local pastor licensing. I am unsure who to contact for DCOM, I know there have been some retirements announced.

Can you guide me through this process. I believe we need to talk.

Blessings,

Beth

Glenn Conaway

Feb. 2, 11:39AM

Hi Beth,

I have not received official notification from the BOOM about the discontinuance, however I was told that I will receive a copy of the letter. At this time you would contact Jim Bolton (Pitman UMC) who is the chair of the DCOM and ask to be placed on the schedule to meet with the DCOM. I know that the schedule is filled for February already. Yes, I think it would be best if we did talk but it will have to be later this week. I am also copying Jim on this email so that he is in the loop why you would be contacting him and DCOM. Keeping you in prayer as you discern God's leading.

Peace,

Glenn

Glenn J. Conaway

Delaware Bay District Superintendent

Beth Caulfield

Feb 2, 1:25pm

Hi Jim,

Hope you are well. When can I get on DCOM's agenda and how do I prepare for the process I'll be entering? Perhaps it is best to talk in person? 908-938-1379.

Blessings,

Beth

forrevjb@aol.com

Wed, Feb 3, 12:35 AM

Hi Beth,

I hope this finds you safe and well. Thank you for your email.

I would like to schedule you to meet with the Delaware Bay District Committee on Ordained Ministry. My understanding is that you will be coming to the Delaware Bay DCOM seeking information and approval to pursue a Local Pastors License.

We would welcome the opportunity to meet with you via ZOOM on **Thursday, March 4, at 2:00pm.**

Please confirm your receipt of this email and if that date and time are good. As requested in your email I will give you a phone call later this week.

May God bless you Beth, your family, and your churches.

Grace and Peace,

Jim Bolton

Delaware Bay District DCOM Chairperson

Beth Caulfield

Feb 3. 7:01 am

Thank you, Jim. Received and on my calendar. I look forward to our conversation.

Beth

All seemed to be set. However, the morning of Tuesday, February 8th, the day after Bishop Schol's cabinet met, I received a call from District Superintendent Glenn Conaway. He stated he was calling to inform me that the District Committee had met and decided that they were not going to license me as a local pastor. When I asked how such a decision could be made without me even going before them, I was simply told that they had decided.

When I asked why this had been decided, I was told it was because I have stated that I will be going to the new denomination when it forms. I said while that may be true, we do not know when or if that will occur at this point. I also said I was surprised that they did not want to wait until the decision that would soon be made by the denomination regarding whether to postpone the General Conference another year or not was made. General Conference would pass the Protocol as most still believed, and a new denomination would be launched. If the conference was again postponed, I do not see why they would not want me to continue serving.

I told Glenn that my intention was, as I always have done, to serve the local church faithfully. He responded by saying I could continue in my appointment until June 30th. Afterwards I could be considered as a supply pastor.

A supply pastor is a lay member who is appointed to serve a church. A supply pastor is not ordained or even licensed. They do not oversee the sacraments. Supply is akin to just keeping the doors open so the congregation still worships. They are paid a minimal stipend.

We had lengthy discussion about my disappointment in my treatment by the Board of Ordained Ministry, the cabinet, and the bishop over the years. I told him that I really did not see a reason, at this point why I should continue under such duress. Eight years was more than enough. He reiterated that I had a job until June 30th and then could be considered as a supply pastor. He told me to let him know what I wanted to do. I said I would.

Saddened but peaceful is the way I would describe how I felt from that day forward. I had hoped, as did many, that the General Conference would proceed forward to occur at the end of August 2021. On February 20th it was announced that it would be delayed yet another year, to August 2022.

At the same time, I knew that we would be announcing the name, a Transitional Leadership Team, a new website, and a draft Book of Doctrines and Disciplines for the new denomination on March 1st. We were declaring to the world that the Global Methodist Church would be launching. The plan was and still is of this writing for that launch to not occur until the passage of the Protocol by General Conference 2022. Nonetheless we are moving forward to prepare for that day. There is still much work to be done to prepare for the coming denomination, especially here in Greater New Jersey, and I have excitement about that work and the calling I have for it.

That week our Greater New Jersey WCA Chapter Council met and approved a new position that we had been working on for months. We also approved that I would go into the position on a fu-time basis, effective March 15th. I cannot tell you the excitement that I felt and still do.

On Saturday, February 27th, I contacted District Superintendent Conaway and the Staff Parish Relations Committee Chairs for both Franklinville and Newfield United Methodist churches with the following email. I also called a Zoom meeting with the Franklinville Pastor Relations Committee.

> **From:** *Beth Caulfield*
>
> **Sent:** *Saturday, February 27, 2021 4:17 PM*
>
> **To:** *Nicole; Dolores Hoffman; Glenn J. Conaway, Delaware Bay District Superintendent*
>
> **Subject:** *Informing*
>
> *Dear Pastor-Parish Relations Chairs of Franklinville and Newfield United Methodist Churches and Delaware Bay District Superintendent.*
>
> *Due to the changes transpiring, and happening quite swiftly in the United Methodist denomination, I was informed by our district superintendent that my clergy ministry will not be supported or certified beyond the current appointment season. Therefore I am resigning my position as your pastor effective March 8th.*

I celebrate and cherish much about our time together and the relationships that have been built with you and the surrounding communities, especially during this very difficult season for all. While this announcement is challenging to make and I'm sure to hear, I am confident it is the Lord's leading at this time.

In Christ's Abundant Love,

Rev. Beth Caulfield

The next day I announced from the pulpit of both churches basically the same message.

I heard nothing from the District Superintendent until the following Monday evening, March 1st.

Resignation Letter

Glenn Conaway gconaway@gnjumc.org

Mar 1, 2021, 4:54 PM

~~to me, Delores, nicole~~

Dear Beth,

The attached letter is acceptance of your resignation letter. The cabinet and interim Bishop have made the effective date as of today, March 1, 2021. I would ask that you please return all keys, computers, credit cards, etc to the SPRC Chairperson, of each church.

May you continue to find God's guidance as you further discern the call of God on your ministry.

Peace,

Glenn

Glenn J. Conaway
Delaware Bay District Superintendent

The next day I followed the instructions from the district superintendent and cleaned out my offices and returned everything. Within a week I received notice that all benefits had ceased effective May 1st. I believe that had been carefully considered in the decision to move my last day up, as a March 7th last day would have extended my benefits through June 1st. But at this point, I had come to expect such decisions from the bishop and his cabinet.

Also, in keeping with his style, I received an endorsement for preaching on my LinkedIn profile from Bishop Schol and the following email from the Episcopal Office Administrator:

From: *Soomin Lee*

Sent: *Wednesday, March 3, 2021 11:22 AM*

To: *bcaulfield710@gmail.com*

Subject: *Thank you from Bishop Schol*

Sent on behalf of Bishop Schol

Dear Beth,

Thank you for your ministry and service in GNJ. Your courageous spirit and determination have helped many ministries move forward. I am particularly grateful for your small group ministry and Team Vital leadership while on staff. I have always believed in your potential.

As you continue to pursue your call, I pray for you and your family. I am grateful that our paths crossed.

Keep the faith!

John

That was it. A process that had begun in 2008 when my pastor had handed me a copy of *The Christian as Minister* (Cokesbury), ended thirteen years later, when I exited the United Methodist church as clergy in 2021. That dream with Jesus pointing me to a toolkit full of papers, dissertations, and credentials telling me "go to seminary," with the angels ascending an elevator with me seemed to be dead. Or at least I had grossly misinterpreted it.

CLARITY

HOW COULD THIS ALL HAPPEN?

In his article, "Loyalty is a Dangerous Virtue, the Church Needs Whistleblowers," Rev. Dr. Michael Jensen asserts that:

> Abusive leadership often happens within toxic cultures. When you listen to people who've come out of abusive churches or organisations, they tell you that the system was toxic. The organisation behaved in a damaging way, and we can't lay all blame at the feet of one leader.[1]

That is indeed my first point regarding the United Methodist Church I have experienced and what happened to me and others like me: The culture is toxic. Certainly, unchecked jealousy is one aspect of this toxicity. "For wherever there is jealousy and selfish ambition, there you will find disorder and evil of every kind" (James 3:16).

The UMC retains a toxic culture that is predicated on a system where, as Christian therapist and professor Rev. Dr. Chuck DeGroat puts it, "unaccountable, narcissistic leaders have free-reign, often choosing staff or elders who are yes-men or yes-women."[2] Dr. Graham Joseph Hill, in his March 2020 article, "Whistleblowing Glorifies Christ: Challenging Narcissistic Leaders And Toxic Cultures," states that a toxic culture "defends narcissistic leaders at all costs, punishes those who speak up, and rewards silence and submission."[3]

Chuck DeGroat also emphasizes that narcissist church leaders, when confronted, deny, blame, express anger, and engage in irrational retaliations. He says that they get away with such behavior because the "people around these narcissistic leaders have often been gaslighted and bullied to an extent they have no will or conviction left. So, whether people challenge the narcissist often depends on checks and balances outside the organisation." These professional observations precisely summarize my experience.

Many do not realize that basic checks and balances that undergird other employers are not applicable to the church in the U.S. and elsewhere when it comes to employing clergy. Specifically, I refer to the to the *ministerial exception,* sometimes known as the *"ecclesiastical exception"* of the First Amendment of the U.S. Constitution. I believe a toxic employment system for clergy has developed in at least the UMC through the *misapplication* of this clause. The *ministerial exception* is:

> A legal doctrine in the United States barring the application of anti-discrimination laws to religious institutions' employment relationships with its "ministers." As explained by the Supreme Court in the landmark case *Hosanna-Tabor Evangelical Lutheran Church and School v. E.E.O.C.,* the exception is drawn from the First Amendment to the United States Constitution, and seeks to both (1) safeguard religious groups" "freedom . . . to select their own ministers," a principle rooted in the Free Exercise Clause, and (2) prevent "government involvement in ecclesiastical decisions," a prohibition stemming from the Establishment Clause. When applied, the exception operates to give religious institutions an affirmative

defense when sued for discrimination by employees who qualify as "ministers"; for example, female priests cannot sue the Catholic church to force their hiring.[4]

The intent of this exception is to ensure religious freedoms are not impeded by the State. That is very important as it guards liberties that were sought in the foundation of this country. It allows churches to set clergy employment standards and practices based on their religious beliefs that might otherwise be infringed upon by secular law. I would never advocate that those liberties be lifted.

But the *ministerial exception* also unintentionally, as it has historically and is currently interpreted, ensures freedom by the Church from responsibility for developing healthy safeguards and protections for those they govern and employ through their own self-regulated ecclesiastical systems and decisions. In other words, when a clergy is mistreated by the Church, other than by sexual abuse or overt racially-motivated violence, there is no protection afforded them through the U.S. court system because of the ministerial exception. The federal Equal Employment Opportunity Commission and its state level equivalents determine whether harassment in the workplace is actionable depending on whether the employer is covered by a state or federal anti-discrimination law, and whether the employee is being harassed due to retaliation or his or her membership in a protected class as defined by any laws that cover the employer. The ministerial exception means the Church is exempt from that coverage for its clergy. You cannot challenge the justice/legality of church clergy systems no matter how toxic, biased, unfair in compensation, advancement opportunities, or any other employment practices. The system you would challenge has been declared not liable for U.S. law and governs itself. Most recently, on January 12, 2022, a Chicago circuit court dismissed an appeal from a former pastor in an Evangelical Covenant-connected church stating:

> Different religious organizations may have different views regarding what constitutes fitness to serve as clergy…We cannot review such decisions without violating the first amendment by approving some views and rejecting others. Thus, because plaintiff's complaint directly challenged defendant's internal investigative and disciplinary procedures, the circuit court lacked jurisdiction and properly dismissed the case.[5]

I was retaliated against for supporting another clergy that was being treated unjustly and for standing up and vocalizing my religious beliefs that I have given vows to uphold. The vows I upheld are a mandated practice for ordination as dictated by the doctrine of the denomination, as evidenced in the UMC Book of Discipline ¶330. I also as described harassment I faced because of my sex. Yet the injustices I share through this book have no legal recourse. I know because I have challenged that assumption by consulting employment law attorneys in more than one state. It is deemed not worth their professional energy to take on matters inadvertently guarded by the *ministerial exception*. Yet I was being retaliated against for supporting another clergy that was being treated unjustly and for my religious beliefs that I have given vows to uphold as a mandated practice of ordination dictated by doctrine of the denomination, as evidenced in the UMC Book of Discipline, ¶330.

Additionally, it needs to be understood that, unlike in secular employment, there is no viable human resources structure or function within the United Methodist Church that operates with an accountability to the well-being of clergy beyond what might be determined by the leaders to whom clergy report. There is no real, independent agency within the UMC ensuring the UMC does not get in trouble with employment law regarding clergy because the UMC is only accountable to itself, not employment law. There is no advocate that is not subject to the powers, influence, and authority of clergy leadership, including the Board of Ordained Ministry.

I say from my own human resources professional experience and based on the treatment I and others have received within the UMC that this lack of oversight is a set up for bad actors to abuse and exploit clergy. Rev. Dr. Chuck DeGroat is correct as he points out that "there must also be external leaders available who have the power and will to act when damaging leadership behavior is identified."[6]

In the current UMC, you cannot go around a bishop and his or her chosen leaders to find help. You must rely on them as your only lifeline within the church. There are no official systems that operate with power and motivation to help you beyond their reach, not the Board of Ordained Ministry, the Book of Discipline, the Council of Bishops, the complaint system, Judicial Council, the Jurisdictional Committee on the Episcopacy, or even agencies such as the General Commission on the Status and Role of Women (GCOSROW) or the General Commission on Race Relations (GCORR). In other words, if you are being mistreated by or have a concern regarding savvy bad actors in power, you have no advocate beyond the very people and practices that may be harming you. My story gives evidence to this.

How are these conditions sustained? Simply because they are not seriously challenged. They thrive under the cloak of oppression.

They are empowered by exploiting and promoting a clergy code that involves a sense of responsibility to boundaries of confidentiality. We are accustomed to keeping sordid tales to ourselves.

Consider this: unless a law has been broken or we suspect one is about to be, clergy have a professional responsibility to our confessors to keep confidences. Somehow, we allow that professional code to supersede protection of ourselves. Add to that a theology that says God is in control, an ecclesiology that has given bishops and other leaders control as God's agents, and a faith that says no matter what, God will see you through, and the abuse of Bible passages such as Matthew 18 and 1 Corinthians 6 to dismantle and attack the reputation of the American legal system,[7] you become a person who publicly glosses over the negatives of the denominational system upon which you rely. In other words, you suck it up and you do not tell. Otherwise, you will be destroyed by the system. That is the fear I witnessed and experienced as a UMC clergy.

Sound preposterous? Please note that I have shared that the Greater New Jersey Annual Conference of the United Methodist Church is governed by a bishop who regularly requires clergy to sign non-disclosure agreements. Non-disclosure contracts have many negative effects, like silencing victims or witnesses of harassment and discrimination. In the real world they are designed to protect trade secrets and, except in very limited circumstances, they have no place in ministry. They are too often used to cover up abuse, preserve secrets and protect the powerful. "Embargoed information" is kept from the press, which is another high price of silence. Clergy are given prejudicing, half-truths and false information to deflect concern over troubling, sometime questionable Episcopal actions. This

467

perpetuates confusion and fear. It warns that if you cross the bishop and his posse, you will be the next one targeted, the next one hurt.

I want to make clear that while bishops are the ultimate responsible parties to the toxic culture that exists. The narcissists among them are not the only ones doing damage. The church is replete with narcissists. In his April 16, 2020 article entitled *Loyalty is a Dangerous Virtue: the Church Needs Whistleblowers*, that appeared in EternityNews.com, Michael Jenson wrote, "I do believe that pastoral ministry may, indeed, be a magnet for those with narcissistic tendencies."[8] It makes sense that this would be the case, for as Wade Mullen states:

> Communities need someone to fill their keystone roles, and narcissistic individuals eagerly search for opportunities to occupy them. We look for charismatic leaders who promise us a grand future. But once found, we often discover these leaders were looking for us before we were looking for them. We willingly provide them with the power they desire because they promise us something we want in return. And over time, narcissistic leaders slowly turn their organizations into monuments to themselves.[9]

My experience of those who felt threatened by my ministry and otherwise expressed jealousies are indicators of a systemic problem with narcissism.

Rev. Dr. Graham Joseph Hill in his article advocates for regular, independent leadership '360s.' These "360s" are workplace reviews by colleagues, congregation members, and others who work with a particular leader. Though not consistently implemented, we do have that tool in the UMC. However, without accountability or consequences for destructive behaviors identified by reviewers and the offending behaviors clearly being shared with perpetrators, the tools are a waste of time.

In the case of bishops, they are accountable only to one another and, with the exception of moral failure regarding sexual misconduct or financial improprieties, they are rarely, if ever, taken to the mat or face serious consequences. Furthermore, the solicited reviews are completed in anonymity. Why? Fear of retribution. Surely the Church should be a place where honest feedback would be welcomed in the spirit of Christian growth and sanctification. Therefore, in my opinion, the 360-review tool is clearly not enough.

In the previously cited article, Rev. Dr. Chuck DeGroat comments, "Narcissistic, toxic, controlling leaders always demand loyalty (and they narrowly define loyalty)." I have experienced such over-the-top personal loyalty being demanded of me. I listened to my bishop's lectures and even a sermon by him to conference staff on being "All in" with his agenda. I experienced rejection, retribution, and shunning when my loyalty was questioned.

Loyalty is a challenging subject for Christians. We know that God is loyal and therefore believe that we should reflect that loyalty. The problem arises, however, when a Christian leader requires loyalty of someone more than to God. That is what I experienced working for Bishop Schol. I had once been fiercely loyal to his leadership. My loyalty derived from both respect of his position and because I believed in his leadership and what I understood he was trying to accomplish for the conference. However, once I could no longer overlook or justify his actions that I perceived conflicted with my faithfulness to God, I could not be "all in" based on those actions. I also saw no opportunity while working in his organization to safely discuss my concerns with him without significant harm being done to me. I look back at evidence of when I did raise concerns and I see the negative responses I received. I began recognizing that there is something awry in this kind of leadership and sought to distance myself from its harmful effects on me.[10] Unfortunately the harmful effects still came.

Early Methodism enjoyed and encouraged pioneering spirits. Those who were willing to not cow at the call of entrepreneurialism, those willing to take risks as directed by the Holy Spirit. I submit that due to the narcissistic culture of leaders within the UMC, the best entrepreneurial leaders do not have much room to succeed or share their spirit and successes. I base this on my Greater New Jersey Annual Conference experience and stories of others elsewhere.

There are outstanding leaders who identify with Wesleyan theology yet do not attempt to enter the UMC ordination process because they know they will never make it through. They do not want to be treated, as I was, by bad actors who bring their own agendas, petty territorialism and insecurities to the forefront to block them. People who are wonderful pastors with United Methodist heritage therefore choose to forgo the UMC process or elect to enter the ordination process for another denomination or religious entity, or leave the UMC process once entering it. Some go to a different conference of the UMC to find better treatment, as I shared in my story. While there is no perfect church, it's difficult to walk with Jesus when a Church and its leadership is not operating true to its mandated function. Today it is not uncommon for excellent, ordained UMC elders and deacons to proclaim that they doubt they would make it through the UMC ordination process, particularly in Greater New Jersey, as it functions today with the leadership that exists on the Board of Ordained Ministry.[11] Clearly such comments are red flags about a system that is not operating true to its mandated function.

Furthermore, those who are ordained or are possibly in the process and do shine in their proclamation of the Gospel and other ministry typically choose to keep as low of profile as possible. Why? Well, in Greater New Jersey I can tell you that it is common advice from clergy to clergy to "never get on Bishop Schol's radar." From seeing the experiences of others (including me), they rightfully believe one of two things will happen. If the bishop is impressed with their ministry, they will very likely be exploited so he can be given more credit for it, even at the expense of the ministry as he puts his own brand on it.

Or, no matter how fruitful, they will be skillfully discouraged, persecuted, and punished if their ministry does not fit his agenda. Therefore, the word on the clergy street in terms of connecting and sharing with or through Annual Conference leadership is not, "get yourself up on a high hill" (Isaiah 40:9), but "keep your head down."

Which leads to those who do put their heads up. The current system in Greater New Jersey leads to mediocrity because those who are rewarded through it, as previously mentioned, often are yes-women and yes-men. Whether they lack the strength and conviction to speak truth to power, or because they choose blind loyalty above the good of the Church; they too are victims of spiritual abuse. Those in the highest positions in the conference resemble blades of grass; willing to blow whichever direction the wind takes them. They are not risk-takers for the sake of the Gospel. They are not willing, or able, to challenge to improve the system, but rather conform to it as it is dictated by the bishop. Hence mediocrity sets in and spirals the ensuing bureaucracy downward to ineptness.

Why are they like this? In my opinion and experience they have been carefully chosen and groomed to, above all else, carry out the agenda of the bishop. Those selected to be his team are well-treated financially and with other perks. Furthermore, if you do not conform, you are ousted, shunned, and made an example of to keep others in line.

The greatest opportunity for bishops and cabinets to operate abusively comes in with the subjectivity in their United Methodist appointment system decisions. The UMC appointment system is a practice in which the bishop, with the aid of his or her cabinet, decides who when and where clergy will go to serve. They take into account through regular consultation with church leadership the needs and desires of each church. They consider the desires, gifts, graces, and limitations of clergy in their decisions.

The appointment process is designed to be Holy as clergy surrender themselves to the needs of the denomination, the local church surrenders itself to the needs and offerings of the connection, and the bishop and cabinet submit their administrative skills to the Holy Spirit in discerning how each church and the entire connection may best be served with the clergy resources available. It is a challenging responsibility for bishops and cabinets and requires an enormous amount of trust from clergy and church leadership.

The Greater New Jersey leadership cabinet prides themselves in having devised a system that is as reasonable, fair, and equitable as possible when they make appointments. They make no claims to it being a perfect system but one in which they work whole-heartedly to best serve the Church. However, in my opinion and experience as detailed in my story, there is too much evidence that the reality is that their appointments are made with personal biases and agendas that have less to do with furthering the Gospel than with rewarding the faithful to the bishop, punishing those perceived as disloyal, and then shuffling everyone else around to plug holes. My experience showed that loyalty is valued over honesty by these leaders. The mentality is, "if you are not with us, you are against us." This narcissistic ethos is key to establishing and maintaining their own personal and spiritual authority.

Too often, little regard is given to the needs and desires of the churches. As my story shows, significant appointment decisions are made without any consultation with incoming churches or with affected clergy at all. Clergy who progress the bishop and cabinet members' agendas, particularly right now around breaking the Book of Discipline's policies on gay marriage and practicing homosexual clergy, are rewarded. Those who defy the cabinet's agendas or are seen as potential threats to it, again, particularly around LGBTQIA issues (but not just those), are punished. Hence the appointment process is utilized as a weapon for abuse of power.

Additionally, the conference in recent years has held significant resources that they themselves utilize to supplement clergy salaries at churches that receive clergy but cannot afford them. This is a very subjective process administered by the cabinet. In my opinion and observation, who gets the bulk of these supplements and who does not frequently have more to do with the theological leanings of those involved than with the effectiveness or potential of the church and clergy together.

A WORD ABOUT PAY

Financials, salaries, and perks are challenging subjects for clergy and that is one reason they are easily used to control us and keep us in fear. When you go into ministry at God's call, there is an understanding that you are not following a path intent on securing riches from pastoring work. Some choose to enter the ordination process as the compensation package is better than that of a local pastor within the system, but overall, you do not enter the ordination process for the money.

And you do not typically find riches within the United Methodist pay structure. We all are taught and believe that pastoring provides rewards and abundant life beyond the shallowness and pitfalls of riches. If you are focused on money, you will forgo much joy in this calling. So, there is a pressure from the onset to not take a stand about your pay. Stand up and you may be deemed petty and materially focused. You also may set up difficulty in your relationships with the cabinet who control your appointments and also with the local church who you have been appointed to serve.

In Greater New Jersey there is a pay equity system that has been developed and is voted on each Annual Conference. My challenge is not that there is no system, it is how the system is administered. The Annual Conference sets a pay structure with ranges and minimums and maximums based on clergy credentials and years of service. Churches then work with district superintendent's approval to set clergy salaries based on those ranges. Churches work to set salaries within those ranges also based on their own budgets and the perceived value and performance of the appointed pastor. The more financially secure the church, typically the better the salary for the clergy. That makes sense. So while it may be a very fulfilling calling to serve a small, financially-strapped church, it can be a very difficult one in terms of supporting yourself.

The key, of course, is the district superintendent and the cabinet as a whole. Their role of ensuring fair, just, and equitable treatment comes to the forefront. How they control personal biases and political agendas strongly affect the lives of pastors. Pastors have no viable intermediary who is beyond the bishop or cabinet's command to intervene on their behalf. There is no Human Resources department to help police the compensation decisions with an eye to equity and fairness issues that may arise in this process.

The reality is that the way compensation is handled within the UMC system where most appointments are too small, low paying churches often causes distress for pastors. While there are minimum pay guidelines put in place by the conference,[12] the pay for clergy can still vary greatly as clergy are shuffled from place to place. This puts undo stress on pastors and their families as long-term planning becomes difficult. It puts stress to do whatever it takes to retain or grow your salary, and those actions do not always line up with the call of the Holy Spirit for how to carry out your ministry. Clergy become easier prey for toeing the line to questionable episcopal agendas without questioning.

Of course, as I see it, my compensation story is more so a reminder of what happens when the bishop likes you, and when he does not and the fact that in Greater New Jersey, that can have nothing to do with your performance. But below I show you my own cash compensation[13] history as an illustration of the great variances and instability clergy face as appointments are made annually and thus compensation can change frequently. The chart also serves as a reminder of the pay afforded to conference staff vs. those with local church responsibilities.[14]

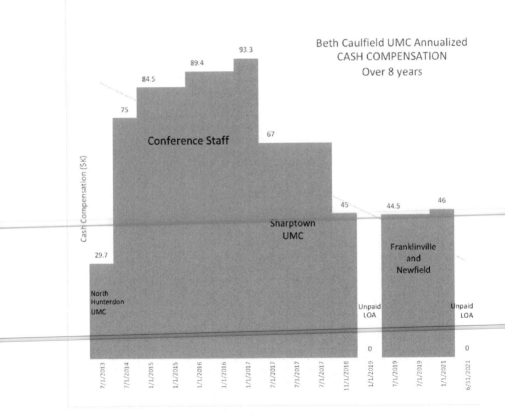

My UMC cash compensation history.

A system that consistently rewards fruitful ministry with greater pay (when possible) sends an affirming message and better accomplishes the stated mission of the Church. A system that rewards political maneuvering first does not bear near the fruit. Why would it? The realities of low pay and instability of pay lures more people to become caught up in moving into positions of greater pay and authority in the system or to positions that are not commensurate with their call rather than focusing first on accomplishing fruitful ministry.

It seems to me that political maneuvering is perceived by many clergy and laity to be rewarded through Bishop Schol and his cabinet in Greater New Jersey. Additionally, if you want to work in Greater New Jersey, as clergy or laity, it is also very good to be friends with or family of the bishop and/or cabinet. Concerns of nepotism have on more than one occasion been raised by brave laity, including attempting legislation to squelch it. Yet there has never been much traction for addressing the concerns as it appears that the bishop controls the process and people for investigating such matters.

Church leaders are frequently sold on a new appointment by being told by district superintendents that they will pay less for the new pastor than for the last. As a female clergy, I faced that scenario on all but one local church appointment I received. In one case, I replaced a highly paid male clergy who, as reported to me, performed minimal ministry, almost vacated the church of members and attendees, and led poor management of its finances. I was then brought in supposedly to rebuild the mess that was dire, but on less than half the pay and with an additional very needy church handed to me to attend to at the same time.

Churches, of course, do want to take care of their pastor. However, in Greater New Jersey, there are appointments to financially strapped churches that are sadly more committed to preserving the church building itself as a symbol of the congregation and to the church's legacy than to taking care of the pastor who is charged to oversee the spiritual growth of the congregation and community. In those cases, repainting the steeple takes priority over an increase in salary to the pastor, as after all, that pastor will most likely be moved anyway. The steeple will continue to represent the local church. Likewise, most churches are aware that shared giving will always be demanded and the concerns of getting a less qualified or less than full-time clergy or worse, being closed, are floated if shared giving is not kept up at the highest possible levels. Therefore, for the many cash-strapped small churches that exist, paying a pastor the minimum necessary seems to make sense in a system with such heavy pressures.

Finally, the Greater New Jersey Cabinet does not hold that churches must even meet the minimum salary requirements that are set by the conference. I know because it happened to me. In my last appointment, a church Pastor Parish Relations Committee Chair reportedly was told by our district superintendent that the church did not have to worry about paying me the minimum salary for my level. Nor did I/they receive any supplement from conference to make up the shortfall. Why was this done? As many of us postulate, it was because I was being persecuted by the conference.

Again, my point is that a system exists that is being administered unjustly and needs to be exposed, renovated, and not replicated.

It has been suggested openly that clergy such as me, who have spouses with consistent income, are not treated with as much concern for our equitable pay treatment as others. I believe this to be true. How many conversations have I had about the fact that I could go part-time and forgo the church and conference paying benefits for me, while at the same time it being very evident that I would still be expected to perform more than full-time work? More than once. One time I was given no other paid option but to do just that. I have heard that clergy couples express similar concerns as the second clergy (usually the wife) is treated as a throw-in whose pay is kept minimal with district superintendent approval.

As a former Equal Employment Opportunity Officer within the corporate world, I am especially nauseated that such thinking and practices exist in the twenty-first century in this country. Again, I believe this would be illegal if it were not for the way the *ministerial exception* of the First Amendment to the U.S. Constitution is currently interpreted and administered. Affected clergy are usually afraid to challenge pay issues as we are taught that ours is to be a life of sacrifice. We see the needs and financial challenges of the local church, and we remember to put our own needs last as an act of service. Who stands up for us? Much comes down to the discretion of the bishop and cabinet. Their integrity to the process is critical. My experience is that although the local church may indeed have limited resources, the Annual Conference, with its ample "shared ministry collections" from the local churches and other resources, have the ability to take better care of clergy's financial needs. That is not their priority, however.

As mentioned earlier, there is a stark difference between the pay of hierarchical administrative staff including cabinet positions and that of local church clergy. There are also plenty of solid clergy who stay in the system and accept the disparities because they do not feel called to administrative work or to be caught up in the highly political world that has evolved around such positions. Hence such staff positions are frequently deemed desirable and obtainable by those who are willing to become yes-men and yes-women. I saw it up close. I also saw the resentment by others of those in such positions. I experienced that resentment personally and the repercussions of it to me as allowed by the system firsthand.

I am not naïve to the reality that the events I describe are in line with the way the world unfortunately works when safety barriers are not in place. The question I ask you to ponder is this: is this the way the Church should operate? Are these the values and goals that should be incorporated in pursuing the commission of the Church? Are we not accountable to a higher standard of the treatment of the people called to serve as clergy?

Wade Mullen points out that "organizations and their leaders are always faced with two choices when abuse happening on their watch comes to light: adopt truth telling and transparency, regardless of the impact on their approval, status, or image; or use the same tactics of abuse in an attempt to retain or regain legitimacy."[15] The following question he asks is also mine, and that of countless other clergy who have or are currently facing abuse, "this is what it comes down to when abuse is exposed: Who will do whatever it takes to overcome a scandal, and who will do all they must to pursue what is right?"[16]

DREAM OF AFFIRMATION SURFACES

That very week of leaving the United Methodist Church, I began cleaning out my home office in preparation for my new focus in New Jersey with the Wesleyan Covenant Association as we prepared further for the launch of the Global Methodist Church. As I sorted through years of materials, I came across one of my old dream journals. The first entry was dated 2/29/2012. This was when I was in seminary and grappling with the call to pursue ordination in the United Methodist Church. Here is what I found:

> Second time I've had a dream with the same young guy who I know as a colleague in seminary. He tells me to come look at a chart he has about something that is happening. He waves me into his house which later is clearly a church. He pulls down the chart – like a window shade that has pictures supposedly of all my new classmates. I think it was my pastoral care class. He seems to be saying "Look, it's happening" or look what's begun" and "see the pattern." He points to an old guy who is very tall and then pulls me over to see the old guy's house. It's a two story, is strange-looking, not flashy but painted with bold black and white-like Holstein cow patterns—and the house is getting a new roof. The young guy is encouraging me to look closely.

> What catches my attention also though is the house across the street. It's a ranch that looks run down but has some of the same black and white patterns, but they are faded. I started thinking that what I was seeing was that the old guy with the strange house was blessed to have family living nearby. But suddenly I am in front of the rundown house with one of my other classmates—Mary Beth, a good friend. She points out to me that the back of the rundown house is burnt

down—and the house itself is abandoned. I am sitting with her in a Lexus SUV she is driving (I have no idea if that is what Mary Beth really drives.) She turns the car around to go back to the guy with the house getting a new roof who has the chart and I notice a pig running from the road to the front yard of the burnt-out house. It just adds to the ugliness of the property.

We pull back into the nice house's driveway and now I can see the house is more of a church.

I am trying to figure this all out and suddenly the dream ends as my home phone started beeping to tell me the battery needed changing. I got up and took the battery out but can't go back to sleep as I'm wondering what this all means.

WOW! When I read this, my heart leapt. I had no idea at the time what that dream meant but I knew it was significant. Now it is clear to me that I was to be part of the plans for a new church that is clear on what it stands for, is different, "strange" as it does a new thing, but maintains the clarity that the old church has faded from. The old church is falling apart but a new home for those who want it is not far away.

Even though I do not exactly understand how at the moment, I get to go to the new church in style (Lexus). But most importantly, I'm going with trusted friends, who are actually a "pastoral care" class.

Hallelujah!! I am encouraged. However, I am not deluded regarding the challenges that lie ahead for all Methodists with hopes beyond the United Methodist Church. The difficulties and costs are great.

HOPES FOR THE FUTURE

While the experiences I have detailed have in many ways strengthened and brought me wisdom, I also still hurt from being hit by so many rocks. Times of self-doubt and regret sneak up and envelop me as misty demons intent on suffocating my very breath. "If only I had been a little smarter ... if I had been better at keeping my head down ... If I had not been intent on shining ... if I had prayed harder ... if I had been more humble ... if I had better listened to the Holy Spirit ... if I had heeded my family ... if I had listened to certain friends ... if I had gotten out in the beginning ... if I had left at almost any juncture before now ... If I had not had such naïve passion for the ministry and dreams for great impact for Christ."

Such reflections are becoming much less frequent as I heal, and time has brought a clearer view of the United Methodist Church leadership systems. I thank Jesus that he is carrying me through. Thoughts about His faithfulness in my life cause me to tear up more than any other.

There are still times when I want nothing more to do with organized religion. Yet the call leads me back. I cannot escape it. When I have been encouraged to do something different with my life, especially by those close to me, I try to envision not being dedicated to bringing a little of Jesus to others with the gifts I have received. I just cannot imagine it. As I have tried exercises to dream of pursuing another vocation, another career, or even just retirement, I just cannot think long about it. This vocation of serving as a church leader is my call. I am getting stronger every day.

I have over twenty years of serving in full-time ministry with many experiences that I celebrate. I hope that sharing some of them with the readers of this book sparks new ministry in others. It is my prayer that the privilege of sharing my experience through this book and elsewhere provokes change and better ministry.

What energizes me currently is lobbying for and being part of birthing a new denomination that better reflects the Kingdom of God for all who enter its service and is robust in its effectiveness in bringing the transformational power of Jesus Christ to the world. It is my passion to see the roadblocks that were in my and others' paths as United Methodist clergy impossible to be replicated in the future. I hope for a denomination where tribalism does not take priority over truth.

I want to encourage those who are waiting for the day that the Global Methodist Church is a viable option for them to hold on and hold out. For those who have no interest in a traditional Methodist denomination of the future, may your eyes be opened to the pitfalls that exist in the current United Methodist system, or even a non-denominational setting, that detract from you following your call. Please remember that we can become what we tolerate. We are all responsible on some level for what the United Methodist Church has become.

For anyone reading this who may believe they have no room in their life for Christianity, my prayer is that what you grasp from this story is that church leaders are human, too. Yet we still hold out for, hold on to, and are abundantly sustained by the hope and love of Jesus Christ.

GLOBAL METHODIST CHURCH SPECIFIC HOPES

In a nutshell, I hope for a Church that does a better job of policing and leading itself and that we resist a toxic culture. That instead we foster a culture that is "redemptive and healing and good," and thereby becomes systematically good.[1] How can we lead others to Christ given the actions that continue in the United Methodist Church I have described? The hopes I hold for the Global Methodist Church include that ample power checks and accountability are put into place at its convening General Conference that include:

- A clear traditional theological approach that is reflected in its doctrines and disciplines.

- All laity and clergy members, including bishops, are covenanted to uphold and adhere to the regulations of the denomination.

- Leaders, churches, and institutions are covenanted to upholding community where loyalty is demanded firstly and primarily to Jesus Christ and no one else. Truth-telling is valued and whistle-blowers are protected and listened to, thereby amplifying the prophetic voices and the voices of "the least of these brothers and sisters."

- An effective judicial system that includes a complaint process whereby bishops may be removed from their positions for expanded definitions of abuse of power when found guilty by church trial. I support a complaint process that uses a strong power authority function that includes persons outside the episcopal and clergy systems who are also outside other church systems that are within bishops' and other leaders' powers.

- A reimagined role for the episcopal office whereby:

  o Bishops are charged to guard the faith, order, unity, liturgy, doctrine, and discipline of the church. Bishops focus the people of God outward toward our mission to make disciples of Jesus Christ in the world. Bishops are to have the witness of personal faith and spiritual maturity.[2]

  o Bishops have term limits. Bishops must move back to the local church or to other positions if not re-elected. After serving elsewhere for a season, they may attempt re-election. This encourages accountability and better performance.

- A separation of powers and authority from the Episcopacy/ Council of Bishops for the administration of the connectional church. This can be achieved through a Connectional Organization made up of Commissions that are overseen by a Connectional Operating Officer who shall:

  o Bear primary responsibility for the fruitful and accountable functioning of the general church and serve as its chief executive and administrative officer. The connectional operating officer shall be directly amenable to the Connectional Council. The connectional operating officer shall assign staff to support and resource any general commission and provide oversight to all general church staff.[3]

- A less subjective ordination process be put into place that focuses on empowering those called to minister as clergy as quickly as possible and building them up to succeed.

- A true human resources support function for clergy within the denomination than currently exists within the United Methodist Church. The current system, which is a loose offering through clergy chain-of-command, the Board of Ordained Ministry, and the complaint process is not sufficient to protect clergy from bad actors who abuse power. My experience is that this is especially true for those who do not have full orders. *There need to be external leaders available who have the power and will to act when damaging leadership behavior is identified.*

- A nurtured culture that is intentional in teaching and maintaining Biblically-based celebration of others' successes as one's own rather than contempt, jealousy, and envy. Emotional intelligence training would include this important facet.

- The Just Ministries area of the currently proposed Commission on Discipleship, Doctrine and Just Ministries is given full attention and appropriate authority to safeguard and root out discrimination for those it is named to protect and promote. That it would indeed function as a resource to those in distress and be beyond the political leveraging of bishops and others in power.[4] I have many ideas on this subject that I would like to work with in the future.

- A deployment process that requires and monitors better accountability to ensure that the local church, clergy, and superintendency all have appropriate checks and balances for clergy staffing decisions made. This can be accomplished through an appointment process, but it needs to be one held accountable to the doctrines and disciplines of the denomination. It needs to include better safeguards and resources for those subject to potential abuse of power and/or ineptness. This would include more local church and clergy consultation to ensure better fits for appointments.

- A more thoughtful pay system for clergy that protects from abuse and the realities of the fluctuating financial capabilities and differences that exist in local churches. I also have many ideas on this subject that I would like to work with in the future.

- Education on narcissism and narcissistic tendencies would be required of church leaders and counseling that includes Christian perspective encouraged for overcoming such tendencies.

- Clergy can operate openly and not in fear of abuse of power or exploitation.

- A denomination-wide taskforce is enlisted, supported and held accountable to address the concerns expressed in the Wespath's Clergy Well-Being Survey published in September 2021 regarding United Methodists.[5]

Laura McKnight Barringer observes that, "a church's culture is not incidental. Your church is its culture, and that culture is your church. Never underestimate the transformative power of culture. If you want to create a culture of goodness (tov), it is profoundly important to understand the type of culture your church has now."[6] I quote her out of a particular concern for the Global Methodist Church in particular. We are being formed by many leaders who have been hurt by the United Methodist Church. It is my prayer that we take intentional time and effort to heal so that we may indeed create a culture of goodness.

FORGIVENESS

Do I forgive those whose deeds I am exposing and those who stood by watching silently? Yes, but also, not yet. I want to and believe that in the long-term I will be able to say that I have done so. I am committed to forgive as Jesus has taught us to do. I know he taught us to do so, in part, for our own heart health and abundant living. Therefore, with great peace I am able to say that my intent is to move on from this protracted experience.

But forgiveness is indeed a process. While I, like many, would like to make forgiveness an immediately obtained goal, I cannot. One challenge is that forgiveness cannot always be accomplished in one easy step. This is in part because it often must be repeated, especially when you have been hurt again and again by the same person or people, which is usually the case when abuse has occurred. Abused people often suffer from some form of post-traumatic stress syndrome (PTSD), which means we continue to relive the pain without control. That makes forgiveness that much more complicated. Saying that abuse should be forgiven, as way too many know, is also counterintuitive.

Telling my story, however, both about what has happened and about my challenge to forgive, are both important steps toward forgiveness and healing for me. Holding myself accountable to God to complete this forgiveness process is another action I am taking. Putting it all in writing for the world to know is as much a part of this personal healing and forgiveness process for me as it is an act of service for others. Telling my story is indeed cathartic.

FINAL THOUGHTS

with Maria Ortiz. Paris, France, July 2009.

In July 2009, the summer I found out I, at forty-three-years-old, was pregnant with my youngest, God introduced a new friend into my life. Maria Vasquez Ortiz brought such comfort and joy at just the right time. I got to know her on a trip that we took together for the cross-cultural ministry credit that we each needed for our Master of Divinity degrees from Drew Theological School. Our class traveled to spend a week at the Taizé Community,[1] an ecumenical Christian monastic fraternity in Taizé, Saône-et-Loire, Burgundy, France. Focused especially for youth, Taize serves as a pilgrimage destination for prayer, Bible study, sharing, and communal work. Our class accompanied Bishop Devadhar, Conference staff, members, and a group of youth that he brought for the experience.

Maria is a most grace-filled, loving person, and we had so much fun together on that trip. We spent much of it laughing and being silly and just enjoying God's gift of humor. She was truly a balm of Gilead for my soul as I was trying to figure out how I was going to adjust to the new life growing within me and what that would mean for my future.

One day, as we were traipsing along a country road in the Burgundy, France countryside just outside of Taizé, Maria prophesied over me that I have "an anointing of new beginnings." She explained this to mean that I thrive in new experiences and that I would have many such opportunities. My mid-life surprise pregnancy and parenting opportunity was the latest example. The words she gave were calming and soothing. They helped me carry on.

Since that time, I have at times cynically chuckled at the creativity of her charismatic imagination while at the same time been warmed by her caring heart that was working overtime to comfort me. But, as I have reflected further, I have come to better appreciate her prophecy. I understand her to mean that part of my blessings in life are many different experiences. It also means that I have a gift for starting and leading others into new experiences. I have always been a pioneer. I can vision, strategize, and mobilize resources quickly to get new offerings out there for others to enjoy and grow closer to God as a result.

I also believe, though, that God gave me that word through Maria to remind me that even when I fail, and I have done so many times, there is always a new beginning. Thus, new beginnings feed my spirit and nourish my soul. No matter what has caused my downfall, I know who lifts me up. The one who hugs my battered body, mends my wounds, kisses my forehead, and ushers me back onto the playing field.

So, when I take in the magic of the wee hours of the morning, I am reminded of that "anointing of new beginnings" prophecy and its promise comes alive for me. I remember that our Lord's "mercies are new every morning, and great is Thy faithfulness." (Lamentations 3:23) Glory be to God!

I also believe that all God's children have an "anointing of new beginnings" when they take off the old and put on the new self in Christ and become renewed in the thinking of their minds (Ephesians 4:21-24). This includes the communities that call themselves Methodists. And God continually renews. As Isaiah 40:31 (CEB) proclaims, "but those who hope in the Lord will renew their strength; they will fly up on wings like eagles; they will run and not be tired; they will walk and not be weary." Hallelujah!

Don't hide your light under a basket (Matthew 5:15)

So even now, after all the pain and suffering I have been through at the hands of leadership within the United Methodist Church, when I wake to the light of a new day, it still brings me great hope. This is because I know within the depth of my being, that even when rocks are thrown at things that shine, darkness never overcomes the light. (John 1:5) Furthermore, the dawn reminds me that when a light is lit, you do not put it under a basket. Instead, you let it burn brightly, putting it on top of a lampstand for all who are in the house to see. (Matthew 5:15)

While I was the Teaching Director for the Community Bible Study class in Paris, one of our class members, Amy Duncan Protonentis, prayed over our leadership team and asked the Lord for a scripture for each of us. She recorded the fruit of her time with the Lord on handmade bookmarks for each of us. The bookmark she gave me, which I still retain, declares: "You who bring good news to Zion, go up on a high mountain. You who bring good news to Jerusalem, lift up your voice with a shout, lift it up, do not be afraid; say to the towns of Judah, "Here is your God!"" (Isaiah 40:9)

Therefore I trudge on, in the race that has been marked out for me. (Hebrews 12:1) I celebrate the journey thus far and thank God for the continued opportunity to grow as Christ's disciple. Though I may at times "walk through the valley of the shadow of death," I will "fear no evil" (even in the Church), "for your rod and your staff, they comfort me." (Psalm 23:4, NKJV) Closing this chapter in life and the recording of my experience through this book brings me "beside the still waters" and to a new beginning.

Praise God! Amen! Selah!

NOT SO FAST... GNJ FINANCIAL DISCREPANCIES... ANSWERED PRAYER?

In the 4th quarter of 2021, after the manuscript for this book was completed and while the book was in editorial review, the United Methodist Church of Greater New Jersey website began prominently displaying under its "Administration" button a "Human Resources" page.

The page predominately includes benefit and conflict of interest policy information. But it also includes a link to a "Whistleblower Hotline" page. The "Whistleblower Hotline" calls attention to a "Human Resources Director," someone who has been handling HR administrative and perhaps employee relations issues for the conference office staff for some time. The website also offers an email for Iona Harding who is the "Chair of the Human Resource/ Personnel Committee."

The Council on Finance and Administration has loosely maintained a personnel subcommittee that has dealt, again, with conference office staff, and has been involved with responsibilities such as updating the office staff employee handbook. They also have developed slates of candidates to serve on the CF&A various subcommittees. Their role has not included employee relations support to clergy. The broader CF&A has rarely, if ever, gotten involved in employee relations issues for clergy other than being apprised of actions with potential or eminent financial implications. Neither CF&A nor the personnel committee have been advertised as being available for employee relations concerns in the past. As of this writing, a "Human Resource/Personnel Committee" is not mentioned on the Conference Website's "Agencies and Committees" page where, presumably, all others are. It is not listed as a sub-committee, even, for the Council for Finance and Administration (CF&A). It was not listed among the Conference committees in the 2020 Conference Journal, the one most recently published.

However, Ms. Iona Harding, a lay person from the Princeton UMC, joined CF&A in October 2021. She was elected chair of the human resources subcommittee upon the start of her tenure. She has extensive human resources experience and owns her own HR consulting firm. It appears that the revamped and highlighted Human Resources function and whistleblower guidelines are in response to an action plan devised by GNJ's Council on Finance and Administration. That action plan, released in April 2021, was derived from findings and recommendations made by an "Independent Financial Review Team." The team had been formed in response to the finding that in 2020, Greater New Jersey had substantial financial discrepancies. CFA summarized the findings as:

> ...designated [ministry] program funds of GNJ started to be used to supplement billings to congregations without the full knowledge or awareness of the leadership of the three finance groups of GNJ board of pensions, trustees, and CFA. Further, GNJ has been paying 100% of general church apportionments while not collecting

100% from local churches. Over the years, this resulted
in a more than $13 million reduction of the corpus of
designated funds...[1]

More specifically, the Independent Financial Report released by
CFA specifically states that their discovery "includes estimates of
restricted and unrestricted assets down $13.1m or 51%. $2.6m average reduction/year over five years." The years identified in the report
are 2014-2019. Additionally, CFA shared that property sales were not
being invested as directed by the annual conference, as also shared
by Bishop Schol.[2] Based on the team's review and recommendations
"that should not be viewed as being exhaustive and conclusive,"[3] the
Council on Finance and Administration put together an action plan
that, among other steps, called for the Conference to:

Review and update all financial, investment and
employee policies and procedures on an annual basis,
tightening controls and delegation of authority as necessary. This includes, but is not limited to:

- Travel/Expense Reimbursement policy (cash and
  credit cards)
- Invoice approval policy
- Investment policy
- Employee Related (Handbook, Conflict of Interest,
  and Whistleblower.)

It saddens me that such a review has unearthed the findings
it has. But perhaps these discoveries and changes are indeed
answers to prayer. I am encouraged that such a team was formed

to address them, that they made significant recommendations, and that the Action Plan was adopted by the Council on Finance and Administration. I applaud the transparency of the Council for releasing the report. I hope that the Annual Conference body holds all leadership accountable to the Action Plan and that, as the Independent Financial Review Team recommended, further examination will be enacted. I am thrilled to know that Human Resources and whistleblower instructions have been added to the conference website and that there is now someone identified as a Human Resources Director.

The website is unclear about this new department's role as a resource for clergy-specific employee relations concerns. I suspect that those concerns are not changing in their handling by the conference. I also suspect that the reason given by leadership would be that there are no such required provisions in the denomination's polity as outlined in the Book of Discipline. It would be wonderful to see a movement for legislation to be passed to avail clergy of a separate Human Resources entity not subject to the powers of bishops.

You never know, God is always on the move ...

Courtesy of Janet Darnell

It would really mean a lot to me if you would leave a review of this book on Amazon.com. Just a line or two would be so helpful. You can also subscribe to my blog and receive updates to my books and ministry at my websites, www.revbethcaulfield.com and www.peoplethrowrocks.com.

PHOTOGRAPH AND ARTWORK CREDITS

Cover and Author Photos: © and Courtesy of Kara Raudenbush Photography

Book Photographs: 1: Courtesy of Waddell Family Archive; 2: Courtesy of Pine Forest High school/Cumberland County School District; 3, 4 © and Courtesy Dorothy Moritz Photography, 1985, 1988; 5, 6, 7, 8, 9, 10, 11, 12: Courtesy of Caulfield Family Archive; 13: Courtesy of Eddie Hatcher; 14 Courtesy of Laura Muskopf; 15: Courtesy of Caulfield Family Archive; 16: Courtesy of Dr. Namjoong Kim; 17, 18, 19, 20, 21, 22 Courtesy of Caulfield Family Archive; 23: Courtesy of the Hunterdon Democrat News; 25, 26, 27, 28, 29, 31, 32, 32, 34, 35, 36: Courtesy of Caulfield Family Archive; 37: Courtesy of Amanda Cosnett; 40, 41, 42, 43, 44: Courtesy of Caulfield Family Archive; 45: Courtesy of Rev. Dr. Jisun Kwak; 46, 47, 48, 49, 50, 51, 52, 53, 54, 55, 56, 57, 58, 59, 60: Courtesy of Caulfield Family Archive; 61: Courtesy of Rev. Dr. Jisun Kwak; 63: Courtesy of Annette Barralet; 65, 66, 67, 68, 69, 70, 71, 72, 73, 74, 75, 76, 77, 78, 79, 80, 81, 82; 83 Courtesy of Shannon Kiser; 84, 85, 86: Courtesy of Rev. Dr. Jisun Kwak; 87, 88, 89, 90, 91, 92, 93, 94, 95, 96, 97, 98, 99, 100, 101, 102, 103, 104, 105, 106, 107, 108, 109, 11, 112, 113, 114, 115, 116, 117, 118, 119, 120, 121, 122, 123, 124, 125, 126, 127, 128, 129, 130, 131, 132, 133, 134: Courtesy of Caulfield

Family Archive; 135, 136, 137: Courtesy of The Sentinel; 138, 139, 141, 142, 143, 144, 147 : Courtesy of Caulfield Family Archive

Artwork: 148, 149 Courtesy of Janet Darnell

Other Images: 24: Poster created by Beth Caulfield; 30: video given to me 1/2014 (fair use); 38, 39 PowerPoint slides created by me; 62, 64: from Beth Caulfield's Facebook Messenger account; 87: Constant Contact emails from our GNJ WCA Chapter; 102: Poster created by Beth Caulfield; 110: Poster created by Beth Caulfield; 146: Chart by Beth Caulfield

As mentioned at the beginning of this book, more than a tithe of its profits will be donated to the United Methodist Committee on Relief (UMCOR). I also want to ask, however, that you offer a donation to the Greater New Jersey Chapter of the Wesleyan Covenant Association. Checks made out to "WCA - Greater New Jersey Chapter" can be mailed to WCA, 213 Maude Ave., Brooklawn, NJ 08030. Or donations may be made online.

Endnotes by Chapter

Introduction

1. https://www.gnjumc.org/about-gnjumc/
2. The WCA connects Spirit-filled, orthodox churches, clergy, and laity who hold to Wesleyan theology. It is an association of individuals and congregations who share a common understanding of our Wesleyan doctrine and a desire to become a vibrant, faithful, growing 21st century church. The WCA has discerned that the best solution to the irreconcilable differences in the UM Church is the "Protocol for Reconciliation and Grace through Separation." It is supported by centrists, progressives, and traditionalists, and it allows for an amicable and orderly separation of the UM Church. It creates a pathway for theological conservatives to start afresh with a new denomination. For more information: www.wesleyancovenant.org and https://www.gracethroughseparation.com/legislation.
3. For more information about UMCOR, see their website at https://advance.umcor.org/p-620-umcor-us-disaster-response-and-recovery.aspx
4. While UMC members are challenged to even agree on what beliefs these labels represent, they are commonly used terms within the denomination at this time. Briefly, traditionalists affirm the core of the Christian faith as revealed in Scripture and its authority along with classical Wesleyan doctrine. Progressives do not as a whole agree with the primacy of Scripture in their theological framework, and instead tend to put primacy on social justice. Centrists assert a preference to be part of a denomination that accommodates both beliefs. Further exploration of these labels and the tensions around them can be seen in Tom Lambrecht's Good News article, "Primary Reasons for Separation," at https://goodnewsmag.org/244074/; Adam Hamilton's response to that article at https://www.adamhamilton.com/blog/a-response-to-thomas-lambrecht/#.YWrGYbhKjD5; and Lambrecht's rejoinder to Hamilton at https://goodnewsmag.org/244110/.

ENDNOTES BY CHAPTER

People Throw Rocks At Things That Shine

1. The mega-sized ministries of Mark Driscol, Ravi Zacharias, John Piper, John MacArthur, Ben Courson, and more have all been exposed for power-abuse-related falls in recent years.
2. The full report and accompanying email can be found at https://www.wespath.org/assets/1/7/5754.pdf. Wespath is the United Methodist Church's provider of retirement plans, investment solutions, and health benefit plans.
3. Ibid.
4. Ibid.
5. I detail chargeable offenses as described in ¶2702.1 in the Introduction to this book. A free version of the UMC Book of Discipline is available online at: https://www.cokesbury.com/book-of-discipline-book-of-resolutions-free-versions.
6. https://wesleyancovenant.org/about-page/#1533314242168-c269fe11-86cb
7. Social Principles, ¶161(G), The Book of Discipline of the United Methodist Church 2016, (Nashville: The United Methodist Publishing House.)
8. Quoting Mary Lyon, founder and President of Mount Holyoke Female Seminary for women. Mt. Holyoke, founded in 1837, was the first institute of higher learning for women in the U.S.
9. For more information about the Protocol legislation: https://www.gracethroughseparation.com/legislation
10. https://globalmethodist.org/
11. Laura Mcknight Barringer *A Church Called Tov: Forming a Goodness Culture That Resists Abuses of Power and Promotes Healing*, (Tyndale Momentum, 2020), pp. 51-52, (ebook).
12. "Here I Am, Lord," Dan Schutte, OCP Publications, 1981.

My Call

1. *Wesley, John (1841). A short history of the people called Methodists. The Complete Works of the Reverend John Wesley, A.M.*, 4th Edition, Vol. 13, pp. 287-360. London: John Mason. Originally published, 1781.
2. https://www.communitybiblestudy.org/
3. This article can be found at https://www.clmagazine.org/topic/other-pro-life-topics/surprise-midlife-pregnancy-burgeoning-trends/
4. https://www.christianitytoday.com/news/2020/september/evangelicals-for-social-action-name-change-christian.html

"She" Preaches Gospel

1. Egalitarianism also affirms that spouses are equally responsible for the family and that marriage is a partnership of two equals submitting

to one another. For egalitarians, roles should be ability-based and not gender-based.

2. https://www.wesleyan.org/a-wesleyan-view-of-women-in-ministry. Accessed numerous times since 4/2017.

3. One resource that I often refer to on these matters is *Encountering God in Tyrannical Texts: Reflections on Paul, Women, and the Authority of Scripture,* by Frances Taylor Gench. Westminister John Knox Press, Louisville, 2015.

4. Dr. Timothy Tennant, current President of Asbury Theological Seminary eloquently summarizes our biblical interpretation as follows:

The redemptive trajectory of the Bible on behalf of women is quite powerful. In the ancient world women had few rights, were frequently exploited and were regarded as property or part of the spoils of war. In cases of adultery, women were penalized more severely than men, and in cases of infertility, it was assumed to be the "problem" of the female. However, in the midst of such a world, the Scriptures begin a process of liberation and cultural transformation. Certain women, like Deborah, Huldah, Priscilla and Junias (Judges 4; 2 Kings 22:14-20; Acts 18:26; Romans 16:7) are lifted up to important positions of leadership. Women are permitted to inherit property (Num. 27:5-8; 31:1-9), purchase land (Prov. 31:16), have their rights protected (Deut. 21:15-17), and engage in public commerce (Prov. 31:24). By the New Testament, Jesus has female disciples (Matt. 27:55, 56; Luke 8:1-3); he protects and defends a woman from capital punishment (John 8:1-11) and grants dignity to many women throughout his ministry by engaging in serious conversations about major matters (John 4:1-30; Matthew 15:21-28; Luke 10:38-42). Despite the prevailing notion in the first century that a woman's testimony was not to be trusted, they were, in fact, the very first to witness and proclaim the resurrection of Jesus Christ (Matthew 28:1-10, Luke 24:1-11). Women are not to be regarded as mere property or as sexual objects, but rather as persons of sacred worth, created in the image of God. (Lev. 19:29; 21:9; Deut. 23:17, 18; I Cor. 6:15-20).... However – and this is the crucial point – no such redemptive movement occurs around the issue of homosexuality. Homosexual behavior, along with a whole range of other sexual sins, is consistently condemned in the Bible. Take time to read Genesis 19:1-11 and Leviticus 18:22 and Leviticus 20:13 and Judges 19:11-24 and Romans 1:18-32 and I Corinthians 6:9-11 and I Timothy 1:8-10 and Jude 7. There is no movement toward relaxing the biblical prohibition against homosexual behavior. In fact, these texts push hard in the other direction. The assumed analogy between slavery, women and homosexual conduct is simply not there. In both covenants, homosexual behavior is regarded as sin. Just to be clear, these texts are referring to homosexual behavior, not homosexual persons, who like all people, are the objects of God's grace and love. https://www.seedbed. com/slaves-women-and-homosexuals/. Accessed most recently 10/06/2021.

5. https://www.kingjamesbibleonline.org/Bible-Verses-About-God-Loves-Everyone/

6. https://www.firstthings.com/web-exclusives/2013/10/sexual-disorientation-the-trouble-with-talking-about-gayness Accessed most recently 10/14/2021.

7. As one example of the science, Dr. Lisa Diamond, of the University of Utah, who self-identifies as lesbian, has done extensive research on sexual orientation. In 2016, she joined forces with a law professor at the Univ. of Utah to write a paper arguing for the rights of self-identified gays and lesbians to marry and other civil protections to be upheld even though (her own) research shows that we cannot scientifically state that "once gay = always gay." Two important quotes from this paper:

> ...arguments based on the immutability of sexual orientation are unscientific, given that scientific research does not indicate that sexual orientation is uniformly biologically determined at birth or that patterns of same-sex and other-sex attractions remain fixed over the life course.

https://dc.law.utah.edu/cgi/viewcontent.cgi?article=1023&context=scholarship, pg 1-2.

8. "Women and racial/ethnic pastors receive lower compensation, not because of education or seniority, but mainly because cabinets consistently appoint women and racial/ethnic pastors to congregations and multi-church charges that pay lower salaries." https://www.gcsrw.org/MonitoringHistory/WomenByTheNumbers/tabid/891/post/women-clergypersons-of-color-earn-less/Default.aspx

9. https://www.gcsrw.org/Portals/13/Archives/WBTN/2017/B.-2015-Salary-Study-Part-II-1-2018.pdf

10. https://gcsrw.org/MonitoringHistory/WomenByTheNumbers/tabid/891/post/2020-geographic-trends-of-gender-disparities-in-composition-and-compensation-for-umc-clergy-the-extent-of-gender-pay-gaps-varies-across-jurisdictions-and-conferences/Default.aspx

Ordination Process Begins

1. For more information about Reconciling Ministries, see their website at https://rmnetwork.org/. The quote is from their "about us" page, accessed on 10/27/2021.

2. https://www.resourceumc.org/en/churchwide/judicial-council/judicial-council-decision-home/judicial-decisions/review-of-a-bishops-decision-of-law-in-the-greater-new-jersey-annual-c

3. The video can be accessed at https://drive.google.com/file/d/0B7aGa6B4t5ic-N0dIa2xzVzUwVlE/view?resourcekey=0-EqDJpUkyxhs13Hdu2fEtPA
4. https://careynieuwhof.com/jealousy-envy-insecurity-and-the-heart-of-a-pastor/
5. Some Boards of Ordination question whether people who serve in staff roles are truly performing duties that fulfill ordination requirements, as their responsibilities look different than those who are serving in local churches. In my and the opinion of many, these concerns are raised by a combination of laity and clergy who do not understand these roles and clergy who resent them. Those who resent can easily manipulate those who do not understand.

Conference Strategy

1. I have retained some of those blogs here: https://bcaulfield710.wixsite.com/mysite/small-groups-blog.
2. https://www.gnjumc.org/news/transformational-leaders-engage-in-northern-nj/
3. Ibid.
4. https://www.facebook.com/watch/?v=10155061743983879
5. If for some reason you find the video has been removed, you can view it here.
6. https://www.gnjumc.org/about-gnjumc/leadership/
7. https://gcsrw.org/
8. https://www.resourceumc.org/en/partners/um-sexual-ethics/home/resources/policy
9. https://www.resourceumc.org/en/partners/um-sexual-ethics/home/resources/policy
10. https://www.resourceumc.org/en/partners/um-sexual-ethics/home/content/bor-2045-eradication-of-sexual-harassment-in-the-united-methodist-church-and-society
11. https://www.facebook.com/beth.caulfield.7/posts/10209614080172928
12. https://www.resourceumc.org/en/partners/gcsrw/home/content/gcsrw-develops-sexual-ethics-resources
13. Examples of other conferences commitments as required by the Book of Discipline regarding sexual ethics: https://www.txcumc.org/seboundaries; https://www.epaumc.org/connectional-ministries/congregational-ministry/ordained-licensed/sexual-ethics-workshops/; https://vaumc.org/?s=sexual+ethics;
14. Book of Discipline, ¶105.4 – Our Theological Task
15. https://nlltribe.com/about-us/

16. https://1stlightmission.blogspot.com/p/about-us.html

17. Chief Gould is a politician and businessman who also serves as Vice-President of the Native American Advancement Corporation. As I have heard him share in presentations and testimonies, "Gould grew up while the tribe was in hiding from United States assimilation and forced removal policies that led to many of the Lenape being removed to Oklahoma. In the 1970s, during the Native American civil rights movement, he and a group of others publicly reorganized the tribe and came out of hiding, incorporating the Nanticoke Lenni-Lenape Tribal Nation as a legal entity in 1978. The Nation quickly became one of the "largest and most vibrant" Lenape groups on their traditional land, and was formally recognized by the state of New Jersey in 1982." https://en.wikipedia.org/wiki/Mark_Quiet_Hawk_Gould

18. https://1stlightmission.blogspot.com/2016/03/pdf-book-on-ministry-challenges-among.html

19. https://www.gnjumc.org/committee-on-native-american-ministries-co-nam/resources/

20. NEJNAMC meets yearly to coordinate and support CoNAM ministries in each local annual conference

21. Interview with Mary Johnson: https://www.bwcumc.org/news-and-views/qa-with-rev-mary-johnson/, interview with Bishop Peggy Johnson: https://www.bwcumc.org/news-and-views/qa-with-bishop-peggy-johnson/.

22. de Vries, Kylan Mattias (2009). "Berdache (Two-Spirit)." In O'Brien, Jodi (ed.). *Encyclopedia of gender and society*. Los Angeles: SAGE. p. 64.

23. Estrada, Gabriel (2011). "Two Spirits, N·dleeh, and LGBTQ2 Navajo Gaze"". *American Indian Culture and Research Journal*. **35** (4): 167–190 as cited in https://en.wikipedia.org/wiki/Two-spirit

24. https://en.wikipedia.org/wiki/Pan-Indianism and Robbins, Dorothy M (30 July 1997). "A Short History of Pan-Indianism." *Native American Information Service*.

25. https://www.dailysignal.com/2019/03/10/i-was-americas-first-non-binary-person-it-was-all-a-sham/

26. https://www.epaumc.org/wp-content/uploads/ActsOfRepentanceLetter.pdf

Politics Of Discrimination

1. The full blog can be found here: https://www.gnjumc.org/50-shades-of-conversation/

2. https://um-insight.net/topics/beth-caulfield/

3. A short insert here: I had so much fun envisioning and producing that video. When it came time to shoot it, I took my son, then a high school senior,

and traveled around the state with a production crew that gave him small volunteer responsibilities. That time with him was a precious gift from God and a reminder to "Let my whole being bless the Lord and never forget all his good deeds." Psalm 103:2 The video, which won the top award from UM Communicators, can be seen here: https://drive.google.com/file/d/1zbWKATKrdzt7W8h8FQYHzSCNfHizORZ_/view?usp=sharing

4. For more information about Reconciling Ministries, see their website at https://rmnetwork.org/. The quote is from their "about us" page, accessed on 10/27/2021.

5. https://www.gnjumc.org/annual-conference-2015/2015-annual-conference-wrap-up/14268-2/

6. The vote count numbers vary slightly. I am reporting 749 as the mode for the six votes.

Cuba Gooding

1. Although there seem to be no official government statistics, various sources estimate that only 1.5 to 5% of identified Catholics actually practice the religion. 2018 Report on International Religious Freedom: Cuba, June 21, 2019 (https://cu.usembassy.gov/2018-report-on-international-religious-freedom-cuba/) United States Commission on International Religious Freedom (https://en.wikipedia.org/wiki/United_States_Commission_on_International_Religious_Freedom)

2. This is my generalization based on statistics and estimates cited from various sources, included Hagedorn, Katherine J. (2001). *Divine Utterances: The Performance of Afro-Cuban Santería*. Washington, DC: Smithsonian Books. ISBN 978-1560989479. P. 171, also Wedel, Johan (2004). *Santería Healing: A Journey into the Afro-Cuban World of Divinities, Spirits, and Sorcery.* Gainesville: University Press of Florida. ISBN 978-0813026947, p.2.

3. This comes from a variety of sources, but all are either old or unclear in their basis, including https://cu.usembassy.gov/2018-report-on-international-religious-freedom-cuba/, and http://www.cubalog.eu/download/pdf/dialogues_38.pdf, and https://www.nytimes.com/1998/01/29/world/cuba-s-protestant-churches-a-growing-flock.html#:~:text=A%20small%20religious%20minority%20before,that%20represents%20non%2DCatholic%20churches.

4. https://www.flumc.org/newsdetail/cuban-methodist-church-sees-massive-growth-12783698

5. https://vimeo.com/37805516

6. Ibid.

7. There are comments I share in this chapter regarding Cuba that come from reliable sources but whose identity I will not divulge.
8. The exchange can be viewed at https://www.youtube.com/watch?v=kwR-8REIkgHY at hour 5:41.
9. Ms. Schol updated her zoominfo profile with this information and more on 12/24/2021. https://www.zoominfo.com/p/Beverly-Schol/1034151538
10. https://www.gnjumc.org/nehemiah-properties/
11. Consider this: the United Way's mission statement is "*United Way* improves lives by mobilizing the caring power of communities around the world to advance the common good." "We envision a world where every community is a strong one, with jobs that pay a livable wage, good schools and a healthy environment. Around the world, we engage people and organizations in innovative solutions that are transforming that vision into reality." https://www.unitedway.org/about# accessed 8/14/2021. Contrast that with the United Methodist mission statement "to make disciples of Jesus Christ for the transformation of the world."
12. https://en.wikipedia.org/wiki/Sloppy_Joe%27s_Bar,_Havana#cite_note-LAT-5. Last accessed on 9/15/2021.
13. https://havanatimes.org/business/two-private-restaurants-closed-in-havana/. Last accessed 9/15/2021.
14. Later in the conference, after approving their own Constitution, Articles of Faith, and Discipline, the Cuban delegates elected Armando Rodriguez as Bishop. When it started, the Cuban denomination elected bishops for only a four-year term. In a fascinating interview in 2008, Rodriguez talks about his own experiences at that time.
15. https://www.gnjumc.org/content/uploads/2015/12/Relay-March-2016-final-3.pdf
16. The video can be viewed at https://www.youtube.com/watch?v=62p6tjsfXbc.
17. The article can be found here: https://www.gnjumc.org/content/uploads/2015/12/Relay-March-2016-final-3.pdf.
18. The video can be seen at: https://www.youtube.com/playlist?list=PLVX8tlT7tl_WqFsYn1joA2DnAZveQ7CnP.
19. https://www.umnews.org/en/news/for-methodists-in-cuba-these-are-good-times Last accessed 9/15/2021. Also https://www.flumc.org/newsdetail/cuban-methodist-church-sees-massive-growth-12783698. Last accessed 9/15/2021.

Turned Down For Full Orders Once

1. Report can be viewed at: *https://drive.google.com/file/d/1nJKzpxrtl23p4ZMn_4qQc-uINnlnLe_S/view?usp=sharing*

2. https://americaskeswick.org/. Last accessed 10/22/2021.
3. The sermon manuscript can be found at People with Abundant Life Plan. https://drive.google.com/file/d/1DOsQrvUY6owKZba99tWUrIL_ExqXHc07/view

Run For Bishop

1. https://www.umc.org/en/content/ask-the-umc-how-are-bishops-chosen-in-the-united-methodist-church
2. https://www.gnjumc.org/news/jurisdictional-delegates-recommend-no-endorsement-for-bishop/
3. http://calms2016.umc.org/Menu.aspx?type=Petition&mode=Single&number=510.
4. http://ee.umc.org/who-we-are/greater-new-jersey-annual-conference-2016
5. https://en.wikipedia.org/wiki/Glide_Memorial_Church
6. https://peopleneedjesus.net/2020/06/09/lessons-from-glide-caution-notes-for-left-and-right-in-church/
7. https://www.glide.org/about/#mission-vission
8. https://religionnews.com/2016/07/19/first-openly-lgbt-united-methodist-bishop-this-is-the-time/
9. https://www.umnews.org/en/news/appointments-leave-glide-without-united-methodist-pastor
10. https://um-insight.net/in-the-church/local-church/disput/
11. Ibid.
12. https://hoodline.com/2020/11/glide-memorial-church-severs-ties-with-methodist-church-after-100-years/#:~:text=A%20settlement%20has%20now%20apparently,property%20at%20330%20Ellis%20Street.
13. https://www.umnews.org/en/news/district-superintendent-suspended
14. Ibid.
15. Ibid.
16. Ibid.
17. https://www.umc.org/en/content/jurisdictions
18. http://www.nejumc.org/pdf/2016-NEJ-DCA-Monday-July-11.pdf
19. http://www.nejumc.org/pdf/2016-NEJ-DCA-Summary.pdf
20. https://us11.campaign-archive.com/?u=b2ab2248b91542a5f476025fe&id=7d53c476ca&fbclid=IwAR0665trc4nqJo68dxox5uPiHXubdrpsaoEuNPzKmzLgEog1Utb_xeRupew

Nowhere To Hide

1. Ocean Grove is known for its tent colony, held over from the original Camp Meeting structures of the 1800s. Beginning in 2020, our family joined that

colony! For more info: https://www.theinnsofoceangrove.com/our-blog/ocean-grove-tents/.

2. Overview-of-Complaint-Process-Jan-11-Clergy-Gathering(1)[117431].pdf

3. You can read my BOM theology response that was questioned here https://drive.google.com/file/d/11NsvNF6txrIkYGQ-7dvTDHURrfHuSDBe/view

4. Support withdrew as those from the main campus who had committed to attend there for a few years to help with its startup felt they had met their obligation. This is understandable at several years into the new campus, a second change in pastor, and that pastor being the first not from the original campus, which is where their loyalties had truly been. I detail other reasons that support withdrawal later in the book.

5. I speak more to the traditional Wesleyan stance on this issue in the next chapter.

6. The comment was referring to a similar controversial statement from Madeleine Albright during the 2016 U.S. Presidential election season. https://www.nytimes.com/2016/02/13/opinion/madeleine-albright-my-undiplomatic-moment.html

7. https://s3.amazonaws.com/Website_Properties/who-we-are/judicial-council/judicial-council-dockets/docket-10-2017-2.pdf

8. https://juicyecumenism.com/2017/11/22/umc-bishop-john-schol-now-favor-church-trials/

Cowtown

1. Interesting fact: the The Main campus is literally next door to the Cowtown Rodeo, which has been claimed to be the longest running rodeo in the U.S. and one of the most well-known.

2. https://www.facebook.com/photo/?fbid=10214050295755545&set=

3. https://www.facebook.com/beth.caulfield.7/posts/10216198746985483

4. https://www.facebook.com/beth.caulfield.7/posts/10216185873223647

5. https://www.facebook.com/beth.caulfield.7/posts/10216191271038589

6. https://www.facebook.com/beth.caulfield.7/posts/10216181669238550

7. https://en.wikipedia.org/wiki/Recognition_of_same-sex_unions_in_South_Korea

8. Here is a fun video we made for the cause: https://www.facebook.com/memories/?source=notification&notif_id=1621277256353240&notif_t=onthisday&ref=notif

Now Shoot Her Dead

1. More info about the day can be viewed at: https://www.facebook.com/beth.caulfield.7/posts/10217712787635553

2. I ended up showing that video to Bishop Schol, my district superintendent and the bishop's executive assistant. They agreed that it was inappropriate and asked for the link to it, which I provided. I'm unaware if the inappropriate behavior was ever addressed.
3. https://www.youtube.com/watch?v=o2G6szkfkKI

Sunshine Through The Clouds

1. https://www.facebook.com/photo?fbid=10159639081996474&set=gm.1001144037360822
2. https://www.cokesbury.com/book-of-discipline-book-of-resolutions-free-versions
3. Taken directly from the RCM web and social media sites.
4. https://mailchi.mp/97c4e066fe5d/message-from-bishop-schol-1000713?e=465ad350a8
5. https://www.umnews.org/en/news/church-courts-finds-clergywoman-not-guilty
6. Ibid.
7. Ibid.
8. https://mailchi.mp/gnjumc/gnj-digest-special-edition-2-7-19?e=f3e4b27bd1
9. ¶2711.2 states "It shall require a vote of at least nine members of the trial court to sustain the charge(s) and nine votes also shall be required for conviction. Fewer than nine votes for conviction shall be considered an acquittal..."
10. https://mailchi.mp/97c4e066fe5d/message-from-bishop-schol-1000713?e=465ad350a8
11. https://www.gnjumc.org/news/cfa-reduces-shared-ministry-formula-and-passes-amended-budget/ https://www.gnjumc.org/content/uploads/2019/03/2019-March-Special-Session-Pre-Conference-Book-pg9-10final.pdf
12. https://wesleyancovenant.org/2019/03/08/reflections-on-the-special-general-conference/
13. Westboro Baptist Church is an American hyper-Calvinist hate group. It is known for engaging in inflammatory homophobic and anti-American pickets, as well as hate speech against atheists, Jews, Muslims, transgender people, and numerous Christian denominations. Wikipedia
14. https://www.inquirer.com/news/united-methodist-church-gay-clergy-ordination-same-sex-weddings-general-conference-20190301.html
15. https://www.nj.com/news/2019/03/methodists-in-nj-grapple-with-vote-to-crack-down-on-same-sex-marriage-and-lgbtq-people-in-ministry.html

First BOM Discontinuation Letter

1. https://www.facebook.com/beth.caulfield.7/posts/10219155041731004
2. I do note that one traditionalist who is clear about his traditional Wesleyan theology had served as a reserve delegate to the 2016/2019 General Conferences.
3. https://drive.google.com/file/d/10PnY_-EUxfEA_FEHI-g44qdFAJV9WYZJ/view

Fresh Expressions US

1. https://freshexpressionsus.org/
2. A video advertising the event participants can be seen at: https://vimeo.com/207325537.
3. We were set to make Team Vital 2.0 more effective than Team Vital. https://www.facebook.com/beth.caulfield.7/posts/10212339080656237. I believe that resource can be resurrected for elsewhere.

Summer Of Praise – Rev. Leo Park

1. https://www.facebook.com/MorrowMemorialChurch/photos/a.664871196892261/2189359404443425/

The Last Stand

1. Except for one item that when thrown out would ensure traditionalists would be overridden by the cabinet when they covenanted to not accept openly practicing homosexual pastors – more explanation is written in the chapter.
2. https://www.facebook.com/beth.caulfield.7/videos/10221082541837302
3. https://www.umnews.org/en/news/conference-charts-way-forward-with-lgbtq-people
4. https://www.facebook.com/WaterlooUMC/posts/2121258324641434
5. https://www.umcredbank.org/way-forward-covenant/
6. https://www.hopewellmethodist.org/greater-nj-annual-conference-approves-a-way-forward-plan/
7. https://www.umnews.org/en/news/diverse-leaders-group-offers-separation-plan and https://www.unitedmethodistbishops.org/files/websites/www/pdfs/signed+umc+mediation+protocoal+statement+-2020.pdf
8. https://wesleyancovenant.org/pc/
9. https://docs.google.com/document/d/1zrHR01f9yG3ifjVb2SVCCEAhnp-kubmOk/edit?usp=sharing&ouid=102933747798495715995&rtpof=true&sd=true

10. Video footage of Beverly's instruction can be seen at: https://drive.google.com/file/d/11_VpO40yRhz-Rey6xwSBqlqvXu-fmiRn/view?usp=sharing

11. https://philadelphia.cbslocal.com/video/4589250-chopper-3-over-peaceful-black-lives-matter-protest-in-franklinville/?fbclid=IwAR1tIxUN-Hv1gBoSv4_EG0YWfxbhjXesnLDumRnHhegixa2Mps7yQuLKO2hU#.XuV13HIz2U0.facebook

12. https://www.nj.com/news/2020/06/peaceful-protest-marches-past-site-of-reenactment-of-george-floyd-killing.html?fbclid=IwAR1Fpy-

13. https://www.fox29.com/video/738354?fbclid=IwAR0txEReIMGEsXefqX-F7isY-N3Amnsi3HFIV-VqzGTQ_Zt3G4WHYoh5YE10

14. https://www.fox29.com/video/890782?fbclid=IwAR307do6Wd0-OPuoeM-CQclLgMh4B6N9dF1Lm435nQQkNQtTvhQuqUDeMTRE

Clarity

1. https://www.eternitynews.com.au/opinion/loyalty-is-a-dangerous-virtue-the-church-needs-whistleblowers/

2. Chuck DeGroat is a Professor of Counselling and Christian Spirituality at Western Theological Seminary in Michigan, USA. He is a licensed therapist with more than 20-years experience, an ordained Reformed Church minister and co-founder of Newbigin House of Studies, an urban and missional training centre in San Francisco. His comment is taken from the article https://www.eternitynews.com.au/world/when-narcissism-comes-to-church/

3. https://www.eternitynews.com.au/opinion/whistleblowing-glorifies-christ-challenging-narcissistic-leaders-and-toxic-cultures/amp/

4. https://en.wikipedia.org/wiki/Ministerial_exception

5. https://ministrywatch.com/church-has-sole-jurisdiction-over-clergy-discipline-chicago-court-rules/

6. Ibid.

7. See Wade Mullen's comments on page 70 (e-book) of the previously cited *Something's Not Right: Decoding the Hidden Tactics of Abuse—and Freeing Yourself from its Power (Tyndale Momentum, 2020)*.

8. https://www.eternitynews.com.au/opinion/loyalty-is-a-dangerous-virtue-the-church-needs-whistleblowers/

9. Mullen, p. 27.

10. In his article on loyalty, Michael Jensen states, "What does this mean for loyalty with the church? It means I can't, as a Christian leader, require a loyalty of someone other than their loyalty to the faithful God. And their loyalty to me might actually be fully expressed in their pointing out my sin – so

that I might be more Christlike." https://www.eternitynews.com.au/opinion/loyalty-is-a-dangerous-virtue-the-church-needs-whistleblowers/

11. I wish I could give names of current pastors who have told me this, but unfortunately it may put them in a tenuous position with the Board as they continue to serve. They include more progressive pastors as well as traditionalists. A traditional pastor who is retiring this year, Alan Darby, is one example of retired pastors who have made that comment to me.

12. https://www.gcfa.org/about-us/affiliates/nacec/

13. This is salary plus housing allowance only. At North Hunterdon and Franklinville I was offered a parsonage but owned my own home and so did not need a parsonage. I was offered medical benefits at all appointments but North Hunterdon, which was part-time. My travel expense account was $12k/yr at the Conference and $2500/yr at all other appointments.

14. In Greater New Jersey we do not have many large churches. Only two have over 1000 members, less than ten have over 500, and the vast majority of the approximately 500 other churches are 100 or less in active worshippers. Thus, most serving in the local church are paid on the lower end of the scale.

15. Mullen, Wade, *Something's Not Right: Decoding the Hidden Tactics of Abuse—and Freeing Yourself from Its Power.* (Tyndale Momentum, 2020), p.6 (ebook).

16. Ibid., p. 128.

Global Methodist Church Specific Hopes

1. Laura McKnight Barringer, "A Church Called Tov: Forming a Goodness Culture That Resists Abuses of Power and Promotes Healing (Tyndale Momentum, 2020), p. 17.

2. DRAFT BOOK OF DOCTRINES AND DISCIPLINE FOR A NEW METHODIST CHURCH ¶608 https://wesleyancovenant.org/wp-content/uploads/2020/12/Doctrines-and-Discipline-Version-1.pdf

3. DRAFT BOOK OF DOCTRINES AND DISCIPLINE FOR A NEW METHODIST CHURCH ¶812 https://wesleyancovenant.org/wp-content/uploads/2020/12/Doctrines-and-Discipline-Version-1.pdf

4. DRAFT BOOK OF DOCTRINES AND DISCIPLINE FOR A NEW METHODIST CHURCH ¶807.2(c) https://wesleyancovenant.org/wp-content/uploads/2020/12/Doctrines-and-Discipline-Version-1.pdf

5. The full report and accompanying email can be found at https://www.wespath.org/assets/1/7/5754.pdf. Wespath is the United Methodist Church's provider of retirement plans, investment solutions, and health benefit plans.

6. Laura Mcknight Barringer, A Church Called Tov: Forming a Goodness Culture That Resists Abuses of Power and Promotes Healing. (Tyndale Momentum, 2020) p. 16.

Final Thoughts

1. https://www.taize.fr/en_rubrique8.html

Not So Fast...GNJ Financial Discrepancies...Answered Prayer?

1. https://mcusercontent.com/b2ab2248b91542a5f476025fe/files/6cbce8b8-dbff-41f9-a7d2-ca0b1cad3aaa/CFA_Release_of_Independent_Financial_Review_Team_Report.pdf

2. https://mailchi.mp/026db738ccf9/conference-leaders-share-billings-concerns-1010494?e=%5bUNIQID

3. The Independent Financial Team's report states, "The team conducted their review over a six-week period." Regarding their efforts, they commented that "The IFT consisted of the part-time efforts of six volunteers with legal, accounting and change-management expertise. The scope, depth and timeline of the financial condition of GNJ could have warranted a year-long engagement of full-time forensic and legal resources absent constraints on time and funding. Accordingly, our review should not be viewed to be exhaustive and conclusive, but as a starting point ..."

Made in the USA
Columbia, SC
16 July 2022

63564569R00289